Rethinking
America's
Security

THE AMERICAN ASSEMBLY was established by Dwight D. Eisenhower at Columbia University in 1950. Each year it holds at least two nonpartisan meetings that give rise to authoritative books that illuminate issues of United States policy.

An affiliate of Columbia, with offices at Barnard College, the Assembly is a national, educational institution incorporated in the state of New York.

The Assembly seeks to provide information, stimulate discussion, and evoke independent conclusions on matters of vital public interest.

Founded in 1921, the COUNCIL ON FOREIGN RELATIONS is an educational membership institution and a forum bringing together leaders from the academic, public, and private worlds. The Council is nonpartisan and takes no institutional positions. It conducts meetings that give its members an opportunity to talk with invited guests from the United States and abroad who have special experience and expertise in international affairs. Its studies program explores foreign policy questions through research by the Council's professional staff, visiting fellows and others, and through study groups and symposia. The Council also publishes the journal *Foreign Affairs*, in addition to monographs.

CONTRIBUTORS

GRAHAM ALLISON, Harvard University

GEORGE BALL

JOHN H. BARTON, Stanford University

BARBARA A. BICKSLER, Institute for Defense Analyses

ROBERT BLACKWILL, Harvard University

MICHAEL BORRUS, University of California, Berkeley

DANIEL F. BURTON JR., Council on Competitiveness

BARRY E. CARTER, Georgetown University

MICHAEL W. DOYLE, Princeton University

RICHARD N. GARDNER, Columbia University

DAVID C. HENDRICKSON, Colorado College

B.R. INMAN

HENRY A. KISSINGER, Kissinger Associates

CHARLES KRAUTHAMMER

CHARLES A. KUPCHAN, Princeton University

CLIFFORD A. KUPCHAN, Columbia University

ERNEST R. MAY, Harvard University

JOHN J. MEARSHEIMER, University of Chicago

WILLIAM E. ODOM, Hudson Institute

PETER G. PETERSON, The Blackstone Group

ALAN D. ROMBERG, Council on Foreign Relations

THOMAS C. SCHELLING, University of Maryland

JAMES K. SEBENIUS, Harvard University

GREGORY F. TREVERTON, Council on Foreign Relations

PAUL D. WOLFOWITZ, Department of Defense

JOHN ZYSMAN, University of California, Berkeley

THE AMERICAN ASSEMBLY
Columbia University

THE COUNCIL ON FOREIGN RELATIONS

Rethinking America's Security

Beyond Cold War to New World Order

GRAHAM ALLISON
and
GREGORY F. TREVERTON
Editors

W · W · NORTON & COMPANY
New York   London

The text of this book is composed in Baskerville.
Manufacturing by the Haddon Craftsmen, Inc.

Library of Congress Cataloging-in-Publication Data

Rethinking America's security : beyond Cold War to new world order /
    Graham Allison and Gregory F. Treverton, editors.
        p.   cm.
    At head of title: The American Assembly, Columbia University [and]
    the Council on Foreign Relations.
    Includes bibliographical references and index.
        1. United States—National security.   2. United States—Foreign relations—
1989–   I. Allison, Graham T.   II. Treverton, Gregory F.
    III. American Assembly.   IV. Council on Foreign Relations.
        UA23.R458   1992   91–3211
    355′.033073—dc20

ISBN 0-393-03059-8 (Cloth)
ISBN 0-393-96218-0 (Paper)

W.W. Norton & Company, Inc., 500 Fifth Avenue, New York, N.Y. 10110
W.W. Norton & Company Ltd., 10 Coptic Street, London WC1A 1PU

1   2   3   4   5   6   7   8   9   0

Contents

Preface   *13*
    DANIEL A. SHARP
    PETER TARNOFF

Introduction and Overview   *15*
    GRAHAM ALLISON
    GREGORY F. TREVERTON

RETHINKING THE CONCEPT OF NATIONAL SECURITY

1   National Security Portfolio Review   *35*
    GRAHAM ALLISON
    GREGORY F. TREVERTON

2   The Primacy of the Domestic Agenda   *57*
    PETER G. PETERSON
    with JAMES K. SEBENIUS

3   National Security in American History   *94*
    ERNEST R. MAY

RETHINKING THE DIMENSIONS
OF NATIONAL SECURITY

4   Technology and U.S. National Security   *117*
    B.R. INMAN
    DANIEL F. BURTON JR.

5   Industrial Competitiveness and National
    Security   *136*
    MICHAEL BORRUS
    JOHN ZYSMAN
    with assistance from DAVID BELL

6   The New Defense Strategy   *176*
    PAUL D. WOLFOWITZ

7   The Global Dimension   *196*
    T.C. SCHELLING

VISIONS OF THE NEW INTERNATIONAL ORDER

8A Disorder Restored   *213*
    JOHN J. MEARSHEIMER

8B Balance of Power Sustained   *238*
    HENRY A. KISSINGER

8C A New Concert for Europe   *249*
    CHARLES A. KUPCHAN
    CLIFFORD A. KUPCHAN

8D Practical Internationalism   *267*
    RICHARD N. GARDNER

8E The Uneven, but Growing, Role of
    International Law   279
        JOHN H. BARTON
        BARRY E. CARTER

8F The Unipolar Moment   295
        CHARLES KRAUTHAMMER

8G An International Liberal Community   307
        MICHAEL W. DOYLE

THINKING BEYOND THE GULF WAR

9A Military Lessons and U.S. Forces   337
        WILLIAM E. ODOM

9B The Hard Realities of the Arab-Israeli Conflict 349
        GEORGE BALL

9C U.S.–Japan Relations in a Changing Strategic
    Environment   362
        ALAN D. ROMBERG

9D The Grand Bargain: The West and the Future
    of the Soviet Union   375
        GRAHAM ALLISON
        ROBERT BLACKWILL

9E The End of American History: American
    Security, the National Purpose, and the New
    World Order   386
        DAVID C. HENDRICKSON

10 Conclusion: Getting from Here to Where?   407
        GREGORY F. TREVERTON
        BARBARA A. BICKSLER

Bibliography   *435*

Final Report of the Seventy-ninth American Assembly   *445*

Steering Committee and Advisers   *467*

About the Council on Foreign Relations   *468*

About The American Assembly   *468*

Index   *471*

Rethinking America's Security

Preface

The beginning of the final decade of the 20th century was marked by a dramatic change in the relationship between the United States and Soviet Union, a relationship that had defined the context of national security and world order since mid-century. In this new environment, The American Assembly and the Council on Foreign Relations joined to commission the chapters in this volume representing a variety of alternative ways of conceptualizing a "new world order" and America's role in it. This volume was used as background reading for the Seventy-Ninth American Assembly on "Rethinking America's Security," which brought together a group of leading authorities from the United States and abroad to consider these issues and to issue a report that has been widely circulated and is included as an appendix to this volume.

The goal of this volume is to lay the groundwork for continued thought about what America's security means amidst the rapidly expanding agenda of new issues raised by the collapse of communism and the emergence of democratic, free market oriented regimes in Eastern Europe, Latin America, and elsewhere. The Council on Foreign Relations and The American Assembly expect that it will stimulate further thinking and discussion among informed and concerned citizens, and encourage the development of a broad consensus about the nature of the recent changes affecting national security, and the kind of a world we, together with other nations, should strive to create.

With the advice of a steering committee whose names are listed in the appendix, our two institutions retained Dr. Graham Allison, professor of government at the John F. Kennedy School of Government, Harvard University, and Dr. Gregory F. Treverton, senior fellow, Council on Foreign Relations, as project codirectors and coeditors of this volume. The Council on Foreign Relations convened a study group in 1990 and 1991 to review early drafts by the authors.

This is the fourth book in a series of American Assembly publications examining U.S. policy options in a world that has been changing faster and more significantly than at any time since World War II. The first volume in the Assembly series was titled *America's Global Interests: A New Agenda* and edited by Edward K. Hamilton. The second volume was *The Global Economy: America's Role in the Decade Ahead* edited by William Brock and Robert Hormats. The third book was *Preserving the Global Environment: The Challenge of Shared Leadership* edited by Jessica Tuchman Mathews.

We are grateful to the following organizations for their support of this project:

The Pew Charitable Trusts
Sasakawa Peace Foundation
The Ford Foundation
Xerox Foundation
Rockefeller Family Fund, Inc.
CITIBANK
Raytheon Company
Volvo North America

Opinions expressed in this volume are those of the individual authors, and not necessarily those of the funders, the Council on Foreign Relations, or The American Assembly.

Peter Tarnoff
President
Council on Foreign Relations

Daniel A. Sharp
President
The American Assembly

Introduction and Overview

GRAHAM ALLISON AND
GREGORY F. TREVERTON

" "L ife, liberty, and the pursuit of happiness": in the wake of
cold war and hot battle, America's goals in the Declara-

GRAHAM ALLISON is Douglas Dillon Professor of Government at Harvard University and director of the Harvard Project on Strengthening Democratic Institutions. As dean of the John F. Kennedy School of Government from 1977–89, he lead the effort to create a major professional school of government. His teaching and research currently focus on American foreign policy, defense, U.S.–Soviet relations, and the political economy of transitions to economic and political democracy. He has tried to structure a useful analytic approach to the intricacies of organizations and politics as they affect governmental choices and actions building on his major work, *Essence of Decision*. He is a codirector of the School's Project on Avoiding Nuclear War, and coauthor of *Hawks, Doves, and Owls: An Agenda for Avoiding Nuclear War; Fateful Visions: Avoiding Nuclear Catastrophe;* and *Windows of Opportunity: From Cold War to Peaceful Competition*. He has served as special advisor to Secretary of Defense Weinberger; a member of the Secretary of Defense's Policy Board for Secretaries Weinberger, Carlucci, and Cheney; vice chair of JCS Chairman Crowe's Committee on Strategy; a director of the Council on Foreign Relations; and consultant to various departments of government.
GREGORY F. TREVERTON is senior fellow for Europe and director of the Pew Project on Global Security at the Council on Foreign Relations. Prior to joining the Council in 1988, he served on the faculty of

tion of Independence now seem ascendant around the globe. America's security—traditionally defined as preserving the United States as a free nation with its fundamental institutions and values intact—has seldom seemed more certain. The political values of freedom and the market inspire the world.

Yet as America approaches its third postwar transition this century, security needs to be redefined. For forty years America knew what national security meant: protection against the overarching threat of the Soviet Union and Communist expansion was priority number one. Now, with the demise of communism and the rise of democracy, the United States finds itself at a moment of re-creation, to paraphrase Dean Acheson, similar to that facing Americans a half century ago.

The need for American leadership on the international stage has not ended. Of that, the Gulf War offers testimony. No one else could mobilize the coalition against Saddam Hussein. Challenges to and instruments of that leadership in this shrinking world, however, are now very much in question. The challenges appear less military and more economic, the instruments less unilateral and more collaborative, the necessity to share responsibilities as well as burdens both apparent and illusive.

Today the question whether America's security begins at home cries out more loudly than it has for forty years. More than three decades ago Dwight D. Eisenhower pointed out the folly of undermining from within what one is seeking to protect from without. Are we consuming our inheritance when we should be investing in our future? Is securing the "blessings of liberty . . . for our poster-

---

Harvard University's Kennedy School of Government for six years and was director of studies of the International Institute for Strategic Studies in London from 1978–81. He is the author of over a dozen books and fifty articles in the areas of European-American relations and security, intelligence issues, and Latin American relations, including *Covert Action: The Limits of Intervention in the Postwar World, Making the Alliance Work: The United States and Western Europe, Nuclear Weapons in Europe,* and *The "Dollar Drain" and American Forces in Germany.* Dr. Treverton is currently completing *America, Germany, and the Future of Europe,* to be copublished by the Council and Princeton University Press.

ity" more at risk from what is happening within America's borders than from anything outside them?

The fundamental implication of this volume is that the United States is required to *think* again, at a depth not required in two generations. Neither the rethinking nor the re-creation will be done soon. This book seeks to contribute to that rethinking. The product of a unique collaboration between The American Assembly and the Council on Foreign Relations, the chapters that follow were refined over a year in a Council Study Group and then served as the backdrop for an intensive, four-day American Assembly.

How should we approach questions this momentous? There are many avenues of approach and something to be said for each. An approach by functions—military, economic, and political—mirrors government's treatment of issues. A geographical approach by region also has the merit of familiarity and permits interactions across functions to be displayed. Focusing on operational choices likely to drive the rethinking assures relevance and, with luck, a lively debate.

Confronted with this Chinese menu of choices, we purposefully hedged, opting for some from most columns. Section I offers a first cut at rethinking the concept of security from several vantage points, actual and historical. Section II is functional, the dimensions of security. In section III we seek to stretch beyond immediate interests and threats to ask what vision of the world should inspire America's imagination and inform its choices. Section IV is topical, using the Gulf War as a springboard for debate about specific issues; three of these are regional, the Soviet Union, the Middle East, and Japan. Finally, the concluding chapter asks how, as the redefining of security proceeds, we might think of the politics of that process and its implications for the way the United States does its public policy business.

Rethinking the Concept of National Security

Imagine the national security establishment of the United States as a giant enterprise whose main competition, the Soviet Union, just filed for bankruptcy. If management consultants were reviewing afresh that U.S. security "portfolio," unit by unit, which units would they now label "stars" to grow, which "dogs" to sell off, which "cows" to be milked for income to spend elsewhere, and which "question marks" for further thought?

This analogy with portfolio analysis as done in the private sector has shortcomings, as we point out. But it is a useful way to think about America's security and how it has changed. For instance, looking across budgets, activities, and infrastructure confirms a common impression: the United States has defined its security very much in military terms. Nearly four of every five dollars the U.S. government spends on "security" go for the military. Perhaps half of those have been spent on the cold war's core task, deterring a Soviet attack on Western Europe. With the Soviet Union in "Chapter 11," perhaps disintegrating entirely, that "unit" requires basic realignment.

The review provokes questions about other units of America's security establishment: the Soviet Union or Russia will still have nuclear weapons, but does America still need to spend $50 billion per year competing in nuclear weaponry? Is the task of sustaining an edge in military technology over potential adversaries less demanding than before? Diplomacy is cheap by comparison to military instruments. Logic argues that as the United States' ability to advance its objectives by military means shrinks, it will have to get smarter, relying on preventive diplomacy sooner to reduce the need for force later.

The Allison-Treverton chapter provides a vantage point for rethinking America's security defined in terms of external interests and threats. By contrast, Peter Peterson and James Sebenius pose a more fundamental question: is America more threatened from within than without? Their answer is emphatically "yes." They do not deny that threats like that posed by Saddam Hussein are real and deserve attention, but their preoccupation is domestic, those "largely self-inflicted *economic* weaknesses [that] now indirectly threaten" national security and those "domestic trends, that if unchecked, may progressively and *directly* threaten the basic character of our society's institutions and values."

The argument is too penetrating to be dismissed. The United

States felt compelled to pass the hat to pay for the Gulf War. Its huge deficits leave it vulnerable in a way reminiscent of Britain during the Suez crisis in 1956, when Washington muscled it, an ally, into line by threatening a run on the pound sterling. The domestic agenda is familiar but no less pressing for it—education, poverty, the underclass, and unmet economic expectations.

Peterson and Sebenius evoke a "choiceless society," one in which by avoiding action the United States, 5 percent of the world's population, consumes a quarter of its energy—and piles up the bills for its children to pay. Whatever the pitfalls of making policy in the traditional national security arena, at least there has been some sense of the "nation" and of national stakes transcending special interests. In domestic policy, by contrast, logrolling has given particular interests—from farmers to pensioners and S&L depositors—some of what they wanted and, worse, created the sense that they are "entitled" to their subventions of public treasure.

At this third postwar transition, it bears examining American conceptions of security in earlier periods. Ernest May's review ranging back to George Washington's time suggests two lessons and three questions. First, the nation's security—"national security" was a post–World War II coinage—always was understood to have both an external and a domestic component, but the relationship between the two varied. For Washington, security was safe borders externally and a safe union internally; what was good for one aided the other. For Eisenhower, by contrast, external security conflicted with domestic, defined primarily as economic health, because of the burden of military spending.

Second, America's conception of its security broadened over time to encompass the traditional interests of other states. The Latin American states were the first nations so encompassed, in the Monroe Doctrine. World War II brought American adoption of Britain and its interests, the cold war Germany and Japan and theirs.

The questions are whether the domestic face of security will continue to be economic, or be broadened to include clean air or less crime; and how domestic and external security will relate. The current public mood, plainly evident in Peterson and Sebenius's chapter, contrasts with the cold war but is like earlier American history: when the external dimension is less pressing, the internal should receive more attention and money.

May's final question is the central one for the later chapters envisioning a new international order. Will America's conception of what is vital to its security continue to expand? That is suggested by the language of a "new world order." But Americans might again shrink their security perimeter to those nations adopted into an "empire for liberty." If so, would the Ukraine, or a Palestinian state, or a Hungary on the brink of collapse be included or excluded? Or the United States might neither shrink its perimeter nor reverse the shrinkage in its capacity; it might simply recognize it needed help from allies or the United Nations.

Rethinking the Dimensions of National Security

The four chapters in this section grapple with the same four questions from one dimension to the next:

- What are American *national interests?*
- What *threats* to those interests impinge externally?
- What *opportunities* are there to advance those interests?
- What *policies and programs* could best defend interests and take advantage of opportunities?

In the *technological dimension,* the chapter by B.R. Inman and Daniel Burton, there is little gainsaying that America has ceded advantage in industrial sector after sector, from consumer electronics to semiconductors. At issue is the consequence for American economic performance and national security.

In their discussion of the effects on the economy, Inman and Burton complement the chapter on the *economic dimension* by Michael Borrus and John Zysman. As the United States retreated from final production in consumer electronics, for instance, it also began to lose the supply base for components, and it deprived itself of the opportunity to master the new manufacturing techniques that provide comparative advantage in other sectors.

For national security the consequences are just as far-reaching.

In the past, American defense technology provided spin-offs for civilian industry, but now the process works very nearly the other way around. In many areas civilian technology outstrips anything the military can offer; the microprocessor in the Patriot missile, for instance, is two generations behind that in the personal computer used to write this introduction. The Pentagon is being compelled to adapt commercial technology to its needs.

As often as not, these commercial technologies have been developed elsewhere, in Japan in particular. That does not mean Japan is the enemy, not necessarily even a potential enemy. It does call attention, however, to how the United States hedges its dependence and, more important, revitalizes its broad base in civilian technology. Inman and Burton offer a number of specific suggestions, all of them aimed at integrating the civilian and defense sectors of American technology.

Borrus and Zysman connect the decline of U.S. technology to the relative decline of the American economy, especially in manufacturing. For them, there is no comfort in the accompanying growth in services, for those sectors usually pay less than manufacturing to which they are, in any event, ultimately linked; moreover, services are not much traded internationally. Nor is it necessarily comforting that the beneficiaries of America's decline are American allies, Japan and Germany in particular. The loss of relative economic position is also a loss of political power. If specific consequences are not always visible, "the American capacity to extract compliance in the security system has diminished."

Indeed, as America's economic competitors have been better at developing new technologies and embedding them in new manufacturing processes, the world is becoming a global economy with three regional poles—east Asia, Europe, and North America. Trade within regions has grown faster than trade among them. The success of Japan and its partners in Asia is most visible, but Europe has advantages as well—a skilled workforce, a foundation in science, and a solid manufacturing base. Moreover, the 1992 program stands as testimony to its commitment to confront its weaknesses.

For Borrus and Zysman, the current security debate is still rooted in the past. If the military world is, for a moment, unipolar, the economic world is multipolar. America's allies have the capacity to act on their own in the international system. The United States is dependent on them in some areas. If it could ever exploit the military area to achieve more favorable terms of trade, it can no longer. Quite the contrary, it is now confronted with how others can exploit terms of trade to impose *their* structure. For Borrus and Zysman, as for Peterson and Sebenius, the American economic position is a matter of national security.

The *military dimension* of security has not gone away: if Americans needed any reminding, Saddam Hussein provided it. Under Secretary of Defense Paul Wolfowitz's chapter is a commentary on how far Washington officialdom has come, as well as on the questions that lie ahead. Notwithstanding the Gulf War, the United States continued with plans to decrease its military forces by a quarter over five years. These plans were based on the virtual ending of Soviet military power as a specific threat to Europe if not (yet) as a long-term fact against which to hedge.

If the United States can afford to be less ready to meet global conflict, it must be more ready to deal with regional conflict outside Europe, and perhaps to deal with more than one such conflict at once. The world the United States confronts will be happier than the glacial stability of the cold war, but it also will be more uncertain. For Wolfowitz, while these arguments can be criticized as conjuring up new enemies to defend Pentagon budgets now that the main enemy is in decline, the Gulf War offers powerful reasons for caution in cutting America's defenses.

The emerging strategy rests on six elements: relying more on allies as a way of extending U.S. power; sustaining forces deployed "forward," especially in Europe and Asia, albeit smaller forces; increasing mobility, including by pre-positioning equipment abroad; sustaining a robust navy; planning for the possibility that the United States might have to dramatically increase its forces at some point in the future, while recognizing that it would have literally years of warning of a renewed Soviet threat; and, finally, sustaining nuclear deterrence while developing future options for strategic defenses.

Saddam Hussein reminded us that old military threats have not gone away. Our newspapers tell us that new problems, or new forms of old ones, are more and more urgent. Do they now threaten America's security? There is no point in splitting definitional hairs over what is or is not "security." At the same time, to call every problem of the day a "threat to national security" is to empty the term of meaning. Just as bad, doing so is a poor guide to policy.

The "war on drugs," for instance, seemed to suppose that national security was at risk. Yet while narcotics abuse is plainly a wrenching problem, it does not yet pose a threat to basic institutions and values for the United States. The same cannot be said of Colombia. Moreover, forty years of the cold war have conditioned us to locate threats to national security abroad, hence the temptation to focus on those who grow coca or traffic in cocaine abroad. The drug problem, however, is above all domestic; the enemy is us, a fact that has intruded only slowly in the American debate.

Thomas Schelling's approach to this *global dimension* of security is characteristically provocative. He asks, first, if the world were to move toward "governing institutions" on a global scale, what might be the basis for comparison? The answer is disturbing: South Africa. We live in a world one-fifth rich, four-fifths poor, with the rich and poor largely differentiated by the colors of their skins and geographically detached from one another.

Atop Schelling's agenda for that globe are population growth and migration; the two are quite distinct in policy terms but linked because the former is a primary engine of the latter. Like other items on the global agenda, both raise questions of sovereignty, of the global community's responsibility for and access to what goes on within a state's borders.

Environment and resources are next on the list. Schelling is more sanguine than most about global warming's effect on the United States and the other industrial countries; its economic consequences will be enveloped by overall growth. Concern will lead to new institutions but not to much by way of resource transfers— the last item on Schelling's suggestive agenda. To bring greenhouse emissions under control in the developing world has been estimated to require transfers from the industrial world on the scale of the Marshall Plan in relation to American gross national product (GNP).

To elaborate the agenda is to underline how far the world is from acting on it. The items do not, in Schelling's view, pose threats to America's security, not yet. But they surely bear on America's values: policy toward immigration, for instance, is about what, and who, we are as a nation.

Visions of the New International Order

Schelling's imaginings of a global agenda are a springboard for thinking about the new international order, a task evoked by George Bush during the Gulf War. The short chapters in this section present sharply varying visions, intended to provoke debate, not stand alone as full-fledged descriptions.

At one extreme, John Mearsheimer looks to the emerging world and finds it wanting. The new order is *disorder restored:* the end of the cold war has removed the dampening hand of bipolarity but left the nation state alive and well. While those states prize prosperity, they will, if need be, subordinate it to national integrity. Hence the world Wolfowitz argued would be more uncertain may also be more disorderly. War is possible, even in Europe.

Henry Kissinger shares with Mearsheimer the view that nation states will be primary actors and that maintaining a favorable balance of power remains the primary security objective. For him, *the balance must be sustained,* in circumstances—both in Europe and the Middle East—that make the balancing harder, not least because America is now more dependent on acting in concert with allies and friends.

Charles Kupchan and Clifford Kupchan make an argument for *concerting power* instead of balancing it. Looking back to the nineteenth-century Concert of Europe, they believe collective security has a future, at least in Europe among the major powers. They envision a core group of the Conference on Security and Cooperation in Europe (CSCE)—the United States, the Soviet Union, Britain, France, and Germany—which would operate, at least for the foreseeable future, alongside NATO.

Richard Gardner's vision is *practical internationalism.* It borrows from the other visions but includes special attention to international law and to the UN. He presumes what Kupchan and Kupchan call for—that after the cold war the major powers will manage considerable cooperation—and he asks whether the UN could build on its success in the Gulf to establish a small, permanent Rapid Deployment Force based on Article 43 of the UN Charter.

John Barton and Barry Carter imagine *the role of law* in another sense, not writ large as in the International Court of Justice but writ small in, for instance, the emergence of the person in international law, not just the state, or the increasing use of arbitration as a way to enforce international contracts. This creeping expansion is not a complete vision of a new order, and it has been most visible where money, not pride or sovereignty, has been the main stake. But the U.S.–Iran Claims Tribunal has been a pace-setting innovation; money is the ostensible stake, but political hostility is not far in the background.

While the other authors emphasize the limits of America's capacity to shape a new order, Charles Krauthammer trumpets its power. This is a *unipolar moment.* The United States is the single, unchallenged superpower; the initials that made the Gulf a success were U.S., not UN. He derides the isolationism he saw in opposition to the Gulf War, and he belittles the idea of America in decline. If it is, the reason surely is not imperial overstretch. For him, the alternative to robust interventionism by the United States is not a balance of power, but chaos.

Krauthammer's exhortation is longer on what America should oppose—Saddam Hussein, the proliferation of weapons of mass destruction—than on what values it should seek to uphold. Values are the heart of Michael Doyle's vision, that of a *liberal community of peace.* Two hundred years ago Immanuel Kant described democracies' peaceful proclivity, and Doyle argues that both in theory and in fact democracies do not make war on fellow democracies. Thus the task for American policy is to expand that community of peace. This is no "crusade for democracy." Doyle would not have America intervene in other states against the will of that state's majority unless basic human rights were being denied.

Thinking Beyond the Gulf War

The Gulf War put the question of shaping a new international order squarely on the agenda. It also left a number of more specific questions about American policy, ones important in themselves but also importantly connected to the vision of the future America seeks. The first and most obvious of these is military: will America be able to guarantee its security with the cutbacks now in train?

William Odom's answer is a qualified "no." In particular, paradoxically, after seeing the value of "heavy" armored forces in the Gulf, the United States is planning to reduce those forces enough to make it difficult, though not impossible, to rerun Desert Storm in the late 1990s. In contrast to Wolfowitz, Odom would make deeper cuts in the Navy—aircraft carriers in particular, whose contribution to the Gulf War was marginal—and shallower ones in Army heavy forces. He would also press both the Air Force and Navy to spend more on equipment to move Army forces around the globe—a neglected mission in both services.

These recommendations are controversial enough. But Odom also argues for measures that cut across other sets of vested interests among the military and their congressional allies—the Marine Corps, Army airborne forces, and the National Guard. While reserve and guard specialists, whose civilian jobs were akin to their military ones, served admirably in the Gulf War, that was not the case of guard combat division. They simply were not ready and, to boot, Odom reckons cost two-thirds as much as active duty units.

Fighting a new enemy in the Middle East also sharpened questions about America's security interests in three regions—the erstwhile paramount enemy, the Soviet Union; the Middle East, where the war was fought; and Japan, like Germany, the ally whose interests were at stake but whose support for the war was criticized.

Graham Allison and Robert Blackwill are surprised by those Americans who, looking at the Soviet Union, conclude that we're too poor to influence its future, that we couldn't anyway, or that its disintegration suits our interests. Having spent $5 trillion to meet the military challenge of the Soviet Union around the globe, they ask, are the United States and its allies to opt out now when the Soviet future is being formed?

American stakes are enormous, beginning but hardly ending
with Moscow's 30,000 nuclear weapons. For Allison and Blackwill,
this moment is a window of opportunity. For Russians it is a
"learning moment," when the country has been pried open to
satellite dishes, fax machines, and the ideas they bring. It may well
be that any effort at influence will fail, but the stakes are too big not
to try.

They call for a *Grand Bargain* of Marshall Plan proportions, put
forward by a coalition of western governments led by the United
States. This bargain would begin with a process that creates incentives for Soviet leaders, both in what remains at the center and in
the republics, to choose democracy and a market economy, the
future consistent with both their own best interests and ours. Western assistance would be strictly *conditional* on continuing political
pluralization and a coherent program for moving rapidly to a
market economy. The context has changed after the failed coup in
August 1991 and the ensuing rush to independence, especially in
the Baltics, but the argument is still apt.

George Ball's discussion of the Middle East is as provocative,
and perhaps more controversial. For Ball, American policy in the
region is contradictory to the point of hypocrisy. While ostensibly
seeking peace, the United States retreats from the idea of an international conference at the first whiff of Israeli opposition. Washington's criticism of Israeli repression in the occupied territories is
not backed by action, and the United States first diverts Soviet
emigrants to Israel, then turns a half-blind eye while U.S. aid is
used to build settlements in those occupied territories. America
preaches restraint in arms sales to the region while selling its
own—unless Israel's allies in Congress prevent sales to Arab countries.

Ball is not optimistic about breaking the impasse. He would
start by reversing the longstanding American desire to monopolize
peacemaking in the region and inviting, say, France to bring the
issue back to the UN Security Council. A UN resolution might
then lay out the principles for a settlement—from the return of
West Bank and Gaza to some Palestinian entity, to a condominium arrangement for Jerusalem, to arrangements for control of
weapons in the region.

The Gulf War also brought to the fore American criticisms of major allies, Germany and Japan, for not doing enough. In Japan's case, the war fueled a broader debate. On one side are those who believe that U.S.-Japan relations are, on balance, a success and can continue to be managed along something like their existing track. On the other side, "Japan bashers" are most visible. This group also includes less polemical critics, like Borrus and Zysman, who are more worried about the pattern and prospects of U.S.-Japan relations. They argue that a different American policy is called for, though the difference is as much domestic as foreign.

Alan Romberg is in the former camp. For him, the American security relationship with Japan remains an imperative in Asia, where Soviet reforms have had much less strategic impact than in Europe and where no state would be comfortable with a sharp increase in Japanese military power. Angry American reactions, especially from Congress—to the controversy over the FSX, Japan's next-generation fighter or to Toshiba selling the Soviet Union equipment that would permit submarines to run more quietly—inevitably washed back on defense. But on the whole the United States, wisely, has kept economics and security at some distance.

The U.S.-Japan security link needs to be "updated" to find ways for Japan to take more responsibility, not just share more burdens—already it pays some 40 percent of the cost of stationing American troops on its soil. The American military presence in East Asia, now 135,000, is scheduled to shrink by 10 or 12 percent in the next several years. But Romberg believes that updating can be done within the current framework of the relationship and, implicitly, within the current definition of security as it applies to Asia.

David Hendrickson's chapter reflects on American use of force in light of the Gulf War. Like May, he sees the world war and cold war as a sharp expansion of America's definition of security—a consensus Vietnam shook but did not break. Rather than defeat in Vietnam, it was victory in the cold war that loosed the foundations of American foreign policy. For Hendrickson, the outcome was a paradox: the ending of the main threat made a new world order possible but at the same time less necessary.

In this context the Gulf War was an ambiguous signal of the intentions of the American body politic. The emphasis on international law and multilateralism, on the one hand, coexisted with temptations to use military power for purposes well beyond what the international consensus would support. The plight of the Kurds underscored the broader point about the devastation of Iraq: America's war was the demonstration of power without the subsequent taking of responsibility that the power implies. No one, for instance, argued that the United States should simply walk away from the defeated World War II powers, no matter how "evil" their leaders had been labeled.

The lesson for Hendrickson is that the United States should be cautious in using force. He supports a "disengagement" of sorts, not abandoning traditional allies but resisting the temptation to take on new security commitments or to become the global policeman, using force on behalf of the independence of all states. He would return to the roots of American foreign policy, imposing limits on the use of force because real national purposes lay elsewhere. America should be an example of freedom, not an enforcer of independence.

Getting from Here to Where?

Ideas and concepts occupy center stage in this book. The debate over a redefinition of America's security is just beginning, and so we asked authors to push the limits of their inquiries, to ask what ought to be while only glancing over their shoulders at what might be politically possible. Those glancings run through a number of the chapters: May wonders how the American body politic will adjust interests in light of reduced capacity; Peterson and Sebenius excoriate the "choiceless society"; and both Ball and Odom in different ways lament that what they deem reasonable seems so far from possible.

In their concluding chapter, Gregory Treverton and Barbara Bicksler draw some of these threads together and raise questions about restructuring *how* the U.S. makes policy as it redefines *what* national security means. The basic institutions of American national security policy—the Pentagon, the Central Intelligence

Agency, or the National Security Council (NSC)—were creatures of the hot and cold wars, adjusted but fundamentally unchanged since. The tinkering mostly took the form of trying to integrate the operations and advice of the separate military services. In the 1970s a spate of proposals for better connecting economics to national security was paralleled by a series of institutional innovations, but none of them endured.

If the rethinking of security implied integrating a broader range of considerations, that might suggest, for instance, a broader NSC or a new domestic council, somehow endowed with comparable stature and claim on presidential attentions. Or new priorities might indicate changing the institutional pecking order. In the 1930s the Agriculture and Commerce Departments would have been thought as weighty as State and War. If Peterson and Sebenius are right about the choiceless society, much more dramatic institutional changes would be in order. It no doubt is too early to implement any of these changes in how America does its public policy business, but it surely is not too early to begin thinking about them.

While it is easy to cover American opinion during the cold war with a gauze of consensus that stretches the facts, the policy of containment did command broad public support and call forth heavy charges on American resources. When Americans argued over Vietnam, for instance, their argument was, as Hendrickson notes, over whether containment necessitated a war in Asia, not over the wisdom of containment itself.

The sea change in American attitudes began before the fall of the Berlin Wall, but its result is neither apparent nor predetermined. Military threats have fallen in the public's concern by comparison to economic issues, the Gulf War notwithstanding. Yet it is a good bet that the public will be as uncertain as the experts, and so there is the risk of volatility in public attitudes, the "crusade of the month." Or, absent the polestar of containment, security policy could come to look more like the domestic policy Peterson and Sebenius portray with pieces of policy captured by specific interests.

To say that much will depend on events is just as trite as to say that, given uncertainty, the scope for leadership is correspondingly great. But both seem the case. If public attitudes remain volatile, they also will be malleable; Americans will be searching for ways to apprehend the dazzling change and comprehend its meaning for their nation's security. The opportunity for President Bush and his successors is exquisite.

We have been struck throughout this project by just how uncomfortable most Americans find the challenge of rethinking of America's security. This applies to foreign policy experts and establishmentarians, perhaps especially so. It requires thinking deeper and wider than is our habit. The changes in the world are staggering, almost too portentous to grasp, and the grooves of cold war orthodoxy run deep. Just keeping up with events is hard enough. At The American Assembly conference, participants frequently suggested as a possibility, or as an impossibility, something that already had happened—for instance, some association of the Eastern European states to NATO or cutting America's military forces by a quarter!

We hope this book contributes to a richer debate. The world beyond the cold war contains some dangers but more opportunities if Americans can but stretch their minds, then their policies, and then their politics to embrace them. The re-creation is up to us.

RETHINKING THE CONCEPT OF NATIONAL SECURITY

1

National Security Portfolio Review

GRAHAM ALLISON AND
GREGORY F. TREVERTON

I magine reviewing the portfolio of American national security expenditures, activities, and assets, much as a management consultant would review a large conglomerate in the aftermath of a dramatic shift in the structure of its market. For forty years the United States concentrated on a single competitor, the Soviet Union. Now we find that competitor filing for bankruptcy under "Chapter 11." What should this mean for U.S. "markets" and the activities by which we seek to advance our interests in them?

The Argument for Reviewing the Security Portfolio

The process of adjusting to the changed environment has begun. In the spring of 1990, the president and Congress agreed to a deficit reduction package cutting defense expenditures by 4 percent per year in real terms for the fiscal years 1991–95. While this reduction was more than some wished—defense spending already had been going down in real terms since 1986—it was less than most expected given the widespread agreement that the cold war had ended. CIA Director William Webster testified to the Senate

Arms Services Committee that "the elimination of the Soviet threat of sudden attack on Western Europe is irreversible." Secretary of Defense Dick Cheney's request for reduced defense funding reflected his judgment that "the threat has declined significantly." The 1990 agreement on reductions stopped what House Arms Services Committee Chair Les Aspin had called the Defense budget's "free fall."

Behind the administration's program for orderly reductions in defense spending lay a serious review of U.S. defense programs in the postwar period, a review led by Colin Powell, the chair of the Joint Chiefs of Staff, and Paul Wolfowitz, the under secretary of defense, whose chapter in this volume describes the reassessment in more detail. The lessons of Saddam Hussein's aggression and defeat will produce specific reassessments but did not fundamentally alter the conclusions of this review.

The Gulf War did serve as a healthy antidote to any imaginings that the waning of the cold war also meant an end to military threats directed at American interests. The chorus of pundits eager to declare the permanent devaluation of military power has been quieted again—for a season. While the victory will tempt advocates to engage in special pleading on behalf of favorite weapons systems, their efforts are not likely to succeed. The administration's commitment to its program for orderly reductions in defense was signaled clearly by Secretary Cheney's announcement of the largest weapons program cancellation in U.S. history, the Navy's A-12 attack fighter, while the war with Iraq was imminent.

The 1990 internal Department of Defense review took a significant first step. But as its authors recognize, the end of the cold war poses a much larger and more daunting challenge. That challenge has not yet been adequately framed. It is a challenge we attempt to conceptualize here as a "national security portfolio review."

The concept of a "portfolio review" emerged in the late 1970s and 1980s as a major idea in U.S. corporate management. The approach begins with the insight that most large corporations, in fact, consist of a number of separable "strategic business units." General Motors' Chevrolet, Buick, and Cadillac divisions are familiar, but apparently more unified corporations, like IBM or Data General, also consist of separable, identifiable units—for instance, large mainframe computers, personal computers, software, and services.

For each of these disaggregated units, a portfolio review first assesses the size of the total market and of the unit's market share, as well as rates of growth in the market and its profitability. Against that backdrop, the analysis then seeks to identify key strategic advantages of the company over its competitors. Following this approach, one of the major consulting firms, the Boston Consulting Group, made famous a two-by-two matrix that classified business units according to market share, growth, and profitability. The units of a firm were thus located in one of four boxes: cash cows (to be milked for income to use elsewhere), dogs (to be sold), stars (to be grown), and question marks (to be further analyzed).

The single most important implication of portfolio analysis for our purposes is this: major change in an enterprise's market (due, for example, to technological change or the entry of major new competitors into the market) will have large, differential impacts on component business units of the corporation. Thus, to continue with the computer example, the recent emergence of personal computers and open architecture for mainframes means that the principal business of most of the large computer companies (namely, the sale of proprietary mainframes) is a waning asset to be milked, but not one that can be sustained. Computer companies are thus refocusing on other strategic business units in the search for competitive advantages.

This brief description hardly does justice to the concept of a portfolio review but perhaps does suggest the relevance of the analogy to the national security community's current challenge. In the aftermath of World War II, defense-dedicated conglomerates, almost all of whose aircraft, tanks, ships, and munitions had been purchased by the U.S. government during the war, confronted a rapid decline of defense spending from half of America's gross national product (GNP) to 10 percent. Plainly, the post–cold war transition will be much less dramatic. But whether defense spending falls from 6 percent of GNP to 4 or to 3, the loss of the Soviet Union as the preeminent adversary will shift the demand for military aircraft, electronics, and other weapons. It will thus reshape the market for, and so reorient the strategies of, defense contractors like General Dynamics, McDonnell-Douglas, or Northrop.

Here, though, the point of the analogy is less firms or even defense spending as a whole than the entire American national security establishment as it seeks to adjust to a post–cold war environment. The portfolio to be reviewed is not just the Defense Department but the national security establishment. This review begins with *budgets* of all entities whose activities are relevant to American national security objectives. Yet since dollars expended are not the only, and in many areas not the most significant, measure of effect, it is necessary to review *activities* as well. And beyond activities, the reassessment needs to include *assets and liabilities* accumulated as a result of the cold war strategy.

A full strategic portfolio analysis would identify strategic business units along several dimensions; ask how the environment has changed for each of these and is likely to change; and then consider whether the current set of activities or some alternative set of activities could better protect U.S. security and advance U.S. interests in this area. For instance, against the most significant change in environment—the declining of the Soviet Union as an imminent military threat to Europe and as an expansionist, revolutionary, global power—how should we evaluate U.S. spending for the defense of Western Europe (approximately $150 billion in the current budget) by comparison to economic aid for Eastern Europe (less than one half of 1 percent of that figure in 1991), or to American diplomacy in seeking to sustain the North Atlantic Treaty Organization (NATO) and develop political institutions like the Conference on Security and Cooperation in Europe (CSCE)? Is NATO a cash cow? Is CSCE a star or a question mark? More broadly, what should the change in environment mean for trade-offs between guns for protection from external threats and investments at home in combating drugs or reducing the federal budget deficit?

The business analogy has its limits, and we point out some of those below. But as a way to think about America's business of national security, it is a useful starting point. It offers perspective on the shape of the national security establishment as it has emerged over the last forty-plus years, and thus provides a base line for assessing possible changes.

Characterizing the
National Security Enterprise:
Dollars, Activities, and Assets

Budgets

One indicator of how America has seen its "business" of national security is how it has spent money. Money is not the only measure, nor an ideal one, but it is a place to start (see Table 1).

One difficulty with these aggregates is that they are *institutional* budgets lumped into functional categories, not programmatic breakdowns. Thus they can be fairly criticized on many grounds. On one hand, it might be said, for instance, that there is much less aid than meets the eye in the foreign aid budget given loan terms and ties to American exports. On the other, big chunks of the defense budget might be called infrastructure or economic development, to the extent they pay people to build buildings, hospitals, or roads. To the extent that defense expenditures transfer resources to groups society might wish to help, they might even be called social spending or pork barrel.

The criticisms are fair. A private sector strategic planner would

---

TABLE 1. National Security Portfolio Review

Rough estimates of federal government expenditures

Activity	1990 Outlays (billions)
Defense	350
Foreign aid and diplomacy	20
Research and development, nondefense	25
(defense, included above	37)
Border control and war on drugs	10
Environment	10
Energy	4
Intelligence (even rougher estimate, much of which is included in defense outlays above)	30

want to spread out spending by programmatic categories. That would be a useful exercise, but it goes beyond our purposes here. Here, we mean only to start discussion from a different vantage point, and for that purpose approximations suffice. Even at that level of crudeness, the numbers are as provocative as they are revealing.

Broader comparisons might be useful in thinking about whether America's "national security" might be more affected by what happened within its borders, in the health or education of its citizens or the state of its infrastructure (see Tables 2 and 3).

Thus the ratio of defense spending to foreign aid was thirty-two to one during the cold war period. This period included the Marshall Plan as well as the 1980s military build-up against the Soviet Union. How should we evaluate the thirty-two to one ratio? Defense clearly was a "star," but was foreign aid a "dog" or just a small "business" unit?

Focusing on current governmental budgets at the federal level is no more than a snapshot. There is double-counting: for example, most of the separate estimate for intelligence is scattered throughout the defense budget. Moreover, this focus leaves out spending by the private sector and nonprofit sectors whose expenditures are sometimes related to national security. For example, aerospace companies finance some research and development (R & D) of weapons systems out of their own resources. Similarly, the American Red Cross spends private donations to care for war refugees.

TABLE 2. Comparative National Expenditures, 1986 (rough estimates, billions of dollars)

National defense	350
Education	270
Health care, including social security	460

TABLE 3. Illustrative Cumulative Totals, 1946–90 (current dollars, in billions)

Defense	11,300
Foreign aid	350

Because the defense "product line" is so large, both absolutely and comparatively, it requires further disaggregation (see Table 4).

Activities

Budgets are one measure of the national security establishment, but not all of what the United States does to safeguard national security means spending a lot of money. Able diplomats, for instance, may reach agreements that limit threats, thus reducing the need for military measures. As in health care, small expenditures of effort on prevention may obviate large commitments of treasure. Alas, cleverness is hard to measure, and so we are thrown back to cruder indicators.

One visual guide to activities is Figure 1. It makes rough judgments about which expenditures should be called "national security," a central question in this book. Thus, all of what the State and Defense Departments do is so labeled, but only a relatively

---

**TABLE 4. Core Military Expenditures
(in billions of dollars)**

	1990 Outlays (estimates)
Nuclear forces	
Strategic nuclear	52.0
Tactical nuclear	2.0
Atomic energy defense activities (DOE)	8.9
Conventional forces by region	
Europe	126.0
Pacific	35.7
Latin America	7.2
Continental U.S.	8.8
Other major functions	
R & D (Defense)	37.0
Intelligence and communications	26.0
Retired pay accrual	21.0
Veterans benefits and services	28.8
Total	353.4

Sources: These and most other figures in this chapter are based on *Budget of the U.S. Government, Fiscal Year 1991.*

FIGURE 1. America's National Security Establishment

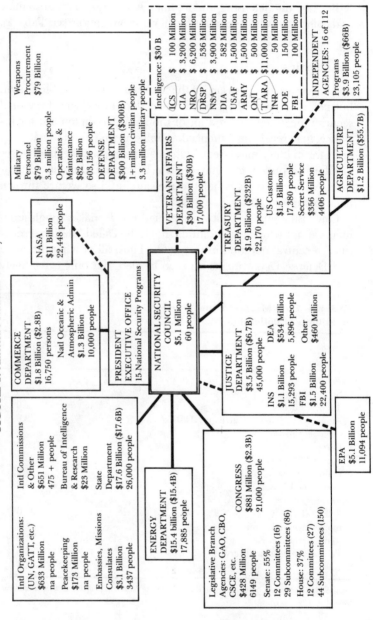

small portion of the Treasury, predominantly the Customs Service. By the same token, for a less "traditional" category, like the environment, most of the federal expenditure and activity goes for cleaning up air and water that is primarily domestic, although the intersections with foreign affairs are present: witness acid rain in relations with Canada or waste water problems with Mexico. Needless to say, the quibbles about budgets also apply to personnel figures, and the estimates are guesstimates, intended to convey orders of activity, nothing more.

Another crude indicator of activity is the count of personnel (see Table 5).

This total is larger than the entire population of New Jersey. And the count is conservative in what it includes, excluding, for instance, private activities that advance (or hinder) the nation's security. Many voluntary activities—CARE or the Red Cross or other relief agencies—might be regarded as mostly humanitarian but not exclusively. America's citizens often pay attention to the league tables of who is providing famine relief in a way that sug-

**TABLE 5. Activities
(as measured by personnel figures, 1990)**

Department or Agency	Personnel
Uniformed military (active and reserve)	3,200,000
Army	1,500,000
Navy	700,000
Air Force	800,000
Marine Corps	200,000
Coast Guard	38,000
Defense Department civilians	1,000,000
Justice (DEA, INS, FBI)	48,000
State, AID, USIA	26,000
CIA	?30,000?
Independent agencies	23,000
Congress	21,000
Commerce	20,000
Energy	18,000
EPA	11,000
Executive Office of President	4,700

gests more than an interest in who is doing what. American firms, U.S. based multinationals, and their subsidiaries abroad affect not only America's economic strength but also developments in foreign countries. So, too, do the purveyors of the culture many Americans regard as distinctly "American" (even while many non-Americans would see it as "international")—from music to movies and television to blue jeans and Big Macs.

The effects of activities need not be commensurate with the numbers of people who do them. Nevertheless, fighting even small wars like Grenada or Panama still requires several State Departments-worth of people. The effects on American security of, say, the Grenada intervention might be less than a successful attempt to open up global trade in agriculture through the General Agreement on Tariffs and Trade (GATT) negotiations despite the fact that the former required thousands of people, the latter no more than a hundred or two.

Relations between the American executive and Congress provide a sharp example of this difficulty. On the face, 20,000 people in Congress engaged in "national security" does not seem a large number by comparison to the executive establishment of 7-plus million. Yet it often seems to executive officials, and sometimes to those in Congress, that the scope of the congressional involvement hampers, not advances, the nation's interest. By one recent estimate, Defense Department officials alone offer fourteen hours of testimony every congressional workday, with additional hours of staff time to prepare for each presentation.[1] At a minimum, again, numbers may not be a reliable index of effort, but at the very least, time is money if not quality.

Assets (and Liabilities)

A third part of America's national security portfolio is capital assets. This, too, ranges from concrete to intangible, with much of it not easy to count, let alone evaluate. In the private sector analogy, much of it, like America's prestige or its perceived firmness or reliability, is more like name recognition of products or goodwill among suppliers than the book value of investment in plant and equipment.

From the tangible to the less so:

• *Military forces and bases.* Table 6 displays American military forces by their basing locations.

• *Diplomatic establishments.* In 1990 the United States maintained some 300 diplomatic establishments abroad—145 embassies, 11 missions and 144 consulates. The locations reflected the numbers of countries weighted by America's traditional interests—accordingly, 78 were in the Americas, 76 in Asia, 75 in Europe, 61 in Africa, and 17 in the Middle East. A full review of facilities would also add intelligence and other purposes.

• *Alliances, like NATO.*

• *Treaties and agreements.* The list of the major U.S. treaties and agreements concluded between 1947 and 1985 runs to nine pages, ranging from the North Atlantic Treaty of 1949 to specific agree-

---

TABLE 6. American Military Forces by Basing Location, 1989

Total, worldwide	2,100,000
United States territory	1,600,000
Continental U.S.	1,250,000
Alaska	25,000
Hawaii	50,000
afloat	200,000
other	75,000
Europe	350,000
Germany	250,000
Britain	25,000
Italy	15,000
Spain	10,000
afloat	20,000
other	20,000
East Asia and Pacific	130,000
Japan	50,000
Korea	45,000
Philippines	15,000
other and afloat	20,000
Rest of world	45,000
Panama	20,000
Saudi Arabia	10,000
other and afloat	15,000

Source: Department of Defense. (Totals may not add up due to rounding.)

ments on particular weapons systems with individual countries. The overwhelming majority of the agreements are in the security area, over weapons, military cooperation, or basing rights. Many of those, not surprisingly, are with those countries with whom the United States has the thickest military connections—NATO partners, Japan, the Philippines, and Australia throughout, Latin American states earlier in the postwar period, and Southwest Asian nations later on, and with the Soviet Union after 1970 and the beginning of arms control.

Again, evaluating this infrastructure is subjective. If agreements are considered infrastructure, in many cases their purpose was also infrastructure, establishing basing or testing rights and so, in many instances, reducing the burden or money cost of doing security "business." To the extent those agreements became controversial, presumably their overall value would be recorded as declining even if their specific military purpose were sustained.

Those agreements-as-national-security-infrastructure whose purpose was not narrowly military are still more subjective in cost-benefit terms. For instance, the 1975 Helsinki Final Act, the beginning of the Conference on Security and Cooperation in Europe, was signed without enthusiasm by the Ford administration, which shared the view of many American conservatives that the West was acquiescing in the ratification of Soviet bloc borders in Europe while receiving in return only fine but empty words about human rights. A decade and a half later, most of those same doubters would agree that the "fine words" gradually put human rights on the interstate agenda and so played a role in liberating Eastern Europe from Soviet imposed regimes.

The infrastructure of nongovernmental activities might also be considered in the national security portfolio. During the cold war, for instance, U.S. commitments to Europe seemed credible, to the extent they did, not just because of nuclear weapons, military deployments, or even the presence of large numbers of military dependents. They were credible also because of the societal connections between the United States and Europe—ranging from U.S. corporate subsidiaries and their managers, exchange students, and tourists, at the tangible end of the spectrum, to the shared history and sense of common destiny at the intangible.

Ideally, many of the less tangible aspects of national power ought also to be considered part of America's national security infrastructure. If measuring them is too hard, distinguishing several overlapping categories is still useful:[2]

• *Political goodwill.* This might be seen as the capital built from previous investments. That this has some effect seems as undeniable as that it seldom leads directly to foreign support for American policy. The United States retains considerable residual respect, if not affection in Western Europe because of its role in World War II; that is especially the case in Britain. America's postwar generosity and steadiness have enhanced that respect, perhaps especially in the enemy-become-friend, the Federal Republic of Germany. Unwavering American support for German unification has added to its political capital in Germany.

Just as a history of resolute support builds capital, so a history of intervention may accumulate suspicion about political motives even as it creates grudging respect. And what is capital for some purposes may be a liability for others: as the United States sought to build a coalition in the Gulf, its identification with Israel was a handicap and the political awkwardness of its past support for Saudi Arabia an uncertainty, while its decade of support for Egypt was a plus. So, too, in Latin America the United States probably acquired political capital among some groups for its support of human rights just as it spent it by appearing interventionist or heavy-handed.

• *Political strengths,* like the attractiveness of American political institutions or economic practices. These derive more from what the United States is than what it does, and so are not easy to treat as an instrument for particular foreign policy purposes.

• *Political consensus and cohesion at home,* in support of particular foreign policies. The Gulf War was a striking example of political consensus played out in national polls about the president and the war, all the way to town-by-town demonstrations of yellow ribbons.

• *Domestic political and economic health*—the "Eisenhower imperative." Even John Foster Dulles's Massive Retaliation speech began with, and repeated, that the first priority of national security is the health of the nation's economy: "It is not sound to become permanently committed to military expenditures so vast that they lead to 'practical bankruptcy.' "

The Implications and Questions

Evaluating America's national security portfolio is more bedeviled by problems of measurement and by intangibles than are private sector analogues. As a first approach, however, several broad observations about the current portfolio seem provocative hypotheses for future exploration. Ideally, the review should look in detail at specific units of the national security establishment and at how changes in their environment should affect their strategy. Here, we can only suggest some general approaches.

• The nation's security establishment is large, but its size is also fairly arbitrary, no doubt inevitably so. In the 1980s the United States spent about 6 percent of GNP on defense, and a broader definition of "national security"—including foreign assistance, diplomacy, and energy, and contributions to the international economic environment added at most another 2 percent. The total amounted to about one-third of the federal budget.

If the world is in many respects less dangerous now than during the cold war, the United States may not need so much for external security. It may be possible to shift the balance from external threats to direct threats to people's security at home, like crime or drugs. By the business analogy, corporations have been known to give some of their capital back to shareholders when they don't feel they can spend it profitably.

• By any reckoning, America's establishment is heavily military. In budget terms, nearly four out of five dollars spent on "security" go for the military. In personnel terms the bias is sharper still; defense work force is perhaps ten or fifteen times the rest of the "security" establishment put together. These numbers may overstate the military emphasis in the portfolio because war is money and work force intensive by comparison to diplomacy or because defense is more tangible than other aspects of the security establishment.

The current magnitude of the military effort is without parallel among democracies during peacetime. By the review's measures, from men and women under arms to bases abroad, the last forty years were tantamount to an imperial effort. How was a democracy mobilized to provide so much treasure, and even on occasion blood, for such a cause? And can a comparable mobilization be imagined for a different conception of national security, one less dependent on a clear and present enemy?

• Allocating the military elements of the portfolio by region or purpose is fairly arbitrary, but nuclear weapons and Europe together account for at least half the budget and a commensurate share of activity and infrastructure. Together, those numbers suggest what postwar history indicates: that the core task of America's national security establishment has been containing a Soviet attack on Europe. Put more sharply, the task has been deterring a Soviet invasion across the north German plain. (A military planner would put the point differently, arguing that other contingencies were lesser included cases: if the United States could stop a massive Soviet attack in Europe on short warning, it could deal with anything else outside Europe.)

• The counterpart to the military emphasis is that the rest of the security effort is small and dispersed. All of that rest shares one-fifth of the budget and a smaller share of personnel, although depending on how activity is defined, its share of that element of the portfolio might be deemed larger than a fifth. In Europe, for instance, by the "revealed preference" of actual effort, other stated American objectives, like promoting democracy and market economies in Eastern Europe, have simply not been pursued very seriously by comparison to deterring that Soviet attack.

More broadly, it is hard to escape the conclusion that whatever the rhetoric, the United States has not been very serious about other aspects of security, whether the war on drugs, energy security, or the economic dimension. The portfolio reviewer might represent this point visually in a "bubble chart," like Figure 2, where the axes represent the likelihood of a given threat and the magnitude of its pain, and the size of the dot (or "bubble") signifies how much effort the United States has expended in safeguarding against it.

The United States has spent enormous money and effort protecting against a very improbable but very damaging Soviet attack

FIGURE 2. Security Threats and American Efforts

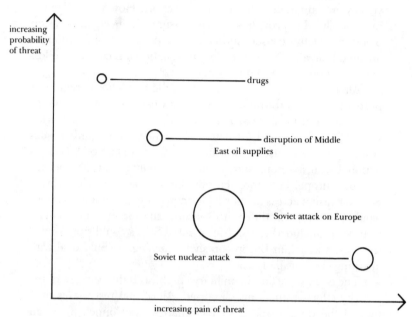

in Europe. By contrast, its preparations for an oil supply disruption in the Middle East, a more likely but less costly threat, have received much less by way of preparations (excepting the sense that, militarily, threats there would be lesser included cases). And drugs, an actual threat, not a probable one, also receives modest attention, comparatively speaking.

• For all the qualifications, it is still striking that the State Department budget is about a twentieth that of the Pentagon. If money talks, then State whispers. And even with regard to the nondefense portion of the portfolio, State's position is relatively weak: nonmilitary instruments are spread throughout the government, in Treasury, Commerce, and Agriculture, not to mention the CIA. How much this institutional dispersion affects the contribution of these instruments to "national security" by a broad definition is a subjective judgment. Still, it is hard to argue that they have been used in any very coherent way.

The implication supports a frequent observation: those nonmilitary instruments have often been managed to support domestic interests, as well as foreign policy purposes. For instance, the portfolio reviewer might imagine food aid—a million dollars in PL 480 funds—to be quintessentially a part of the kitbag of statecraft. But it is operated by the Department of Agriculture and seems to be used as often to help American farmers as to alleviate foreign famines or for any other foreign policy purpose.

• Indeed, the picture of national security that emerges from the portfolio review is one of mixed incoherence, especially on the nonmilitary side. That is especially marked when the reviewer asks what notion of economic security might have been pursued. There, the total money spent is small by any reckoning, and scattered across a dozen department and independent agencies. The conclusion is inescapable that the economic dimension of American national security has not been high priority. Yet the "rate of return" to the creation of basic international economic structures just after World War II—GATT, the International Monetary Fund (IMF), and the World Bank—was extraordinarily high. It permitted the most rapid expansion of the world economy in history.

Beneath these broad observations, the review suggests that the "return" to some specific units, activities, or instruments of the American national security establishment has changed. We start with defense and move to other units:

• *Strategic nuclear forces.* If the driving force behind America's nuclear forces, the Soviet Union, begins to lag behind, how much more will the United States need? To be sure, Soviet forces remain enormous, and so the United States needs to retain its guard. But the pace of Soviet militarization is likely to slow. There is a new concern about the risk—perhaps, paradoxically, growing—of nuclear weapons being used less in premeditation than desperation, in a Soviet civil war or by Third World states or groups. However that threat is judged, though, it is unclear how additional sophisticated American nuclear offensive forces add to our ability to deter it.

• *Advanced conventional forces.* By the same logic, if the new generations of Stealth airplanes and other high-tech forces were driven by the need to maintain an advantage over the Soviet Union, that advantage is in hand. If keeping an advantage over possible non-Soviet adversaries, like Iraq, is the objective, that is less demanding. On that score, the F-117 advanced fighter seemed to prove its worth in Iraq. The case for the B-2 Stealth bomber is much weaker, not only because of its expense, but because the mission for which it was designed, namely delivering nuclear bombs against the Soviet Union, is less demanding. If the objective is retaining an advantage in competition with America's allies, that would have still different implications. Pushing the technology envelope is extremely expensive. For instance, in 1989, after a decade-long build-up, the United States had about the same number of weapons systems as at the beginning, but most of the weaponry embodied much higher technology and was thus much more expensive per unit.

• *Technology and the national economy.* If maintaining technological superiority in the military realms is less demanding than it has been, consciousness of the cost to the economy is also rising. When the U.S. found a formidable foe with larger quantities of troops and weapons, the U.S. concentration on technological, qualitative advantages was understandable. It led the United States to devote nearly half its R & D to the military.

While there are occasional spin-offs from military R & D to the civilian economy—teflon, for instance—defense executives have argued more and more forcefully in recent years that the long lead times of military products, plus their secrecy, combined with the narrow specialization of defense products sharply limits those spin-offs. Most military R & D is, from the perspective of the civilian economy, a diversion.

Moreover, civilian technology is now overtaking military technology in many areas. The development and application of computer chips, for example, was led by military purchases, which accounted for 70 percent of the market in the 1960s. Today, 92 percent of all chips are supplied to civilian markets. Ironically, the Pentagon sustains a company producing an earlier generation of chips that it alone continues to use.

To the extent that spending on military R & D is a pure loss to U.S. commercial technology, that is an additional—and strong—argument for reducing it to the lowest level compatible with maintaining a reasonable margin of American technological superiority over possible military adversaries. It is also an argument for re-shaping how America does its defense business. Rather than al-ways tailoring technologies to meet military needs, the reverse should be the preference, taking commercially available technolo-gies to make the best possible weapons. Japanese defense already follows this practice.

• *Overseas basing structure.* The network of American bases over-seas was constructed to meet the need to deploy forces to contain the Soviet Union worldwide. To the extent that the containment is now less urgent or less demanding, the value of those bases dimin-ishes. Europe and Japan are special cases, but U.S. bases in, say, the Philippines simply are less valuable than they were during the cold war—a fact already reflected in U.S. negotiations with Ma-nila over continuing the base presence. Many of these bases look more like "dogs" than "stars."

On the other hand, to the extent the United States contemplates another large deployment in the Persian Gulf, the value of land bases there was starkly demonstrated by the war against Iraq. Because the big aircraft carriers dared not venture into narrow, mined waters, and had to spend, in any case, most of their air-power defending themselves, the massive U.S. led air war would have been all but impossible without the network of bases in Saudi Arabia.

• *European alliance and arms.* The United States has made an enor-mous postwar investment defending Europe. The waning Soviet threat indicates the need for much less in purely military terms. Yet rather than just "less," the review would suggest the need to trim and refashion this unit of the enterprise in order to capitalize on the investment already made. Along the military dimension, this would indicate restructuring the American military force in Europe to provide reassurance to a Europe in transition while enhancing flexibility for using those forces outside Europe, as was the case during the war with Iraq.

Perhaps more important, postwar American support for Europe and more recent American steadfastness in pursuit of German unification are seen in the portfolio review as intangible assets. If their value were judged to be significant but waning, how would

U.S. diplomacy and its conceptions of future European order capitalize on those assets? Is it worth making the intangible assets more tangible by financial investments in Eastern Europe that are perceived by some to be long-range "stars"?

• *Intelligence.* So much of the expense of intelligence collection, by satellite and other remote sensors, was driven by the closed nature of would-be American adversaries. Now, though, many of those nations are not adversaries and most are less closed. To evaluate Soviet industrial production, it is no longer necessary to photograph output from miles up or intercept communications about supplies and orders: you can simply go look at the plants. The days are almost here when many traditional spies can come in from the cold.

But not everything is open. Monitoring nuclear weapons, both in the Soviet Union and in their global spread, will remain a concern; nations will not frequently allow looking. So, too, tactical intelligence during the war with Iraq, some of it provided by satellites, was invaluable. Yet even in some sensitive areas, like monitoring nuclear weapons, technology can be helped by diplomacy. The cooperative on-site arrangements agreed to by Washington and Moscow for the intermediate nuclear forces (INF) agreement are an example. The conventional forces in Europe (CFE) agreement will make the western Soviet Union essentially transparent to Western observers in the air and on the ground.

• *Energy security.* The Iraq war reinforced a lesson the United States has thrice been taught but has yet to learn: crises in the Gulf would be less damaging if the United States were less dependent on oil from that region. Preventive measures would make military cures less necessary. Of course, the Gulf War was not just about oil, but to the extent it was, other ways of safeguarding that interest—from conservation to stockpiling to foreign policy arrangements with nearer oil suppliers—could have played a role. The war cost $75 billion or so, quite apart from human costs. By contrast, the energy unit of the security establishment was receiving, by a generous calculation, no more than $4 billion per year.

• *The value of preventive diplomacy.* This review demonstrates what the Gulf War underscored: diplomacy is very cheap in comparison to military measures; if it can make military force unnecessary, it is a great bargain. It can have the corollary benefits of demonstrating America's competence, hence leadership, along with the preference for peaceful solutions. The implication of this observation is that "working smarter" both in devising strategy and conducting diplomacy will have a higher value in the years ahead.

The Gulf War illustrated both the costs of diplomatic failure and the value of its success. If careless American diplomacy played some role in tempting Iraq to attack, just as it had North Korea two generations earlier, diplomacy later kept together a coalition that many Arab specialists deemed impossible. Whatever one thinks of Secretary of State James Baker's passing the hat for contributions from friends, the "mother of all fundraisers" all but covered the out-of-pocket cost of the war. And whatever American complaints over German behavior during the war, it is undeniable that the earlier virtuoso American performance in supporting German unification built capital with America's most important European partner.

To reach back to earlier diplomacy, think how much harder the last decade of the Middle East would have been for American policy without the Camp David Accords of 1978, which to be fair probably would not have been possible without the 1973 war. Or consider Central America's agony if the Panama Canal issue had remained unsettled. When the United States sought to depose Manuel Noriega, whether Panama could run the canal was a test of its governance; without the treaty, the canal would have been the nationalist rallying point against the Americans Noriega tried to make it.

In all these instances, wise policy was the crucial factor. But another common denominator was sustained attention at the top of government—from President Bush's hours on the telephone to President Carter's weeks at Camp David. Both paid a price, one most notable in Carter's being caught unaware by the fatal weakness of Iran's shah—a case that is yet another example of the costs of flawed intelligence and diplomacy.

American policy toward Japan seems to be a push-pull between those, on the one hand, whose dominant image remains Pearl Harbor and those, on the other, whose eyes are fixed on Japan's remarkable economic success. Forty years ago U.S. policy was conditioned by Japan's status as a defeated military enemy, like Germany but without surrounding allies. Now there is the question whether that continuing security relationship is anachronistic in the absence of a mutually beneficial economic connection. Artful diplomacy to bridge the military and economic realms would cool the sparks in the relationship that now seem perpetual.

The Middle East is the paradigm of an unresolved, perhaps unresolvable, problem in which American diplomacy seems both an art form and a sensible policy but is also perceived by major regional actors as a contradiction in terms. Nonetheless, the cost of the Gulf War to the Arab states in money, people, and political pride was very high. Having spent the military capital, it would be a shame for the United States not to realize a "return on investment" by trying to forge small steps toward resolution of the region's conflicts.

The larger lesson seems clear. As the overall American national security enterprise shrinks, the United States will need to be smarter as it gets smaller, substituting thought and skill in planning and negotiating—and attention at the top of government as well—for money. Just as the military elements of the portfolio need to change as well as shrink, so the nonmilitary aspects also need to be reconceptualized as they expand, in importance and probably in size as well.

Notes

[1] Cited in Adelman and Augustine (1990), p. 211.
[2] Many of these are what Joseph Nye (1990) calls "soft" attributes of power.

2

The Primacy of the
Domestic Agenda

PETER G. PETERSON
WITH JAMES K. SEBENIUS

The legislative mandate of the National Security Council
(NSC) on its creation in 1947 was to serve as a forum for
integrating "domestic, foreign, and military policies relating to the
national security." First articulated in the early 1950s, the NSC's
working definition of our national security is as appropriate now as
then: *"to preserve the United States as a free nation with our fundamental
institutions and values intact."* This goal implied a combination of
military, political, and economic objectives. These were explicit in
the early years of the NSC, when issues such as America's role in
rebuilding the shattered economies of Europe and Japan were
routinely discussed as priorities on a par with the creation of
NATO, the U.S.–Japan security agreement, and other cold war

PETER G. PETERSON, a former U.S. secretary of commerce, is chairman of The Blackstone Group, a private investment bank. He also chairs
the Council on Foreign Relations and the Institute for International Economics.
JAMES K. SEBENIUS is an associate professor at the John F. Kennedy
School of Government, Harvard University, and a special advisor to The
Blackstone Group.

military matters. Moreover, the concept of national security has historically encompassed domestic threats, such as armed insurrections, as well as foreign considerations.

In practice, however, national security policy in the 1970s and 1980s came to mean *foreign* policy in general and *military* policy in particular. Rarely, if ever, were domestic economic challenges seriously considered to be a significant part of the national security agenda. When I joined the government in the early 1970s, "high politics," to Henry Kissinger and its other masters, meant the metaphysics of MIRVs and other more seductive issues of managing the superpower balance of terror. By contrast, as the president's assistant for international economic affairs focused on trade, productivity, and the dollar, I was consigned to the realm of "low politics." Indeed, Kissinger once chided me about being preoccupied with "minor commercial affairs." I retorted with surprise that he was being uncharacteristically redundant; in his world view, were there any *other* sorts of commercial affairs? (In fairness, the problem was not just that the military-strategic experts ceased to be very interested in industry and commerce. It is also that the economic experts ceased to be very interested in geopolitics and history.)

In the postwar period, whenever "economics" clashed directly with military "security policy," the U.S. instinctively opted to give precedence to the latter. Economic factors often heavily entered, constrained, or even dictated the foreign policy "choices" of other, then less affluent countries, whose military security costs we often paid. Now something similar is happening to us; our own economic constraints are beginning to influence, if not dictate, America's relations with others. For some time, it has been clear that U.S. national security interests *must* include the development of policies that will increase our economic strength and domestic stability. Now, I believe a new definition of national security that recalls the vision of 1947—and augments it with more forceful economic and domestic policy components—is urgently needed. Indeed, I suspect that no foreign challenge of the 1990s will affect America's security as much as what we do, or fail to do, at home on a range of economic and social issues. We should not forget Eisenhower's admonition not to "undermine from within that which we are seeking to protect from without." In this spirit, I will advance two propositions.

Proposition 1. After four decades of the cold war, failure to make progress on a "domestic agenda" now threatens America's long-term national security more than the external military threats that have traditionally preoccupied security and foreign policy. While the world remains a dangerous place requiring us to maintain military strength, our failure to invest in productive capacity, research and development (R & D), and infrastructure; the crisis in American education; the exploding underclass, and other domestic problems may have greater *direct* impact on "the United States as a free society with its fundamental institutions and values intact" than the threats from abroad, such as the possibility of Soviet nuclear attack, which have traditionally preoccupied the national security community. Moreover, continued failure to address these domestic priorities may entail a progressive loss both of political will and economic capacity to take actions abroad that promote our real national security interests.

Proposition 2. America has demonstrated a debilitating incapacity to face and make the kind of hard trade-offs needed for progress on this expanded national security agenda. In key areas of concern—for example, energy, fiscal policy, entitlements—we have become a "choiceless" society, substituting denial and rhetoric for meaningful action. Issues that on the surface appear to be economic are, at bottom, deeply political. Only fundamental political changes, such as the formation of a broad and deep bipartisan coalition on behalf of an expanded national security agenda, can get us back on the path to real choices.

Together, these propositions argue that those traditionally concerned with our foreign policy and national security must broaden their focus. To separate "foreign" and "domestic" policies is increasingly untenable. And as these policies are more effectively integrated into a larger and more coherent view of "national security," the primacy of the domestic agenda in our national security becomes evident. This broadened and more integrated national agenda, along with a sustained effort to explain and address our incapacity to make effective choices, can no longer be treated as incidental to our "real" national security policy; it must now play a central role.

Changing Threats to
U.S. National Security

No one can dispute the fact that the postwar world has been a dangerous one for the United States. With Soviet nuclear weapons and military adventurism (especially through proxies), North Korean and Chinese aggression, assorted menacing regional conflicts, an expanding nuclear club, terrorism, and so on, "eternal vigilance" has been a military necessity. Iraq's malevolence and military capacities sound a current warning against complacency, or neoisolationism. Yet the world is changing. One need not belabor the importance of the powerful East-West thaw and the spread of democracy to conclude that some of the "old threats" have diminished.

Beyond the now-defunct Warsaw Pact, consider China as a specific example of a receding threat. Quaint as it may sound today, much of our Southeast Asian defense policy was formulated with a keen remembrance of "hordes of Chinese" pouring across the Yalu River. Indeed, even in the late 1960s, as a private citizen member of the president's Arms Control Advisory Board, I vividly remember presentations by the Joint Chiefs of Staff about the threat of a Chinese nuclear first strike against us. China was an unambiguous and dangerous enemy, and was a key part of discussions about the Southeast Asian "conceptual balance of power" vis-à-vis the Soviet Union during the Vietnam War.

As just this single example illustrates, traditional external threats to our security are changing and require reassessment. Yet it is not just the geographic sources of the threats that are changing: it is their nature. Today, the threats are far more likely to be from regional aggressors like Saddam Hussein, contagious conflict arising from ethnic/religious problems, or nuclear proliferation in Third World countries. All these threats of conflict require very different responses than those for which we have traditionally prepared. In this chapter, however, I am concerned with emerging security threats of a still different character. In particular, largely self-inflicted *economic* weaknesses now indirectly threaten our national security. After sketching these economic factors in the context of the first proposition stated above (the primacy of the domestic agenda in our national security), I will then consider "domestic threats."

Economic Weakness as a National Security Threat

Despite the euphoria over America's success in the war in Iraq, the 1990s will be a decade of new and increasing tensions for the United States between international needs and economic constraints. These constraints are caused by budget deficits, balance-of-payments deficits, growing foreign debts, debt service costs, paltry levels of investment, anemic productivity growth, a loss of technological leadership in key cutting-edge industries, and a general decline in our global competitiveness. The awkward but enduring fact is that, taken together, the claims of our various national interests and global obligations will far outrun our available resources to sustain or defend them. As the full implications of being the world's largest debtor dawn on us *and* on the rest of the world, the gap between our interests and our capacities will become larger, more obvious, and more painful. As Eisenhower sought to teach us, military and economic security over time depend on each other; countries that lose control of their economic destinies lose control over their foreign policies.

New Resource Constraints. Apart from the anomaly of Uncle Sam brandishing a saber toward Iraq in one hand while rattling a tin cup in the other, we have already seen the effects of chronic budget stringency on foreign policy interests: State Department allocations (even to maintain embassies and consulates abroad) dropping and under further siege, administration proposals for massive cuts in foreign aid (except to Egypt and Israel), 10 percent real cuts in all our international budgets, our virtual inability to offer meaningful financial support to a newly democratic but fragile Philippine government (a meager $50 million at a time

Corazon Aquino appeared before a joint session of Congress), our financial paralysis in the face of enormous Eastern European changes (the president's embarrassing offer of $25 million at the time of his visit to Hungary), as well as our inability to make essential investments in economic growth and social harmony in our own hemisphere. Just as cutting back on subway and infrastructure maintenance during its 1970s fiscal crisis ended up costing New York vastly greater sums to later repair the damage, the costs to the United States of its increasing inability to respond constructively to changing opportunities and threats abroad will become dramatically higher. The U.S. faces constraints on policy that are unprecedented for a great power. Spreading slowly like a silent progressive disease, the long-term effects are both cumulative and debilitating.

One could well argue, for example, that Mexico presents a veritable cauldron of potential threats that could easily become immense national security problems for the United States. Political, social, demographic, economic, and financial trends combine to make an "explosion" south of our border at least as likely as the detonation of a nuclear bomb. If Mexico fails to grow economically in step with its population—which before long will grow to twice its current size—Mexico's problems will become our problems. Some 60 million *more* Mexicans, many unemployed and just across our effectively open border, for example, could rapidly become our immigration problem.

If we were thinking in a "zero-base" mode, this set of conditions might easily place Mexico—as well as other Latin American countries—near the top of the external threats and opportunities that we face in terms of our national security. Beyond the valuable, though partial, step of a Mexican free trade agreement, this kind of thinking might easily lead to compelling proposals for comprehensive and bold programs to include further debt restructuring and/ or relief, immigration reform, investment flows, economic development programs, as well as a major, coordinated attack on drug problems. Though I believe that most observers sense the importance of such initiatives, there seems to be a conspiracy of silence. Even at the cost of ignoring a major developing threat to our national security, virtually everyone avoids the issue since proponents of such initiatives are soon confronted with the awkward question: *where will the money come from?*

Before the decade of the 1990s is out, I predict a surge of domestic budgetary pressures to bring home costly U.S. troops from Europe, Korea, and from far-flung bases and ships. Ideally, this fiscal necessity may present major opportunities for enhanced security at lower economic cost, but there is a far less desirable likelihood that we take these steps as a result of fiscal crisis and in an atmosphere of severe trade tension. Keep in mind that these pressures to cut our military commitments will likely intensify just as the United States is desperately striving to increase its share of world exports and to further reduce its current account deficit. Undoubtedly, the Japanese and Europeans—who, especially after Iraq, will increasingly be seen by resentful Americans as the affluent beneficiaries of long-time military free rides—will also be straining to retain their trade positions. As GATT's (General Agreement on Tariffs and Trade) late 1990 deadlock warns us anew, competitive attempts to win global share could give way to an "antagonistic mercantilism." These economic conflicts will put serious strains on the cohesiveness of our military and political alliances. Truly acrimonious debates over allied burden sharing that turn into fundamental questioning of collective purposes are already becoming an unwelcome feature of the foreign policy landscape. It will be very difficult to keep trade wars limited to trade issues alone.

If we get our own budgetary house in order and begin attempting to increase our exports further, we will need to exert strenuous diplomatic efforts to induce other countries simultaneously to adopt complementary economic policies that expand world trade. (The alternative of deep global recession or depression would also "solve" our trade and current account problems; recall that we had a trade *surplus* every year during the 1930s.) But such coordination will be exceedingly difficult to sustain in an atmosphere strained by foreign policy disagreements.

New Vulnerabilities. Moreover, there are specific risks inherent in our passive decisions to run huge deficits and to rely on foreign investors to fund them. Though it is unlikely to occur in a brazen form, a decision by investors or central bankers to cease buying additional dollars—for economic *or* political reasons— would put us in deep trouble. We have generally downplayed such possibilities, often pointing to our potential leverage over Japan, a generally unflagging purchaser of dollars. After all, almost 40 percent of Japanese exports have come to our markets in recent years. Yet if we took serious protectionist measures aimed at the Japanese, they could threaten powerful retaliation by ceasing to fund our deficits. This could cause a dollar plunge, an interest rate surge, and a deep recession along with a host of other unpleasant consequences.

Such an action by the Japanese or others could parallel a dramatic 1956 foreign policy incident. Shortly before the U.S. elections that year, the British surprised the United States by spearheading, in tandem with the French and the Israelis, an invasion of Suez, responding to nationalization of the canal by Nasser. Opposing this "risky, imperialistic" gambit, the United States forced the invading armies to withdraw by threatening to dump the pound sterling and cut off British access to international credit— measures that could have caused a steep devaluation of the pound and highly unpopular gasoline rationing. (And remember, we were alliance partners and "special *friends*" of the British.)

Monetary historian Susan Strange has examined some of the consequences of Britain's unprecedented growth in foreign debt. She observed that "by the time of the 1967 devaluation Britain had become, in effect, the ward of the other developed countries of the non-Communist world. They constituted a creditors' club exercising the same watchful concern over the British economy that the Aid Consortia exercised over those of India, Indonesia, or Turkey."

"Given the stream of postwar balance of payments crises to which Britain has been subjected," noted British financial expert Michael Stewart, "I am amazed at the insouciance with which the United States has quietly amassed such an astronomical foreign debt." In my view, our passivity has become pathological. Perhaps Stewart should not be so amazed. The painful lessons of great debtorhood were hard for the British to perceive. Susan Strange eerily noted that "at a time when the British had amassed by far the largest government foreign debt per head of population of any country in the world . . . comment in Britain . . . tended to stop short at expressing regret for the necessity to borrow so heavily, and hope that the loans may soon be repaid, so that the 'crushing burden' of debt may be lifted from British shoulders." Most Britons, however, did not seem too sensitive to the "crushing burden"—either on their pockets or on their consciences. Their regret seemed a trifle perfunctory, their concern superficial, and their appreciation of the scale and urgency with which the creditors required repayment very vague indeed. Economic reality, however, soon translated into harsh wage freezes and incomes policies as well as unpleasant constraints on public expenditures—much as has been the case with developing country debtors in recent years trying to work their way out from under staggering debt loads. These domestic economic costs for Britain, of course, only added to the foreign policy vulnerabilities so painfully illustrated earlier by the 1956 Suez crisis.

The United States, of course, is not postwar Great Britain. Among many differences, our debts are in our own currency. Indeed, Charles de Gaulle used to lament the "extravagant privilege" accorded the U.S. from our reserve currency status—our ability to repay borrowings from foreign lenders in our own currency. This special position allowed us to avoid taxation to pay for the Vietnam War and permitted our recent defense build-up, entitlement increases, and tax cuts to occur without a surge in interest rates. (Arguably, the capacity to have both guns and butter resulted in increased inflation that ultimately led to the breakdown of the international monetary system.)

Further, should the Japanese (or other major buyers or holders of dollars or dollars-denominated assets) seek to exert direct foreign policy leverage on the United States today as a result of their new-found creditor position, they would simultaneously inflict grave costs on *themselves* from the resulting dollar plunge, huge foreign exchange losses, the likelihood that their exports would be sharply curtailed, the risk of global recession, and worse. But nowhere is it written that countries, in emotional political spasms, will not act in ways that prove to be counterproductive. And though governments and central banks tend toward relatively measured action, the herd mentality and psychological panics may sweep the private investing community, adding to underlying volatilities and dangers. (Recall the South Sea Bubble and "tulip-mania.") In sum, worldwide economic risks are sharply increased by the predicament in which we now find ourselves. Ironically, with the possibilities of lethal economic and financial actions, reactions, and counter-reactions, we now face an economic version of MAD, or *M*utually *A*ssured *D*estruction, with which we have uneasily lived in the military "security" realm.[1]

Yet there is a broader point here. It is not so much the threat of a creditor strike per se. Instead, continued U.S. economic weakness will cause a subtle but very real worldwide shift of *political* perceptions. Perhaps ironically, in a world that is increasingly multipolar and complex, the need for collective action puts an increasing premium on the capacity for effective leadership. As the Gulf War coalition underlined, the United States is virtually the only candidate for such a role. Yet our capacity to exert leadership may be undermined to the extent that increasing domestic and economic failures cause us to be taken less seriously. An extreme but instructive analogy, of course, is the effect of domestic failure in the Soviet Union on the reality and perception of Soviet influence. Despite the surge, perhaps temporary, in worldwide admiration for U.S. military capacities generated by the Persian Gulf War, perceptions of relative U.S. economic decline could well mark a psychological turning point in others' perception of our long-term ability to back allies and oppose enemies, of our vulnerability, and of our unreliability. And since perceptions can govern actions, I believe that we would see our "friends" take more independent stances, our enemies act with less restraint, and, generally, our presence, stature, and security diminished.

Direct Domestic Threats to National Security

When I survey the changing postwar sources of threats to our national security, I certainly do not see external threats as having vanished. Rather, I am struck by the emergence of a series of powerful domestically generated trends that increasingly seem to pose direct and indirect threats to our fundamental institutions and values. The first of these trends—economic weakness and relative decline—may *indirectly* constrain essential actions abroad and increase our vulnerabilities. I will now turn briefly to some domestic trends, that, if unchecked, may progressively and *directly* threaten the basic character of our society's institutions and values. Not surprisingly, these include education, poverty, the underclass, and economic expectations.

Education. One-quarter of school-age children can neither read nor write at a satisfactory level. Since 1985 every fourth student in high school has failed to earn a diploma and has dropped out. *Every year*, 2 million Americans leave school without having learned to read and write. The 1985 White House Commission headed by John A. Young, chief executive of Hewlett-Packard, concluded that this is particularly bad news, because the highest dropout rate—from 40 to 45 percent—is found among blacks and Hispanics, the fastest growing segments of the population. "It is clear that the competitiveness of American industry is threatened when many young workers lack the basic skills for productive work," he says. We have the largest number of functional illiterates in the world—nearly one in five American workers falls into this tragic category. Indeed, it is almost incredible that we, unlike the Japanese, fail to *act* as if we believed in the intimate connection between an educated society and a competitive one. "If a hostile foreign power had attempted to give America the bad education that it has today," the National Commission on Excellence in Education has warned, "we would have viewed it as an act of war."

Poverty and the Underclass. Almost a fourth of all children younger than six, and about half of all black children younger than six, live beneath the official poverty line. In urban areas, infant mortality rates rival those in traditionally agrarian, less developed countries. Overall, some 31.5 million Americans live below the official poverty line. Minorities are particularly affected: more than 30 percent of blacks and 26 percent of Hispanics earn less than this amount. Many of them are working at full-time jobs;

about 7 million Americans do not earn enough from their jobs to escape poverty.

Not *coincidentally*, the U.S. leads the world in crime. Explanations abound: the symbiosis of poverty and poor education, the drug catastrophe, racism, guns. Since 1975, more American citizens have met their deaths through firearms than the U.S. military lost in World War II. Partly in response, some 3.7 million Americans, constituting nearly 2 percent of the adult population, are under continual supervision by prison or police authorities. The number of prisoners in federal and state penitentiaries has almost *tripled*, from 250,000 in 1975 to 710,000 in 1989. (Japan has 50,000.) Incredibly, the average black male child today is more likely to go to prison than to college. Beyond crime, our litigious society (about two-thirds of all the lawyers in the world practice in the U.S. with their number growing at about four times the rate of population growth) and the related insurance costs have now added significantly to our uncompetitiveness. (The cost of our tort system was estimated at 2.6 percent of gross national product (GNP) in 1987, over three times higher than the next highest industrial country.)

Expectations. From the mid-1970s through 1986, the median income of young males without some college education plummeted by 35 percent in real terms. For those who do not finish high school, the corresponding decline is an incredible 42 percent in real terms. Since approximately half of young Americans do not ever attend college at all, this downward mobility is pervasive and deeply disturbing. More generally, as Senator Daniel Patrick Moynihan of New York has noted, the wages of production and nonsupervisory workers, after Social Security taxes and adjustment for inflation, are *lower today than the week that Eisenhower left the presidency*. After a careful study of income and wealth accumulation trends, Frank Levy and Richard Michel concluded that it is highly unlikely that Americans born in or since the 1950s will *ever* achieve the same level of real household net worth currently held by now-retiring Americans born in the 1930s.

"Our country used to have dreams," said journalist John Chancellor recently. "We dreamed of independence, and we got it. We dreamed of becoming a continental power, and we became it. Our immigrants dreamed of a different life in prosperity, and they created it. We dreamed of the moon landing and carried it out. But where are our dreams now?" Without hope of improvement, without dreams of a better life for our children, what kind of society will we have? Can a stable center hold in the face of such unprecedented income gaps? Will citizens at the bottom exercise their civic and political responsibilities when their basic economic security is threatened? Will our freedoms as well as our fundamental values and institutions—that is to say our national security— remain intact?

I know of no more perceptive spokesperson on these questions than Daniel Yankelovich, public opinion researcher and social commentator, whose words bear repeating:

This situation is a formula for social and political instability. The history of this century shows that there is no more potent negative political force than downward mobility. If the American Dream becomes a mockery for tens of millions of vigorous young Americans who, it should be remembered, represent mainstream American youth, not just inner city minorities, the nation can expect rising levels of violence, crime, drug addiction, rioting, sabotage, and social instability. The surge of racial tension between young whites and blacks is already an expression of it. We will be lucky if this is the worst of it.

Let me summarize the first proposition: the world is still a dangerous place that requires us to maintain military strength. Yet failure to make progress on a domestic economic and social agenda now threatens America's long-term national security more than the traditional preoccupations of security and foreign policy such as the menace of Soviet nuclear bombs or conventional attacks on our territory or vital interests. To put this first proposition a bit more concretely, suppose we were now deciding where to spend, say, an *additional* trillion dollars to enhance our national security, broadly construed. Faced with this decision, would not these domestic economic and social agendas have a strong claim to primacy over additional efforts to mitigate traditional external threats?

The Choiceless Society

My second proposition is painfully simple: America has demonstrated a debilitating incapacity to face and make the kind of hard trade-offs needed for progress on this expanded national security agenda. We have become a "voiceless" society, substituting denial and rhetoric for meaningful action. We tolerate that which we declare resoundingly to be "intolerable"; we are passive in the face of "imperatives" that are universally described as "compelling."

One might recall how a Roman historian complained about the decadence of his time: the citizens of Rome, he wrote, "can neither bear their ills nor their cures." In short, these are not merely economic and social policy failures; they are major political failures. Let me illustrate this proposition with examples from the areas of energy policy as well as the linked questions of deficits, investments, and entitlements.

A Dangerous, Choiceless Energy Policy

Many experts are saying today that oil will go down below $15 a barrel, given overproduction at a time of declining demand. In my view, this is an overly simplistic and short-term picture. Now that some stability has been restored in the Persian Gulf, and now that Kuwait and Saudi Arabia have had to expend so much of their financial reserves, incentives for finding ways to cut production and raise prices are already growing.

This is particularly significant in light of the drift of U.S. policy toward ever more oil consumption, ever less production, and ever more dependence on imported oil. Let me offer a very brief history. When the Organization of Petroleum Exporting Countries (OPEC) overplayed its hand in 1979 and sharply raised prices, the U.S. temporarily decreased its oil consumption and domestic oil production rose. But the decrease in consumption was over by 1983—ironically just as many Americans were convinced that they were entering a period of painless national prosperity. U.S. oil consumption has since risen by 12 percent. And the good news about increased domestic energy production was over by 1985. Between 1985 and 1989 U.S. production declined by 12 percent, and it was expected to decline another 4 or 5 percent in 1991. From net crude oil imports of about 4 million barrels a day in the mid-1980s, our oil deficit has lately been increasing; it exceeded 7 million barrels a day in 1990. The warning signs are clear. The U.S. now depends on oil imports for about half its needs. In 1987 Persian Gulf producers accounted for only 6 percent of U.S. oil imports. In 1991 they were supplying 28 percent and could reach 50 percent by 1995. Moreover, increased U.S. imports have accounted for more than half of the growth of OPEC exports. Thus, however unwittingly, the United States has been a principal force in restoring the basis for a potentially resurgent OPEC, and the likely decline—or even reversal—in Soviet oil exports only magnifies this danger.

Projections indicate that U.S. oil imports will rise to perhaps 10 million barrels by 1995. At $20–25 per barrel, such an increase would add about $15–20 billion to our annual trade deficit. By 1995, at the level of $20–25 per barrel, our oil deficit *alone* would be $75–90 billion—approaching the size of the entire U.S. trade deficit in 1991. (Even with oil at $15 per barrel, these trade deficit effects would be massive.) And to this we must add the new melancholy dimension that our foreign debt service will increasingly overwhelm our overseas investment income, adding ever-increasing amounts to our current account deficit.

The U.S. has been lethargic in devising ways to reduce its oil gluttony. In Europe and Japan, governments have raised the price of oil to the consumer and have continued to invest both in more efficient energy use and in different energy sources. As a result, they will be able to keep increases in oil imports under some degree of control during the next decade. France now gets over 70 percent of its electrical power from nuclear energy, and it has set a goal of 100 percent by 1995. Its nuclear industry has had no major safety problems so far, enabling the French to avoid some of the worst effects of fossil fuel generating plants.

Japan—which has no oil of its own to speak of—has nonetheless managed to render itself less vulnerable to the economic consequences of rising oil prices. Japan has done a much better job than we have in terms of energy conservation and efficiency. Aside from the obvious lower consumption of energy in automobiles, the Japanese get 2.5 times more manufacturing output per unit of energy than we get in the United States, and 2.4 times the real output with the same amount of energy as in 1977. Through conservation, efficiency, and increasing of nuclear capacity, Japan is today scarcely more dependent on imported oil than the United States is, when viewed in GNP terms. The American bill for imported oil now stands at about 1.1 percent of our GNP. Japan's bill is almost identical—and down by two-thirds from past levels. What's more, because Japan has such a large trade and current account surplus, it can much more readily absorb whatever oil price increases may lie down the road.

The U.S. faces a choice. On the one hand, we can eschew any meaningful action to bring national oil consumption more in line with national energy production. And when our children ask us why we saddled them with vast debt obligations to our overseas creditors, we will have to tell them: "Despite the fact that in 1990 our national appetite for oil was far out of proportion to our population or our productivity—in 1990, with less than 5 percent of the world's population, the U.S. consumed fully one-quarter of the world's oil output, including *one-tenth just for our automobiles*—we deemed any reduction on your behalf to be too great a sacrifice for us to make." Or, better: "We left the outcome up to the free choice of the American consumer and, too bad, you lost!"

Clearly, we will be unable to tell our children that our appetite for imported fuel was good for their health, for the air they breathe, for the climate in which they live, or, indeed, for their economy. Other industrial democracies have confronted similarly difficult political problems and have made real choices instead of the cost-free "choices" we persist in making. Why not the United States? We could, in my view, work out a farsighted energy policy that would increase our productive use of energy, improve the environment, avert the risk of crisis being imposed by foreign energy producers (whether through a sudden cutoff or a "slow bleed"), and do much to minimize our trade and budgetary deficits.

A main component of such a policy should be an energy consumption tax, or at least a tax on petroleum products, such as a sales tax on gasoline of 25 to 50 cents a gallon that would be phased in over several years.[2] A primary benefit and purpose of such a policy would be to reduce the federal deficit. But a significant gasoline tax would lower the volume of the trade deficit in oil by restraining total U.S. oil consumption. Indirectly it would help to lower the dollar trade deficit by boosting national savings and bringing down world oil prices. This last effect is important. While fearing OPEC's power to push up prices, Americans have seldom understood that the U.S., as the world's largest oil consumer, possesses sufficient buying power to pull down prices, if only we care to use it. With an energy tax, we could at least try to do just that—playing the OPEC game in reverse. A farsighted energy policy would also go much further in encouraging conservation of petroleum and the development of clean energy sources. Here, we should consider not only the risks of dependence on imports and the dangers of a swollen foreign debt, but also the growing national consensus that fossil fuels pose serious environmental hazards, possibly including the greenhouse effect.

Gasoline taxes could raise at least $25 billion and perhaps as much as $40 to $50 billion more yearly in new federal revenue. They could cut our oil import deficit by perhaps $5 to $15 billion yearly, and would still leave us with by far the lowest heating oil and gasoline prices of any major Western nation. Even with an added U.S. gasoline tax of 50 cents a gallon, Americans would still be paying only 40 percent of what consumers pay in other leading industrialized countries, where the average gasoline tax is about $2. During the 1990 U.S. budget "crisis," it was considered a major political triumph that Washington settled on a paltry 5 cents per gallon gas tax. Contrast that to the recent German imposition of an additional *50* cent per gallon tax to pay for their efforts to rebuild East Germany.Eschewing conscious, meaningful choice, we have come to regard cheap gasoline as yet another entitlement.

"Choiceless" Policies on Deficits, Investment, and Entitlements

Solving the budget deficit in the United States has never received the serious political attention it deserves. In the wake of the Gulf War, it has become virtually impossible to attract focused attention to this crucial problem at all. Yet the red ink continued to spill forth from Washington as we headed toward a record federal deficit in the range of $300 billion in 1991.

The deficit is likely to remain very high regardless of the exact number. One might well ask: why is this the case, in view of the supposedly "Draconian" efforts to reduce the deficit we have read about? Well, the dirty little secret is we did not do very much about the *big spending items* that have been ballooning out of sight. These include, of course, the vast entitlement programs for the elderly, and other transfer payment programs for the relatively well off. To give you some historical perspective, if you look back twenty-five years, the entitlement programs have *increased* by 6.1 percent of the GNP. Just the *increase* alone is larger than our entire defense budget.

On these issues, as with energy conservation and so many others relating to our real national security, we are refusing to face the problem head-on and make the necessary choices. We have become the "choiceless society," a label inspired by the American poet Peter Viereck who captured something of the national preference with the plea to "suspend me in the choiceless now." One might ask: don't Americans know better? Don't we know that savings and investment are the fuel of productivity and competitiveness? Don't we know that if the Japanese economy invests two and a half times per capita what we put into capital investment, and installs ten times the number of industrial robots per capita as we have in our manufacturing systems, that Japan will be more competitive? Don't we know that education, R & D, and technologically sophisticated investments are required to reverse our lost lead in critical fundamental technologies? Don't we know, living in a society where the phrase "crumbling public infrastructure" has become the ultimate redundancy, that if the Japanese invest ten times what we do in public infrastructure per capita, it is they and not we who will have not just bullet trains, but magnetic-levitation trains running at even higher speed and even more efficiently? And if we Americans know all this, what does it say about the courage of our convictions? Everyone agrees that America has a crying need for public and private *investment,* in both physical and human capital. Indeed, our *rhetorical* investment "imperatives" enjoy a uniquely bipartisan consensus of support that extends from education of the workforce, to infrastructure, to R & D. Everyone agrees except on one brute question: where do we get the *resources* for this consensus investment agenda?

To invest, there must be savings—ours or those of more thrifty people elsewhere. Unfortunately, our largely consumption based deficits constitute negative savings. Counting the S&L bailout and the illusory social security "surpluses," we now face deficits that, incredibly, could average over $300 billion annually between 1991 and 1995. From 1985 through 1989, with federal borrowing wiping out over half of all private sector savings, the U.S. net savings rate fell to 2.2 percent of GNP, less than *one-third* the equivalent rate for the rest of the industrial world.

There were few visible effects of the 1980s "deficit decade" largely because savers from abroad "bailed us out"—even if it did mean borrowing nearly a trillion dollars from them. During the 1990s, however, the two biggest "surplus savers" of the Western world, Japan and Germany, will be less ready lenders. Japan's available savings pool will continue to shrink, as a rapidly aging population saves less, and as the Japanese invest more at home, and spend ever more on consumer goods (both at U.S. urging). Likewise, German savings are now flowing toward the reconstruction of Eastern Europe and the Soviet Union. And reconstruction of the war-ravaged Middle East will be yet another major capital claimant: some estimate that bill will amount to over $100 billion dollars.

As we seek to cut deficits and fund investments, the hard choice between "less spending" and "more taxes" will continue to be interpreted by politicians as a false dichotomy—when our third option is more borrowing. And borrow more we will to fund our deficits. These deficits will increasingly be driven by non–means tested entitlements—benefits passed out regardless of financial need—which have ballooned from $27 billion in 1965 to $472 billion in 1990 and continue to spiral. In addition to current budget deficits, the "pay-as-you-go" financing of our vast entitlement edifice has created *unfunded liabilities* that almost certainly exceed $10 trillion, a hidden debt of $100,000 for every American worker that will be borne by our children.

Our national interest is best served by programs that direct public resources toward *investment* and *youth*—not toward consumption and age. Perversely, we squeeze the former each year, while the latter are Gramm-Rudman "exempt" from cuts and protected with automatic cost-of-living allowances (COLAs). Americans under age eighteen have the highest poverty rate of any age bracket, yet in recent years have received only $1 per capita in federal benefits for every $11 going to Americans over age sixty-five (who have the lowest poverty rate, when all benefits are included as income). From subsidies to rich farmers to free medical care for old millionaires, we have massive "welfare for the well off."

The structural aspects of our entitlements must be put on the table. Setting aside interest costs (a genuinely uncontrollable 16 percent of the budget) and "discretionary expenditures" (which should be raised to the extent they represent genuine public investment), *non—means tested entitlements virtually constitute half of everything left over in the federal budget.* Most of the rest, national defense, is already projected to fall to 4.8 percent of GNP by 1995—the lowest level over the entire postwar era—and the Iraqi adventure reminds us there are clear limits. This latter point bears elaboration. It is commonly felt that spending a dollar less on defense will free up a dollar for "social programs." In reality, there is a complex four-way trade-off among defense, private investment, private consumption, and the various forms of nondefense government spending.

To ensure that the right redirection of resources toward investment is made, we should move from age based to need based transfer payment programs by progressive taxation of benefits, gradual reduction in COLAs for the nonpoor, lower initial benefit levels for upper-income retirees, gradually increasing retirement ages, and increased cost sharing for health benefits. For upper-income beneficiaries like myself, above some threshold, such as an annual income of $50,000, an additional sliding-scale rate of up to 100 percent should be used to tax away the full value of benefits in excess of total contributions plus interest; there should be no more "welfare for the well off." When the Japanese government recognized in 1986 that their versions of these programs were unfair to the young and the cost of its public retirement system was quickly rising to unaffordable heights, it made a clear choice and reduced average future benefit levels by roughly 20 percent. Choicelessly, however, we say it is "politically impossible" to change entitlements. Tomorrow, we may have to relearn—quickly and painfully—the true meaning of impossibility.

The "Reagan Revolution" was no revolution in terms of the largest social entitlement programs; it merely ratified and preserved them, while paying for them not with taxes but with debt and hidden inflation. Tax increases such as the gasoline tax I discussed above must play a role in a *real* revolution. But such taxes will provide only a short-term stopgap solution. Without structural entitlement reform, but with greater longevity, earlier retirement, low birth rates, and medical hyperinflation, the cost of our federal entitlements system could climb by a colossal 11.5 percentage points of GNP between 1991 and the year 2025, necessitating a tax of 20 to 40 percent of worker payrolls to pay for it. Even if the public consensus were suddenly to shift to allow such an unsustainable level of new taxes, these increased revenues would at best simply cover entitlement cost increases—leaving nothing to meet the needs of the new "imperative" investment agenda in other crucial areas such as education, R & D, and infrastructure, which lie at the heart of what I believe are our real national security interests. Here, too, our rhetoric overwhelms reality. We may say that regaining our competitiveness is "essential" to our economic security, but we ignore the awkward question: what are we willing to give up to get it back?

It is said that our current deficit debacle is a tragic political gridlock, between those who want high spending and those who want low taxes. In fact, no one is truly choosing and both sides are getting just what they want: *high spending* and *low taxes.* Judged by our actions, what we really want is to protect *ourselves*—at the expense of our children.

Why This Choiceless State of Affairs?

Across these issues of energy, deficits, and entitlements, *choicelessness* is a constant theme. This same choiceless quality underlies

our apparent inability to make real progress on the broader domestic agenda that I have argued should be central to our true
national security. Of course, the decision *not* to decide explicitly is
itself a profound decision. Our refusal to make overt choices is the
biggest choice of all. It makes a mockery of the political system that
was once the world's most advanced and capable. It means that
problems that have solutions will continue to go unsolved, making
the society poorer and more polarized over time. It means that our
national security, in the broadest sense of the term, may be deeply
eroded.

Indeed, since a society defines itself as much by the values it
forgoes as well as those it preserves at great cost, we will have defined ourselves almost by default as a diminished nation. In the
end, our choicelessness means that history will choose for us, and I
doubt it will be kind. To avoid this outcome, we must understand
and address the underlying causes of our debilitating incapacity to
face and make hard trade-offs. Though a deeper analysis of the
interlocking causal factors goes well beyond the scope of this chapter, a few of the most important ones merit brief mention.

Throughout most of the past two centuries, the world regarded
America as a society in which economic growth and material improvement were an overriding obsession. If there were any choice
to be made between enjoying today and investing in tomorrow,
Americans could always be counted on to choose tomorrow.
Around the turn of the century, we outperformed all other nations
in our rate of savings, our investment in education and R & D, our
child-favoring commitment to public health and durable families.

Today, of course, we have largely reversed direction. The country that once had the highest rate of savings and productivity
growth now has the lowest of any major industrial nation. The
country that once pioneered public vaccinations for children now
has the highest infant and child mortality rate—at the same time
that we enjoy the highest life expectancy at age 85. The country
that once equated "posterity" with a generations-long time horizon now struggles to focus attention on next year's budget deficit.
As for culture and ideas, what the supply-side revivalists point out
is true: America is indeed now influencing the world, from MTV
and country-western music to "no free lunch" lectures on free

enterprise and economic growth. Ironically, we have become more persuasive in describing the "traditional" American way of life at the same time that we have become less capable of practicing it.

Other industrial democracies have been able to make many of the future oriented choices that now tie Americans in knots. It has not always been this way for us; our impressive previous capacity to address these issues underlines just how much we have changed.[3] In my mind, several factors have contributed to this drift.

Postwar Hubris and the Demand-Side Economy. When did we veer from one extreme to the other? Why did it happen? Perhaps one early cause was the enormous hubris felt by most Americans in the aftermath of World War II. Americans began to believe that our industrial might and technological prowess made us "exceptional." We saw ourselves exempt from the rules of history, believing we could have everything at once—a cornucopia of guns and butter—without the necessity of choices or even hard work. In Japan, as in Germany and elsewhere, plants were destroyed and industries devastated by the war. Japan required a set of postwar economic policies that would enhance the stock of physical and human capital. (Thus the Japanese experience was a *real* supply-side miracle of investment, and nothing like the phony "supply-side" fantasy of America in the 1980s, that in fact masked a demand-side reality and slipped a huge hidden bill to our children.)

Yet after the war, U.S. plants were undamaged. If anything, their efficiency had been greatly spurred by the innovations and productivity improvements that occurred during the war years. With our world dominating industrial plant capacity intact and our technological leadership in place in virtually every field, economic competitiveness was not something we had to strive for, because it seemed to be a given. Especially following the depression, we saw the lack of *demand* as our problem, not lack of investment and capital formation. As a result, we built a demand-side economy. We made housing cheap through government guaranteed mortgages and tax deductions. We encouraged borrowing and consumption in virtually every way possible—from the advertising messages on TV to the premises of our tax code. We didn't just glorify consumption, we implicitly declared savings to be bad and penalized savers. Believing ourselves economically invincible and virtually entitled to ever-rising national wealth, ever-improving living standards, and ever-more leisure time with ever-less work, we lost perspective on the objective limits facing a society, even one as rich and blessed as ours. In the 1960s, we believed we could fight a huge and costly war in Vietnam at the same time that we tried to eradicate poverty at home and vastly extend universal entitlement programs—leaving unanswered the awkward question: if we all got on the wagon, who would pull it?

In short, our arrogance after winning World War II, combined with a kind of pop Keynesianism, led to the feeling that consumption was good, savings bad, and that we could have it all. Sufficient *production* came to be taken for granted. Vance Packard and John Kenneth Galbraith influenced many in the 1950s and 1960s when they argued that the *distribution* of wealth had become our main economic problem now that our "affluence" was assured. We seemed so effortlessly rich that a high and rising standard of living was built into our expectations. Our political system easily came to reflect and embody those expectations. The standard of living became the responsibility of the politicians rather than of we ourselves as producers. Yet long after the seemingly automatic economic growth engine had sputtered and stalled during the 1970s, our political leadership continued to reinforce a particularly selfish version of this "no need to choose, you can have it all" consumptionist/borrowing philosophy, especially in the 1980s.

Triumph of the Special Interests. In recent years our political system has pushed pluralism to extremes. Though American politics is typically centrist, avoiding the ideologies of the left and the right, the "center" has been steadily losing its intellectual coherence on its way to becoming merely a collection of intensely parochial and self-interested groups. In step with the declining capacity of political parties to mediate among diverse interests and forge more unified coalitions, every group became an entrepreneur for its own private advancement. Political energies in America increasingly coursed through ever-more narrow channels. Deep loyalties often developed around single social issues—clean air, women's rights, abortion, the nuclear freeze, food labeling, school prayer, porpoises, and the like. Out of this evolving political culture came the "Entitlements Revolution," a pervasive, grievance oriented conviction that each organized group—such as farmers, textile companies, auto unions, weapons contractors, civil servants, military pensioners, S&L depositors, and Social Security retirees—has a "right" to a prearranged award, regardless of what the economy can afford. The budget and tax systems evolved as an inventory of benefits and subventions for groups claiming particular grievances and rights. Production was taken for granted, while ensuring one's share of the consumption pie became the central political concern.

Once underway, the revolution of entitlements swiftly entrenched itself. Each program acquired and nurtured a public, bureaucratic, and congressional constituency, which in turn protected the program and assured its continuous expansion. Between 1965 and 1981, the number of staffers per U.S. senator climbed from sixteen to thirty-six; the number per U.S. representative climbed from nine to seventeen. During the 1970s alone, the House Committee staff grew from 702 to 1,843. In 1971 New York City still had twice as many trade associations as Washington, and only five state governments had D.C. offices. By 1981 Washington had 3,136 associations—500 more than New York—employing about 80,000 people, and thirty-four state governments had D.C. offices. Rather than checking and balancing each other, the special interests making up our pluralistic polity joined together in a tacit conspiracy against the general interest, and the entire fiscal system acquired a strong bias favoring budget deficits and current consumption.

As for the power that entitled constituencies can exercise over politicians, consider but one suggestive example: the American Association of Retired Persons (AARP). With its 28 million members and more than 5,000 state and local chapters, AARP is not just the most important force in the "gray lobby," it is unquestionably the nation's largest and most powerful interest group. Its voluntary membership, which includes one in every four registered U.S. voters, is larger than that of any other organization in America aside from the Catholic Church; it is *twice* the size of the AFL-CIO; and it is growing by several thousand members daily. With an operating budget of $200 million, AARP is also the largest single business entity in the Washington, D.C. metropolitan area; its annual cash flow (now about $5 billion) would put it near the top of the Fortune 500 if it were a public corporation. AARP's mail order drug business is the nation's largest; its health insurance programs, driver education courses, and tax advisory services are among the nation's largest; and its magazine, *Modern Maturity,* now has a circulation second only to *TV Guide.* When AARP speaks—and it speaks loud and clear on the question of entitlements—you can bet that Congress listens.

American individualism used to honor community values. Now it seems to be a quest for unlimited personal advantage. As consumers rather than citizens, we seem to have become a nation of silent players and special interests in which few speak effectively for the common good. In this political contest, saving and investing in tomorrow has no constituency. For many, government is like a giant vending machine, with the central purpose of political action to get to the front of the line. The question of stocking the machine to ensure that it will not run out of goods generates no particular fervor and, accordingly, is neglected. Unfortunately, moreover, the weakest moral claims are typically made by those claimants with the greatest political strength. Farm price supports are more fiercely defended by lobbyists than are food stamps. Civil service pensions are far better protected in Congress than aid to families with dependent children (AFDC) payments. More generally, amidst the din of special pleadings, we have lost a workable political and economic consensus.

Contrast postwar Germany as a case study in consensus building. One of the most valuable learning experiences for me as a member of the Brandt Commission in the 1970s was the opportunity to listen to Willy Brandt in highly informative breakfast conversations on the subject of building of long-term economic consensus. He emphasized the profound difference between the "institutionalized hostility" that existed in our country between labor and business, for example, and the attitude that exists in his country. Mr. Brandt once added, "You Americans simply have never experienced the hell that can take place in a country if it doesn't get inflation under control. It is what brought us Adolf Hitler; it's what transformed, in a hideous way, our entire values and society." Brandt told stories about the devastation of the 1920s, which he said still conditions today's economic consensus within Germany. As a schoolchild, he had to pack the family's lifetime of savings of D-Marks in bags and take them to the local orphanage, where they were used to start a fire so that the children could be kept warm.

I listened with equal interest to Helmut Schmidt's report of discussions with German labor and business leaders in which both "sides" accepted four fundamental economic premises: (1) the vital importance of significant productivity increases, including the capital investment to help make those productivity improvements possible; (2) wage increases related to productivity increases; (3) orderly, moderate increases in the money supply; and (4) the crucial importance of global competitiveness and capturing a large share of export markets.

The truth is that we don't have the glimmerings of such a long-term economic consensus. Thus Germany and Japan each developed a consensus, forged out of their own separate and deeply painful political experiences: perhaps their common purpose was born of common misery. But we in this country have had no common purpose, no common misery, no common fear. Thus, since we had no problem, we needed no solution. It is difficult to have a collective vision of the future without a collective vision of the present.

Cynicism and Withdrawal from Public Life. Along with the extremes of pluralism and the loss of consensus, we have witnessed an ebbing spirit of national community (what William Raspberry calls "the unraveling of America" and Arthur Schlessinger Jr. calls "the De-Uniting of America"). The link between individual well-being and that of the community as a whole has frayed. The decline of the intact, nuclear family has removed a centrally important source of communal *values* and sense of the future for many children. Since 1960 the likelihood that a child lives in a single-parent family has tripled, and the Urban Institute now estimates that 70 percent of white children and 94 percent of black children born in 1980 will spend at least some time in a single-parent family before reaching age eighteen.

One might also point to the shattering effects on public faith in government and institutions occasioned by Vietnam and Watergate that led to a kind of political withdrawal and cynicism. This breakdown in trust in our public institutions added a certain toxicity to our tendency toward an unbridled quest for individual consumption: "Don't be a sucker. Don't produce it. Grab it. There's plenty there and beside you deserve it." The multiple shocks of this era seemed to have severed our common bonds of citizenship, our "sense of the platoon." When one combines these corrosive effects with a system of campaign financing that seems absolutely loaded against challengers, it is perhaps no wonder that political participation, especially by the young, is so thin or that so little meaningful choice seems to be exercised. The spectacle of political action committees (PACs) feeding bloated TV budgets and apparently wielding undue political influence is hardly calculated to encourage grassroots participation.

Such lack of engagement has been reinforced by patterns of television watching by young people. American children have been offered unlimited TV and relatively limited schoolwork, while children in our competitor nations were permitted only limited TV and had much heavier schoolwork. Not only do the endless hours before the tube lead to a reduced capacity of American children to distinguish between reality and image, but also to far shorter attention spans than are required by complex real problems. Further, the continual message of most television is a glorification of instant gratification and endless consumption while implicitly discounting any need for long-term concern or painful trade-offs. The "Consciousness Revolution" was triggered by postwar baby boomers who came of age ridiculing the very notion of deferred consumption as a pathology of their parents' "mindset."

Cynicism is especially acute among today's (postboom) youngsters, those who came along too late for a seat at our entitlements banquet, but whom we expect to pay off our debts and shoulder the growing cost of our "have-it-all-today" mentality—regardless of whether we have trained or educated or protected them. No generation in living memory has come of age sensing how little adults care about their fate. We sent hundreds of thousands of twentyish Americans to the Persian Gulf to risk their lives—in part to ensure the flow of oil to large American cars and houses that very few of them will be able to buy at the same age as their parents. Then we howl in indignation over depositing nuclear waste in salt caverns within 500 miles of our home or over acceding to a pennies-per-gallon tax on gasoline—or any other inconvenience that might keep us from having to risk young American lives again.

Implications

I have urged that the concept of "national security" be interpreted broadly to mean the preservation of the United States as a free society with its fundamental institutions and values intact. If this characterization is accepted, then my first proposition implies that there is a strong *national security* case for the primacy of the domestic economic and social agendas as I have described them above. Making the necessary progress on these agendas, however, requires that we make some very hard choices as a nation. Yet my second proposition indicates just how far we are collectively from the capacity and willingness to face and make such trade-offs. While I briefly noted a number of possible reasons for this state of affairs, my purpose has neither been to resolve the issue definitively nor to fully explain its causes, but to put it squarely on the national security agenda.

Together, these propositions argue that if those who have been traditionally concerned with our foreign policy and national security are to have maximum effect, they should broaden their focus. Separating "foreign" from "domestic" policies is increasingly untenable. And as these policies are more effectively integrated, the primacy of the domestic agenda in our national security becomes evident. Though not among the most-traveled paths in the conventional world of "national security," this agenda, along with a sustained effort to explain and address our incapacity to make effective choices, can no longer be treated as incidental to our "real" security policy; it should now move to center stage. In this regard, what should be some of the special responsibilities of those in the traditional world of security policy, who have often been especially farsighted, enlightened, and sophisticated in their out-looks?

First, members of the foreign policy "establishment" must look afresh at subjects that have traditionally been outside their pur-view. The security links to intensely domestic and "political" top-ics must not be overlooked; in general, action is needed to strengthen and unify our political culture, our system of govern-ance, and our collective problem-solving capacity. Even "grubby" and unfamiliar particulars of our national political life can matter a great deal to the attainment of the broader national security agenda. We may conclude, for example, that major campaign financing reform to limit the explosive growth of special interest PACs is an essential building block. Or, we may decide that it is essential to make adequate free TV time available to political can-didates. (We have the most expensive political campaign system in the world. In 1988 the average candidate for U.S. Senate raised and spent $3.7 million in his or her election bid.) The general point, however, is clear: national security demands a focus well beyond things "foreign" and "military"—in other words, to things "domestic" and political. (In this same vein, those in our society who have up to now focused on things overtly economic and fiscal must broaden their angle of view to include national security con-cerns.)

Second, foreign policy specialists tend to be very comfortable with the notion of necessary *trade-offs* within the national security spectrum (as between MX missiles and submarines for example, or even between foreign aid that contributes to security versus a di-rect military presence or military aid). In line with my first point above, I would urge that this same logic and style of analysis be extended from traditional national security concerns to encompass the larger agenda that I have outlined above. For instance, is our real national security better served by an additional $10 billion spent on selected aircraft systems or on the programs that the Committee on Economic Development (CED) deems essential to

attack the problems of our children? True generalists are needed
to begin making, in a nonpolemical way, the kinds of trade-offs
that bear on *all* aspects of our national security.

Third, and more broadly, we must create an *overall,* balanced
plan to achieve our wider national security goals. Such an "integrated national security budget" should combine both foreign and
domestic priorities. It must lay out the true financial and intellectual requirements for military security, as well as economic secu-
rity/competitiveness (including education, the underclass, infrastructure, research and development, productivity-enhancing
investment, etc.). It must include a realistic plan to pay for the
associated costs (e.g., spending cuts, tax increases, etc.). Inciden-
tally, security specialists trained in cost-benefit analyses are well-
equipped to assess the cost effectiveness of domestic programs such
as prenatal care and Headstart. Moreover, along with an integrated national security budget should come serious consideration
of the *institutional changes* that would foster its formulation and execution. Should a revamped and broadened NSC be set up that
includes members concerned with competitiveness and productivity, such as the Commerce Department and the Office of Management and Budget? What institutional changes may be needed in
the structure and operation of the associated congressional committees? These are the kind of questions that need to be asked—
and answered.

Fourth, to this substantive agenda must be added a *moral* dimension. For years, national security and foreign policy goals have
attracted domestic support not only from naked self-interest, but
also from a sense of equity and compassion. The response to the
plight of the Kurds is but one recent example of this theme in U.S.
foreign policy. One humanizing element of our foreign policy has
always been to narrow the gap between the haves and the have-
nots. As we strive to develop the concept of a new *world* order, can
we permit the *domestic* equivalent of this gap to continue to widen?
Can we succeed in the world economy, let alone as a democracy,
with such internal disparities and discords? In my view, as we seek
to forge a domestic consensus, it must be within the context of a
larger moral purpose—a familiar element for those who have contributed to and relied on the consensus "beyond the waters' edge."

Some worry that we may continue indefinitely trying to look away from the future. Since Americans have always reached for greatness in the midst of travail, I think that an equal danger may lie in our waiting for a very painful crisis as an excuse to assert and rebuild our national priorities. Indeed, national consensus has often resulted from war or historic crisis. Unfortunately, for Americans, the only remotely parallel economic crisis was the Great Depression, and one of the lessons learned—that total demand should not be allowed to collapse—has little application to our contemporary problems. Along with cynicism, apathy, and waiting for galvanizing crisis, polls show that a growing number of Americans are attracted to apocalyptic solutions and are resisting half-measures that (it is said) merely delay the inevitable. It is my hope that we might learn that "civilization" means striking a consensual balance and thinking ahead—without choicelessly lurching from sackcloth to gluttony and back again. Without such a consensus, I very much doubt we will be able to achieve anything coherent or long term in the broad national security agenda.

We need a new broad based, bipartisan political coalition to shape and give powerful political expression to a new American consensus that transcends special interest politics and constituencies. In imagining such a coalition, the example comes to mind of a determined Harry Truman, an energized bipartisan effort of congressional leaders, and an American elite of business, labor, and intellectuals. In the late 1940s America was the world's leading creditor, but a provincial American people were reluctant to take up the responsibilities of a central global role, let alone paying for them. Truman's potent bipartisan coalition put together an array of initiatives that led to the postwar complex of institutions from the Bretton Woods agreements to NATO, the UN, and the Marshall Plan. It was perhaps our finest hour as a nation. Looking back on that era, I am struck by today's need for leadership to craft a new coalition around the general interest that transcends special interests. Certainly the task of a new bipartisan coalition of informed generalists will be formidable given the powerfully organized interests defending every entitlement and other special interest program, however ill-justified.

Let me say a few words about the shape of this new bipartisan coalition I envision to lead the way in defining and implementing the new broad national security agenda that I have outlined.

First, it must begin with an approach that soberly reckons with the magnitude of the problems before us, accepts the need for sweeping, structural reform of many of our programs and institutions, and adopts a *long-term focus* and a *long-term action plan.* Only by concentrating on the *future* can we rid ourselves of the short-termitis, the now-nowism, and the constant search for quick fixes that fracture and divide the nation, while raising the cost of real solutions in the future.

Second, this coalition must advocate goals and principles that can unify a broad range of concerned citizens who are now scattered across today's traditional political spectrum of Democrat and Republican, left and right. This means, for example, that the coalition must find the way to incorporate *both* historic "liberal" concerns about fairness and compassion for the truly needy in our society with historic "conservative" support for policies that encourage investment-led economic growth and keep business from becoming tied down in a constricting web of regulation and onerous taxation.

Third, as a force for turning today's choiceless society into one that once again confronts and makes intelligent choices, the coalition must also not only have principles, programs, and priorities, but it must also be able to say "here's how you pay for them." In developing the "integrated national security budget" I have discussed, I favor starting in a zero based mode. We should not begin with a trillion dollar–plus budget on the table as a given and then start to fight over what to add and what to cut *at the margin.* Instead, the leadership of this new bipartisan coalition should make an extraordinary effort to develop a new budget that begins at zero, compares investment in conventional national security—say X thousand less troops in Europe—with equivalent investment in domestic economic security—say the CED's comprehensive program for investment in our children. Then this process should carefully and critically proceed to include only those programs our society absolutely needs over the next decade. Then, we should implement this new vision by way of multiyear budgets.

In this context, even given the decline of traditional external military threats to our security and the rise of internal economic and social ones, we certainly cannot allow ourselves to become so preoccupied with the domestic threats that we *ignore* the continuing need for adequate military resources. Indeed, there can be no greater or more important role for government than insuring that the nation is safe from external attack. I believe, however, that if we rebuild the military budget from the ground up to meet today's and tomorrow's threats, not yesterday's—we can obtain a military capability that is at once less costly than today's force structure *and* more suited to the threats we are most likely to face. Achieving this double blessing would result (1) from a moderate shift in emphasis from today's focus on high-expenditure troop deployments and nuclear weapons delivery systems aimed primarily at the Soviet Union to the less costly needs of regional and mobile deployment forces, and (2) from enhancing and institutionalizing the system of financial burden sharing with our allies.

Fourth, if one looks around the world at all the high real growth economies of recent years—Japan, Germany, Singapore, Taiwan, etc.—one finds high savings rates and strong capital investment levels in each case. If we are to have the much needed decade of investment, the coalition I propose must *focus* on *investment* and *savings* that stimulate real, long-term, sustainable growth. Currently, apart from burdening our children with staggering debts, we have only two real tools available to deal with the government's explosive deficits. We can cut spending, and in particular, *subsidized consumption* for the relatively well off —whether business people, farmers, homeowners, elderly, civil servants, or military pensioners, and others from the broad middle class—and we can raise taxes. I believe we will need to do both.

As advocates of choice rather than choicelessness, the coalition I propose must not beat around the bush about the fact that policies that favor savings and investment mean less growth in today's consumption. But we must avoid being cast in the role of opponents of consumption and improved quality of life. Just the opposite: we must make the case forcefully that savings and investment today will lead to a sounder economy tomorrow, which, in turn, will generate *more* consumption and improved quality of life in the future. By contrast, the current policies of dis-savings and disinvestment will lead to *less* consumption and perhaps a disastrous decline in the quality of life and the stability of our society in the future.

Fifth, and finally, this coalition must not be simply an intellectual or moral force—it must become an organized force. This will require imaginative, sustained leadership as well as massive resources and an organization that exists not just in Washington but is truly rooted in the states, cities, and communities of America. It must coalesce people and organizations that are not now part of the special interest infrastructure, or that are willing to make the requisite shift from special interest to the genuine national interest and the public good.

Can we mount a new and powerful coalition that—unlike the current patchwork of special interests that screams, threatens, and grabs for particular benefits and payoffs—is a coherent mosaic of citizens infused with our society's *general interest,* the interests of our children, and of *our* collective future? It would be an extraordinarily difficult and even more frustrating task.

Despite difficulties, we have mounted such a coalition before. Can we do it again in the face of even greater obstacles? The answer to that central, if haunting, question will have more to do with whether we will achieve true national security in this increasingly competitive future than anything else I can think of.

There is much talk today about the need for leadership. Curiously, politicians, by and large, are clear on the right things to do. Yet they have decided that to do the right thing given the current political system would be to commit political suicide. What we need, as Herb Stein has said, is to make it "safe for politicians to do the right thing." We might say that courageous leadership requires "enlightened followership." Instead, we have a bad case of collective denial and a leadership vacuum to match. We have what E.J. Dionne Jr. calls the politics of "false choices." (Regardless of one's views on the merits of flag burning, the pledge of allegiance, Willie Horton, ACLU membership, snail darters, or spotted owls, none of these issues would have a priority claim for inclusion on our integrated national security agenda.)

The mystery for those of us past age fifty is why our parents never slipped into comfortable denial of their responsibilities to the future. As a group they were much less affluent than we are today. Yet from 1940 to 1955 they pulled America out of a depression, fought and won a world war against fascism, led another war against communism in Korea, gave prodigious sums of foreign aid to Europe, supported massive outlays to young veterans on housing and education—and yet still managed a level of net national savings more than double ours. Many opposed government spending, but when spending rose, few advocated borrowing instead of taxing. Many disliked the Marshall Plan—an investment in world peace that cost over $50 billion in today's dollars and consumed 16 percent of the federal budget—but even its opponents would have been astonished today that we cannot spare one-fiftieth that amount for Eastern Europe. Many were poor, but no one suggested making any public benefit rise "automatically" without regard to need or economic growth. Certainly no one justified current consumption by promising away a third of their children's future payroll. Our parents' generation took the future, and their choices, seriously, and today we thank them for it. As a result, we enjoyed a long period of national security in the full sense of the term.

Someday, our children will look back on us. When they weigh our material affluence against the challenges we faced, they will surely take a dim view of how few sacrifices we deemed worth taking for their benefit, and how we sleepwalked, choicelessly, through critical years.

Notes

[1] Less dramatic than our "debt mountain," but, over time more troubling in some ways, is the gradual but significant decline in America's technological leadership, which is the subject of another chapter.

[2] One idea that still merits consideration is to impose the tax when oil prices drop below a predetermined level. In other words, the tax would get larger as oil prices fall below a floor price, thus providing the price stability necessary for encouraging investment in energy while discouraging the easy consumption of cheap oil.

[3] It is for this reason that I am suspicious of "structural" solutions that, for example, would replace our presidential-congressional structure with a parliamentary one. But I doubt that the root problem is as simple as the division of federal powers prescribed by the U.S. Constitution. There are, to begin with, many counterexamples: countries with unified governments that have bad track

records (for instance, Great Britain, whose economic "disease" has been much discussed for at least half a century). Such structural explanations would also be more persuasive if, in our own country, the separation of powers were blocking a clear consensus within each branch of government or among the electorate at large. Yet the generally muddled messages we have heard over the last couple of decades both from the White House and from Congress are evidence to the contrary—that we are getting just the sort of choiceless policy "leadership" with which the electorate is passively comfortable.

3

National Security
in American History

ERNEST R. MAY

N ational security may mean "preserving the United States as
a free nation, with its fundamental institutions and values
intact." The key terms, however, have not kept constant meanings. In George Washington's day, the "nation" consisted chiefly
of scattered farming settlements where people had, as Washington
said in his Farewell Address, "the same religion, manners, habits,
and political principles." American institutions included Negro
slavery. Over time, even in short living memory, American institutions and values have changed enormously. They will continue to
change.

This chapter sketches American notions of national security
from George Washington's time to George Bush's. For discipline,

ERNEST R. MAY is Charles Warren Professor at Harvard University.
Former dean of Harvard College, he is the author of numerous books on
U.S. foreign policy. In 1988 he and Richard Neustadt received the
Grawemeyer Award for Ideas Improving World Order. Professor May is
currently American chairman for an American-British-French-German
Nuclear History Program, collecting data and sponsoring research on the
roles of nuclear weapons in international relations.

the chapter uses as reference points the yearly presidential messages to Congress required by the Constitution. During most of American history, these were known simply as the president's annual messages. Since the 1930s they have been called State of the Union messages.[1]

In these messages, presidents plugged their programs. They spoke as party leaders. Often, they spoke lines written by others. George Washington used drafts prepared by Alexander Hamilton and other advisors. Since the 1930s the White House staff has included professional speechwriters. Reminiscences by some of these writers give details of Byzantine infighting over the texts.[2] Nonetheless, most presidents tried to make these messages addresses from the throne, appealing to and speaking for the nation as a whole.

In these messages, presidents usually said something about security, not necessarily "national security," for that phrase became common only after World War II. Theodore Roosevelt, for example, almost never used it. Statements about the subject were couched in terms of "safety" or "tranquillity" or opposites such as "insecurity," "danger," "threat," or "peril." Used flexibly rather than mechanically, the series of speeches can be taken as a rough index of the evolution of national thinking.

Phases

The series of annual presidential messages suggests that American ideas about national security evolved in four stages. The stages were not sharply separate. The chrysalis of a new concept appeared long before it became dominant. The general pattern of evolution was nevertheless plain.

Safe Borders and Union

From the 1790s to the 1870s, presidents described national security as dependent on two factors: the safety of national borders and the preservation of the union of states.

In Washington's presidency, the British maintained a hostile presence in Canada, and British warships patrolled the Caribbean. Spain had Caribbean islands and owned Florida, the mouth of the Mississippi, Mexico, and most of the Americas. Powerful Indian nations ringed the borders of the United States from the Great Lakes to the Gulf of Mexico.

Washington's annual messages dwelt on the need for "defense and security of the Western frontiers." Almost half of his messages for 1792 and 1794 concerned wars with Indian nations. The prevailing sense of menace is conveyed by Jefferson's first annual message, which urged the states to strengthen their militia because of how "uncertain . . . we must ever be of the particular point in our circumference where any enemy may choose to invade us."

Washington and his successors emphasized the importance for national security of holding the United States together. In his special Farewell Address of 1796, he said to the nation that "unity of government . . . is a main pillar in the edifice of your real independence, the support of your tranquillity at home, your peace abroad, of your safety, of your prosperity, of that very liberty which you so highly prize."

By the 1820s presidents no longer expressed so much fear of immediate neighbors. The United States had escaped safely from the War of 1812, sometimes termed the Second War for Independence. All factions in Britain seemed finally reconciled to the former colonies being independent. Spain no longer posed a threat. It had ceded to the United States Florida, the mouth of the Mississippi, and disputed territory to the west. Its American colonies had mostly become independent, and the British navy prevented any continental European power from helping Spain reconquer them.

Monroe's annual message of 1823 said that any change in these new conditions in the Western Hemisphere would make the United States less safe. In what became famous later as the Monroe Doctrine, Monroe said of the monarchies of Europe: "We should consider any attempt on their part to extend their system to any portion of this hemisphere as dangerous to our peace and safety." He warned guardedly that if any European powers were to aid Spain against her former colonies, Americans might conclude that intervention was "indispensable to their security."

As has often been pointed out, neither Monroe nor his seventeen immediate successors gave body to this doctrine. The United

States watched unprotestingly a series of European punitive expeditions in Latin America. Even when French armies were patrolling Mexico in the 1860s, Lincoln and Andrew Johnson made only mild protest.[3]

Through most of the nineteenth century, presidential annual messages echoed the themes of Washington. Zachary Taylor in 1849 was still warning of the "exposed frontier." Presidents year after year stressed to Congress the importance of coast fortifications for protection against invaders.

Presidents spoke also of the peril of national division. They said most about this peril, of course, when it was most real—in the periods of the Missouri Compromise, the Compromise of 1850, the Kansas-Nebraska Act, and actual Southern secession. Long after the Civil War, however, sectional division ceased to dominate presidents' descriptions of conditions that could imperil the national safety. Not until after the 1890s, when the wind had gone out of Western agrarian protest movements, did mention of this fear begin to drop out of annual messages.

Hemispheric Independence and Social Order

From the 1880s to the end of the 1930s, presidents tended to speak of national security (or its equivalents) in terms similar to those of Monroe in the 1820s. They talked of American safety in terms of the safety of other American republics. At the same time, they began to identify as the major source of insecurity the possibility of domestic class conflict.

With the British government in conflict with Venezuela over the boundary of British Guiana, President Grover Cleveland in 1895 demanded that the British agree to arbitration. He said in his annual message that "the traditional and established policy of this Government is firmly opposed to a forcible increase by any European power of its territorial possessions on this continent." He was able to report subsequently that the British had yielded to his demand.

When Theodore Roosevelt gave his first report on the state of the union in 1901, he said: "Our people intend to abide by the

Monroe Doctrine and to insist upon it as the one sure means of securing the peace of the Western Hemisphere." In 1906 Roosevelt added, as his corollary to Monroe's doctrine, the proposition that the United States should police the hemisphere to ensure that American republics honored their financial and other obligations to non-American states. "That our rights and interests are deeply concerned in the maintenance of the doctrine is so clear as hardly to need argument," he explained.

Woodrow Wilson said in 1914:

We have made common cause with all partisans of liberty on this side of the sea, and have deemed it as important that our neighbors should be free from all outside domination as that we ourselves should be; have set America aside as a whole for the uses of independent nations and political freemen.

Franklin Roosevelt, warning in 1935 that wars might be in prospect in Europe or Asia, asserted that, if such wars came, "the United States and the rest of the Americas can play but one role: ... through adequate defense to save ourselves from embroilment and attack."

As concern for the safety of American republics superimposed itself on concern for the United States proper, so concern about possible domestic class conflict began to dominate concern about possible sectional conflict. Theodore Roosevelt warned in 1905 of "the growth of the class spirit . . . [which] in the past has proved fatal to every community in which it has become dominant." Harding said in 1922, "It is no figure of speech to say we have come to the test of our civilization. . . . I am not speaking at this moment of the problem in its wider aspect of world rehabilitation or of international relationships. The reference is to our own social, financial, and economic problems at home." Franklin Roosevelt in 1938 identified as one of the nation's gravest weaknesses a tendency to put "class consciousness ahead of general weal."

The reason for shift in concern from disunion to class conflict is obvious. As the industrial revolution came to the resource-rich United States, a few entrepreneurs, managers, and financiers became very rich. A prolonged agricultural depression and flooding immigration from Europe created a buyer's market for labor. The nation had increasingly large concentrations of poorly paid workers. With people of many nationalities now crowded into cities and with discontented workers sometimes protesting their condition, many Americans began to worry lest the country dissolve, not in a conflict of section against section, but in one of poor against rich.

Free World Independence;
Prosperity at Home

From World War II through the 1960s, presidents tended to define national security as dependent on the continued independence and freedom of a number of countries, many outside the Western Hemisphere. They also defined security as dependent on the general health of the American economy and the American political system.

As Monroe's address of 1823 had prefigured trends after the 1890s, so Woodrow Wilson's addresses during World War I prefigured the trends that appeared after World War II. Wilson had asserted that American security needed thenceforth to be seen as dependent on conditions outside as well as inside the Western Hemisphere. But presidents of the 1920s, and Franklin Roosevelt in the 1930s, explicitly rejected Wilson's formulation. In a characteristic example of what he himself styled "bloviation," Harding said in his inaugural:

We do not mean to be entangled. We will accept no responsibility except as our own conscience and judgment, in each instance, may determine. . . . This is not selfishness, it is sanctity. It is not aloofness, it is security.

After Pearl Harbor, Roosevelt revived the theme Wilson had broached more than twenty years earlier. "We are fighting today for security, for progress and for peace," he said in January 1942, "not only for ourselves, but for all men, not only for one generation but for all generations." Truman in 1948 applied to the whole world words similar to those previously applied to the Western Hemisphere: "The loss of independence by any nation adds directly to the insecurity of the United States and all free nations."

By 1951, with the Korean War in progress, Truman both amplified and narrowed his language, saying:

We believe in independence for all nations.

We believe that free and independent nations can band together into a world order based on law. . . .

Our own national security is deeply involved with that of other free nations.

In time, the phrases "free nations" and "free world" came to embrace practically all states that rejected Communist rule and association with the Soviet Union.

As earlier in the Western Hemisphere, so in this wider world, the United States gravitated toward interpreting any change in the status quo as potentially threatening. The government had acquired capabilities for responding to unwelcome changes by covert action. It used them. Iran, Guatemala, and Laos were major examples. Also, on occasion, it brandished or used military force. In 1955 and again in 1958, the Eisenhower administration threatened war to protect the Nationalist Chinese state on Taiwan from the Communist Chinese state on the mainland. In 1958 it committed troops in Lebanon. In 1961 the Kennedy administration deployed troops to Thailand as a gesture of support for a non-Communist regime in Laos.

The logic of the Vietnam War came from the definition of national security prevailing in the period from 1940 to the 1970s. In his State of the Union message for 1967, President Lyndon Johnson acknowledged that it was "a very costly war . . . and the danger to us is seemingly remote." He explained that, otherwise, there could develop a larger war. Meanwhile, the "peoples of Asia . . . know that the door to independence is not going to be slammed shut."

During the same period, presidents stopped speaking of peril from class conflict. Since the Great Depression had produced nothing more radical than the New Deal, the danger of social upheaval had come to seem a chimera. Presidents now spoke of a healthy domestic economy as the domestic complement of national security. Truman said in 1948, "We have learned that a healthy world economy is essential to world peace—that economic distress is a disease whose evil effects spread far beyond the boundaries of the afflicted nation." Americans saw the cold war as one waged as much economic as with military resources. Kennedy said in 1963, in the last State of the Union message he was to deliver:

We shall be judged more by what we do at home than by what we preach abroad. Nothing we could do to help the developing countries would help them half as much as a booming U.S. economy. And nothing our opponents could do to encourage their own ambitions would encourage them half as much as a chronic lagging U.S. economy. These domestic tasks do not divert energy from our security—they provide the very foundation for freedom's survival and success.

Stability and Economic Growth

In the 1960s presidents began to modify the prevailing definition of national security. After the Bay of Pigs fiasco and the Cuban Missile Crisis, the United States acquiesced in practice in a condition that, by traditional criteria, should have been seen as incompatible with national security. An American republic had, by U.S. lights, lost both its independence and its freedom, and the Soviet Union had extended its system into the Western Hemisphere. Yet the United States government did little besides grumble.

In the painful process of ending the Vietnam War, Johnson and successors said that independence for South Vietnam, Laos, and Cambodia had turned out not to be as essential to American security as previously supposed. The "Nixon doctrine" of 1969 made it explicit that the United States would protect other nations against nuclear attack but would not necessarily regard a non-nuclear attack as so threatening to U.S. security as to require commitment of U.S. troops.

State of the Union messages of the 1970s and later echo much of the earlier rhetoric. What distinguishes these messages from most of those of the earlier cold war period is the addition or coupling of comments on the importance to American security of keeping any armed conflicts within narrow bounds.

This apparent cutting back was obviously related to awareness that, though the American frontier had expanded all the way to central Germany and central Korea, the national homeland had become vulnerable as it had not been since the early nineteenth century. As Eisenhower said in 1960:

With both sections of this divided world in possession of unbelievably destructive weapons, mankind approaches a state where mutual annihilation becomes a possibility. No other fact of today's world equals this in importance—it colors everything we say, plan, and do.

The missile crisis had put in high relief the new conditions surrounding definitions of what made the United States secure and insecure. When Johnson defended the importance of the Vietnam War, he had simultaneously to explain why it was a limited war. Truman had explained the limiting of the Korean War in terms of priorities. He identified the Soviet Union as the real enemy and Europe as the crucial theater. Regarding Vietnam, Johnson said simply that "the temptation to 'get it over with' is inviting but dangerous." In the same message, he had already called attention to reported increases in Soviet long-range missile forces and had said, "My first responsibility to our people is to assure that no nation can ever find it rational to launch a nuclear attack or to use its nuclear power as a credible threat against us or against our allies."

The shift beginning in the 1960s involved expansion as well as contraction in the definition of national security. Nixon voiced an interpretation of external security almost as broad as Wilson's or Franklin Roosevelt's. Those presidents had said that the security of the United States was affected by internal conditions in all nations. Truman had retreated to linking it only with conditions in free nations. Stating publicly the rationale of "containment" as developed in key policy documents such as the "long telegram" of 1946 and NSC-68 of 1950, Truman said in his final State of the Union message:

As we continue to confound Soviet expectations, as our world grows stronger, more united, more attractive to men on both sides of the iron curtain, then inevitably there will come a time of change within the communist world. We do not know how that change will come about, whether by deliberate decision in the Kremlin, by coup d'etat, by revolution, by defection of satellites, or perhaps by some unforeseen combination of factors such as these.

But if the communist rulers understand they cannot win by war, and if we frustrate their attempts to win by subversion, it is not too much to expect their world to change its character, moderate its aims, become more realistic and less implacable, and recede from the cold war they began.

Nixon shifted to saying, in effect, that American security benefited from certain *existing* conditions in the Soviet Union and in the People's Republic of China. Jimmy Carter echoed Nixon, saying in 1979, for example: "In our relations with our potential adversaries, it is a myth that we must choose between confrontation and capitulation. Together, we build the foundation for a stable world of both diversity and peace."

President Ronald Reagan seemed to move back toward Truman's line, but it is hard to be sure. Reagan's State of the Union messages appear to have been almost entirely the creations of speechwriters, other White House staff, and bureaucrats. Memoirs of his administration indicate that he meddled with these texts no more than he had meddled with scripts when in Hollywood. He read the lines handed him. Often, the lines had been crafted as combative statements of position rather than as parts of a magisterial tour d'horizon. His message for 1987, for example, described the long-defunct Monroe Doctrine as still "historic bipartisan American policy." He argued for aid to the Nicaraguan contras in terms appropriate for a partisan appeal but not usual for State of the Union messages. Even President Reagan, however, spoke of the utility to American security of "constructive relations with the Soviet Union."

A modest shift had occurred meanwhile in definitions of the domestic requirements of national security. From Truman to Nixon, presidents had usually emphasized the importance of domestic prosperity, assigning the American economy the key role in fostering prosperity elsewhere. From the later 1970s onward, presidents came more to speak of American security and American prosperity as keyed to global, not necessarily American, economic growth. Reagan, in his 1988 State of the Union message, put first among the nation's key objectives "to expand a growing world economy."

Lessons?

As to what this history suggests for the future, I offer two loosely
connected sets of observations.

*First: national security has always been understood as having both external
and domestic components, but these components have sometimes been seen as
complementary, sometimes as in competition with one another.* For Washington, safe borders and union were inseparable. Whatever Washington deemed needed for border security, he held to be needed for
union, and vice versa. Thus, for example, Washington could argue
in 1791 for more spending on the post office and post roads on the
ground of "their instrumentality in diffusing a knowledge of the
laws and proceedings of the Government, which, while it contributes to the security of the people, serves also to guard them against
the effects of misrepresentation and misconception."

In the nineteenth and early twentieth centuries, presidents did
not make such a close connection between protection of American
republics and the avoidance of class conflict at home. Instead,
presidents tended to congratulate the nation on not facing serious
military threats in the hemisphere; then they would go on to say, in
effect, that this made possible greater attention to the requirements of order at home.

After World War II, Truman spoke of preserving the independence of "free" nations and maintaining domestic prosperity
much as Washington had spoken of safe borders and union—as
separate faces of the same coin. Truman said in 1950:

> Our success in working with other nations to achieve peace depends
> largely on what we do at home. We must preserve our national strength.
> Strength is not simply a matter of arms and force. It is a matter of eco-
> nomic growth, and social health, and vigorous institutions, public and
> private. We can achieve peace only if we maintain our productive energy,
> our democratic institutions, and our firm belief in individual freedom.

Eisenhower, by contrast, tended to characterize the demands of
external security and of domestic strength as in competition with
one another. This mirrored, of course, the chronic problem of his
two administrations—the high cost of maintaining military forces
ready to defend all the frontiers of the "free" world. "Beyond a

wise and reasonable level, which is always changing . . . ," said Eisenhower in 1957, "money spent on arms may be money wasted. . . . National security requires far more than military power. Economic and moral factors play indispensable roles. Any program that endangers our economy could defeat us."

Second: as the United States identified its security with the security of other states, the American conception of security broadened to include the traditional interests of those states.

From the American Revolution through the War of 1812, Americans were concerned with preserving their own national independence. With some reason, they feared British revanchisme. They worried lest Britain or France so exploit divisions within and among the states as to create rival satellites. After the treaties of Vienna and Ghent of 1814–15, Americans had much more reason for confidence in their own national survival. In 1822 the British secretly proposed an alliance. It was debate about this proposal that led to the Monroe Doctrine. It was the fact of the proposal, and of Britain's position as protector of the Spanish-American republics, that permitted the Monroe administration to speak so boldly.

The new American republics were at the time in the situation of the United States a generation earlier. While they seemed to have won their wars of independence, they could not be sure of not having to fight again. They faced the problem of solidifying societies long torn by internal warfare. For each republic, the paramount interest was preservation of independence.

The Monroe Doctrine implied that the United States was adopting as its own interests the primary interests of these Spanish-American republics. Said Monroe:

With the Governments who have declared their independence and maintained it, and whose independence we have, on great consideration and on just principles, acknowledged, we could not view any interposition for the purpose of oppressing them, or controlling in any other manner their destiny, by any European power in any other light than as the manifestation of an unfriendly disposition toward the United States.

In the background were three distinctive strands in American thought about international relations. "Distinctive" because their

exact counterparts were not to be found contemporaneously in
Europe; worth singling out here because they continue to echo in
American thinking about foreign and national security policy.

One strand was that captured in Thomas Jefferson's phrase,
"empire for liberty."[4] From the Revolution onward, Americans
thought of their nation as one destined to be a great empire, but
not an empire on the European or even Roman model. The
United States would not acquire and rule colonies. It would instead grow organically, expanding by adding states, each as free
and autonomous as all the others, each with a proportionate share
in ruling the whole. This was the concept first implemented in the
Northwest Ordinance of 1787. The power of the concept explains
why, though American troops occupied Mexico City, President
James K. Polk and Congress rejected proposals to annex all of
Mexico. They could not satisfactorily imagine areas predominantly Indian and/or Roman Catholic becoming states of the
union. This concept consistently frustrated champions of annexing
Cuba. It explained why, when the Philippines were taken as a
colony, proponents and opponents of annexation agreed that the
status would be temporary and that the Philippines would eventually have independence.

The ideal of the "empire for liberty" informed American promotion of self-determination both in World War I and in and after
World War II. It influenced the strength of American reaction
against the "iron curtain." It influenced American efforts to shape
regional cooperation in Europe and elsewhere.

The second and third strands were intertwined in Henry Clay's
rhetoric, during the early 1820s, about an "American system."
Clay argued that there was a natural affinity between the United
States and the new Spanish-American republics because they were
republics. They shared an ideology of republicanism. They had an
interest in protecting one another. Clay also argued that there was
some natural affinity among states that were American. Even if
monarchical or only dubiously republican, these states had something in common with the United States.

There developed a myth that the line of demarcation drawn by
Pope Alexander VI in 1493 had permanently separated two political spheres—one in Europe and one "beyond the line." It was

1963 before the historian Garret Mattingly looked back and determined that this notion derived not from actual history but from Sir Walter Scott's novel, *The Pirate,* published in 1822.[5] But the myth had had great power. In the year when Mattingly published his findings, the two dominant textbooks on the history of American foreign relations, Samuel Flagg Bemis's and Thomas A. Bailey's, both spoke still of the historic separation of "the two spheres."

Though crucial passages were drafted by Secretary of State John Quincy Adams, who would defeat Clay in the 1824 presidential contest, the Monroe Doctrine embodied the "empire for liberty" concept and both strands of Clay's "American system"—the natural affinity of republics and the natural unity of states "beyond the line."

When Grover Cleveland and later presidents finally began to give life to the Monroe Doctrine, they did so on the presumptions of Clay's "American system." In effect, they said that the American republics formed a single security zone because they were republics and because they were American.

At the time, as when Monroe first published his doctrine, the chief concern of those republics was their national independence. This was the time of Europe's great new burst of imperialism. The Latin republics were nearly all poor and in debt. Many were in situations not dissimilar to that of the United States in its early years. When Cleveland and his successors invoked the Monroe Doctrine to define American security interests, the effect was to enlarge the definition of United States interests to encompass the apparent interests of other American states.

Like Monroe, Woodrow Wilson initiated a process that would ultimately add still further to the interests amalgamated with those of the United States. All along, there had been Americans holding that there were common interests between the United States and not only all republics but all nations aspiring to freedom. One of the complications facing Monroe and John Quincy Adams in 1823 had been finding a way of expressing sympathy with Greeks who had just won independence from the Ottoman Empire without, in doing so, jeopardizing relations with the Sultan and his European supporters. The lives of later presidents and secretaries of state were similarly complicated by Americans urging support of other national independence movements, including those of the Hungarians, the Poles, the Armenians, and the Irish.

Wilson took the position that there was, indeed, some identity between the interests of the United States and those of other nations, no matter where, aspiring to independence and freedom. During and after World War II, when presidents began consistently to take this position, the United States began to adopt as its own interests the interests of a number of states, some of them actual or erstwhile great powers.

The first non-American nation to be thus adopted was Great Britain. Franklin Roosevelt in 1941 identified Britain as a first line of American security. He said of the possibility of direct invasion: "As long as the British Navy retains its power, no such danger exists." By the time of the Korean War, Truman had extended the line to the continent. "Strategically, economically, and morally the defense of Europe is part of our own defense," Truman said in 1951. In 1953 Truman specified that "free Germany is on its way to becoming . . . a partner in the common defense."

Though presidents used somewhat similar language regarding other nations with which the United States had alliances, they usually spoke more of common concerns and aspirations than of their having a role in American defense. By 1960 President Eisenhower was, however, distinguishing as a special set "America's partners and friends in Western Europe and Japan." By President Ford's time, the hierarchy of relationships had become unmistakable. He said in January 1976:

> Today, the state of our foreign policy is sound and strong. . . .
> Our military forces are capable and ready. . . .
> Our principal alliances with the industrial democracies of the Atlantic community and Japan have never been more solid. . . .
> Our traditional friendships in Latin America, Africa, and Asia continue.

As earlier in the Americas, the United States tended to take as its own interests the primary interests of the nations now associated with the "empire for liberty."

Historically, Britain had identified as <u>two</u> of its key interests the preservation of a balance of power in Europe and maintenance of imperial sea communications, particularly those through the Mediterranean connecting the United Kingdom with India. The United States took both goals as its own. Looking backward in his State of the Union message of January 1950, Truman said that the "greatest danger" of the preceding three years had been "the possibility that most of Europe and the Mediterranean area might collapse under totalitarian pressure." The Greek-Turkish aid program of 1947, the Marshall Plan, and the North Atlantic Treaty had, of course, been the principal measures designed to avert that danger. These measures were based on a presumption that the traditional interests of Britain were now major interests of the United States.

Germany, as the Bismarckian Empire and as the Weimar Republic, had had as two obvious interests the avoidance of "encirclement" and the achievement of what Emperor William II had termed a "place in the sun"—recognized status as a power not only in Europe but in the world. Japan's obvious interests, from the time of its emergence from isolation in the nineteenth century, had been safety from its immediate neighbors and access to raw materials and markets.

From the 1950s onward, American presidents tended to define American interests as including in some degree not only the traditional interests of Great Britain but also those of Germany and Japan.

American presidents, of course, noted differences between U.S. interests and those of allies. They did not, however, differentiate convergent interests. That is: presidents (or others) usually did not say: "The United States has an interest in free communication through the Mediterranean. Great Britain has a similar interest. Our reasons are thus and so. Hers are partly the same, partly different, as, for example, ..." In the spirit of the "empire for liberty," the interest of the ally became the interests of the United States, just as, after statehood, the interests of Ohio, then Kansas, then California had become the interests of New York and Virginia.

Questions

These observations about the past suggest some questions about the future. More precisely, they confirm that certain obvious questions are the right questions to ask.

1. *What will be the domestic face of national security? What should it be? To what extent will, or should, the nation's domestic agenda be determined by security concerns?*

The United States faces large, obvious domestic problems. Those much debated include deficits, debt, the state of the schools and of research and development, costs of health care, crime, poverty and homelessness, decaying infrastructure, and pollution.

In the spirit of George Washington, the United States would give priority to those domestic weaknesses that most obviously affect the strength of the nation in comparison with its actual or potential competitors. The exact choices would be open to debate. Theodore Roosevelt, who shared Washington's belief that "the general welfare" should be interpreted as counterpart to "the common defense," justified in terms of national security nearly all proposals for domestic amelioration—breaking up trusts, limiting strikes, conserving natural resources, even promoting childbearing. Roosevelt said in 1906:

There are regions of our land, and classes of our population, where the birth rate has sunk below the death rate. Surely it should need no demonstration to show that willful sterility is, from the standpoint of the nation, from the standpoint of the human race, the one sin for which the penalty is national death, race death; a sin for which there is no atonement.

There is, however, an equally respectable alternative approach. When Abraham Lincoln spoke of security or safety or the avoidance of peril, he concentrated almost exclusively on the domestic scene. In his first annual message, he said little of relations with foreign nations, explaining: "Whatever might be their wishes or dispositions, the integrity of our country and the stability of our Government mainly depend not upon them, but on the loyalty, virtue, patriotism, and intelligence of the American people." From this emphasis he never wavered. His second annual message voiced the theme to be heard in his Gettysburg Address and repeated in his second inaugural: "We shall nobly save or meanly lose the last best hope of earth."

Harding and Calvin Coolidge took a similar approach. They said, in effect, that what mattered most was what happened at home. Like Lincoln, they tended not to look on external security as something needing reinforcement through domestic policy but rather as a by-product of policies aimed at making America and Americans better or richer or both.

Looking toward the future, one can foresee renewed debate about priorities, with Washington's approach and Lincoln's pitted against one another. And it will not be enough to say that security has a domestic face while domestic betterment has an external face. The choice affects the precedence of issues to be addressed. It also affects the ends to be sought. What makes the nation stronger abroad may not be what makes consciences most easy. Nor what makes life most comfortable. And what eases consciences at home, or creates comfort, may not conduce to making the United States stronger or more competitive abroad.

2. *What will be the commonly accepted measurements of national strength?* The extent of conflict between opposing approaches to the domestic agenda will depend in part on what is assumed to contribute to national strength. Historically, the criteria have changed and varied. This has been true of military strength. The capital ship remained a leading element until the two world wars proved otherwise. For a long time after World War II, nuclear arsenals were taken as significant measurements even though it became increasingly difficult for anyone to envision their actual use.

Economic measurements of strength have been similarly inconstant. At different times or places, emphasis has gone to, among other factors, population, trade, wealth, productivity, savings rates, and managerial capacity. Rankings of nations according to summary numbers such as gross national product (GNP) produce results against common sense. The Soviet Union doesn't make it onto the roster of major powers; Saudi Arabia does. And political measurements of national strength have never had precision. National political unity was thought in Washington's time to be a key to national power. His Farewell Address counseled against political parties partly because he thought they would jeopardize unity.

By the twentieth century, the existence of political parties counted
among forces giving a nation unity and strength, leading Harding
to say in 1921:

We divide along political lines, and I would ever have it so. . . . There is
vastly greater security, immensely more of the national viewpoint, much
larger and prompter accomplishment where our divisions are along party
lines, in the broad and loftier sense, than to divide geographically, or
according to pursuits, or personal following.

By Harding's time, social cohesion had become a gauge of power.
Nations were thought weak if they experienced riots or waves of
strikes. And after World War II economic growth became a major
gauge in part because it was a dynamic measurement of all the
elements that had entered into the mobilization of economies in
World War II.

What the world thinks in times to come will greatly influence
what Americans see as the sources of their security, both externally
and at home. If great power competition seems primarily economic competition, the domestic emphases counseled by concern
for security would be those most obviously affecting productivity,
exports, and research and development. If competition comes to
be more in the realm of good works, as some Japanese have recently proposed, then there would be stronger security arguments
in favor of improving medical capabilities or capacities for alleviating poverty or controlling crime. (While the second of these possibilities may seem far-fetched, it is worth remembering that, during
World War II, two of the most secure political entities in the world
were Switzerland and the Vatican, neither of which ranked high in
either military power or aggregate GNP.)

3. *How may—or should—our inherited conceptions of national security
change?* In the past, the requirements of American national security
periodically expanded. Will they expand again? Will they stay as
they are? Will they contract?

First indications suggest another stage of expansion. As the cold
war dissolved, President Bush began to speak of pursuing "a new
world order." His first steps toward defining that order were his
police action against the Noriega regime in Panama and his organization of a UN action to counteract Iraq's invasion of Kuwait.

One might infer that the United States was in the process of associating most of the world with its "empire for liberty," with the District of Columbia destined to be de facto capital of a world government. While the United States might not become the policeman of the world, presidents of the United States might arrange the world's policing. National security would lose most meaning, in the sense that, like the Roman government in the ancient Mediterranean, the American government would concern itself with *any* disturbance of peace.

Possibly, however, the working definition of national security will revert to being what it has been. President Bush and his successors will take as threats to security only menaces to the independence or freedom of nations that the United States has adopted into the "empire for liberty." If so, the key question will be: who belongs within the circle and who does not? An independent Ukrainian Republic? A Hungary facing collapse? A Palestinian state established by negotiation but slipping into extremist hands? A Zulu enclave in South Africa? Hong Kong?

Or could Americans come to see the requirements of security as less than in the past? There are few models. Britain, Germany, and Japan came to recognize that they could not achieve security on their own, but they did not downsize their conceptions of what their security entailed. They found a powerful protector who would make their security its own. The old Austrian-Hungarian and Ottoman Empires did the same. As of 1914 they were acting on conceptions of national security not much different from those of their most palmy days. They simply accepted that they needed help. Only after World War I, when so reduced in size and stature as to be different selves, did these two states come to define their security in more limited terms. Whatever consensus emerges from debate over whether or not the United States is in decline, it is hard to imagine its being transformed into something like the Austrian or Turkish republics of 1918.

One supposes it unlikely therefore that the United States will cease to define its security in terms of the independence and freedom of a large number of nations. The only downsizing that seems in the realm of reality would be some counterpart to that of the British, Germans, and Japanese. Conceivably, Americans could come to see the United Nations as an entity with authority and resources sufficient to take over the defense of some interests now primarily under American guard.

If history is a guide to the future—which it usually is not—the answers to bet on would seem to be the following. The domestic face of national security will continue to be economic growth. If the president and the Congress agree to address any domestic problems, not just debate about them, priority will go to those seemingly most closely related to international strength and competitiveness. The definition of what national security requires will expand. President Bush and his successors will enlarge the roster of American security concerns. The most interesting uncertainties will have to do with particular choices when and as administrations in Washington face the question: shall we act as if there were a world government, with the president of the United States its chancellor? Or shall we say that some of the world's disorders are not American concerns? If so, by what test?

Notes

[1] A handy collection is Israel (1966). It has an admirable introduction by Arthur M. Schlesinger Jr. Messages of later presidents can be found in their *Public Papers*, published annually by the Government Printing Office.

[2] As examples, Rosenman (1972), Safire (1975), and Noonan (1990).

[3] The standard study is still Perkins (1963).

[4] See Tucker (1990).

[5] Mattingly (1963).

RETHINKING THE DIMENSIONS OF NATIONAL SECURITY

4

Technology and U.S. National Security

B. R. INMAN AND
DANIEL F. BURTON JR.

F or the past century, technology has been a major driver of U.S. economic and military success. It has created millions of jobs, spawned entire new industries, and been a major factor behind U.S. export strength. Moreover, it has carried the nation to victory in two world wars and, more recently, helped win the war in the Persian Gulf. In many respects, technology has been America's ultimate comparative advantage. Because of its great techno-

Admiral B.R. INMAN served in the United States Navy from 1952 until his retirement in 1981. He was director of naval intelligence from 1974–76; director of the National Security Agency from 1977–81; and deputy director of the Central Intelligence Agency from 1981–82. From 1986–90 he was chairman of the board and chief executive officer of Westmark Systems, Inc., Austin, Texas. Admiral Inman is a trustee of The American Assembly.
DANIEL F. BURTON JR. is the executive vice president of the Council on Competitiveness and directs its technology program. Prior to joining the council, he was the executive director of the Economic Policy Council, UNA-USA, and a fellow in the U.S.–Japan Leadership Program. Mr. Burton has edited three books on the global economy and written numerous articles on international economics.

logical superiority, the United States has enjoyed unparalleled economic and military advantages, which have translated into a rapidly rising standard of living and strong national security.

During the past two decades, however, America's relative technological superiority has eroded. This decline has undermined America's competitiveness in world markets and forced a reevaluation of U.S. national security. Moreover, this erosion has been accompanied by a fundamental shift in the relationship between civilian and defense technology. Today, civilian industry—not the military—is emerging as the driver of many state-of-the-art technologies. The erosion of U.S. technological superiority and the shift of technological leadership from the military to civilian industry have had a profound impact on U.S. national security. As a result of these two trends, the national security debate is increasingly preoccupied with issues related to technology and industrial competitiveness.

This chapter will examine these shifts. It will analyze how the relative decline in America's international technological leadership and the growing importance of civilian technology are changing how the United States views national security. It argues that as civilian technology becomes more and more important to military performance, it is forcing a fusion of economic and defense issues. Indeed, where advanced technology is concerned, it is increasingly difficult to separate civilian from military technology and to separate strategic economic issues from national security concerns.

The analysis in this chapter will focus primarily on electronics, since this technology is essential to both America's economic and military performance. Moreover, electronics provides a good case study of the new strategic concerns driving much of the debate about U.S. national security.

The American era of electronics manufacturing began with Edison's invention of the phonograph in 1887. This breakthrough was followed by a string of other U.S. inventions, including wireless transmission of speech (1900), radio broadcasting (1920), television receivers (1923), magnetic wire recorders (1947), transistors (1947), color televisions (1954), and semiconductors (1959). Until 1970 U.S. industry dominated all of these fields. During the 1970s, however, the U.S. consumer electronics industry was virtually eliminated by foreign competition. Today, American owned companies have less than 5 percent of the consumer electronics market, despite the fact that it has more than tripled in value during the past decade to $25 billion.

The decline of the American owned consumer electronics industry was one of the early signals that the United States was facing a challenge to its technological leadership. Until 1980, however, many other segments of the U.S. electronics industry continued to maintain a commanding market position. In 1980 U.S. firms controlled all of the world market for supercomputers, three-quarters of the market for fiber optics and semiconductors, over 80 percent of the market for silicon wafers, and over 60 percent of the markets for computer equipment and microprocessors. That same year, the U.S. enjoyed an $8 billion trade surplus in electronics.

By 1988, however, the U.S. share of the world market for supercomputers had fallen to 75 percent, its share of the market for fiber optics was down to 42 percent, semiconductors was down to 36 percent, silicon wafers was down to 20 percent, and computer equipment and microprocessing units were below 50 percent. In 1988 the United States had a $10 billion trade deficit in electronics.[1] Clearly, U.S. industry no longer enjoys the international technological superiority it once did. What are the consequences for American economic performance and national security?

The Economics of Technology

The electronics industry provides a good illustration of the economic dividends that flow from a strong industrial technology base. Jobs and economic growth are perhaps the two most widely recognized national benefits. For example, the electronics industry is the nation's largest manufacturing employer. Over 2.6 million Americans are now directly employed in electronics manufacturing—more than three times the auto industry and more than nine times the steel fabrication industry—and many of these are high value-added jobs. In addition, electronics is a fast growing industry. From 1983–88 the growth rate for the electronics industry was 50 percent greater than for the U.S. economy as a whole. Rapid growth and high value-added jobs mean profits, exports, and a rising standard of living for American citizens. By contrast, the erosion of U.S. industrial competitiveness means a loss of jobs at home, a shift of profits overseas, and a drop in America's exports.

It would be wrong, however, to view job creation, profits, and exports as the only economic dividends of a strong civilian technology base. By providing tools for other sectors of the economy, technology-intensive industries also have a major impact on productivity. U.S. strength in computers, for example, has helped such diverse industries as aerospace, pharmaceuticals, and financial services increase their productivity and, therefore, their competitiveness in world markets. Indeed, some economists argue that technology is responsible for two-thirds and perhaps as much as 80 percent of U.S. productivity growth since the depression.[2]

As pervasive as the economic impact of electronics has been, however, the industry is built on a fragile foundation of relationships. The electronics industry has been likened to a food chain. The survival of each unit in the chain—materials, manufacturing equipment, semiconductors, circuit boards, computers, software, and systems—is critical to all of the other elements. For example, semiconductors depend on materials and manufacturing equipment. Access to leading-edge semiconductor technology, in turn, is essential to the success of all of the technologies further up the chain. A lag in access to this technology ultimately means a loss of competitiveness for the businesses that rely on this technology.

The economic repercussions of U.S. industry's exit from the consumer electronics business provide a dramatic illustration of this interdependency. U.S. industry's decision to quit consumer electronics in the 1970s was based on the fact that it was a "lousy business." Profit margins were low, economies of scale were high, and foreign competition was intense. These pressures led American companies to view the consumer electronics industry as a low-tech, commodity business in which a high-wage country like the United States simply could not compete.

In hindsight, it is clear that the strategic importance of consumer electronics was not fully appreciated. Consumer electronics provides two critical advantages to industry. First, it is an important mass market for electronic components. Companies that supply components to this market enjoy dramatic economies of scale that allow them to offer their products at very low prices. Second, it allows companies to develop volume manufacturing expertise. The combination of low prices and high volume manufacturing expertise gives companies in the consumer electronics market tremendous competitive advantages in the broader marketplace. As a result, they can successfully move into other segments of the electronics market.

Semiconductors provide a good example of the linkages among different electronics technologies. Consumer electronics is a big user of semiconductors. Because of its exit from consumer electronics, U.S. industry soon discovered that it faced significant problems in semiconductors. When U.S. companies dominated the consumer electronics industry, they provided a ready market for U.S. merchant semiconductor firms. Once the consumer electronics market had been taken over by the Japanese and Europeans, U.S. merchant semiconductor firms found that the demand for their products fell sharply. Instead of going to U.S. firms, orders for semiconductors went to foreign companies that had strong relationships with the Japanese and European consumer electronics industries.

At present, there is growing concern that a similar story is unfolding in computers. Just as the exit of American producers from consumer electronics hurt the U.S. semiconductor industry, the problems of the U.S. semiconductor industry may spell trouble for the U.S. computer industry. Weaknesses in the U.S. merchant semiconductor industry have forced more and more U.S. computer firms to rely on their overseas competitors for semiconductors. This reliance means that many U.S. computer companies are dependent on the same companies that they compete with in end markets for the components necessary to build their products. There is a very real question about how long these foreign companies will see it in their best interest to supply U.S. computer firms with timely, state-of-the-art components at competitive prices. By withholding advanced components or simply delaying delivery to American firms, foreign companies could gain an important market advantage over their U.S. rivals.

These technological interdependencies demonstrate how strategic considerations are beginning to dominate discussions about technology and economic policy. The economic debate surrounding technology is no longer limited to jobs and exports. It now includes larger issues about industrial structure and competitive position.

The National Security Implications of Technology

If there is one lesson from the war in the Persian Gulf, it is just how critical technology is to national security. Whether it is precision guidance systems that allow missiles to find their targets with pinpoint accuracy or advanced materials that allow planes to avoid detection by enemy radar, technology creates incredible military advantages. The irony of the Gulf War is that, notwithstanding America's overwhelming technological success, its edge in many critical military technologies has eroded sharply.

Since World War II, superiority in military technology over potential adversaries has been a fundamental tenet of U.S. national security policy. Technological leadership over our allies has been an implicit part of that policy. Moreover, U.S. policy has assumed that defense technology is more advanced than civilian technology. The erosion of U.S. technological leadership and the emergence of civilian industry as the driver of many state-of-the-art technologies therefore has had a profound impact on the U.S. defense establishment. As a result of these shifts, the Department of Defense (DoD) is facing two major new challenges. First, DoD is being forced to address a new set of issues related to protection of and access to advanced technology. Second, DoD is being drawn into a debate about the consequences of weaknesses in the domestic technology base and how to redress them. These issues are discussed below.

During the immediate postwar era, the United States dominated the world technologically. Consequently, the national security challenge facing the U.S. military was straightforward—prevent advanced U.S. technology from falling into the hands of potential adversaries. The solution was equally straightforward—impose export controls. Although U.S. industry complained about lost overseas sales, its grumblings were not taken too seriously because it enjoyed a dominant position in world markets, and export controls were widely accepted as a legitimate price to pay for national security.

With the erosion of U.S. technological superiority, the challenge facing the U.S. defense establishment is much more subtle. DoD must not only prevent advanced American technology from falling into the hands of adversaries, but also must limit their ability to obtain advanced technology from U.S. allies. At the same time, DoD must assure that the U.S. military maintains timely access to allied technology.

The complex game surrounding protection of and access to critical technology is only part of the quandary facing the defense establishment. Today, DoD must also deal with another problem—how to make sure that the United States maintains a strong civilian technology base.

In the past, DoD has spearheaded many of the breakthroughs that paved the way for new commercial technologies. There is mounting evidence that this trend is changing. Today's leading-edge technologies in microelectronics, computers, and telecommunications are found not in DoD laboratories, but in private industry. Even the top-billed U.S. defense weapons used in the Persian Gulf were not as modern or as sophisticated as much commercial technology. The much-acclaimed Patriot and Tomahawk missiles were developed over ten years ago, and many of their parts are even older. For example, the 8088 microprocessor used in the Patriot missile was developed by the Intel Corporation fifteen years ago. This technology would not be competitive with the commercial technology at the corner Radio Shack store today.

As markets for commercial technology have taken off, they have driven advances in civilian technology that outstrip anything the military can offer, not only in terms of price and quality, but often in terms of performance. Instead of industry adapting defense technology breakthroughs to commercial markets, DoD is increasingly faced with the challenge of adapting commercial technology to its needs.

The interdependence of defense and commercial technology means that industry problems can quickly become national security headaches. As a result, DoD finds itself interested in the vitality of certain commercial industries that produce dual-use technologies with both commercial and defense applications. The erosion of the U.S. position in these industries has raised concerns about whether DoD will continue to have timely access to state-of-the-art technology. Increasingly, DoD is being forced to rely on overseas suppliers for critical technologies. During times of international conflict, however, it is not certain that DoD will be able to secure all of the necessary technologies. Although DoD maintains extensive stockpiles, it cannot stockpile against every eventuality. It will inevitably remain vulnerable in certain key areas. In this respect, there is no substitute for a strong domestic technology base.

Although DoD is being drawn more deeply into the policy debate about the impact of industrial competitiveness on national security, its technology practices are increasingly at odds with successful commercial practices. When the United States enjoyed undisputed international dominance in technology, the Pentagon forced a strict separation between defense and commercial applications in an attempt to keep key military technology out of the hands of America's adversaries. Moreover, DoD developed detailed specifications for military technology in order to ensure quality standards that did not exist at the time in many commercial products. These practices drove up costs. In order to keep prices down, DoD instituted a complex procurement process based on competitive bidding that emphasized fixed price contracts. The complexity of the procurement process also hurt productivity and innovation and dramatically increased the cycle time of the defense products.

As a result, the U.S. defense industry lost touch with the relentless push for improvement in quality, cost, and time-to-market that characterize competition in commercial markets. Cost-plus contracts, quality control based on inspection rather than process improvement, highly specialized products, limited production runs, and restricted markets are the dominant features of defense technology management. By contrast, flexibility, high quality at low cost, volume manufacturing expertise, lean production, and access to many different markets are the primary concerns of managers in the private sector.

Because of the way commercial markets have evolved and the way DoD's technology programs are currently structured, it is doubtful whether DoD will provide as many economic benefits to the country in the future as it has in the past. The divergence between DoD's needs and those of commercial markets has simply become too pronounced. The major shifts in DoD's role are summarized in Table 1.

DoD must achieve a more integrated approach to the development and deployment of technology that draws on the strengths of civilian industry. Otherwise, DoD's ability to incorporate leading-edge technology into defense systems in a timely, cost-effective

TABLE 1. The Defense Department's Changing Role in Technology Development

1950s	Today
Defense technology more advanced than civilian technology.	Civilian technology more advanced than much defense technology.
Defense R & D highly relevant to commercial industry.	Defense R & D increasingly specialized and of limited relevance to commercial industry.
Flexible policies allow defense procurement to facilitate the development of new technology-intensive industries.	Rigid policies render defense procurement of limited value for new technology-intensive industries.
Defense technology standards consistent with many industrial needs.	Defense military-specifications at odds with industrial practices and irrelevant to industrial needs.
Defense export controls acceptable because of U.S. industry's technological dominance.	Defense export controls are often ineffective and undermine U.S. industrial competitiveness because of worldwide distribution of technological competence in many industries.
Defense R & D creates breakthroughs that advance U.S. industrial performance.	Defense R & D does not contribute to the integrated process improvements driving international competition in many industries.

Source: Council on Competitiveness

manner will be severely compromised. The message is clear. Not only has America's relative technological superiority eroded, the relationship between civilian and defense technology has fundamentally changed. Today many civilian technologies are more advanced than defense technologies. As a result, it is no longer possible to maintain leadership in defense technologies by defense research and development (R & D) alone. A strong civilian or dual-use technology base is essential to leadership in defense technologies and, therefore, to U.S. national security.

Just how deep are America's technology problems? And what should we do about them? The rest of this chapter will examine these two questions.

Scope of the Problem

In 1989 the private sector Council on Competitiveness launched a major effort to determine the extent of the technology challenge facing American industry. It assembled a group of top technology experts from companies, universities, and labor unions around the country to determine which technologies will be critical to America's industrial competitiveness over the next decade and where the nation stands in them.[3]

The council identified a core group of technologies that is vital to the overall competitiveness of U.S. industry. Advances in the following five areas are driving innovations and superior performance in virtually every industry: (1) materials and associated processing technologies, (2) engineering and production technologies, (3) electronic components, (4) information technologies, and (5) powertrain and propulsion technologies. In fact, there is a broad domestic and international consensus about which technologies will drive industrial performance during the decade ahead. The council's list of technologies corresponds closely to the list compiled by the U.S. Department of Commerce, the U.S. Department of Defense, the White House Office of Science and Technology Policy, Japan's Ministry of International Trade and Industry, and the European Community.

It is important to note that these technologies include not only emerging technologies that will create new industries, but also technologies that will improve performance in existing ones. Many of the most important are not dramatic breakthroughs, such as high-temperature superconductors, but incrementally evolving technologies, such as materials processing and the design of manufacturing systems.

In addition, it is important to recognize that organization systems related to managing the design, commercialization, and production process are key areas of knowledge for companies to master. In other words, not all critical technologies involve hardware or computer software. Many depend on human know-how.

In total, the Council on Competitiveness was able to identify ninety-four generic technologies that are critical to U.S. industrial competitiveness. Had this survey been conducted a decade ago, the United States would have been leading in virtually all of these technologies. Today, it is in trouble in one-third of them. A list of the technologies where the United States is weak or losing badly is provided in Tables 2 and 3.

TABLE 2. Technologies in which the United States Is Weak

Materials and Associated Processing
Technologies
  Advanced Metals
  Membranes
  Precision Coating
Engineering and Production Technologies
  Design for Manufacturing
  Design of Manufacturing Processes
  Flexible Manufacturing
  High-Speed Machining
  Integration of Research, Design, and Manufacturing
  Leading-Edge Scientific Instruments
  Precision Bearings
  Precision Machining and Forming
  Total Quality Management
Electronic Components
  Actuators
  Electro Photography
  Electrostatics
  Laser Devices
  Photonics
Powertrain and Propulsion
  High Fuel Economy/Power Density Engines

Source: Council on Competitiveness

TABLE 3. Technologies in which the United States Is Losing Badly or Has Lost

Materials and Associated Processing
Technologies
   Display Materials
   Electronic Ceramics
   Electronic Packaging Materials
   Gallium Arsenide
   Silicon
   Structural Ceramics
Engineering and Production Technologies
   Integrated Circuit Fabrication and Test Equipment
   Robotics and Automated Equipment
Electronic Components
   Electroluminescent Displays
   Liquid Crystal Displays
   Memory Chips
   Multichip Packaging Systems
   Optical Information Storage
   Plasma and Vacuum Fluorescent Displays
   Printed Circuit Board Technology

Source: Council on Competitiveness

Although there are no definitive explanations for why the United States is strong in some technologies and weak in others, several rules of thumb apply. In general, the United States tends to be strong in technologies that have the following characteristics:

- They are close to basic research or are the direct result of basic research without the intervening steps of lengthy development (e.g., biotechnology).
- They do not have heavy capital investment needs (software).
- They can be initiated largely by individual innovation (computer-aided engineering).
- They are strongly aided by U.S. government investment in basic research (genetic engineering), defense procurement (rocket propulsion), and environmental regulations.
- They have been supported by high levels of private sector R & D (materials and information technologies).

By contrast, technologies in which the United States is weak or losing badly tend to have the following characteristics:

- They have not had sufficient private or public investment in the underlying technology (display materials).
- There is inadequate risk sharing among companies in technology development (electronic packaging).
- They have high capital needs and low capital investment (automated equipment).
- They need extensive investment in technology for an extended period of time (optical information storage).
- They have a significant manufacturing focus (integrated circuit fabrication equipment).
- They have been targeted by foreign government and industry (memory chips).

It is important to bear in mind these strengths and weaknesses in developing policy responses. Generic solutions that treat all technologies the same will meet with marginal success. Instead, policies and programs must be designed that address the specific characteristics of individual technologies, and they must build on the unique strengths of U.S. government, industry, and universities.

What to Do?

U.S. government technology policies and programs are still based largely on the assumption that the United States dominates world technology markets and that defense technologies are more advanced than civilian technologies. It is imperative to recognize these assumptions are being challenged. Government policies and priorities must come to grips with the fact that the United States is no longer the leader in many key technologies and that many civilian technologies are more advanced than defense technologies.

Although the U.S. government spends in excess of $70 billion on R & D, little of it is directed toward strengthening the U.S. industrial technology base. Instead, it focuses primarily on basic scientific research and weapons development, testing, and evaluation. New policies are needed that focus on developing generic industrial technology and on diffusing it throughout the private and public sectors.

No line agency in the government has broad responsibility for research and other activities related to technology. In Congress, the civilian science budget alone is divided among nine of thirteen different appropriations subcommittees. In the executive branch, R & D is dispersed among twelve agencies. The primary goals of these agencies do not directly address issues related to commercially relevant technologies, and they have tended to subordinate initiatives related to industry.

The largest civilian R & D agencies include the National Aeronautics and Space Administration with a FY 1990 budget of $12 billion; the Department of Energy with a budget of $7 billion; the National Institutes of Health with a budget of $7 billion; and the National Science Foundation with a budget of $2 billion. In addition, there are 726 federal laboratories. Combined, these labs have a budget of $20 billion, but, like their lead agencies, their focus on technology and competitiveness is limited.

The National Institute for Standards and Technology (NIST) at the Department of Commerce is the main U.S. laboratory with a specific mission to support U.S. industry. For many years, however, it has had to cope with level or shrinking funding while the demand for its services grew. Recent budget increases and new programs have expanded its focus on technologies that are critical to U.S. competitiveness. With a budget of only $215 million in FY 1991, however, NIST's capacity to help U.S. industry develop critical generic technologies is limited.

The bulk of U.S. government R & D funds is devoted to defense. In FY 1990 DoD spent $37 billion on R & D. More than 90 percent of this total went to weapons development, testing, and evaluation, which provide little benefit to the U.S. civilian technology base. About $1.1 billion went to the Defense Advanced Research Projects Agency (DARPA), which conducts most of the more fundamental research on dual-use technology that provides the greatest contributions to commercial industry. It is important to note that although the U.S. defense R & D budget increased substantially during the 1980s, the parts of the R & D budget that are the most relevant to industry—basic and applied research (line items 6.1 and 6.2 of the DoD budget)—did not share in the build-up.

In the decades ahead, U.S. national security will depend increasingly on leadership in key dual-use technologies that are driving both military and industrial performance. The United States still has the finest research base in the world, but its ability to commercialize technology rapidly, to maintain a strong market position, and to preserve a strong industrial technology base is being severely challenged. In order to safeguard U.S. national security, government and private sector must work together to develop coherent policies to ensure American leadership in the development, use, and commercialization of technology.

In order to rise to this challenge, U.S. policy should focus on greater integration of the defense and civilian technology sectors. For DoD, integration implies greater reliance on commercial products, processes, and buying practices. For industry, it implies that the same technologies, personnel, administrative procedures, R & D, and production facilities could be employed for both commercial and military customers. The result would be a larger, more competitive industrial base that would offer greater economies, lower costs, and higher quality for defense technologies.[4]

Government, industry, and universities all have an important role to play. Government must make sure that the priority of technological competitiveness is reflected in its budgetary decisions, procurement practices, and broader economic policies. Industry must improve its ability to commercialize technology. And universities must make sure that their research and education programs adequately address the technology needs of industry. Working together, the public and private sectors can revitalize U.S. technological leadership. In doing so, they can bolster the nation's industrial competitiveness and national security.

The recommendations that follow address how to strengthen the technological leadership that underpins U.S. national security. They focus on the responsibilities of government, industry, and universities.

1. *The president should act immediately to make technology and competitive-*

ness a national priority. Current federal R & D programs have limited relevance to the technology needs of the U.S. industrial base. Although defense related R & D has helped U.S. civilian industries in the past, these benefits are likely to decline in the future because the DoD is a technology leader in a diminishing number of industries. The United States is already losing badly in many critical technologies. Unless the nation acts today to promote the development of generic technology that is important to both U.S. industrial competitiveness and national security, America's technological position will erode further.

The federal government should view support of generic industrial technologies that apply to many different sectors as a priority mission. It is important to recognize that this mission would not require major new federal funding. If additional funds for generic technology programs are required, other federal R & D programs, such as national prestige projects, should be redirected or phased in more slowly to allow additional resources to be focused on generic technology. The president should move quickly to take the following actions:

- Announce his intention to increase dramatically the percentage of federal R & D expenditures allocated to support for critical generic technologies and present a five-year implementation plan as part of his next annual budget.
- Direct the Office of Science and Technology Policy to establish the Critical Technologies Institute expeditiously. This institute would work with industry to set priorities in critical generic technologies, translate these priorities into specific action plans, and cooperate with key agencies and departments to implement these programs.
- Direct key technology agencies, such as DARPA, NIST, and NSF (National Science Foundation), to work closely with industry to advance U.S. leadership in critical generic technologies.
- Implement decisions to ensure that the federal laboratories' contribution to U.S. technological leadership is commensurate with the national investment in them.
- Make the cost of capital for the development of priority technologies competitive with that of America's major competitors.

- Promote capital formation programs, regulatory guidelines, and trade policies that are conducive to U.S. manufacturing and investment in technology.
- Ensure that key policy-making bodies, such as the National Security Council, are more closely involved in issues related to strengthening the U.S. industrial technology base.
- Revise federal procurement policies so that they boost U.S. industrial technology performance. The National Institute for Standards and Technology, working with industry in an open standards-setting process, should be given the responsibility for adopting within government dual military-industrial standards. A reasonable goal would be to replace half of DoD mil-spec standards with dual military-industrial standards by 1995 and three-fourths by 2000. In addition, government contractors should be encouraged to qualify for the Malcolm Baldrige Quality Award.
- Assess the nation's technology infrastructure needs, benchmark what foreign governments are doing, and develop strategies, programs, and implementation plans to make sure that the United States has a world-class technology infrastructure.

2. *U.S. industry should set a goal to meet and surpass world-class commercialization practices.* There is no question that American management needs to improve its ability to commercialize technology. U.S. companies should understand and build on the successful commercialization practices of their domestic and foreign competitors. To achieve this goal, U.S. firms should benchmark their competitors, set appropriate goals, and allocate the necessary resources. They should also motivate, train, and empower their employees to take responsibility for achieving these goals. Action in the following areas is especially important:

- Match the administration's goal to increase dramatically the R & D allocated to critical generic technologies and develop a five-year implementation plan.
- Institute total quality management and continuous improvement.
- Strengthen process engineering and accelerate time-to-market to competitive levels.

- Improve the ability to share risks and spread costs for technology development across a broad base.
- Continuously upgrade the skills of the work force.
- Work with industry associations to strengthen their competence in technology issues, improve their ability to identify, assess, and disseminate information about generic technology and world-class commercialization practices throughout the U.S. private sector, develop technology road maps, and build cooperative supplier networks.

3. *While keeping their basic research programs strong, universities should develop closer ties to industry so that education and research programs contribute more effectively to the real technology needs of the manufacturing and service sectors.* America's research universities are one of its greatest technological assets and should be strengthened. In pursuit of new knowledge, however, many universities have lost sight of issues related to technology and manufacturing that affect U.S. competitiveness. Universities should strengthen their focus on the manufacture, use, and commercialization of technology. In the process, however, it is important not to jeopardize the basic research contributions of universities. They should concentrate on the following actions:

- Develop close ties with U.S. industry and make efforts to ensure that important technology advances are communicated to potential U.S. users on a priority, expedited basis.
- Make efforts, in cooperation with employers, to ensure that education programs in engineering and management reflect the real needs of industry. It is especially important that universities promote understanding and competence in the process by which a product is carried from conception through design and manufacture to market.
- Keep basic science and engineering programs strong and strengthen research capabilities so that they can adequately address fundamental, long-term technology issues that are relevant to industry.

Conclusion

The framework for U.S. national security is changing. Although attention is currently riveted on events in Eastern Europe and the Soviet Union, the dramatic impact of technology on national security cannot be overestimated. America's technological superiority has eroded sharply, and many civilian technologies are now more advanced than defense technologies. As a result, U.S. policy makers must broaden their view of national security to include issues related to strengthening the U.S. civilian technology base at home and access to advanced technology overseas.

Technology alone, however, is not the answer. Although it is essential to generate new technology, it is perhaps even more important to develop new relationships between government and industry, enhance America's manufacturing expertise, and improve U.S. management's understanding of the commercialization process. By building these strengths, the United States will be able not only to create new technology, but also to do more with existing technology. In the process, it will strengthen the technology base that drives U.S. industrial competitiveness and, increasingly, underpins America's national security.

Notes

[1] Computer Systems Policy Project, *Perspectives on U.S. Technology Policy, Part I: The Federal R & D Investment*, February 1991; American Electronics Association, *America's Future at Stake: Winning in the Global Marketplace*, 1989.

[2] The first effective effort to measure the impact of technology on the U.S. economy is credited to Robert Solow (1957). Many economists have since expanded on these concepts.

[3] Council on Competitiveness, *Gaining New Ground: Technology Priorities for America's Future*, March 1991.

[4] For a full discussion of this issue, see "Integrating Commercial and Military Technologies for National Strength," Center for Strategic & International Studies, Washington, D.C., March 1991.

5

Industrial Competitiveness and National Security

MICHAEL BORRUS
AND JOHN ZYSMAN
with assistance from David Bell

T he debate on U.S. competitiveness must become a debate about national security. Relative decline in economic posi-

MICHAEL BORRUS is a director of the Berkeley Roundtable on the International Economy at the University of California, Berkeley. He also teaches in the joint School of Engineering-Business program on the management of technology. A member of the California State Bar, Professor Borrus has worked on high-technology and trade issues for the last decade. He regularly consults on technology policy and business strategy issues with various governments and firms in the U.S., Asia, and Europe—including, most recently, the National Advisory Committee on Semiconductors.
JOHN ZYSMAN is professor of political science at the University of California, Berkeley, and codirector of the Berkeley Roundtable on the International Economy. He has written extensively on the politics and policy of European and Japanese business and economic development. His most recent works include *Manufacturing Matters: The Myth of the Post-Industrial Economy* (with Stephen Cohen) and *Politics and Productivity: How Japan's Developmental Strategy Works* (with Laura Tyson and Chalmers Johnson). This chapter is drawn from chapter 1 in *The Highest Stakes: Technology, Economy and Security Policy*, Oxford University Press, 1991. The authors wish to acknowledge support of the Alfred P. Sloan Foundation and the MacArthur Foundation for making this work possible.

tion and the erosion of technological leadership will soon undermine the exercise of American power. The problem is not that U.S. foreign policy commitments have exhausted the economy's resources.[1] Nor is it that in an increasingly sophisticated and interconnected world economy, U.S. security must partly rest on foreign technological and industrial capacities that lie outside of direct U.S. control.[2] Rather, U.S. industrial and technological decline has eroded the economic foundations of the postwar security system at the same time that industrial and technological initiative abroad is creating the basis of a wholly new system that minimizes U.S. influence.

These concerns may seem laughably distant coming on the heels of America's military triumph in the Persian Gulf. To be sure, the Gulf conflict demonstrated the vast difference between a great power and the modest capabilities of a regional Third World power. But U.S. military success in the Persian Gulf rests on past industrial strength; it is not a reliable indicator of future capacities. Even the U.S. weapons mastery rests on electronic components and subsystems largely designed in an era when U.S. industry dominated the civilian computer and semiconductor industries. That era is fading rapidly. Continued mastery is by no means assured, because the economic base on which the U.S. international political position rests is at risk.

For four decades, the security system presumed a fundamental Soviet enemy, a U.S. controlled military umbrella over allies in Western Europe and Asia, and an international system of trade and finance organized around U.S. economic strength. Change in this third pillar, the economic foundation of the security system, is the central concern of our analysis. To be sure, the U.S. economy remains the world's largest and its technological and scientific resources are still deeper and broader than any near challenger in Europe or Asia. But the relative U.S. position has changed substantially. In 1970 the ratio of U.S. gross domestic product (GDP) to that of Japan and Germany was 2.5:1. By 1990 this ratio had dropped below 1.3:1. Simply put, there has been an undeniable shift away from the U.S. in the relative capacity to generate and deploy economic and political resources.

There is now constraint where there was once leverage in finance, trade, and technology. U.S. capabilities to shape discussion and outcomes—through cajoling or coercion—are fundamentally circumscribed by allied toleration of American aims. Take finance: in 1956, during the Suez crisis, the U.S. was able to change British, French, and Israeli behavior by threatening a run on the pound. Compare today's situation, when Japan or Germany has the capacity to shape American fiscal and monetary policy—and when the U.S. president's plea for lower interest rates abroad to stimulate economic recovery at home is resoundingly rejected by the other members of the Group of Seven. Similarly, compare the enormous influence the Marshall Plan once permitted the United States with America's relative financial inability to invest to shape Central Europe's redevelopment today.

The U.S. is similarly constrained in its ability to use an open domestic market to secure compliance in the security realm, something that used to be relatively cost free given the dominant position of American industry in the decades after the world war. Now U.S. owned industry is unable to compete without government protection in a growing number of industrial sectors from textiles to microelectronics. The stubborn U.S. trade deficit also reflects the exit altogether of U.S. producers from industries like consumer electronics and large segments of machinery and materials. In traded industries today, other countries look to emulate the Japanese model of production, not U.S. practices, which further limits U.S. influence especially in Asia.

U.S. freedom of action is also limited technologically. Where once the U.S. was the only significant source of advanced technologies with commercial or military relevance, today there are equally competitive or superior technologies available from Asia and Europe. Indeed, especially in the broad range of component, machinery, and materials technologies that underlie much industrial production from auto to military electronics, the U.S. economy is increasingly dependent upon foreign supplies. At best, as in the Toshiba Milling Machine case, technology dependence makes it very difficult to punish clear contraventions of U.S. security interests; at worst, it leaves the U.S. susceptible to subtle technological leverage.

In our view, relative changes in the economic sphere are undermining the postwar security system though not determining the structure of the new order. We argue below that innovations in policy and production abroad are creating an alternative industrial basis for security. America's superior military technology will not rescue U.S. influence; but commercial weakness may very well undermine military strength. As a consequence of these changes in relative position, the American, European, and Asian regions each has the political capacity and technoindustrial foundations for independent action. In our view, the technological and economic foundations that are emerging could support any of a number of security structures, from a benign, U.S. led managed multilateralism to a confrontational geomercantilism. We conclude by assessing U.S. choices given the new constraints. But we start by charting how America has come to find itself in such a new and precarious position.

The Emergence of Vulnerability: America's Deteriorating Position in the Global Economy

How deeply eroded is the American capacity to exact compliance either directly or through its position in the trade and financial system? There are two interpretations.[3] One view is that decline is mostly the result of industrial catch-up abroad that ended in the mid-seventies, and therefore leads to a tolerable economic interdependence with continued U.S. political leadership.[4] The second view, presented here, is that the decline is more fundamental, and has been disguised by the process of catch-up, stagflation, and European economic troubles in the late seventies and early eighties.

The Pattern of Decline

We see the overall picture like this: an emerging competitive weakness in manufacturing, increasingly visible in the 1970s, was accelerated and amplified by mistaken macroeconomic policies in the 1980s.[5] America's shifting position began in the 1950s and 1960s with textiles, footwear, apparel, and shipbuilding. These were labor intensive sectors at the time, and seemed to indicate only a change in the composition of American domestic production. However, steel soon followed with growing imports in the 1960s, culminating decades later when American firms became importers of steel technology and even then were not at the frontier. The 1970s then saw the decline of the consumer electronics, automobile, numerically controlled machine tool, and other manufacturing and capital equipment sectors. Now, in the 1980s and 1990s, a range of advanced technology sectors face intense international competition—including electronic materials and manufacturing equipment, semiconductors, displays and other component technologies, and electronic systems like computers and office automation equipment.[6]

There was a characteristic story of retreat culminating in decline in all of these sectors. First, global market share began to drop, especially at home as imports flooded the domestic market. Firms usually responded by moving offshore to lower production costs through cheaper labor (if they had the resources) and simultaneously by securing some form of bilateral restraint on imports to protect their waning domestic market position. The bilateral agreements, quantitative restrictions on imports, usually accelerated competitive decline. Such supply restrictions permitted foreign producers to raise prices and encouraged them to move toward higher value-added goods to maintain profit margins. Consequent higher prices restored domestic profit levels, thereby deferring the competitive adjustment of the troubled U.S. industries, even as they meant that U.S. consumers were subsidizing ever more competitive foreign firms. For those who went offshore, the respite was short-lived. As production processes became more and more spatially fragmented, integration of product and process innovations became ever more difficult. Finally, as the competitive position of U.S. firms waned, so did their capacity to spend on research and development (R & D) and new product and process development. The principle sources of innovation and advanced technology development began to move abroad to competitors.

The problems in electronics bring this story of troubled adjustment into the 1990s and suggest some of the significance for American security of the loss of U.S. industrial position. Postwar U.S. dominance of electronics was premised on companies producing complete products, such as computers, while having access to a highly competitive domestic market of independent component, machinery, and materials suppliers. Even the most vertically integrated firms such as IBM depended on this supply network. Over time, those independent suppliers have been disappearing under competitive pressure from domestic Japanese producers. Today large, integrated Japanese electronics firms control the supply of many of the essential underlying technologies, either directly through ownership or indirectly through group affiliation.[7] An increasing number of American companies from high-end suppliers like Unisys and Honeywell to micro suppliers like Compaq, Sun, and Apple, sell name brand computers that consist almost entirely of hardware technologies supplied by their major Japanese competitors.[8] As competitive dependence in the supply base undermines computer product development, the technological initiative is increasingly passing to Japanese industry, which dominates most of the fastest growing market segments.[9]

This story is repeated in other sectors of the U.S. industrial base. The U.S. is increasingly dependent on foreign supply of a broad range of industrial technologies including manufacturing machinery, tools and robotics, precision mechanical and magnetic components, displays, optoelectronics, power supplies and control systems, and many advanced materials like ceramics and ultra-pure silicon. All of these technologies are militarily significant. Advances abroad in all of them have come primarily through civilian markets rather than military spending.

A very different spin has been placed on these shifts by a succession of analyses beginning in the early 1980s. Then, a positive face was placed on trade deficits in older industries. The deficits were supposed to represent a shift upward out of declining labor intensive into expanding technology intensive industries, a shift out of sunset into sunrise industries.[10] The apparent decline in these supposedly mature sectors was claimed to be a source of strength for the economy as a whole. Unfortunately, the sunrise-sunset distinction simply misinterpreted many of the processes of industrial development. Sunrise sectors largely make producer goods that are applied across the economy to help transform production and products in traditional and consumer industries. The U.S. inability to maintain position in "mature" sectors, conjoined with the success of Germany and Japan in the same sectors, suggests that U.S. firms have a limited ability to reorganize manufacturing and apply new technology. This has simultaneously weakened the advanced technology sectors of the domestic economy by eroding their customer base.

A related benign cast was put on U.S. industry's industrial difficulties by the argument that the U.S. economy was shifting from a manufacturing based industrial to a postindustrial service economy. This issue has been examined in detail by Cohen and Zysman.[11] Our position is that services can not substitute for manufacturing as a means of supporting either the relative domestic standard of living or the U.S. international trade position. Critical parts of the service sector are linked to manufacturing, and their capacity to support income growth erodes as manufacturing loses position. Indeed, a two-decade-long stagnation in real U.S. wages in part reflects the shift from manufacturing to services employment.[12]

Finally, analysts have argued that there is little cause for concern because the U.S. industrial base has not in fact eroded: the share of manufacturing in U.S. GDP, while declining until the mid-1980s, has since recovered to previous highs of the 1970s.[13] The implication is that particular cases of industrial trouble were simply isolated though visible instances that did not describe the broad patterns in the American economy. The export boom of the late 1980s and substantial direct foreign investment in U.S. industry would appear to support this position. Is there, then, no cause for concern?

Recall first that the export boom and the growth in manufacturing have been accomplished with stagnant wages and a hugely devalued dollar. This means that U.S. industry is no longer competitive enough to support rising wages or to prosper internationally at the exchange rates of the past. Thus by 1989 the U.S. was able to regain the share of world exports it held in 1972 when the dollar was more than twice as strong, and, despite devaluation, 1972's trade surplus had become 1989's $113 billion deficit. Any country can have balanced trade and produce a boom in manufactures; the question is at what real exchange rate and at what real income levels. The trick is to maintain balanced trade and industrial boom with high and rising real incomes.[14] The U.S. has failed that test for close to twenty years.

Indeed, sectoral evidence from the recent boom suggests that American manufacturing surged especially in lower value-added segments of particular industries. Apart from a few stellar performers like Boeing and chemicals, the domestic composition of production is shifting toward becoming a low-wage, low-technology manufacturing and raw materials economy.[15] In our view, the shifting composition of production matters mightily to economic performance. Employment and output in industry may grow, but if the composition of production shifts as indicated, the domestic economy may slowly be ceding the market segments and core competences on which future competitive advantage, long-term growth opportunities—and, ultimately, national security—lie.[16]

Innovation Abroad and Constraint at Home

After World War II, the United States made things others could not produce, and what others could make, American firms often made better and cheaper.[17] The dominant industrial position rested on a system of mass production and divisionalized management that emerged in the late nineteenth and early twentieth century, and that was strongly supported by U.S. policies favoring consumption.[18] These real innovations in the organization of production and corporate control were responses to the particular circumstances of American economic development. Other countries tried to catch up. They sought to imitate what the U.S. did; they saved and invested to do so. But they never really did imitate the United States. Rather, the most successful innovated and built the basis for advantage in global markets.

Two aspects of postwar development in the foreign advanced countries concern us: policy and production. The two stories intermesh. Our most successful competitors, like Japan and Germany, chose to emphasize investment in production over consumption, creating macro conditions for rapid growth. In both, government encouraged the rapid adoption and widespread diffusion of technology acquired abroad, and helped to provide the skilled work force necessary to adoption. In Japan, the government went a step further. Not only did policy help to stimulate new investment through a variety of tax incentives but it reserved the growth in domestic demand for Japanese producers by formally closing the domestic market to foreign firms. As technology followers, Japanese firms borrowed, implemented, and improved foreign technologies through continuous rounds of reinvestment in the rapidly growing domestic economy. In essence, Japanese firms faced conditions in quite traditional industries that Americans associate with high-technology industries—rapid growth and technological development forcing dynamic adaptation through investment and learning. Learning economies dominated, making the pursuit of market share a necessity to sustain short-term profits.[19]

As a result of these developments, real innovations in production, production organization, and technology development were generated and entrenched in Japan and Europe. Our hypothesis is that these breakthroughs are of sufficient scope and power to alter the relative position of nations.[20] What is emerging is not incremental or even radical improvement in the older American production systems, but a new approach, a new paradigm. Elements of these breakthroughs are found in the United States, but the evidence is that the new approaches are not well established or broadly diffused in this country.

The detailed character of this production revolution is increasingly understood and documented.[21] The central codewords of the new manufacturing are flexibility, speed, and quality. The popular notions of quality circles, just-in-time delivery, and automation— slogans of the new approach—are simply organizational or technological elements of the whole. Though implemented in a variety of forms, the most powerful involve flexible volume production (labeled variously as flexible automation, flexible mass production, and lean production).[22] Until recently, high-volume production has been dominated by the rigidities of scale economies: expensive equipment dedicated to specific tasks in which the costs could only be recouped by large production runs of the same items.[23] Variety could be very costly because it disrupted long production runs and incurred significant costs in long set-ups and substantial down time. Now, organizational innovation, reinforced by microelectronics, has removed the past constraints. The new approach creates the capability of producing a variety of tailored products with costs, quality, and market responsiveness far superior to mass production.

Principal features of the new approach include shorter production runs staffed by smaller teams of multiskilled workers operating less expensive general purpose machinery that can be rapidly changed over for new production set-up with minimal downtime.[24] Line workers are given responsibility for strict process control to systematically eliminate variability in manufacture (the major source of defects). In turn, elimination of defects and rapid changeovers eliminate the need for carrying inventory and permit parts to be delivered as needed, "just-in-time" for production, further reducing costly inventories. Tight process control and the multiskilled work team also eliminate the costly layers of supervisory, maintenance, housekeeping, and quality control personnel that characterize mass production. In a variety of ways that tend to speed up design and production cycles, the new system extends beyond the shop floor into product development and to suppliers.

Overall, significant gains in product quality and variety result, without increased costs, but with great flexibility in production and greatly reduced total cycle times, thus enabling superior market responsiveness. Indeed, the flexible, speedy production capability permits the leading firms to do their market research by introducing new product and then accommodating to customer reaction, fine tuning product configurations and volumes to actual demand.[25] Conjoined with the policy innovations described earlier, the new practices are already transforming traditional industries, generating vertical disintegration in many cases, new entry in others, and prying open established industrial structures. The observed forms of new production suggest a sharp break from practices dominant in the middle part of this century and pave the way for realizing the huge gains in productivity that have been promised but not yet delivered by the application of information technology to production.[26]

In our view, America's relative decline reflects a failure to understand, access, and adopt the innovations in policy and production that underlie superior industrial performance abroad, and especially in Asia. Successive U.S. administrations continue to deny the relevance of interventionist policies abroad. And many industrialists continue to believe that technological leadership can be maintained indefinitely even as manufacturing mastery is ceded to competitors, or that cheap foreign labor and capital costs rather than production innovation lie behind superior performance abroad, or even that refined techniques for financial management make long-term strategic planning, production reorganization, and technology investment unnecessary. A few U.S. firms are slowly undertaking a strategic reconceptualization of the firm and its place in the market and the community, the necessary prerequisite to adoption of the new production innovations. But policy makers and the bulk of American industry have barely begun to acknowledge the need for fundamental changes in policy and industrial practices.

Diffusion and Adjustment: The Risk of Competitive Dependence

The decline in U.S. industrial position will be difficult to reverse even with significant changes in policy and practice, because far more has been lost than simple market position in specific sectors. Rather, the supply base of the economy is unraveling: the component and parts technologies, materials and machinery sectors, and related industrial skills necessary to sustain competitive manufacturing and development are eroding, or are already gone. For example, competition in the past decade has devastated domestic producers of manufacturing machinery, including advanced industry segments like computer-numerically controlled machine tools, robotics, and semiconductor-photo-lithographic equipment. U.S. dependence on foreign supply of such machinery has increased dramatically since 1980, with imports rising from 14 percent over 40 percent of domestic consumption.[27]

Table 1 similarly shows that, in electronics, U.S. producers are broadly dependent on foreign supply of a huge and growing list of essential component, materials, and machinery technologies. Indeed, most U.S. computer firms can no longer produce consumer-

---

TABLE 1. Gaps in the U.S. Technology Supply Base

Precision-mechanical
>> Motors—flat, high torque, subminiature
>> Gears—subminiature, precision machining
>> Switch assemblies—subminiature
Packaging
>> Surface mount, plastic
Media
>> Magnetic disk
>> Optical disk
Displays
>> Electroluminescent
>> LCD, Color LCD, LCD shutter
>> CRT—large, square, flat
>> LED—arrays
>> Projection systems
Optical
>> Lens
>> Scanners
>> Laser Diodes
Feromagnetic
>> Video heads
>> Audio heads
>> Miniature transformer cores
Copier-printer
>> Small engines for laser printers

Source: National Semiconductor

like products, e.g., laptop and smaller PCs, without an alliance with Japanese firms to provide the necessary components, microdesign know-how, and relevant manufacturing skills—Compaq with Citizen Watch, Apple with Sony, Sun with Fujitsu and Toshiba, and TI with Sharp. Even IBM is not immune from this trend. The U.S. General Services Administration recently noted that IBM's RISC System 6000 model 7013-540 computer has a foreign content in excess of 88 percent.[28]

In electronics, existing dependencies appear slowly to be creating a cumulative knowledge gap that is profoundly disturbing in its security implications: even where they can procure technology inputs from abroad, U.S. firms no longer retain many of the design and manufacturing skills necessary to use them in a competitive fashion. For example, Japanese producers have painstakingly acquired, iteratively over several product generations, the precision mechanical design expertise embedded in products like VCRs, or the precision machining know-how in auto-focus camcorders. A leading U.S. industrial laboratory recently reverse engineered such products and concluded that the embedded precision mechanical skills probably no longer exist anywhere in the U.S.

These are serious problems for America's security position because, in the leading-edge technologies of the future, component, materials, and equipment manufacturers control the technological advances in product and production know-how that help to shape competitive performance. Competitive dependence will increasingly constrain the competitive adjustment of U.S. producers by deterring access to appropriate technologies in a timely fashion at a reasonable price.

The Architecture of Supply and the Trajectory of Technology

It is not the fact of dependence on foreign producers itself that concerns us. It is rather the "architecture of supply"—i.e., the structure of the markets through which component, materials, and equipment technologies reach U.S. producers. Again, by the supply base of an economy, we mean the parts, component, subsystem, materials, and equipment technologies available for new product and process development, as well as the structure of relations among the firms that supply and use these elements.[29] The supply base can be thought of as an infrastructure to any given firm, in the sense that it is external to the firm but broadly supports the firm's competitive position by helping to delimit the range of its possibilities in global markets, while providing collective gains (e.g., technological spillovers) for the economy as a whole.[30]

The supply base shapes the possibilities confronting users by enabling or deterring access to appropriate technologies in a timely fashion at a reasonable price. The architecture (or structure) of the supply base matters precisely to the extent it influences such technology access, timeliness, and cost. Domestic industry that is significantly dependent on a foreign supply base (i.e., on imports of key inputs) will not be overly constrained wherever markets are open and competitive, and foreign suppliers are numerous, geographically dispersed, and not in the same lines of business as their customers. This was essentially the case for European electronics systems producers from the 1950s to the 1980s: they relied primarily on U.S. components suppliers, who were themselves competitive, numerous, located in both Europe and the U.S., usually not in competition with their customers, and accessible through relatively open markets for trade and investment. Indeed, it was not until the competitive problems of U.S. chip producers threatened a much more constraining architecture of supply for Europe in the 1980s that European companies moved at great cost to re-create a locally controlled supply base.[31]

By contrast, domestic producers should be concerned where the architecture of supply includes closed markets, oligopolistic and geographic concentration, and especially wherever such concentrated suppliers compete directly with their customers. When suppliers have the ability to exercise market power or to act in concert to control technology flows, or when markets and technologies are not accessible because of trade protection, then the architecture of supply can significantly constrain competitive adjustment to the disadvantage of domestic industry. Such an architecture is emerging today in electronics for U.S. producers: a small number of foreign suppliers, principally Japanese, are more and more driving the development, costs, quality, and manufacture of the technological inputs critical to all manufacturers. Most of those suppliers of electronic components, manufacturing equipment, and subsystems are also competitors in a range of electronics systems from TVs and portable phones to computers.[32]

The supply base architecture thus becomes a crucial element of international competition for domestic industries. It has an even greater significance, however, for the domestic economy. The architecture of supply and the character and composition of domestic production together delimit the technological opportunities that are perceived and pursued within a domestic economy.[33] They define a technological development trajectory that reflects the community and market context within which technology evolves.[34]

Such development paths are not dictated alone by technical

knowledge. Technology development is a path dependent process of learning in which tomorrow's opportunities grow out of product, process, and applications activities undertaken today. Consequently, the pace and direction of technological innovation and diffusion are shaped by production and market position. In this view, technological know-how cannot simply be acquired through international market mechanisms; otherwise, there would be no possibility for distinctive national development trajectories. But most technical knowledge involves additional, often subtler insights that coalesce only in conjunction with experience in development and production. The process is simultaneously cyclical and incremental—rather than a dramatic leap up to the next rung in the ladder of technological progress, advances are driven through iteration and cumulative learning-by-doing in production.

The speed and degree to which such embodied technical know-how flows across national boundaries depend crucially upon the character of these local and national institutions. In the U.S., employee mobility is very high, firms can be purchased outright, and short-term capital market constraints often push firms to license proprietary technologies. In general, U.S. technology accrues locally but diffuses rapidly even across national boundaries. By contrast, in a country like Japan, skilled labor mobility is low, acquisitions are virtually impossible, patient capital is available, and relevant networks and national institutions are extremely difficult to access. As a result, considerable accrued technologies know-how is retained locally in Japan and never diffuses readily or rapidly across national boundaries.

Because know-how can accumulate and be retained locally, the character of the domestic economy and the architecture of the supply base supporting it can dramatically shape the availability of national technological opportunities. It is our suspicion, take it as a research hypothesis that we elaborate more fully below, that within the global economy three regional supply architectures will emerge in Asia, America, and Europe. The structure of each—the mix of skills, components, subsystems, equipment, and technological ideas—will powerfully affect the terms on which international competition evolves. Rather than global markets displacing national economic foundations, we foresee regional restructuring.

In our view, the American architecture of supply is increasingly limiting. Capacities to access and adopt the new production model are severely constrained, as is access to the technologies essential to the new model's future evolution. This is occurring at precisely the wrong time for America's security concerns: the innovations abroad in production and policy that have helped to create competitive dependence are simultaneously providing a new and different technological foundation for the security system. Because it is constrained industrially in the ways suggested above, the U.S. also has a limited capacity to participate in shaping the new foundation.

Spin-off to Spin-on: High-volume Digital Electronics and the New Defense Technology

The industrial economy is eroding at precisely the wrong time for America's security concerns. American military technology will not rescue the commercial U.S. position. Rather, a weakening commercial position will almost surely affect U.S. capacities to develop military technology and systems. The links between military and commercial technologies are shifting, and so is the relative contribution of each to security. Consequently, national military capabilities must be reassessed and their compass redefined.

Commercial factors have always influenced the technological opportunities available to support the U.S. security position, even as military spending has shaped the civilian economy's composition and character. Early on, development of mass production and interchangeable parts was accelerated by military demand for rifles during the Civil War. The two world wars saw the organizational and technological innovations of commercial mass production underpinning America's relative ability to churn out huge numbers of tanks, guns, and planes. In those days, the defense production base grew directly from the commercial production base. The precursor to a new model of technology development was taking shape however, as directed government spending created new defense technologies including radar, artificial rubber, the atomic bomb, and the rocket.

The new model fully took hold in the U.S. after World War II, helping to create a new technological development trajectory. This was premised on belief that pouring in investments in science at the front end of the development pipelines would produce technology out the other end. Military and related spending (e.g., space exploration) supported the enormous development costs of relevant new technologies. Initial applications were developed for, and procured by, the military, and later would diffuse—"spin off"—into commercial use. In this way, U.S. defense spending promoted the rapid development of jet aircraft and engines, microelectronics, computers, complex machine tools, advanced ceramic and composite materials, data networks, and a host of other relevant technologies. In the jet aircraft and semiconductor industries, in particular, government priorities helped to set the functional characteristics of the emerging technologies, R & D funds accelerated the development of the technology, and military procurement at premium prices constituted a highly effective initial launch market.[35] That kind of technology development trajectory continues in some instances to be successful for the U.S. Recent commercial spin-offs from military spending include local area networking, gallium-arsenide components, massively parallel computing, and algorithms for data compression.[36]

But there are other, competing, technology development models. Massive resources committed in specialized defense contractors to technology produced in batch processes for initial use in military projects constitute one development trajectory. Massive resources committed to commercial development produced in volume for consumer markets constitute a separate trajectory. The former is the development model that has underpinned U.S. leadership of the postwar security system. The latter has underwritten increasing Japanese success in commercial markets. The problem for the security system is that the latter trajectory is proving to have increasing military relevance.

From Spin-off to Spin-on

A completely alternative military technology development trajectory is emerging from the innovations in production and consequent reshuffling of markets examined earlier. The alternative drives technological advance from commercial rather than military applications. Technology diffuses from civilian to defense use rather than vice-versa, a trajectory characterized as "spin-on" in contrast to its predecessor. The new alternative is prospering most fully in Japan, where an increasing range of commercially developed technologies is directly, or with minor modification, finding its way into advanced military systems.[37] In particular, militarily relevant subsystem, component, machinery, and materials technologies are increasingly being driven by high-volume commercial applications that produce leading-edge sophistication, extremely high reliability, but with remarkably low costs.

The case is clearest in electronics, where a new industry segment is being defined in Asia, largely outside of U.S. control and with only limited U.S. participation. Its distinguishing characteristic is the manufacture of products containing sophisticated, industrially significant technologies, in volumes and at costs traditionally associated with consumer demand. Such products include the latest consumer items like camcorders, electronic still cameras, compact disc players, and hand-held TVs, and new microsystems like portable faxes, copiers and printers, lap-top computers, optical disk mass storage systems, smartcards, and portable telephones. This "high-volume" electronics industry is beginning to drive the development, costs, quality, and manufacture of technological inputs critical to computing, communications, military, and industrial electronics. At stake is a breathtaking range of essential technologies from semiconductors and storage devices to packaging, optics, and interfaces.

Such products contain, for example, a wealth of silicon chip technology, ranging from memory and microprocessors to charge-coupled devices (CCDs), and have been a principal factor behind the drive for Japanese semiconductor dominance. Over the past decade, emerging high-volume digital products have grown from 5 percent to over 45 percent of Japanese electronics production, accounting for virtually all of the growth in domestic Japanese consumption of integrated circuits (IC). With this segment continuing to expand at 22–24 percent per year, more than twice as fast as the approximate 10 percent per year average growth rate of the electronics industry as a whole, high-volume electronics will constitute an ever-larger part of the electronics industry of the next century. Its impact on the component technologies that military systems share is just beginning to be felt.

Aside from silicon integrated circuits, militarily relevant optoelectronic components like laser diodes and detectors, LCD shutters, scanners, and filters are also present in the new high-volume products. For example, the semiconductor lasers that, at different wavelengths, will become the heart of military optical communications systems, are currently produced in volumes of millions per month, largely for compact disc applications. Displays and other computer interface technologies provide yet another significant overlap between high-volume and military markets. Miniature TVs from Japan are the leading-edge users of the flat-panel, active matrix, liquid crystal display technology that is just beginning to infiltrate military systems. Map navigation systems beginning to appear in automobiles are the functional equivalent of military digital map generators.

Optical storage was refined for consumer compact and laser discs, but is beginning to spread into military applications, as are the latest miniature commercial power technologies like batteries for portable phones. High-volume requirements are also driving a wealth of imaginative packaging technologies that range from tape automated bonding and chip-on-board to multichip modules. Producers of hand-held LCD TVs already use packaging technology as sophisticated as that being used in advanced U.S. defense systems. The new electronics products are driving similar innovations in precision mechanical and feromagnetic components like motors, gears, and switch assemblies and recording heads, transformers, and magnets. Ball bearings used in videocameras, for example, are now of equal precision to those required for missile guidance systems.

Successful production for high-volume markets also requires mastery of several different kinds of highly responsive product development, materials, and manufacturing skills. For example, Japanese consumer producers like Matsushita now supply the most advanced manufacturing equipment for IC board-insertion, a capability essential for military systems production. Similarly, because elaborate repair and maintenance is not cost effective in consumer markets, high-volume producers deliver product reliability levels that often now surpass military products at far less cost.

In sum, the basic technological requirements of new consumer products now approach, equal, or at times surpass those needed for sophisticated military applications. They have begun to share a common underlying base of component, machinery, and materials technologies. There are several significant implications. First, by spreading the huge development costs across many more units, high-volume markets can support the development of advanced technologies previously initiated only by military spending.

Second, however, price sensitive consumer applications demand that the unit cost of the underlying technology components be very low. For example, auto producers will pay an order of magnitude less for semiconductor component technologies than would contractors applying the same or similar products to military systems. Low consumer product costs cannot be achieved by reduced functionality or reduced reliability, because a real time processor for engine or brake control on an automobile is a very sophisticated element incorporated in systems that must not fail in operation. The necessary low costs can only be achieved by the scale, scope, and learning economies of the revolutionary production approaches detailed previously. The end result is that new, militarily relevant generations of cheaper but sophisticated and reliable technologies emerge from high-volume commercial markets.

Moreover, the new production model's emphasis on speed of product development and rapid cycling of technology introduction has additional, critical, military consequences. Using the strategies and production capabilities of the new manufacturing, Honda and Toyota can now take an automobile from design to showroom in less than three and one-half years. This is twice as fast as with traditional mass production. Imagine the possible implications for military system development, plagued as it is with cycle times that incorporate technologies often two generations old—advanced as design begins but old when production starts.[38]

It is a plausible hypothesis that civilian developers who have mastered the new manufacturing can move complex systems from design to battlefield faster than traditional military suppliers. They are better organized to do so. The very concept may have to change of what the fastest route is to the most advanced but reliable military systems in the field. The quickest route may no longer be to jump to the extreme limits of the technically feasible at the moment a system is conceived. Rather, the most effective route may well be the iterative innovation that Japanese firms have mastered. As IBM's former chief scientist, Ralph Gomery, puts it:

In the process of repeated incremental improvement . . . an existing (not new) product gets better and develops new features year after year. Though that may sound dull, the cumulative effect of these incremental changes can be profound. . . . If one company has a three-year cycle and one has a two-year cycle, the company with the two-year cycle will have its process and design into production and in the marketplace one year before the other. *It is the speed of the development and manufacturing cycle that appears as technical innovation or leadership. And it takes only a few turns of that cycle to build a commanding product lead.* (emphasis added)

Will America Adapt?

The American military technology system is not well positioned to accommodate the new alternative—neither to timely integrate the new high-volume technologies into military systems nor to support the commercial development on which military technology now heavily depends. Neither the financing nor the organization of the American R & D effort adequately comprehends the emerging reality of high-volume commercial technology development. While the level of American R & D remains high, expenditure is dominated by military needs. Conversely, by international standards, the civilian effort is low, and the part financed privately is very low.

The old system has created a domestic military-industrial enclave that is profoundly unlike the commercial world and organizationally unprepared for the emerging competition. Project bidding and accounting procedures involve selection criteria that amount to highly politicized speculation on future cost, performance, and procurement, and inherently limit incentives to develop the most cost-effective technologies. The consequent process of control for abuse compels highly bureaucratic management approaches. Indeed, firms dependent on the military for research and production contracts adapt their organizational structures to the problem of marketing to the Pentagon.[39] This leaves them with business strategies and organizational structures ill suited to the commercial world.

Civilian and military initiative for now represent two different ways of developing advanced technology. Technical sophistication driven from commercial market success, high reliability, low costs, and superior speed in development and execution, together comprise a distinctive technology development trajectory. It is a trajectory rooted in a different community and market context than the military spending trajectory that still dominates U.S. policy. It is an alternative that may be better suited than traditional military spending to respond to the unpredictable regional conflicts that are likely to characterize the next century.

For the United States the shift from spin-off to spin-on and the potential conflict between commercial and military trajectories pose severe policy issues. The American approach to military development may well be obsolete for its own purposes and counterproductive for the long-run development of the national industrial base on which militarily relevant technology development rests. Military spending and military technology development are not going to rescue the civilian economy from its competitiveness problems. Nor can they assure sufficient national technological development even for security purposes. These are most damaging conclusions for U.S. interests in a world economy increasingly characterized by regional autonomy from U.S. influence.

Autonomy with Interconnection: The Regional Economic Structure of Security

The preceding sections have argued that U.S. capacities have declined and new capacities have arisen abroad. This section contends that, as a consequence of those developments, new patterns of economic dependence and autonomy are emerging that amount to a fundamentally new industrial foundation for security:

the international economy is becoming a multipolar system organized around three distinct regional groupings. This alters not only the American security problem, but the very structure of international politics as profoundly as the changes in Eastern Europe or developments in the Gulf.

The structure of the international system—the distribution of national capabilities—has changed. The purposes to which the new capabilities will be put are yet to be defined for Europe or Japan, and may be defined anew for the United States. The alliances formed to pursue as yet undefined threats are not evident. But if our argument is right, the international system that emerges will be very different than the one constructed by American hegemony, and perhaps much less congenial to U.S. interests.

A Multicentered Global Economy

A more global international economy is visible in trade, direct investment, and finance. Products, companies, and investments from each of the major industrial regions can be found in almost every market on earth. But multinational corporations and global finance do not sweep away the national foundations of trade, finance, and technology; they have not yet created a borderless, homogenized, global market. Responses to the new competition are still rooted within particular places; governments still shape the character of MNC activities, and, with local industry, create and influence trajectories of development.[40] Global financial institutions do not erase national technology distinctions since, as we argued earlier, national technology trajectories do not rest on aggregate conditions.

Despite global interconnection, there are three coequal and distinct regional economies in the West: Asia, North America, and Europe.[41] The United States/Canada and Western Europe each represents about 25 percent of global GDP. In 1987 Japan accounted for 12.4 percent, and Japan plus the NICS 15.8 percent, of global GDP. The latter region will continue to expand in relative size because growth rates in Japan and Asia are substantially higher than in the United States or Europe. Foreign trade (i.e., from one region to another) is a quite limited part of the GDP of both Asia and Europe. Trade within those regions has now begun to grow more rapidly than external trade. Direct foreign investment over the last decade in Asia has constructed a Japan-centered industrial economy and pushed the United States out of its position of preeminence.[42] Europe's move toward greater integration with the 1992 plan and its financial and political concomitants (e.g., the EMS, perhaps a European Central Bank) are creating an equally autonomous region.

National and regional differences will shape the character of international trade and investment flows. Europe and Japan are both seeking and increasingly establishing independent technological bases. They are attempting to assure the foundations of national autonomy through domestic action. The conviction is widespread in Japan that it will be the dominant technological power by the end of the century, if not before.[43] European governments, the European Community, and major European companies are increasingly investing the resources required to overcome existing weaknesses and play to technological strength. The suspect case is the United States. Our concern is that the United States is substituting dependence for dominance, while thinking it is establishing an interdependent world of managed multilateralism.

The Asian Economic Region

Consider first the Japan-centered Asian trade and investment region. Japan's economy is itself less dependent on exports, thereby reverting to its historical form of domestic demand-led growth.[44] Japan, rather than the U.S., is now the dominant economic player in Asia. Japan is the region's technology leader, its primary supplier of capital goods, its dominant exporter, its largest annual foreign direct investor and foreign aid supplier, and increasingly, a vital market for imports (though the U.S. remains the largest single market for Asian manufactures). In 1989 Japan's trade with Asia (imports and exports) surpassed its trade with the United States.

Trade within Asia has grown faster than trade between Asia and other regions since 1985.[45] Increased intra-Asian trade between 1985–89 has permitted the NICS to reduce their dependence on the U.S. market, with U.S. bound exports falling from one-half to one-third of their total exports. Financial ties further reinforce intra-Asian trade trends. By 1990 Japanese industry was investing about twice as much in Asia as American industry.[46] Japanese investment in the Asian NICS grew by about 50 percent per year, and by about 100 percent per year in the ASEAN nations.[47] Moreover, the use in Asia of the yen as a reserve currency is expanding sharply.

The result of such trade and investment trends is a network of component and production companies that make Asia an enormously attractive production location. That regional production network appears to be very hierarchically structured and dominated by Japan. Japanese technology lies at the heart of an increasingly complementary relationship between Japan and its major Asian trading partners. Japanese companies supply technology intensive components, subsystems, parts, materials, and capital equipment to their affiliates, subcontractors, and independent producers in other Asian countries for assembly into products that are sold via export in third country markets (primarily in the U.S. and other Asian countries). Conversely, nonaffiliated labor intensive manufactures, and affiliated low-tech parts and components, flow back into Japan from other Asian producers. Summarizing these trends, Japan's Ministry of International Trade and Industry (MITI) noted in 1987 the "growing tendency for Japanese industry, especially the electrical machinery industry, to view the Pacific region as a single market from which to pursue a global corporate strategy."[48] Now a production core essentially independent of American technology and know-how, though tied for the moment to American markets is emerging in Asia. As Asian incomes rise, a growing Asian market may further disconnect Asian growth from its tie to the U.S. market.

There is resistance to these patterns by other Asian countries. The Koreans, the Taiwanese, the Thai, and the Malaysians, among many others, all seek to emulate some of the developmental policies and business strategies responsible for Japan's success. This developmental competition is likely to reinforce Asian autonomy even if it relaxes Japan's control over the division of labor.

For the foreseeable future, however, the character of Japanese development and policy is crucial to an understanding of the region's potential for autonomy. The basic elements of Japan's autonomous development strategy are still in place. As Japanese firms have become dominant in some sectors in world markets, the Japanese economy has become more open. However, in the advanced technology sectors, old patterns have continued, especially domestic closure combined with intense internal competition to develop products and technologies originating in Japan or borrowed from abroad. Relative autonomy is readily apparent in trade, investment, and technology. Japan still tends not to import in sectors in which it exports and, despite progress, its overall level of manufactures' imports is still quite low.[49] Moreover, the recent upsurge in imports is at least as much a story of the regional adjustment of Japanese industry to the yen shock as of the opening of the Japanese economy.[50] Japan is an increasingly prolific foreign investor, but it has not permitted comparable foreign ownership of its domestic economy. Though direct investment into Japan has increased substantially over the past decade, less than 1 percent of the Japanese industrial base is foreign owned.[51]

Overall, in sum, the prospect for Japan and Asia is for increasing autonomy conjoined with real capacities to handle constraints arising from outside the region.

The European Region

The indicators of growing Asian regionalism find a counterpart in Europe. In Europe, though, there is an overt political as well as economic dimension to the story. Economic and political challenges have pushed the national powers of Europe to consolidate their markets and their influence. The movement to create a single market of Europe is driven not only by the emergence of Asia, but by the perceived real decline of the United States as a source of technology, production know-how, and hegemonic influence. European elites are rethinking their roles and interests in the world, reconsidering their relations with the United States and within the European Community.

For the last two generations Europe's economic position has rested on a set of implicit bargains with the United States in technology, finance, and trade built inside of the explicit security bargains.[52] If Europe was not first, it was second, and the activities of European governments and companies could suffice for generating economic growth and significant geopolitical influence. Over the last fifteen years, however, that situation changed dramatically. Japan's rise, America's perceived decline, and the failure of national policies and firms to revive growth and handle unemployment within Europe meant that the region's existing options were much more constrained. Crucial technologies suddenly appeared to be available only from Japan. Tokyo moreso than Washington was suddenly shaping international finance. American legislation and bilateral arrangements aimed at Japan were disadvantaging European industry, while the Japanese market remained relatively impermeable.

Set aside arguments about culture or history. America and Europe share a security problem and structure, but Europe and Japan do not. To be even modestly dependent on Japan in finance, trade, or technology—or even to be less geopolitically influential—was unacceptable without the integrated defense and economic ties that linked the Atlantic partners. Asymmetrical access in technology investment and trade without integrated security ties made it wholly unattractive to exchange America for Japan as hegemon. The result was an increased move toward European unification, economically and politically—the creation of an integrated region that could take its rightful place as an equal alongside the U.S. and Japan.

With the retreat of Soviet power from Eastern Europe, the abrupt reorganization of Europe has confronted the ongoing European Economic Community (EEC) process. Germany has been unified and a Central Europe reconstituted. While these political developments initially risked splintering an emerging Europe back into squabbling national powers, they now appear to have generated an increased commitment to the European project. The clear evidence of that increased commitment is to be found in the agreement to pursue European monetary union that will almost certainly reinforce German economic leadership, the project for increased political union, and the effort of the European Free Trade Association (EFTA) members to negotiate increased accommodation. At least some of the reasons seem evident. A reunited and increasingly powerful Germany can be safely anchored only in a strengthened European community. NATO always provided two containments, an overt containment of the Soviet Union and an implicit containment of Germany. The EEC was founded in part to serve as an anchor for Germany in the West. Now as NATO recedes in political significance the community bargain in economics and politics may be recast again to ensure that a reunited and sovereign Germany remains an integral part of Europe.

On the economic front, Europe already exists as a relatively self-contained unit. Rather than the image of a set of small and medium-sized countries increasingly opened to the global economy, Europe should be seen as nations (including the EFTA countries) that have successfully moved from interlinked national economies to an integrated regional economy. Trade within the EEC has grown faster than the trade between the community and the rest of the world since the establishment of the European Community in 1958.[53] These trends are likely to continue with the creation of the single market and the adherence of the EFTA countries to it whether they formally join or not. As in Asia, financial ties now also reinforce regional trade ties. Even the British, initially so recalcitrant under Margaret Thatcher, are now committing to increased monetary integration.

Europe's regional capacities and fundamental strengths have often been underestimated. They rest in an educated and highly skilled workforce, a sound foundation in science, and the enormous wealth built up through a long and successful industrialization. They are particularly strong in traditional and scale manufacturing, from textiles to chemicals, and in manufacturing equipment and materials. In these industries, European firms have been very effective, often at the forefront, in applying advanced technology to hold market position—much more successful than their U.S. counterparts.

Europe is by no means a single political actor. It will remain a set of national, political communities, and as a region, a bargain among governments. Nonetheless, in a growing number of domains, including trade and increasingly finance and technology,

European governments are able to act jointly to create regional capabilities. In a world of autonomous regions, Europe would have significant advantages—not least collective wealth, size, education, and political will. Like Japan/Asia, Europe appears to have both a technological/industrial base capable of providing for itself in the international system and the political will to maintain that capacity and respond to external constraints. How should the U.S. react to these developments?

Converting Economic Power into Political Influence: Toward a New Security System

A new distribution of economic resources, of industrial and technological capacities, alters, almost by definition, the constraints and choices for the major nations. Do the developments explored in the preceding sections point to a manageable multilateral security system with continued U.S. leadership, or to something entirely different and less congenial to U.S. interests? The retreat of Soviet power from Central Europe, the Persian Gulf aftermath, and political changes in Asia all leave Europe, Japan, and the United States with different concerns. For example, major movements of people may be provoked by upheaval in the Soviet Union and the Gulf, and Europe—not the U.S. or Japan—will be a primary destination. As the security problem shifts, becomes differentiated, and takes new forms, visions of security and conceptions of interests will be redefined. Predicting the evolution of the security system is impossible, but several issues that the U.S. must confront emerge from our discussion.

Military Potential and Security Interests

At the moment, Europe and Japan are regional economic powers that have the technological and industrial capacity to put a strategic military machine in place. While the machine does not now exist, Europe and Japan can achieve significant political leverage with the potential to move toward autonomous security positions. Their military potential and changed sense of threat may alter what Europe and Japan will pay for security.

The military potential is very substantial. As suggested earlier, Japan has the component and subsystem expertise to put in place almost any military equipment it chooses. It already builds sophisticated weaponry like tanks and smart missiles, and is developing systems expertise in aerospace. Recall that the FSX was an American alternative to independent Japanese development of a fighter plane. Many Japanese believe that Japan could have built a better plane on its own. The increasing electronics content of weapons may well provide Japan an opportunity to quickly establish an advanced weapons position by trading expertise in avionics for expertise in aeronautics.[54] Already, Japanese military electronics are more reliable, with longer times between service or failure. Japanese industry and policy makers are quite aware that they are likely to be able to produce systems less expensively than the United States. In short, the restrained Japanese military position is a matter of political choice not industrial or technological constraint.

Europe's situation is quite different. European countries and industry can build varieties of military systems of all types—indeed, too many varieties. Combined and coordinated, Europe would be a formidable military player. Amid conflicts and doubts, there is identifiable, if tentative, evidence—in planning, procurement, and industry consolidation—of increased European commitment to common defense structures. At the moment, each nation within Europe is dependent on the United States for important technologies. Exactly complementary to Japan's strengths, Europe is weakest in the underlying component technologies, strongest in systems expertise. Needless to say, Europe-Japan industrial alliances that are emerging could provide a formidable challenge to U.S. leadership in military systems—even if such collaboration arose only as a consequence of joint commercial projects with substantial spin-on technology.[55] Again, what Europe does is now a matter of political choice rather than industrial constraint.

Just as important, as Francois Heisbourg argues, the postwar security structure was defense oriented, clear-cut, comprehensive, and rigid. In the new system, confusion and complexity will prevail, defense will lose its centrality, and the nature of threat will be ambiguous and shifting. Consequently, Europe and Japan may not need fully autonomous military capabilities to assert and defend autonomous security positions. They may achieve significant political leverage with their mere potential. The circumstances that would spark a reformulation of Japanese or European policy are diverse and could become compelling. The push could come from conflicts and civil wars, likely with the disintegration and reorganization of Central Europe. Or it might start with the Gulf crisis's cost and consequences. The European discussion of a common defense policy has already begun. It is a discussion in which the place of America is by no means clear.

A situation in which U.S. leadership and managed multilateral security continue because our allies choose not to define an alternative is radically different from one in which U.S. leadership is produced by strength. That situation persists at a time when the rapid changes in Eastern Europe and the Persian Gulf will almost certainly force a redefinition of the relations between the advanced countries, whether or not that redefinition comes within existing alliance institutions. The character of any new security system will depend on the distribution of capacities and the perception of threat, on the balance of external constraints and opportunities perceived in each region. That will define the objectives and alliances likely to be pursued.

There is an emerging intellectual basis for interpreting the particular trade, technology, and investment frictions among competing regions or nations as security threats. A multipolar security system build around a world of mercantilistic competition can be conceived, and justified from increasingly established reasoning. So-called new trade theory argues that in oligopolistic industries governments can reshape the structure of global competition and global industry to the benefit of national welfare, increasing firms' market share and creating external social economies. If we marry the implications of the new trade theory to those of the technology trajectory arguments developed earlier, the result is explosive. Then, the outcome of strategic trade conflicts is not simply a matter of one-time gains or losses that result when one government's policies assist its firms to gain share in global markets to the disadvantage of its trading partners. At stake are future gains and losses in terms of each nation's dynamic potential for long-term growth, increased standards of living, and technological preeminence. Trade and domestic technology strategies quickly become the stakes in international conflict.[56]

A New Security Era

Although a new security era is upon us, the current security debate is still rooted in the past. It has been an argument about the level and form of American contribution to a Western security system with America at the center and its allies ceding the definition of crisis and response because they are dependent on U.S. action for their own security. The new reality confronts us in pieces, in fragments and isolated controversies, not yet as a whole. The reality is that our major allies have the range of capabilities required to act on their own in the international system, to behave as great powers. The reality is that the possibility of American dependence on our allies in a range of significant policy arenas is real. Whether they use their capabilities to pursue their foreign policy preferences is increasingly a matter of their political choice.

The U.S. economy is no longer so disproportionately large or so distinctively structured around advanced production and technology as to create a fundamental foreign policy advantage. The domains in which the U.S. used to exert influence to extract security compliance—trade, technology, finance—can no longer rescue American autonomy. Those former domains of action have become binding constraints in their own right. Industrial innovation is no longer the preserve of the United States. The areas of significant industrial weakness are extensive and growing. Financial power rests in institutions outside the United States, though for the moment the system is still organized around the dollar and American dominated international institutions.

Nor, as we have emphasized throughout, will U.S. security preeminence be maintained by current military systems advantages or by a new focus on rebuilding the defense industrial base. The dominant U.S. model of military technology developed through military spending faces a less costly, more reliable, more responsive commercial alternative. The architecture of the domestic supply base is consequently shifting from autonomy to dependence on regions whose political interests may diverge from those of the U.S. If present developments go unchecked, thoroughgoing dependence on foreign sources of military components and subsystems will become a reality. The possibility is real that technologies only obtainable abroad will be sufficiently critical to provide leverage on American foreign policy.

The bipolar era is ending. The U.S. is now confronted with the problem of managing relations with two other, roughly equal regions, each with the capability of acting autonomously in matters of technology, industry, finance, and security. At a minimum the formation of Western security policy will become more complicated. Real differences about the organization of the international economic system, as well as the risks and potentials in the remarkable events in Eastern Europe, could become the basis of serious divisions. At a maximum, badly diverging interests could create the basis of real conflict between the regions.

The nature of threats to the U.S. position in this multipolar world must also be reconsidered. In the world we are describing, the continued erosion of America's international economic position is a national security issue. We are past the point where America's security dominance can be exploited to impose more favorable terms of trade. Rather, we are confronted with precisely the reverse: how others can exploit terms of trade to impose dominance, how they can structure and play the international system through economic means. In that world, the only secure America is a competitively able one. The U.S. must regain its competitive standing in trade, technology, and finance if it wants to be in a credible position to effectively manage the changing security system.

Think what the Persian Gulf War might have been like if our adversaries had the technologically advanced planes, night warfare capabilities, and smart weapons. Think of the military systems a combination of Japanese componentry and manufacturing skills with European systems integration know-how might produce. Then think of the emergence of autonomous regions with the political will and capability of pursuing interests that diverge from a competitively weakened U.S. Those flights of fancy are increasingly possible. America needs to act now from the belief that we are and can remain dominant, but from an understanding of how we can be effective in circumstances in which we no longer are.

Notes

[1] This is the essential position argued historically by Kennedy (1987) and analytically before him by Gilpin (1981). Many of the forces they depict are at work in the American case, but those forces are not central to the deterioration of the American position.

[2] This problem is very well analyzed by Moran (1990). Again, much of Moran's analysis is directly apposite; it is his presumption of globalization and interdependence with which we take issue.

[3] This section draws on much work done at BRIE, especially collaborations with Stephen S. Cohen and work of Laura Tyson. See in particular Cohen and Zysman (1987), (1988a), and (1988b).

[4] See, for example, Moran (1990), Kennedy (1987), Nye (1990), Keohane (1984), and Nau (1990).

[5] Office of Technology Assessment (1988). This is the position argued in Cohen and Zysman (1987) and foreseen in Tyson and Zysman (1983).

[6] Overall, as an MIT study affirmed, the troubled sectors together represent a broad range of industries, often the entire industrial complex within those industries, and a substantial chunk of total U.S. output. (See Dertouzous et al. (1989).

[7] The integrated or group character of the enterprises is important. Even if components and subsystems are sold on the market, they will almost certainly be made available within the Japanese firm or group first. On the group structure of the Japanese economy, see, for example, Gerlach (1989).

[8] In late 1990 ICL passed into Fujitsu's hands largely as a consequence of its hardware dependence.

[9] On this issue, see the remarks of Andy Grove, president of Intel Corporation, in the *New York Times*, May 2, 1990, p. D17. This problem is also the central motivation behind formation of the Computer Systems Policy Project, a new trade association and lobby of all of the top U.S. owned computer producers.

[10] See, for example, Lawrence (1984).

[11] Cohen and Zysman (1987).

[12] Some authors have taken comfort in the fact that the American share of global GDP, after declining until the mid-1970s, has since remained stable. See the data and arguments in Nye (1990). But these figures are deceptive. The continuing U.S. position rests mainly on an economic slowdown in Europe in the 1980s. By contrast, growth rates in Asia have remained higher than in the United States; the U.S. position relative to Asia and Japan has continued to decline. For security purposes, that relative decline matters. That the U.S. has been able to "hold its own" with a temporarily sclerotic Europe is hardly reassuring.

[13] The original statement was that manufacturing's share of GDP had remained roughly constant even during the early 1980s. See, for example, Lawrence (1984). That data set was challenged, notably by Mischel (1989), which provoked a recalculation. The new data set reveals a distinct decline in manufacturing's share

of GDP through the mid-1980s, with subsequent recovery to historical norms by the end of the decade.

[14] Cohen, Teece, Tyson, and Zysman (1984). The definition of competitiveness given here is as follows:

Competitiveness has different meanings for the firm and for the national economy. At the level of the individual firm, competitiveness is a fairly easy concept to define and understand. A firm's competitiveness is its ability to increase earnings by expanding sales and/or profit margins in the market in which it competes. This implies the ability to defend market position in the next round of competition, as products and production processes evolve. If the market is international in scope, so is the concept. Clearly, competitiveness is almost synonymous with a firm's long-run profit performance relative to its rivals.

An analogue exists at the national level, but in our view it is much more complicated. A nation's competitiveness is the degree to which it can, under free and fair market conditions, produce goods and services that meet the test of international markets while simultaneously expanding the real incomes of its citizens. International competitiveness at the national level is based on superior productivity performance and the economy's ability to shift output to high productivity activities, which in turn can generate high levels of real wages. Competitiveness is associated with rising living standards, expanding employment opportunities, and the ability of a nation to maintain its international obligations. It is not just a measure of the nation's ability to sell abroad, and to maintain a trade equilibrium. The very poorest countries in the world are often able to do that quite well. Rather, it is the nation's ability to stay ahead technologically and commercially in those commodities and services likely to constitute a larger share of world consumption and value-added in the future. Clearly, a nation's ability to compete internationally is reflected by its ability to maintain favorable terms of trade, which in turn governs the ease with which its citizens can maintain their international obligations while enjoying steadily rising real incomes.

National competitiveness will, of course, rest on competitive firms generating the productivity levels needed to support high wages, especially in growth sectors. The competitiveness of firms depends upon the quality and quantity of physical and human resources, the manner in which resources are managed, the supporting infrastructure of the economy, and the policies of the nation. National and corporate competitiveness are analytically distinct but practically intertwined. p. 2.

[15] Some sought reassurance in data suggesting that the American problem was not its companies, which were believed to be globally competitive, but its weakness as a production location. In fact, however, the data demonstrated something else—that U.S. firms were able, temporarily, to hold market position by moving production offshore to cheaper labor locations. There were, in fact, hints of serious problems later to come in sectors such as automobiles and electronics as firms delayed introducing innovative production technologies. The moves offshore often proved to be signs of weakness that generated greater weakness. And in any case, the competitiveness of the U.S. as a production location is of direct relevance to the security debate, as we elaborate below. Recent studies of trade patterns of all the advanced countries have recategorized all the sector-level data to examine this problem. They show a radical loss of U.S. position in traditional and scale-intensive industries like textiles and consumer durables, and in production equip-

ment (capital goods) and materials sectors, where, for two generations, American producers have dominated. The latter sectors in particular embed substantial industrial know-how, and, as we will argue below, provide an important foundation for future growth. By contrast, Germany and Japan have maintained or gained position in traditional, scale-intensive, and production equipment/materials industries. Moreover, relative to the U.S., Japan has claimed position in advanced technology sectors. The relative inability of American producers in diverse sectors to compete in global markets has shaped the composition of our trade deficit as well as of our industrial base. While America's position in global manufacturing competition changed abruptly, the roots of this dilemma lie in a long process of industrial development overseas. See Dertouzous et al. (1989). This report of the MIT Commission on Industrial Productivity develops many of the same arguments on manufacturing changes advanced in this section. Many of these same positions were argued in Cohen and Zysman (1987).

[16] Our interpretation that the resurgence of American industrial production does not indicate a return to an equivalent competitive position is supported by recent comparisons of the advanced industrial economies. The United States is certainly one of the wealthiest countries in the world. But it is revealing to decompose the measures and sources of its wealth, and to compare those with the sources of wealth of the other twenty-five richest countries. First, consider gross national product per resident. Here the United States ranks number two. In a second measure, however, gross domestic product per resident—which excludes imports and exports—the United States ranks only fourth. The gross domestic product in manufacturing per inhabitant tells a worse story. The United States ranks number eight, behind France and barely ahead of Denmark. This position is a radically new development. In 1965 the same measure placed the United States in the first position. By 1973 the U.S. had fallen to third position. In 1981 the U.S. had fallen to fourth position and by 1984 to tenth. The U.S. fell nine places between 1965 and 1984; the current resurgence in U.S. manufacturing has recaptured only two of the nine places lost.

[17] See Maier (1977) for a fuller explanation of the early postwar bargain between the U.S. and its allies.

[18] Policies favoring consumption and demand management are necessary to mass production because they increase the likelihood that production will be at near full capacity—the only way that mass producers are profitable. This point is made explicitly with respect to Keynesean policies by Piore and Sable (1984).

[19] For a fuller version of this argument see Tyson and Zysman (1989).

[20] In a 1990 detailed analysis of Japanese production innovations in the automotive industry, *The Machine that Changed the World,* the authors explicitly reach an identical conclusion based on their findings.

[21] See, for example, Hayes, Wheelwright, and Clark (1988), Jaikumar (1988), and Drucker (1990).

[22] Manufacturing flexibility consists of two important capabilities: static flexibility is the capacity to vary product mix on a single production line or to automate batch production; dynamic flexibility is the capacity to introduce new production methods and wholly new products without significant disruptions to existing set-ups and practices. The organizational and technological innovations that permit flexibility have actually been implemented in a variety of forms. One form in evidence in Northern Italy and parts of Germany is so-called flexible specialization. This model involves an attack by smaller firms on niche markets. It

is built on craft skills and on local community infrastructures that permit shifting ties between firms that compete one day, collaborate the next. Piore and Sable (1984) first elaborated this model in English, emphasizing Italian variants. For the German vision, see Herrigel (1989). Industrialists like Romano Prodi, the former head of the Italian state holding company IRI, express concerns about the validity of this latter model. As a production system, we believe it is far less significant than the largely Japanese model described below.

[23] There is a broad literature on these matters. See, for example, from Europe, Coriat (1990); from the U.S., Hayes, Wheelwright, and Clark (1988); from Japan, Monden (1983); and from the business press, Drucker (1990).

[24] Rapid, cheap changeover is accomplished in a multitude of clever, relatively modest ways that include simple jigs, easy recalibration, and innovations in tool transport that increase mobility.

[25] This characterization comes from a lecture by IBM's director of technology, James McGroddy, at Cornell University's Graduate School of Engineering, Distinguished Lecturer Series, May 1, 1989.

[26] The latter potential is strongly underlined in the remarkable work of Jaikumar (1988) depicting the historical evolution of the technology and management of process control.

[27] Hatsopoulos, Krugman, and Summers (1988).

[28] It is of course an open question of just how significant this problem of competitive dependence is, particularly where required technologies are readily available from abroad, such as in textile production. It does appear, however, that dependence in parts and components supply has played an important role in the downfall of the U.S. electronics and automobile industries.

[29] This notion of the supply base is drawn from forthcoming work of Borrus, from which we derive the definition and concerns set out here. For a very brief preliminary statement, see Borrus (1990).

[30] The economics of infrastructure is quite underdeveloped. In general, infrastructure is defined as being outside any individual firm, ubiquitously available, indivisible, and as generating broad externalities (social gains that are not fully capturable by private firms). By this definition, our supply base notion (especially given technological spillovers in advanced sectors like electronics) qualifies as an infrastructure with the caveat that the open question remains of precisely how nationally "indivisible" it is. This is, of course, precisely the issue we examine in the text.

[31] For example, Siemens executives confirm that the danger of dependence on Japanese competitors was one of the explicit rationales for Siemens's expensive move into memory chip production in the early 1980s.

[32] As we suggest in a moment, the very largest firms are often able to obtain technology wherever it emerges and from whomever it is developed; the small and medium-sized firms are much more dependent on national channels of technology flow.

[33] Contrary to the arguments of some analysts, industries are linked in more than simple input-output relations of no special significance. Our work suggests that the composition of domestic production and the specific character of links among firms and sectors matter to technological and industrial development. See, for example, Cohen and Zysman (1987) and Silverberg et al. (1988). In our view, recognition of this fact has been a central component of Japan's remarkable postwar economic transformation.

[34] See Freeman (1987) for the analysis applied to Japan.

[35] This is not to deny that R & D funds were often spent on activities that failed to produce winners. For example, the military funded many different efforts to build miniaturized electronic components that were unable to compete with the eventual winner, the integrated circuit—in part because it was prudent to back several competing approaches in a situation of great technological uncertainty. Even the IC, whose creators generally credit their civilian R & D effort for the relevant advances, benefited from know-how spilling over from the detailed defense efforts, from defense funding of graduate education and research in electronics, and from funding of prototype electronic systems that demonstrated the efficacy of the fledgling technology. See, in general, Borrus (1988), chapter 4, and the numerous sources cited there.

[36] Even in the heyday of U.S. technological leadership, this development model had occasional problems in moving from defense to civilian markets in a timely and competitive fashion. See Stowsky (1986). For example, the U.S. Air Force supported the development of numerical control technology for machine tools building advanced aircraft. The programming language proved too complex for general commercial use, producing only a commercially vulnerable U.S. industry that was squeezed by Japanese competitors from the low end and German firms from the high.

[37] Vogel (1989).

[38] It is a well-accepted fact that military product development cycles are gruesomely long, usually resulting in military systems incorporating electronic components that are several generations behind the existing state of the art. For example, it took eleven years for products incorporating the military's first very high speed integrated circuits (VHSICs) to appear on the market *even though the VHSIC program's major purpose was RAPID insertion of advanced components in weaponry.*

[39] More generally, dominant organizations that control a critical resource shape the structure of subordinate organizations that require that resource. The subordinate organization adapts itself to obtain the critical resource. Those adaptations generally involve mimicking the structure of the dominant organization in order to provide better communication with those who make decisions. See Zysman (1977).

[40] See Zysman (1991).

[41] Needless to say, this argument is widely disputed. For the skeptical view, see Segal (1990) and Shott (1989). For a view parallel to ours, see Krause (1990a).

[42] This has been widely reported, and we elaborate it below. See, in general, the discussion in Japan Economic Institute (1990), especially pp. 5–6.

[43] The conviction is captured in Ishihara and Morita (1989).

[44] Japan's export dependency dropped from a high point of 13.5 percent of GNP to 9.5 percent in 1990. Figures from a presentation by the Keidanren's Kazuo Nukazawa in the U.K. at the Royal Institute of International Affairs, July 27, 1990.

[45] Inoguchi (1989). By 1988 intra–Pacific Basin trade had risen to almost 66 percent of the region's total trade, from about 54 percent only eight years earlier. Data calculated from various sources by Krause (1990b). The major source of imports for each Asian economy is usually another Asian economy, most often Japan. In the late 1980s, for example, Japan supplied on average about one-quarter of the NICs imports (vs. the U.S.'s 16–17 percent). Indeed, Japan supplied well over 50 percent of Korea's and Taiwan's total imports of technology products

in the late 1980s, more than double the U.S. share. Conversely, the NICs are increasing their share of Japan's imports of manufactured products, from 14 percent to 19 percent between 1985 and 1989.

[46] From 1984 to 1989 there was as much direct Japanese investment in Asia as in the previous thirty-three years, thus doubling the cumulative total.

[47] Perhaps even more indicative, in several emerging Asian economies cumulative NIC direct investment in the second half of the 1980s surpassed the cumulative U.S. total (by as much as five time greater in Malaysia).

[48] Ministry of International Trade and Tourism (1987). In automaking and electronics, there appear to be two key elements to the strategy. One is to spread subsystems' assembly throughout Asia, while persuading local governments to treat subsystems originating in other Asian countries as being of "domestic origin." The second element is to keep tight control over the underlying component machinery and materials technologies by regulating their availability to independent Asian producers and keeping advanced production at home. The two elements together would tend to deter too rapid catch-up by independent producers to the competitive level of leading Japanese producers, while simultaneously developing Asia as a production base for Japanese exports to the U.S. and Europe to avoid bilateral trade frictions.

[49] Although manufactures have doubled to account for about 50 percent of Japan's imports, that figure is still far below the U.S. and Germany, each with 75–80 percent. Some analysts agree that Japan's trade structure differs from that of the other advanced countries. Other quantitative studies of Japanese imports suggest that in technology-intensive sectors imports are tied to Japanese firms, a point backed up by MITI surveys indicating that perhaps half of manufactured imports reflect intrafirm transfers between Japanese companies and their affiliates in foreign countries.

[50] Comparisons of the purchase of equipment by the subsidiaries of Japanese, European, and American firms in Australia show that European and American firms buy equipment widely on global markets, while Japanese firms buy almost exclusively from Japanese suppliers, returning to Japan for equipment.

[51] This and the following percentages are from U.S. Department of Defense (1990).

[52] This perspective is drawn from Sandholtz and Zysman (1989). See also Krasner (1977).

[53] From 1967 to 1987 the ratio of EEC–EEC exports to EEC–non-EEC exports rose from 79 to 115. Moreover, intra-EEC trade has been a dominant proportion of each member nation's trade. Discounting intra-European trade, Europe's percentage of world exports and imports drops, exports from 44.6 percent to 13.8 percent and imports from 42.6 percent to 11 percent. Add the EFTA-EEC trade in, and the picture is even clearer. In 1967 intra-European trade accounted for 50 to 60 percent of Europe's total trade; by 1987 the intra-European share had risen to 60 to 75 percent. These figures vary in the range given depending upon whose data set is used. Our figures were obtained from national account statistics: main aggregates and detailed tables, 1987.

[54] Yakushiji (1985).

[55] Such outright collaboration on military systems does not require a formal alliance structure: when the FSX deal was negotiated with the U.S., Dassault and the French were exploring a similar venture with the Japanese.

[56] Success in trade is not simply an alternative to a security strategy. Trading nations have lived in very particular balances of military power. More importantly, a trading strategy can serve as a means of creating the wealth to provide security directly, and the emerging military potential of Japan suggests just that.

6

The New Defense Strategy

PAUL D. WOLFOWITZ

The Bush administration has adopted a new defense strategy to meet the requirements of a changed international environment. President Bush first outlined the new approach in his August 2, 1990, address to the Aspen Institute—paradoxically the same day that Iraq invaded Kuwait. The president called on the Defense Department to formulate a strategy that, in his words, "adapts to the significant changes we are witnessing without neglecting the enduring realities that will continue to shape our security strategy."

PAUL D. WOLFOWITZ is under secretary of defense for policy. Formerly, he was U.S. ambassador to the Republic of Indonesia. Before assuming that post, he was assistant secretary of state for East Asian and Pacific affairs. Ambassador Wolfowitz also has served in the government in various capacities specializing in political-military, arms control, and strategic defense policy issues. He has also been visiting associate professor and director of security studies at the School of Advanced International Studies in Washington, D.C. and assistant professor of political science at Yale University.

A new defense strategy was mandated because of three key interlocking developments: (1) the transformation of the Soviet Union and Eastern Europe; (2) changes in the nature of regional conflicts; and (3) the evolution of increasingly capable American friends and allies. These developments are major successes for the United States, but they also present new challenges.

The Transformation of the Soviet Union and Eastern Europe

For forty years American defense strategy was designed to meet the challenge posed by a Warsaw Pact threat of a sudden, massive assault on Western Europe. At various times, defense planners contemplated that this invasion would occur in conjunction with or following the initiation of hostilities in other theaters. For example, through much of the 1980s, Defense Department planning focused on a global war commencing in Southwest Asia and spreading to Europe and elsewhere. The most important new element in U.S. conventional force planning is the shift in focus away from a global Soviet threat to other contingencies, a shift that has dramatic consequences for U.S. force planning.

Today, the Warsaw Pact has ceased to exist. The Communist domination of Eastern Europe is no more. Central and East European states embarked on the path of democracy, and a united Germany is a North Atlantic Treaty Organization (NATO) member. The Soviet Union has undertaken unilateral force reductions, has agreed on terms for broader reductions of forces in Europe, has withdrawn its forces from Czechoslovakia and Hungary, and continues to withdraw them from Poland and Germany.

In the future, if the Soviet Union wished to undertake aggression on a global scale, it would face an entirely new set of conditions. It could not launch an offensive using the allied forces it once controlled under the Warsaw Pact. It could not begin an attack from forward positions in Eastern Europe. It would draw on a considerably smaller force structure than it had in the mid-1980s.

Thus while Soviet forces could pose a serious threat to individual regions—especially the northern or southern flanks of

NATO—they can no longer conduct the traditional "theater strategic offensive" against all of NATO's three regions without taking action that should provide significant warning.

Regional Contingencies

The end of the cold war has mixed implications for regional conflicts. On the one hand, though U.S. interests around the world were not immutably linked to competition with the Soviet Union, the U.S.–Soviet rivalry gave many regional conflicts added impetus and urgency, and raised the specter of a regional contingency escalating into global war. This was illustrated most graphically during the 1973 October War, when the United States placed its forces on a DEFCON 3 alert.

One result of the new era in superpower relations is that such regional conflicts can now be treated more independently of the East-West context. In some cases, for example in Southern Africa, Central America, Cambodia, the Arab-Israeli peace process, and the Gulf crisis, the United States has found a Soviet Union willing to cooperate with the U.S. and others in efforts to solve regional conflicts.

Another consequence of a less aggressive Soviet policy abroad is a reduction in military supplies and ideological support for anti-Western insurgencies. At the same time, the many regional, ethnic, and national antagonisms around the world, for which the Soviets have not been the driving force, feed on distinct and diverse local sources of oppression, instability, and grievances.

It should be readily apparent from recent history that regional threats can arise and embroil the United States in conflicts with very short warning. As the new U.S. strategy shifts its focus from global war to threats to individual regions (whether in Europe, Southwest Asia, East Asia Pacific, or Latin America), the size and shape of the conventional forces necessary for the future will change. The new force structure will focus on a smaller forward defense presence and a crisis response force to meet these challenges.

When this new defense strategy was adopted in 1990, some critics suggested that this was merely a ploy to create a new post–

cold war rationale to protect Defense Department spending and
force levels and frustrate the emergence of a "peace dividend."
However, the appropriateness of the new approach was demonstrated almost immediately. Fortunately, the Gulf War reduced by
half the forces of Iraq—one of the most serious regional threats.
Moreover, the coalition's success in Desert Storm should cause all
potential aggressors to think twice before attacking an American
friend.

But dangers will persist. It is likely that more states in areas of
potential conflict will acquire or develop unconventional weapons
and the means to deliver them. Iraq employed Scud missiles
against American forces and against Saudi Arabia and Israel.
Moreover, the United States faced the first real prospect that
weapons of mass destruction might be used against American
forces. This problem will only worsen in the future. By the year
2000 at least fifteen developing nations will be able to build ballistic missiles, and eight of these countries may have nuclear weapons
capability. Thirty countries may have chemical weapons, and ten
will be able to deploy biological weapons as well.

Paradoxically, while the United States can relax its warning
time assumptions for global war or conventional conflict in
Europe, it may need to respond more rapidly than before to the
outbreak of conflicts in other theaters.

In the conventional realm, the United States may face an increasingly difficult time defending its interests. To be sure, American strategy and tactics were effective in Operation Desert Storm.
But the U.S. will not be the only one studying the lessons of that
campaign. Other potential Saddam Husseins, armed with sophisticated aircraft, armor, air defenses, and missiles, may be determined not to repeat Iraq's mistakes. They will ask how the United
States would have fared if it had not had several months to build
up its forces in theater. They will ask how the United States would
have fared had it not been allowed to build up its forces without
opposition. And they will ask how the United States would have
fared had it come under unconventional weapons attack, especially during the critical early weeks of the deployment.

The United States must also consider the possibility of facing
more than one contingency concurrently. It was spared such a

major challenge during the course of Operation Desert Shield/ Storm, although it did have the diversion of having to conduct significant evacuations of U.S. and other civilians during insurrections in Liberia and Somalia. The United States must preserve the capability to respond to multiple crises—including those requiring the use of force—in what may be an increasingly complex and militarized world.

Greater Allied Participation

A third development is the increasing ability of American allies to play a greater role in defense of shared security interests. A remarkable international coalition assembled during the Persian Gulf crisis, and the forces of many nations took an active part in combat operations. Friends and allies elsewhere are also making growing contributions.

Apart from combat capabilities, the unprecedented foreign contributions to U.S. expenses during the course of Operation Desert Shield/Storm are noteworthy as well. For calendar year 1990, America's coalition partners absorbed over 80 percent of U.S. incremental costs incurred in Desert Shield. In 1991 allied contributions covered most of incremental expenses. The amount pledged—more than $53 billion—would easily rank as the world's third largest defense budget, after that of the United States and the Soviet Union. Few would have imagined this level of foreign participation.

In other contexts, a changing security environment and the increased abilities of our allies are making it possible for the United States to reduce its forces in particular areas and adjust its role. For instance, the expanded defense efforts of Japan and South Korea will help enable the United States to reduce its force levels in Asia by 15,250 by the end of 1992. Such increased allied capabilities will enable the United States to sustain its critical regional security commitments and balancing role, while reducing force structure and budgets.

General Uncertainty
and Future Trends

The early 1990s have dramatically highlighted the difficulties of
accurately forecasting the international environment. Indeed, any
review of modern history would accent the challenge of predicting
the pace and nature of change as dramatic transformations have
attended nearly every decade of this century. Who among the
experts foresaw Hitler's accession to power? The outbreak of the
Korean War? Or, moving closer to the present, the Iraqi invasion
of Kuwait?

Some of these shifts have been political. For example, the Gulf
War followed in the wake of profound alterations in the political
alignments of Iraq, Iran, and others in Southwest Asia. The war
itself will, no doubt, significantly impact future alignments. The
cold war, for four decades the central feature of international relations, confounded many when it emerged and more when it de-
parted.

Other profound changes have been technological. Today, there
is uncertainty with respect to the future nature of warfare itself.
Operation Desert Storm vividly demonstrated that advanced technology and equipment, high-quality personnel to utilize them, and
innovative doctrine to guide their employment are critical to military success.

The developments and counterdevelopments of long-range
bombers, radar precision-guided munitions, advanced sensor
technologies, guided missile defenses, and Stealth illustrate the
strategic importance of technological change. Arguably, the pace
of such changes is increasing, a phenomenon often referred to as
the military-technological revolution.

To plan forces and capabilities now for the immediate and distant future, the U.S. must be sensitive to inevitable uncertainties
about the international environment and political and military
threats. This is particularly true given the long lead times—sometimes a decade or more—required to develop, build, and field
major systems or new capabilities.

Despite uncertainties, America must strive to maintain its technological and operational edge—as well as educating the next

generation of youth to perform as well as the outstanding soldiers of Desert Storm. This is necessary both to deter future aggression and to provide our future forces with the tools for success on the battlefield should deterrence fail.

Residual Concerns About the Soviet Union

In his address before the NATO Council in March 1991, Czechoslovak President Vaclav Havel noted both the euphoria and disappointments of the past year:

When the totalitarian systems collapsed in Central and Eastern Europe and democracy won, everything seemed to us, in the first exciting weeks and months of freedom, clear and simple. . . . A year full of dramatic events has passed, and we now see that history is going, after all, through a much more winding and complicated path than we thought in the first moments of excitement.

Secretary of Defense Dick Cheney has frequently described the continued turmoil and troubling trends within the Soviet Union that continue to cause concern to the Defense Department. The Soviet Union faces staggering economic and political problems. Indeed, uncertainty plagues virtually every aspect of Soviet society. The economic situation is particularly bleak. We foresee further economic decline and continued political, national, and social unrest.

Internal political trends in the Soviet Union have been mixed. The resignation of Foreign Minister Eduard Shevardnadze and the crackdown in the Baltics appeared to signal a reversion to repression and authoritarianism. However, Mikhail Gorbachev changed course with his rapprochement with Boris Yeltsin—whose popular election as president of the Russian Federation may have been a watershed in the realignment of political forces in the Soviet Union—and the "nine-plus-one" agreement. This agreement marks yet another coalition between Gorbachev and reformist and nationalist forces, but it has not solved the Soviet Union's fundamental problems: the crisis of legitimacy at the center, the failure of the economic system, and the future shape of the

Soviet Union and of relations between the center and the republics. Aside from the fact that six republics have chosen not to participate in the process leading to the adoption of a new Union Treaty, it is conceivable that the negotiation of the treaty would introduce new elements of instability.

Of course, mounting instability within the Soviet Union would have been likely regardless of the policies Soviet leaders were pursuing—including the genuine market oriented and democratic reforms that the United States believes offer the only hope for a productive future. The transition from totalitarianism to democracy is virtually inconceivable without difficulties.

The international coalition's success in the Gulf War has had its own effects on Soviet politics, and will have further ramifications in the future. Soviet cooperation furthered success in countering Saddam Hussein's aggression. But some in the Soviet military saw the U.S. vanquishing of a longstanding client so near the Soviet border as a threat to traditional Soviet interests, rather than proof of how much can be achieved when cold war patterns are abolished. In a 1991 *Izvestiya* article, Chief of the General Staff Mikhail Moiseyev complained about U.S. "attempts to secure military superiority and to demonstrate its superpower status in relations with the Soviet Union."

President Bush has often said that the United States hopes the process of reform in the Soviet Union will succeed. This hope continues despite setbacks within the Soviet Union, and the United States is willing to help the Soviet leadership in many ways to ensure success. However, the absence of ongoing democratic reforms could dramatically diminish the prospects for a thoroughly transformed U.S.–Soviet relationship. This would not mean a return to the darkest days of the cold war, but could frustrate hopes for moving from persistent confrontation to wide-ranging cooperation.

The implications of conflicting trends within the Soviet Union—both positive and negative—on the nature of the Soviet military threat must be weighed in several areas. On the negative side, these include uncertainty about future stability in the Soviet Union and Eastern Europe, and continuing Soviet military modernization.

In this regard, the Soviet Union retains a significant strategic capability and continues to modernize it across the board. By the mid-1990s it is expected to field fully modernized strategic forces, including Typhoon/Delta IV submarines, SS-24 and SS-25 missiles and follow-ons, a highly accurate SS-18, and ALCM-bearing Bear H, Blackjack, and Backfire bombers. Five to six long-range ballistic missiles are under development, and upgrading of strategic defenses continues.

The Soviet Union will also continue to field modern, well-equipped conventional force, including the largest national army by far in Europe. The victory of advanced technology in the Gulf War will likely strengthen those within the Soviet military who advocate allocating greater resources to the military and especially to the research and development that will enable the country to master the military technological revolution now underway.

Nonetheless, these worrisome developments have not erased the positive changes witnessed during the early 1990s or altered basic American assumptions about the reduced Soviet threat that underlie the new defense strategy. An independent East Europe still offers NATO the strategic separation from Soviet forces that it always lacked. The promise of Conventional Armed Forces in Europe (CFE)–like levels of parity greatly shifts a historical conventional arms imbalance, and the Soviet military will not be able to fully insulate itself from the economic decline of the surrounding society.

At the same time, it is prudent to recognize the still formidable capabilities that the Soviet Union retains. Rather than adopting sweeping and radical long-term reductions in military capabilities, the Soviet Union so far has attempted to maintain a high level of military spending even in the face of massive economic challenges; whether this can be sustained in the future remains to be seen. Though Soviet policy is unlikely to return to the aggressiveness that marked the depths of the cold war, it would be unwise to ignore how rapidly policies or intentions can change. Certainly, there is no doubt that these can change more rapidly than America's ability to rebuild imprudently dismantled military capabilities.

Elements of the Strategy

Under the leadership of Secretary Cheney and General Colin Powell, the Defense Department has placed a new stress on the strong and vital link between strategic planning and the budgeting process, particularly at this time of major changes in the international environment. The Office of the Secretary of Defense and the Joint Staff have undertaken an extraordinary effort to redirect U.S. strategy and reduce U.S. force structure in a fashion as dramatic as the changes in the strategic environment.

The Defense Department began to reexamine its traditional strategy of containment and preparation for global war in the context of the historic changes in Eastern Europe and the Soviet Union in 1989. This reassessment led to a new defense strategy, outlined by Secretary Cheney in his testimony before the Senate Armed Services Committee on February 21, 1991, which in turn has led to proposed force reductions of over 500,000 men and women.

The Importance of Alliances to U.S. Global Strategy

Secretary Cheney's FY 1991 annual report states:

> Strong alliances are fundamental to U.S. national defense strategy. The shared values, mutual defense concerns, and combined economic strength of friendly countries have provided a strong foundation for collective security that has served our nation well. . . . Strong alliances remain critical in the post–cold war security environment.

The U.S. system of alliances and less formal arrangements with friends throughout the world promotes cooperation for common defense. This collaboration manifests itself in a number of ways, ranging from industrial base cooperation to the overseas basing and access so vital for enhancing deterrence and facilitating crisis contingency operations. U.S. defense strategy relies heavily on the assumption of international collaboration in the pursuit of mutually agreed defense and foreign policy goals.

The United States is party to seven formal alliances:

- The North Atlantic Treaty Organization;
- The Australia–New Zealand–United States (ANZUS) Alliance (although U.S. obligations to New Zealand are suspended);
- The Treaty of Mutual Cooperation and Security between the United States and Japan;
- The Mutual Defense Treaty between the United States and the Republic of Korea;
- The Mutual Defense Treaty between the United States and the Republic of the Philippines;
- The Southeast Asia Collective Defense Treaty (which remains in effect on a bilateral basis with Thailand); and
- The Inter-American Treaty of Reciprocal Assistance (the Rio Treaty).

In addition, the United States maintains informal arrangements with many other states to meet emerging challenges. During Operation Desert Storm, the United States and international coalition forces worked in Saudi Arabia and other Arab countries to reverse Iraq's aggression. United States–Israel defense ties enabled our two countries to cooperate in the most productive way to address the crisis and the military threat posed by the launching of Iraqi Scuds against Israel.

Europe. NATO has functioned as the most successful peacetime alliance in history. As the political situation in Europe continues to evolve, NATO will still play the central role in preserving regional security and stability. As President Bush has indicated, the United States will maintain significant forces in Europe for as long as they are wanted. One of the most heartening elements of Operation Desert Storm was the military and economic cooperation between the United States and many European allies. We and our NATO allies will continue to confront security questions within Europe and globally.

We and out allies agree that any European system for collective security must provide for a strong Atlantic connection. Without a significant American role and presence, Europe will be unable in the foreseeable future to maintain an effective counterweight to Soviet military potential. Though the Western European Union, the Conference on Security and Cooperation in Europe, and the European Community will all make valuable contributions to European security, a strong NATO remains central to defend Western interests. NATO also remains a vital forum for transatlantic consultations on a wide array of security issues.

In response to changing developments, NATO undertook a major strategy review. Two of its most important guidelines were announced at the July 1991 NATO summit in London: (1) reduced reliance on nuclear weapons, which in the future will be weapons of last resort, and (2) increased reliance on a smaller, mostly multinationally organized NATO defense posture in Central Europe.

Asia. In the Pacific region, more than any other, U.S. security interests and effectiveness depend on a series of bilateral relationships. Unlike in NATO, there is no overarching alliance system in which each nation contributes to the common defense. Yet, unmistakably, American national interests in Asia are enormous and growing steadily.

A strong, complementary security relationship with Japan continues as the key to America's strategy for long-term stability and access to the Asia-Pacific region. Japanese support facilitates the U.S. ability to forward deploy in Asia. In early 1991 Japan pledged both to increase its support for U.S. forces and its own defense capabilities. Japan has agreed to assume over 70 percent of U.S. stationing costs (excluding military salaries) over the 1991–96 period. Japan also made an important economic contribution to Operation Desert Storm, including pledges of more that $13 billion.

Korea has also increased its contributions to the cost of mutual security. Although the balance of forces still favors North Korea, the Republic of Korea (ROK) is steadily increasing its relative strength—facilitating the withdrawal of some 7,000 U.S. military personnel by the end of 1992. We have agreed with the ROK that it should assume the leading role in its own defense. Seoul has also more than doubled its cost-sharing support for U.S. forces, and provided over $500 million in the context of Operation Desert Storm.

Despite an improved political environment exemplified by the establishment of diplomatic relations between the Soviet Union and the Republic of Korea, a U.S. presence remains important for the preservation of peace and stability on the Korean peninsula. Indeed, Korea is the most likely place in the region where hostilities might erupt. Kim Il-Sung is one of the few Communist ideologues remaining in the world, and he continues his offensive military build-up. Of greatest concern are North Korea's nuclear development program and its refusal to accede to International Atomic Energy Agency (IAEA) safeguard inspections.

In the Philippines the protracted sense of crisis that followed the December 1989 coup has abated. The Philippine government's reaffirmation of its interest in a sustained defense partnership has been a pivotal development. The U.S.–Philippines base negotiations process has been lengthy, difficult, and at times contentious. But at this writing, the prosects are still good for a new agreement. The U.S.–Thai treaty relationship is based on continued mutual goals and Thailand's central importance to stability in Southeast Asia.

Australia today remains the southern pillar of the East Asia and Pacific region's security network, and bilateral U.S.–Australian defense relations were strengthened during the Persian Gulf crisis when Australia dispatched naval ships and assistance teams to the region. Despite New Zealand's contributions during Desert Shield, its break with its ANZUS Treaty obligations continues to strain relations with the U.S., and there is little chance in the near term that New Zealand will resume its treaty obligations.

Outside the formal alliance structure, the most promising development in East Asia has been the improved cooperation between the United States and Singapore. In November 1990 the U.S. and Singapore signed a memorandum of understanding permitting U.S. use of Singaporean military facilities. The anticipated increased American presence will help foster regional stability and security.

Middle East. The United States has no formal alliances with Mideast states. But as Operation Desert Storm demonstrated, the United States is willing and able to assist its friends when they face aggression. American action, in conjunction with an international coalition, has restored Kuwait to its people. And timely American action helped protect Israel and Saudi Arabia from the threat posed by Iraqi Scud missiles.

The United States will continue to have a vital interest in the Middle East of the 1990s, including preservation of access to the region's oil and the survival and security of Israel and friendly Arab states.

During the 1980s the United States began a number of cooperative programs with Mideast states, including Egypt, Israel, Oman, and Jordan. In the wake of Desert Storm, the United States hopes to expand such cooperation with these states and others in the Gulf Cooperation Council to deter future aggression.

Latin America. In Latin America, the United States seeks to ensure a stable security environment as more American allies reinstitute democratic systems. With the global interest of Soviet power, the threat to the U.S. from Cuba has diminished, but has not disappeared. Cuba continues to be a base for Soviet intelligence activities, as well as a threat to regional stability. Because of growing economic and political problems, Cuba has entered a period of severe crisis—posing new challenges and opportunities for the U.S.

The U.S. is working to strengthen alliances and foster the proper role of defense establishments in a democracy through training, leadership by example, and the provision of defense equipment. Through these means, the destabilization of Central American states by extremist forces has been contained, though the fragile democracies of the region remain vulnerable. The U.S. supports the efforts of the Andean governments to control cocaine production and distribution, concurrent with efforts to reduce demand in the U.S. In Secretary Cheney's words, the U.S. is pursuing a "peacetime engagement" strategy, consisting of coordinated political, economic, and military measures aimed at promoting democratic stability.

The Continued Importance
of Forward Presence

Forward presence will remain one of the enduring principles of U.S. security policy. Its importance to our strategy is fundamental and goes far beyond its military role for deterrence and war-fighting, as important as that is. In addition to their military role, forward deployed forces play a vital but less visible role in maintaining stability, preserving regional balances, and demonstrating U.S. commitment. Forward deployed forces and overseas basing are critical for both peacetime operations and crisis response.

Because it is possible to depend on increased warning time for a major European contingency and because Asian allies can make a greater contribution to the common defense, it will be possible to reduce U.S. forward deployed forces significantly over the next decade. In Europe, there will be a dramatic reduction—roughly 50 percent—in keeping with revised requirements and arms control agreements. In East Asia, there will be a 10 to 12 percent reduction by the end of 1992 in the 135,000 forward deployed personnel.

It is important to ensure that the U.S. does not draw down its forces too precipitously, undermining regional stability. Reducing one's forward presence is a little like walking on thin ice—one only knows one has gone too far when one slips through. Accordingly, the U.S. should maintain a sufficient presence in Europe and East Asia to deter aggression and meet our security commitments.

In the Middle East, the U.S. will increase forward deployments above levels of the past few years. As the president has stated, the United States does not seek to base ground forces in the Middle East. But because the security arrangements prior to August 1990 failed, the U.S. must be prepared to maintain an appropriate presence, consistent with the wishes of local friends, to protect American interests. The United States must be prepared, if necessary, to deploy significant forces to the region even more quickly than during Operation Desert Shield. Thus, for example, it will be necessary to pre-position more equipment in the region than was possible before. The United States will also want to conduct additional combined exercises and strengthen its planning with local states.

Force Structure and Mobility
for Crisis Response

Regional crisis response wherever required is another key element in U.S. strategy and force sizing requirements. The U.S. must maintain the capability to deploy both light and heavy forces of significant size at great distances. Pre-positioning, either on land (POMCUS) or afloat (MPS), can greatly expedite and facilitate such deployments, especially for heavy forces.

U.S. forces may face many and varied conflicts, presenting different challenges in terms of quality of opposition, climate, terrain, distance, infrastructure, and host nation support. One element is likely to be a constant in many conflicts: short, ambiguous warning. Thus a portion of U.S. forces will need to be highly mobile and ready.

Reserve and National Guard forces played a vital role in providing airlift, sealift, and other support for Operation Desert Shield/Storm. They would be expected to play a similar role in the future. However, short warning times demand that the bulk of combat forces remain in the active component.

Desert Storm also demonstrated that even regional crisis can require a very large U.S. military operation. Nonetheless, the new Defense Department strategy in a changed international environment permits further force structure reductions. Over the period 1991–96, DoD will cut Army divisions from twenty-eight (of which eighteen are active) to eighteen (of which twelve will be active); will reduce Air Force tactical fighter wing equivalents from thirty-six (twenty-four active) to twenty-six (fifteen active). The U.S. Navy will retain twelve aircraft carriers (plus one training carrier), but will decrease the fleet to 451 ships and Navy carrier air wings to thirteen (eleven active). Finally, strategic bombers will be reduced from 268 to 161.

Such cuts are part and parcel of the Defense Department's overall budget reductions. DoD outlays as a share of America's GNP are projected to fall to 3.6 percent in FY 1996, the lowest level in half a century. Altogether, DoD will cut about 25 percent of its force structure.

As the Defense Department undertakes budgetary and force reductions, it remains determined to support adequate pay and other incentives aimed at retaining high-quality personnel in the U.S. military. If Desert Storm showed nothing else, it demonstrated that the quality of military personnel can make a critical difference in performance. DoD cannot sacrifice quality as it reduces quantity. A principal reason for cutting force structure is to perserve and enhance the quality of what remains.

Our forces also must be sized to provide an adequate rotation base to support overseas commitments. As critical as forward presence is to U.S. defense strategy, we must recognize the toll that overseas duty takes on U.S. personnel and their families. Therefore, we must ensure that the force is sufficiently large to provide a reasonable amount of time in the U.S. between overseas tours.

To enable forces to meet multifold contingencies, we will also require enhanced mobility capabilities—such as that represented by the C-17 aircraft. We have also undertaken a study of defense mobility requirements that addresses sealift issues. The objective for non-European contingencies is to be able to deploy about five Army divisions, along with tactical fighter and naval forces, in about six weeks.

Finally, because the United States is separated by vast oceans from most potential areas of conflict, it is vital that we control the air and sea lanes that connect us. Moreover, the United States is the world's premier maritime power and depends upon freedom of the seas for its economic well-being. While changes in the Soviet threat permit significant reductions in force structure, the U.S. must retain strong naval and land based air forces to maintain maritime and air superiority whenever required. Maritime forces also play a critical role in our ability to respond to crises in regions where we do not have a forward land based presence, a consideration that could become more important if global trends confront us with diminished access to bases and facilities ashore.

Force Reconstitution against a Renewed Global Threat

Our force structure reductions are based on the premise of considerable warning time—measured in years rather than months—before the U.S. would have to face a massive Soviet conventional threat in Europe or an equivalent challenge elsewhere. A prudent approach, however, dictates beginning to plan now for the possibility that a dramatic expansion in U.S. force structure could be required.

Secretary Cheney outlined the principles that will govern DoD force reconstitution policy in his February 21, 1991, testimony before the Senate Armed Services Committee. We will stress the retention of weapons systems and capabilities that take a long time to rebuild (e.g., large weapons platforms), as well as the retention of highly skilled personnel, unit commanders, and specialized technicians. We will also maintain some reserve forces in a "cadre" status, with greatly reduced personnel and training. Plans currently include two cadre divisions in the Army, plus creation of a new status for some Navy frigates.

Another vital element of a reconstitution strategy will be U.S. technological superiority, and a healthy industrial production base. One of the reasons we are willing to accept reductions in force structure is to preserve resources for technological development. Operation Desert Storm demonstrated the value of advanced technology in battlefield effectiveness and saving lives. We must maintain a robust R & D program to advance our competitive edge in key warfare areas through innovations in platforms, sensors, and subsystems.

Of course, a reconstitution strategy could require important political decisions based on early strategic warning indicators. This underscores the need both for improving intelligence and warning support to policy makers, as well as other measures designed to allow a prompt response without unacceptable risk of escalation.

It is important to emphasize that our reconstitution strategy is based on certain key assumptions. In particular, the Soviets must complete their withdrawal from Eastern Europe and must reduce to CFE-like levels of parity. Beyond this, we cannot be insensitive to the success of reform in the Soviet Union, because the internal order of a state is intimately reflected in its external behavior. Finally, Western forces must retain sufficient cohesion for defense, even at reduced levels. As Secretary Cheney has emphasized, if trends prove less favorable than projected, we may not be able to move as fast or as far as planned.

Strategic Deterrence through a Balance of Offensive and Defensive Capabilities

The deterrence of strategic attack against the U.S. remains the most critical mission of the Department of Defense. The Soviet Union is the only nation on earth that can destroy America within a matter of minutes. Here, the United States can take little risk. It must maintain a diverse mix of survival and capable strategic offensive nuclear forces and command and control assets, and pursue defensive systems to provide global protection against limited ballistic missile strikes whatever their source.

Nonetheless, the U.S. will continue to scale back strategic forces in keeping with expectations regarding arms reduction agreements and in an effort to maintain essential deterrence at the least cost. B-52 bombers will be retired and FB-111s transferred to tactical use. Retirement of the veteran Minuteman II force will begin in FY 1992, and retirement of mid- to late-1960 vintage submarines with the older Poseidon missile will be accelerated.

Those strategic modernization programs that remain represent the Department of Defense's highest priorities. These include the B-2 bomber, Trident, the small mobile ICBM, SRAM-II, ACM, B-1 upgrades, and command and control systems that support strategic forces.

The United States will have to be able to deploy defenses against ballistic missiles—whether it be against the theater threat of Scuds or far more sophisticated systems. At President Bush's direction, we are restructuring the Strategic Defense Initiative Program to provide global protection against limited strikes. This program will provide an essential capability for American forces, wherever they may need to deploy.

Conclusion

We are clearly at the dawn of a new era. For much of the past forty-five years our primary security concern was a global Soviet threat originating out of a possible Warsaw Pact attack on Europe. We met that challenge successfully. The threat to Western Europe has diminished. But as the war in the Gulf demonstrates, meeting more limited threats can still be quite demanding, even when we can marshall international cooperation.

In the coming years, we will seek to preserve our unique international role, consolidate the changes in Europe, and promote a cooperative effort to contain and defeat possible regional threats. Given current trends, we can meet these challenges with a significantly reduced force structure. However, we must sustain an appropriate level of military strength. Strength of the kind we relied on in the Persian Gulf cannot be built overnight. Continued investment in America's defense is a must, as we look forward with confidence to the years ahead.

7

The Global Dimension

T. C. SCHELLING

A s the burden of East-West rivalry lifts from the earth, a familiar world structure disappears. From the time of the Bandung conference of 1955, developing countries, mostly former European colonial areas, attempted to define their position in world affairs as "nonaligned." This definition by negation—what they were not, by comparison with the "aligned"—later gave way

THOMAS C. SCHELLING, president of the American Economic Association, is distinguished professor of economics and public affairs, University of Maryland, and Lucius N. Littauer Professor of Political Economy in the John F. Kennedy School of Government, Harvard University. Prof. Schelling served in the Economic Cooperation Administration in Europe from 1948–50, and in the White House and the Executive Office of the President from 1951–53. He has been a consultant to the Departments of State and Defense, the Arms Control and Disarmament Agency, and the Central Intelligence Agency, and a frequent lecturer at the Foreign Service Institute and the several war colleges. Prof. Schelling is the author of several books as well as numerous articles on military strategy and arms control, energy and environmental policy, foreign aid and international trade, conflict and bargaining theory, racial segregation and integration, and ethical issues in policy and in business.

to a more symmetrical notion, that of a "Third World." Which of the three worlds was first and which second didn't matter; the claim or the pretense was that these nations might constitute a distinct world. Still, the reference base was the complementary pair of worlds to which these nations aspired not to belong.

Now there cannot be a Third World: the first two have dissolved. Nations cannot be nonaligned; there is no alignment to repudiate.

Nonalignment was never a tight bond. It could not cement relations between India and Pakistan; and over the years even nations self-described as nonaligned became recognizably aligned, the alignments usually corresponding to regional antagonisms, as between India and Pakistan or Egypt and Iraq.

But any structure provided by the basic antagonism of East and West is being lifted, and even the effort further to replace "Third World" with "North-South" is being confounded by the identification of parts of Eastern Europe, and even some if not all of the Soviet Union, as among the underdeveloped.

I cannot tell whether the development of international political institutions was retarded by the cold war. There have been institutional developments in health, food and agriculture, environment, and scientific cooperation; the World Bank and the International Monetary Fund (IMF) remain an important part of the landscape; the General Agreement on Tariffs and Trade (GATT) remains a major institution within which nations may try, and sometimes fail, to govern their trade relationships. But there have been no profound developments, on a universal or global scale, of institutions that would bind nations formally into any more intimate relationship than that of independent nation states.

Europe in contrast is proving that the grandest dreams of unification can be realized even if the patience required is measured in decades rather than in years.

Globally there is some redistribution of income from wealthy nations to poor; it remains discretionary on the part of grantors, and modest in scope compared with the redistribution of wealth and income that occurs within nations. (Some $50 or 60 billion in aid to the developing world is barely half a percent of the developed world's gross national product [GNP]; the Marshall Plan was three times as large in relation to U.S. GNP.)

It can be argued that the economic and political integration of some kind of world system could not proceed in the presence of the East-West rivalry that dominated international politics during all these decades. That is not to argue that in the absence of that rivalry anything profound might have occurred. Nor does it argue that moving toward some system of potential world governance would have been, or might still be, an improvement deserving American encouragement and support. Europe has had the benefit of dramatic increases in cultural and economic homogeneity, as well as enforced cooperation beginning with the Marshall Plan and continuing under the North Atlantic Treaty Organization (NATO).

One of the issues along the global dimension of national security is whether the world would be safer for most of its inhabitants and for the institutions and values that we most appreciate, as well as safer for American interests, if institutions were to develop that could attempt to cope collectively with problems that beset nations, and especially problems that provoke conflict among nations. It can easily be argued—not necessarily correctly, but easily—that the kinds of problems that threaten to destroy India as a unified entity indicate that autonomies are more viable than collectivities, that disintegration may be more salutary than integration, and that smaller, more homogeneous nation states may handle their external relations in a more civilized way than larger heterogeneous nations can handle internal affairs. Experiments in Balkanization may soon provide evidence.

What I have in mind is not the possibility of dramatic progress toward a unified globe, but rather looking ahead to the possibility that the demise of the cold war opens a possibility to move toward what I would call "governing institutions" on a world scale. Considering how ripe Western Europe appeared to be for some such development forty years ago and how long it is taking, and considering all the reasons why it has been easier in Western Europe than it could be on a global scale, I think all we can have in mind on the global scale is a few seeds that may grow over the decades or centuries.

A more urgent question is whether we think it in the interest of

the United States that there be movement toward a more systematic way of coping with global issues, and especially whether the
United States would be wise to take a leading role in that development. In thinking about this question I have to try to get some
perspective on what the events in the Persian Gulf since August
1990 imply about U.S. leadership in world affairs. My current
assessment is that from here to the horizon the United States has
no rival in the role of world leadership.

Whether this is a status that was recently earned, or just recently
displayed, I am not sure. I am not thinking of American popularity
but of acceptance of American leadership by the governments of
Western Europe. That community responded to American leadership. The European Community is a long way from being a
United States of Europe. Among other things, we have a president
and they do not.

There are three strategic questions to address. First, what are
the main developments, problems, issues on a global scale that are
going to preoccupy national governments and influence international relations? Second, to what extent should we hope for the
development of integrative institutions that formally and expressly
address these issues as a matter of global international responsibility? And third, what profile does it behoove the United States to
adopt in confronting these issues?

I do not think we can answer the third or even the second until
we have surveyed the contents of the first. The role the United
States should wish to play depends on the kinds of issues that will
dominate the agenda, on whether the problems are potentially
solvable, on whether universal institutions are any good at coping
with the particular problems we identify, and on whether the
United States has a comparative advantage.

These are not rhetorical questions. It is not my intention to
discover that the United States would be well advised to claim and
exercise a leading role, and it is not my intention to discover that
some collective and formally integrated attack on those issues can
do a better job than coping piecemeal, ad hoc, unilaterally, oppor-
tunistically. My caution about formal institutions of potential
worldwide governance is somewhat stimulated by a mental exercise that goes as follows.

If we were to think about a "new world order" that might embark on the gradual development of some constitutional framework within which the peoples of the globe would eventually share collective responsibility and reciprocal obligations, somewhat analogous to what we expect in a traditional nation state, and if we were to think about political mechanisms that might be developed, what actual nation, existing now or in the past, might such an incipient world state resemble? If we were to contemplate gradually relinquishing some measure of sovereignty in order to form not a more perfect union, but a more effective world legal structure, what familiar political entity might be our basis for comparison?

I find my own answer stunning and depressing: South Africa.

We live in a world that is one-fifth rich and fourth-fifths poor; the rich are segregated into the rich countries and the poor into poor countries; the rich are predominantly lighter skinned and the poor darker skinned; most of the poor live in "homelands" that are physically remote, often separated by oceans and great distances from the rich.

Migration on any great scale is impermissible. There is no systematic redistribution of income. While there is ethnic strife among the well-to-do, the strife is more vicious and destructive among the poor.

For the purpose of this book we have defined national security as "preserving the U.S. as a free nation with our fundamental institutions and values intact." "Values" is a wonderfully ambiguous word. I believe it must include what we *possess* as well as what we *appreciate*. It includes our material standard of living. We protect those institutions and values by, among other things, protecting our national boundaries.

Population and Migration

The two issues I put at the top of that world agenda are related. They are migration and population growth. Policies to deal with migration and policies to deal with population growth have little in common, but pressures for migration in large numbers during the coming century will be reinforced, if not mainly generated, by population growth.

Population growth bears directly and heavily on the third area of my agenda, environment and resources. In this area population plays a dual role. It is a major determinant of environmental degradation and resource exhaustion, especially in the use of carbon fuels with the attendant risk of climate change. But population size will also be a main determinant, in the event of adverse climate change, of the severity of that adversity. A major concern about greenhouse induced climate change is the impact it may have on agriculture, specifically food production. Any adverse impact on global food production will be measured largely by the number of people there are in the world to be fed. Global populations projected for the second half of the coming century range from as low as 9 or 10 billion to as high as 14 or 15 billion people, the difference being identified with the parts of the world that are now considered underdeveloped. With continuing worldwide improvements in agriculture over the next seventy-five years, a population of 9 billion would be a cause of little alarm compared with a global population of 15 billion.

Besides constituting a global issue of potentially great magnitude, in terms of the collective sustainability of a decent match between earth resources and human needs, population growth will for many countries be an important determinant of economic development. The People's Republic of China, the largest of nations in population, has adopted the most Draconian policies to curb population growth. It has done so in a manner that most developing nations would probably not choose to emulate if they could, but that most probably could not. Indeed for many countries, a dramatic example being Nigeria with 120 million people and doubling every twenty years, population growth is as intractable as it is alarming.

Policy toward population growth continues to suffer from two inhibitions. One is that, with occasional important exceptions, what happens to population in a country is considered by the country to be the country's own business, not any matter of global or international responsibility. Second, but connected, programs and policies to control birth rates conflict with the most powerful traditions, dogmas, and family institutions. These conflicts evidently constrain policy and programs not only in developing countries, but within the governments, like that of the United States, to which some developing countries look for assistance.

The conclusion I reach on this momentous subject of world population growth is that international policy will remain for the foreseeable future at the level of technical assistance. It is not a subject that can currently support any overarching policy framework. I see no likelihood that a U.S. government will play a leading role in elevating population growth to the status of a major threat to international peace and security or to preserving the United States as a nation with our fundamental institutions and values intact. Probably our "values" are elastic enough to accommodate the prospect of another 150 million births in Nigeria during the coming two decades.

Migration comes next on the agenda, and relates to where all of those people are going to live. In the modern era most migration is within nations, not between them, and is primarily from rural areas to cities. That migration will not cease; but in many developing countries the natural growth of urban populations will come to predominate over migration of those born in the countryside. Ten million inhabitants barely qualify as a major city any more, and Beijing and Mexico City are continuing experiments in how much environmental degradation the human race can produce and tolerate as these dense and immense urban concentrations increase.

But it is the pressure for migration across national boundaries that may provide the greater challenge to traditional international relations and sovereignties. It is an interesting characteristic of democracies, especially the United States, that however assiduously they attempt to limit immigrants to those with official approval, the rules of the game allow almost anyone who can get in, legally or illegally, to begin acquiring rights of residency and even of citizenship. It is also characteristic of democracies that they are attractive places to work and live and that, within limits, they can be selective about whom they admit, by age, family status, education, ethnic origin, and ties to residents and citizens already in residence.

Capital has been increasingly free to migrate internationally during the last few decades, and the corporate entities that do much of the world's business have become less and less identified with national origin. In Western Europe the same is becoming true

for people, whether as workers or as residents or students. Of all
the relinquishments of sovereignty to go with the formation of a
new "community," from national airlines to central banks and
currencies, the most far-reaching, with the possible exception of
language itself, may be the movement of people. Europe is in the
midst of a great experiment in the survival and persistence of local,
regional, and ethnic cultures and values.

For the United States the issues involved in migration are of two
kinds, which might be labeled international and domestic except
that the domestic has international dimensions. The international
aspects are mainly in the future; but events in Eastern Europe and
in the Persian Gulf have heightened international interest in what
happens to people who, in the hundreds of thousands or even
millions, are displaced or choose to migrate. Hong Kong has been
in the news with its Vietnamese refugees, but is itself becoming a
port of embarkation for people seeking new nationalities elsewhere. Further in the future are migratory pressures due to increasing population in areas like Bangladesh and Nigeria. While
the sovereign right to hold against their will people who want to
emigrate has regularly been challenged—the Berlin wall, Soviet
Jews—the sovereign right to exclude foreigners from the privileges
of residence and citizenship remains remarkably intact in principle. The United States has to explain and try to justify its policy on
immigration, but the subject is entirely under the heading of diplomacy, not of a regime or governing system. That situation seems
stable.

The United States' own immigration policy, or lack of policy, is
a different matter. Since the time of the McCarran Act the United
States has not reexamined its immigration strategy. It has had ad
hoc policies for dealing with legal and illegal residents, policies
toward refugees and toward spouses and children, and a system of
quotas, but there has not been a commission or a congressional
study oriented toward the long-run role of immigration into the
United States in relation to population, the labor force, education,
public health, Social Security, and all the demographics of the
U.S. economy. Immigration can have a major impact on the age
structure of the population and the labor force participation rate,
and on the retirement and Social Security System. Immigration is

already having a major impact on the ethnic composition of the United States and even its ethnic identity. Immigration is having a significant effect, if a gradual one, on "our fundamental institutions and values."

This is a difficult subject on which to have a national dialogue. We cannot talk about immigrants without talking about some of "us" here in the country as well as about "them" over there. Immigration is part of the larger picture of the racial, ethnic, linguistic, and religious composition of our population, and those have a powerful influence on our values and institutions.

This issue of immigration into the United States is "global" in that we have to think and plan globally in contemplating where our immigrants may come from during the coming decades, both where we wish they would come from and from where we may be unable to resist their coming. Our ability to influence world migration in coming decades will be severely restricted by our need to maintain undiluted sovereignty over immigration into the United States. Immigration, furthermore, is not only part of our current relations internationally but influences the national heritage and identities of our future citizens. To devise an immigration plan for the future, especially if the plan allows a large role for immigration, is to plan not only on how many we shall be, but on who we shall be.

Environment and Resources

We have seen in the Gulf that energy resources can generate not only threats of military action but military action itself. This chapter is not about military implications; my question is whether there are natural resources or environmental issues that pose on a global scale threats to our freedom, our institutions, and our values.

There are at least two developments to consider as potential global threats to security. Both relate to energy, one to nuclear energy and one to fossil fuels.

Nuclear energy, a favorite alternative to fossil fuels not so long ago, is currently unpopular in many parts of the world. But nuclear energy will be with us for many decades and may undergo a renewed growth in years to come. Two environmental hazards deserve mention. One is exemplified by the Chernobyl disaster; the other is the prospect for world trade in plutonium fuel.

Little needs to be said about the former. It is not hard to imagine the international repercussions of a Chernobyl-type disaster if the reactor were located in Luxembourg with the radiation casualties distributed among four or five adjacent countries. Reactor safety is a regional national security interest. But except for Three Mile Island and Chernobyl, nuclear energy has been well behaved, and most countries' reactors have not been perceived as major hazards to neighboring countries. Nor has the disposal of nuclear wastes. With care and luck the problem need not become a source of international conflict.

The other nuclear development is the prospects for the separation of plutonium and its recycling as a reactor fuel. The United States discontinued development of this technology in 1980, but it is proceeding in Europe and Japan. The risk is that material that is capable of being used in the production of nuclear explosions will be shipped between processing plants, fuel assembly plants, and reactors. The subject receives remarkably little attention in this country, probably because for the past ten years there has been no U.S. plutonium separation program to keep attention alive. As a nonparticipant in any international plutonium fuel regime, the United States may not be in a position to take a leading role in developing international safeguards. There may be no cause for alarm; but the subject could suddenly arouse intense concern.

The environmental issue that is most internationally active is the one usually identified as "global warming," or global climate change. Because the primary emission that may lead to a greenhouse effect is carbon dioxide from fossil fuels, the issue has the potential to become a division between developed and developing countries, the latter wanting to be able to emit their share in the process of development. In Western Europe and Japan there are popular movements and numerous governmental pronouncements and resolutions about reductions in carbon emissions or, at least, in rates of growth of carbon emissions over time. The United States has not been in the forefront of an antigreenhouse campaign. What is the likelihood that international friction over what to do about this awesome prospect of global climate change will pose a threat to U.S. security, and what is the likelihood that unchecked carbon emissions (and emissions of other greenhouse gases) will lead to environmental damage severe enough to threaten our freedom, institutions, and values?

On the latter—potential catastrophe through climate change—it is too early to tell and will probably remain too early to tell for another decade. That being so, it is unlikely that dispute and disagreement over how seriously to take global change, how much to do about it, and who should do it will severely aggravate international relations. Developing countries have more pressing issues. They will mainly want to avoid being coerced into jeopardizing their development by reducing their consumption of energy; and they will be eager to receive carbon-efficient technologies financed by the countries that can afford to provide it. But there is going to be no coercing for the next few decades and probably no great provision of carbon-conserving assistance, and it is likely that for the next few years all the enthusiasm that has been mobilized to do something about the greenhouse problem will be channeled into institutions rather than into commitments. I think that it is unlikely that the current crescendo of activity will be maintained.

On the more substantive issue of how serious climate change is likely to be for different parts of the world, there will need to be two kinds of progress. One is scientific progress on the character of the global changes to be expected, and especially on whether climate change will be slow and gradual and surprise-free or may instead entail sudden and unexpected and possibly calamitous events and phenomena. The second kind of investigation, of which much more needs to be done, is the study of just how vulnerable, and in what ways, the societies and the economies and the values of fifty to seventy-five years from now will be to changes in local and regional climates.

Modern industrial economies are remarkably immune to the effects of weather and climate. The economic impact on those countries is likely to be eclipsed by the economic growth and change that will be occurring simultaneously with any climate changes over the next fifty to seventy-five years. But even the modern industrial societies may be vulnerable to other kinds of loss and damage, and most assessments of that vulnerability have so far been purely intuitive.

Developing countries are inherently more vulnerable economically because they are so dependent on agriculture. For them there may be a trade-off between investing in carbon abatement and investing in economic development; and they must consider whether the best way to insure against the damages of future climate change will be to invest in holding back the climate change or to invest in economic development and reduced dependence on agriculture. Many of these countries, furthermore, along with the countries of Eastern Europe, will be facing immediate threats to health through environmental degradation and pollution, and may have to give higher priority to emissions other than carbon dioxide.

International Income Redistribution

A central feature of any global framework resembling the incipient formation of world governing institutions would be some formal mechanism establishing or acknowledging the responsibility of prosperous nations to share their wealth with the poorer ones. For half a century the state in Western democracies has been identified as the welfare state. While the concept of "insurance" has been used to legitimize the redistribution of income from the advantaged to the disadvantaged, the fundamental principle has been some sharing arrangement, whether exemplified by income taxation, inheritance taxation, Social Security, unemployment compensation, welfare assistance, or national health coverage provided on a nonactuarial basis. If one were to identify four or five dimensions characteristic of a modern democracy, one would be a constitutional provision for redistributing income.

One of the interesting measures, therefore, of how world society may have progressed in the direction of unification would be whether, in the past half century, formal acknowledgment of redistributive responsibilities, and the development of redistributive mechanisms and criteria, had made progress.

The answer is negative. If anything, there has been retrogression during the past forty years. There are two evidences for this observation. One, mentioned earlier, is that the aggregate of resource transfers from the well-to-do countries to the poor and aspiring countries is on the order of half a percent of the GNPs of those countries that contribute, while the United States alone forty years ago provided nonmilitary assistance, of grants and loans, close to 2 percent of the American GNP. There are explanations for this comparison, but the quantitative expression of responsibility for economic reconstruction, improvement, or development has not flourished.

Furthermore, earlier there were formal attempts to identify principles governing the contributions of the more fortunate countries to the less fortunate. The United Nations Reconstruction and Rehabilitation Administration (UNRRA) negotiated a formula, as did the IMF and the World Bank. The Marshall Plan struggled to identify criteria for the division of aid among recipients, and NATO attempted, not altogether successfully but also not without result, to establish criteria for sharing the burden of defense among the countries of Western Europe and North America. In the 1950s, when greater optimism prevailed about the impact of potential foreign aid on the developing world, authors like Max Millikan and Walt Rostow could publish and attract attention to a proposal that assistance from the developed to the developing nations should be available in amounts limited only by the absorptive capacities of the recipients.

There never was a formula for distributing Marshall Plan dollars; there never was an explicit criterion, such as equalizing living standards, equalizing growth rates, maximizing aggregate output or growth, or establishing a floor under levels of living. Nor was any formula ever developed in connection with NATO burden sharing. But in both cases there was a procedure of critical examination, comparison, and debate, in the course of which there emerged some consensus on what the relevant variables were and what criteria were legitimate.

That period from the end of World War II, with the establishment of the United Nations budget and UNRRA, through the middle 1950s was one in which precedent and tradition appeared to be developing with respect to the claims of recipient countries, the obligations of providing countries, and the sharing of common costs in institutions ranging from the International Postal Union to the United Nations and NATO. I actually published an essay on this development in 1955 and included it in a textbook in 1958, in the belief that I was discussing the emerging foundations for some international fiscal regime. But that development stagnated for thirty-five years.

Again the question can be asked, to what extent was the international financial rivalry, especially in the developing world, between the Soviet Union and the United States responsible for the retrogression into ad hoc bilateral arrangements. Equally pertinent is the question, how much of the disintegration into ad hoc and opportunistic financial arrangements was due to the emergence of prosperous developed nations in Western Europe and Japan that had unilateral reasons, often competitive with the United States, to share their prosperity with developing countries outside the tradition that had been built substantially around American economic leadership.

Whatever the diagnosis, there is currently little system, and little evidence of growth yet in any system, for coordinating and formalizing the felt responsibilities of developed countries to assist the developing. Of all the features, for example, that characterize potential aid to emerging Eastern European democracies in contrast to the aid to Western European democracy forty years ago, the most striking may be the multiplicity of independent potential aid grantors with their own motives, expectations, and obligations toward Eastern Europe as a whole or to particular nations in that region. (An interesting question analytically is whether a greater number of potential contributing nations, simply by their greater number, will lead to a larger or a smaller total of aid forthcoming.)

The lack of accepted principles for the global distribution of available assistance is highlighted by the recently vocalized concern of the countries traditionally characterized as "developing" over the sudden competitive appeal of the developing countries of Eastern Europe.

The possibility of a formal regime for the channeling of assistance from developed to developing countries, with criteria both for contributions and for claims, has had superimposed on it recently the prospect of some organized and explicit regime for sharing the burdens of environmental protection. On a very small scale this appeared in connection with the Montreal Protocol governing the phasing out of the ozone-destroying chlorofluorocarbons

(CFCs). Developing countries successfully negotiated leniency in their own restrictions, and further negotiated modest funding, upwards of $200 million, from the developed nations to alleviate the burdens of phasing out CFCs. The Bush administration, which participated only reluctantly after first declining, was reportedly concerned about the precedent that might be established for global financing of a regime to discourage emissions of carbon dioxide. It is widely recognized that the magnitude of any comparable effort with respect to carbon dioxide could easily be two or even three orders of magnitude larger, and permanent, compared with CFCs.

Indeed, early preliminary estimates of what it might cost to bring carbon emissions under control in the developing world over the next half century, and estimates of where the financing for such a program might come from, suggest resource transfers from the developed to the developing world on a scale comparable to that of the Marshall Plan in relation to the U.S. GNP. A serious program to keep carbon emissions increasing by only a percent or two per year rather than 4 or 5 percent per year in countries like China, India, and Brazil, financed by the developed countries, could easily be several times the magnitude of all current aid to the developing world.

These are just preliminary glimmerings of the possible sizes of resource transfers from rich to poor countries over the next five or six decades in the event the more alarming visions of global change should be scientifically verified over the years to come.

Resource transfers of that magnitude will undoubtedly call for—not necessarily receive, but call for—integrated coordination and planning and the development of express criteria both for contributions and for benefits. Interestingly, the criteria for allocating resource transfers might have more to do with which nations can, with assistance, reduce carbon emissions than with which nations could most benefit, or most deserve to benefit, in terms of economic development.

These are some of the items on the global agenda for American national security. They do not exhaust that agenda, but they should provide a springboard into the new world order.

VISIONS OF THE
NEW
INTERNATIONAL
ORDER

8A

Disorder Restored

JOHN J. MEARSHEIMER

M any Americans and West Europeans believe that the prospects for creating a stable new world order are excellent. These optimists usually do not spell out the basis for their sanguine view, but instead, they tend to write and speak as if the prospects for international stability will automatically increase in the wake of the cold war. Nevertheless, close examination of the optimists' rhetoric reveals that it is based on a handful of key ideas about the nature of international relations.

Two of the optimists' most important beliefs challenge the very essence of the state system. First, some hold that the territorial state, the principal actor on the international stage since the birth of the European state system in 1648, is either a dinosaur flailing

JOHN J. MEARSHEIMER is professor and chair of the Department of Political Science at the University of Chicago. He is also a consultant to the RAND Corporation. Professor Mearsheimer is the recipient of several distinguished awards and serves as officer to renowned organizations and associations. He has written many articles for leading publications and is the author of two books, *Liddell Hart and the Weight of History* and *Conventional Deterrence*.

about on its last legs, or at the very least, an organization with a severely circumscribed capacity for causing trouble. Second, others argue that the military competition between states, which has been a constant feature of international politics as well as a profound source of instability, is now a thing of the past, or at the very least, subordinated to economic competition, which according to the optimists' logic, rarely results in war.[1]

Although these purported changes took place during the cold war, the optimists argue they were in large part blocked from view by the enduring competition between the superpowers, which failed to grasp the revolution taking place before them. However, with the cold war now relegated to the dustbin of history, those changes are rapidly becoming apparent to all. Most important of all, optimists believe these changes can serve as the basis for a more peaceful world in the twenty-first century.

In fact, however, there have been no fundamental changes in the nature of international politics since World War II. The state system is alive and well, and although regrettable, military competition between sovereign states will remain the distinguishing feature of international politics for the foreseeable future. Furthermore, the conventional wisdom notwithstanding, there is likely to be more—not less—disorder around the globe in the wake of the cold war.

The Future of the State

Is the territorial state finished, or at least severely constrained? Three arguments usually underpin the claim that sovereignty is at bay.

Some optimists claim that powerful international institutions or "regimes" are emerging as important actors on the world scene, and that they have the capacity to seriously constrain state behavior. States, so the argument goes, are no longer the principal actors in the international system. The most frequently cited example of this phenomenon is the European Community (EC), which purportedly has coercive influence on the actions of West European states.

Other optimists emphasize that states have lost large amounts of control over their societies because direct ties between individuals and organizations in different societies are growing at a spectacular rate. These transnational links shift the primary loyalty of citizens away from central governments toward actors in other societies, thus making it difficult for states to command their own citizens. States are anachronistic in a world that is fast becoming a global village.

Finally, some optimists argue that economic interdependence among states is growing, and that the resulting integration of national economies will eventually lead those states to political integration. Presumably, this integration will reduce the number of states over time, until there is eventually one giant super-state, which has no rival to fight with. The early evidence of this emerging trend, so the argument goes, can be seen in Western Europe, where ongoing economic integration is slowly but steadily eroding national boundaries.

On close inspection, each of these arguments is flawed. Let us first consider the empirical evidence, and then turn to their conceptual shortcomings.

There is what social scientists call a "selection bias" problem in the optimists' case. Specifically, proponents of the claim that states are either withering away or losing their autonomy invariably point to Western Europe alone as evidence for their position. Optimists cannot point to any other region of the globe, including the rest of Europe, where similar trends are at work. In fact, the state system is thriving outside of Western Europe. Virtually all Third World states are fiercely determined to maintain their sovereignty, and it is difficult to imagine the East European states allowing their independence to be challenged after forty-five years of Soviet occupation. Moreover, the number of sovereign states in the system continues to increase.

Even in Western Europe, however, the state system is intact. There has certainly been considerable economic integration in that region during the past decade, but there is little evidence that serious political integration is following in its wake. The Persian Gulf crisis was an important test of that trend. The European states failed to coordinate their responses, and acted very much like the sovereign actors they are. Also, the West Europeans have not made much progress in their efforts to design a common security policy. There is certainly a lot of high-sounding rhetoric, but fundamental disagreements among the major powers have effectively stymied the development of concrete policies.

There are two conceptual shortcomings in the "sovereignty-at-bay" thesis that raise further doubts about it.

First, nationalism makes it likely that states will remain the principal actors in international politics. Nationalism is a political ideology that assumes the world can be divided into nations or tribes, and that each of these nations should have its own territorial state.[2] Nationalism has been an extremely powerful force for two centuries. It will be difficult to transcend the state system as long as nationalism is a potent force in world politics. There is little reason to think that nationalism is a spent force. Not only is it a thoroughly modern phenomenon, but as events in Eastern Europe make clear, a force with considerable staying power.

Nationalism is widely recognized to be a potent force in both the Third World and Eastern Europe, but it is thought to be absent from Western Europe, where ever-increasing numbers of citizens supposedly see themselves not as Germans or Britons, but as Europeans. In fact, nationalism remains a dominating force in Western Europe, and Margaret Thatcher's was not the only evidence of this phenomenon: German unification was another clear manifestation of nationalism—albeit in a benign form. German unification was predicated on the twin beliefs that underpin nationalism: there is a German nation and all members of the German tribe should be free to live in a German state. The recent controversy caused by some prominent Germans advocating a return to greater nationalism in historical education is further evidence that nationalism remains a force to reckon with in Germany, as it is elsewhere.[3] Finally, it is difficult to imagine the French, who remain deeply committed to their own culture, allowing their nation to be subordinated to some greater European entity—especially since the Germans would probably play the dominant role in shaping that new polity.

Second, the sovereignty-at-bay argument fails to recognize that the cold war was largely responsible for the unusually high levels of economic integration and political cooperation in Western Europe over the past forty-five years. Old-fashioned balance-of-power logic mandated cooperation among the Western democracies to meet the Soviet threat. Britain, Germany, and France no longer worried about each other because all faced a greater menace from the Soviets. In fact, each Western democracy had a vested interest in seeing its alliance partners grow more powerful economically and militarily, since each additional increment of power helped deter a Soviet attack. Furthermore, America's hegemonic position in NATO guaranteed that no EC state would threaten the others. For example, France did not have to fear Germany because the American presence in Germany meant that the Germans were not free to attack anyone.

Relations among the EC states will be fundamentally altered in the wake of the cold war. Without a common Soviet threat and without the American night watchman, Western European states will begin viewing each other with greater fear and suspicion, as they did for centuries before the onset of the cold war.

In sum, it is much too soon to cheer the passing of the state system in Europe, to say nothing of the rest of the world. States are likely to remain the principal actors in international politics for a long time to come.

The Future of Security Competition

States have historically competed with each other for military security in circumstances best characterized as a zero-sum game. That competition, which sometimes leads to war, has long been the defining characteristic of international politics. Many optimists maintain that states are becoming increasingly less concerned about security issues, and focused instead on economic concerns. Post–World War II Germany and Japan, not the United States and Soviet Union, are seen as the appropriate models for the future.

Optimists usually employ two lines of argument to support their claim about the shrinking importance of military competition among states. Some focus on the horrors of war to make the case that war is rapidly becoming an obsolescent enterprise. Others offer an economic argument based on the assumption that modern states are more concerned about prosperity than security.

The Obsolescence of War

Optimists often claim that war had become so deadly by the early twentieth century that it was on the verge of becoming an unacceptable form of state behavior.[4] Like dueling and slavery, war was about to fall into the category of outmoded social activities that civilized states no longer pursued. States, so the argument goes, are inexorably learning that lesson and are therefore increasingly less disposed to "reach for their revolvers" when tensions develop between them. Consequently, states do not have to pay much attention to security issues, thus greatly ameliorating the traditional military competition among them.

It is certainly true that modern war can be extremely deadly. The horrors that would attend a nuclear war are well understood in the West and require no elaboration here. Conventional war can also be terribly destructive: for example, the U.S. fire-bombing campaign against Japan from March to August 1945 destroyed virtually all of Japan's major cities.[5] The war on the Eastern Front in Europe (1941–1945) was even more deadly. Not only were many millions of combatants killed in brutal combat, but millions of prisoners of war and millions of innocent civilians were systematically murdered by the Nazis and their allies.[6]

As war has become increasingly destructive over time, it has become less frequent. War was more commonplace, for example, in the eighteenth century than in the nineteenth and twentieth centuries.[7] However, war is not obsolescent.

Consider the evidence. Since World War II, numerous statesmen have chosen to go to war. The United States has fought three major wars in this period: Korea, Vietnam, and the Persian Gulf conflict. Israel has fought major wars in 1948, 1956, 1967, 1973, and 1982. Furthermore, Egypt and Syria attacked Israel in 1973 knowing that the Israelis had nuclear weapons. In fact, there have been a number of wars during the past forty-five years involving a nuclear-armed state.

There is an important conceptual flaw in the obsolescence of war argument that points up why war remains a central feature of world politics. The claim that *conventional* war has become so costly that states can no longer consider it a serious option rests on the assumption that all conventional wars must be long and bloody wars of attrition. It is evident from several wars since 1945, as well as several campaign-ending battles of the Second World War, that it is still possible to gain a quick and decisive victory on the battlefield and avoid the devastation of a protracted conflict. This point was certainly made clear in the Gulf War, where the United States and its allies won a stunning military victory against Iraq, and suffered remarkably few casualties in the process. As long as the possibility remains that states can win a conventional war at an acceptable cost, the threat of conventional war will remain a serious concern for states.[8]

The World War II cases described above support this point. Japanese leaders did not attack the United States in December 1941 thinking that in less than four years the American military would smash and strangle their country to the point of ruin. If they had known the war's outcome, they surely would not have struck at Pearl Harbor. Although many Japanese policy makers recognized the odds of victory were slim, they believed that there was still a reasonable chance that Japan could win a military victory against the United States. Moreover, they clearly saw continued peace leading to ruin under pressure of the U.S. embargo. Adolf Hitler and his lieutenants did not invade the Soviet Union in June 1941 thinking that Germany would suffer a devastating defeat in the ensuing war. In fact, the Nazi leadership thought that the Wehrmacht would win a striking victory against the Soviet Union, similar to the victories achieved against Poland in 1939, and France in 1940. The central point here is that conventional wars can sometimes be won rather cheaply, and national leaders occasionally recognize that fact, and as long as that situation obtains, states must pay careful attention to their security environment.

One might argue that this discussion about conventional war misses the fundamental fact that we live in a nuclear world in which war between great powers is no longer a viable option. Nuclear weapons surely reduce the likelihood of war between rival states, but there are two reasons why the threat of war remains a serious concern even in a world of nuclear powers.

First, there is always the possibility that a conventional war might start between two nuclear-armed states because one side does not believe that the other side's threat to use nuclear weapons is credible. The logic is straightforward: if both sides have a robust nuclear retaliatory capability, there is little to be gained by going nuclear, and a powerful reason—avoiding incineration—for keeping the war conventional. Thus a state under pressure to go to war might be willing to bet that an adversary will not use nuclear weapons if attacked, but will fight conventionally.

Second, there is a well-developed body of strategic literature that lays out plausible scenarios where nuclear weapons are used in a war. Let us consider four of the most prominent scenarios. *Crisis Instability:* A heated crisis develops between two states with vulnerable nuclear forces. There would be powerful incentives for each side to strike the other's vulnerable nuclear arsenal before the other side struck first. *Preventive War:* One of two potential adversaries has nuclear weapons, but the other side is on the verge of acquiring nuclear weapons. The state with the nuclear arsenal would have strong incentives to use nuclear weapons to destroy its rival's burgeoning nuclear capability before it became operational. After all, the victim would not be able to retaliate in kind. *Nonnuclear Adversary:* Again, we have two potential adversaries, but only one has nuclear weapons. If a major crisis broke out between them, and the conventional balance of power was roughly equal, the nuclear-armed state would surely think about using nuclear weapons against the non-nuclear state. *Nuclear Escalation:* In the event of a conventional war between two nuclear powers, there is always the danger of accidental or inadvertent escalation, or the purposeful use of nuclear weapons by one side to rescue a losing situation on the conventional battlefield.[9]

The claim here is not that these scenarios are likely, but instead that there is some small but reasonable possibility of nuclear use. That simple fact, coupled with the horrors that would attend a nuclear war, leaves states no choice but to worry much about their security environment.

The events of World War II on the Eastern Front highlight another reason why states must be deeply concerned about possible military threats. Modern nation states sometimes go berserk and murder vast numbers of noncombatants from the defeated state. These massacres occur because powerful ideological forces—be they fascism, nationalism, or religious fundamentalism—can produce deep-seated hatred between states, and because modern nation states usually have the technology and organizational wherewithal to build formidable killing machines. Thus losing a war in the twentieth century might involve much more than simply getting beaten on the battlefield, or even bombed from the air. Military defeat can result in the death and destruction of a society. Had the Nazis won World War II, for example, Polish society, not to mention the Polish state, would have been eliminated from the face of the earth.[10] Although such completely barbaric behavior is not commonplace, the fact that there are a number of similar cases means that no state can afford to take the chance that a potential rival might go berserk. This logic compels states to worry about their security, and thus to compete among themselves for advantage, or at least to prevent others from achieving advantage.

Economic Liberalism

Optimists also employ an economic argument to make their case that interstate competition for security has waned greatly in recent years. They start with the assumption that modern states are essentially welfare states, in which governing elites are prisoners of consumer oriented populations that demand economic prosperity. Prosperity, not security, is the principal goal of modern states, because wealth, not martial glory, is the chief aim of most citizens. At the same time, statesmen have come to recognize that prosperity can easily be achieved without conquest in an interdependent world. Indeed, they have learned that imperialism leads to overextension, which leads to economic decline, not prosperity. Japanese and German behavior in the cold war, in contrast to Soviet and American actions, shows clearly that conquest does not pay. By this logic, the key to achieving prosperity is to establish and maintain a liberal economic order that allows free economic exchange between states.

The main flaw in this argument is that the principal assumption underpinning it—states are primarily motivated by the desire to achieve prosperity—is wrong. States are surely concerned about prosperity, and thus economic calculations are hardly trivial for them. However, states operate in both an international political environment and an international economic environment, and the former dominates the latter in cases where the two come into conflict. The reason is straightforward: the international political system is anarchic, which means that each state must always be concerned to ensure its own survival.[11] A state can have no higher goal than survival, since profits matter little when the enemy is occupying your country and slaughtering your citizens. Therefore, when push comes to shove, international political considerations will be paramount in the minds of decision makers.

Germany and especially Japan were exceptions to this rule during the cold war. They mainly concentrated on achieving prosperity in the decades after 1945, while security was a second-order concern. This situation, however, was highly unusual and is likely to end with the passing of the cold war. The devastation inflicted on Germany and Japan in World War II, coupled with the intense superpower rivalry that developed in the late 1940s, forced the United States to provide security for both states, alleviating them of the burden of protecting themselves from the Soviet threat. At the same time, the United States had a vested interest in encouraging and fostering economic growth in Germany and Japan, since both states could be powerful cold war allies. Thus security concerns tended to take a back seat to economic concerns in Germany and Japan over the past forty-five years. That situation will change once the cold war order is torn down and Germany and Japan no longer rely on the United States to provide them with security, but must provide it for themselves.

Furthermore, economic interdependence, which is a central ingredient of a liberal economic order, tends to foster security competition among states. Interdependence is defined as a situation in which two states are mutually vulnerable; each is a hostage of the other in the economic realm. Interdependence, according to the optimists' logic, allows states to compel each other to cooperate on economic matters, much as mutual assured destruction allows nuclear powers to compel each other to respect their security. However, states will struggle to escape the vulnerability that interdepcndence creates, in order to bolster their national security. States that depend on others for critical economic supplies will fear cutoff or blackmail in time of crisis or war; they may try to extend political control to the source of supply, giving rise to conflict with the source or with its other customers. Interdependence, in other words, will probably lead to greater security competition.

Finally, welfare states operating in an interdependent economy might be pushed toward war for prosperity reasons. Economic interactions between states often cause serious frictions, even when the overall consequences are positive. There will invariably be winners and losers within each state, and losers rarely accept defeat gracefully. In modern states, where leaders have to pay careful attention to their constituents, losers can cause considerable trouble. Even in cases where only winners are involved, there are sometimes squabbles over how the spoils are divided. At the same time, there will be opportunities for blackmail and for brinkmanship in a highly dynamic economic system where states are dependent on each other. For example, although mutual vulnerabilities may arise among states, the actual levels of dependence are likely to be unequal. A less vulnerable state will probably have greater bargaining power over its more dependent partners and might attempt to coerce them into making extravagant concessions. Furthermore, different political systems, not to mention individual leaders, have different capacities for engaging in tough bargaining. Elites under pressure to provide prosperity for a demanding populace, who feel that the actions of another state are undermining their efforts to provide it, might very well think about employing force to rectify the situation. It is not certain that the people, seeing their prosperity threatened, would oppose war. Again, we see evidence that interdependence is likely to promote rather than eliminate security competition.

The Future World Disorder

The foregoing analysis challenges the optimists' rosy assessment about the prospects for creating a stable world order. I shall now go beyond that critique and explain why the end of the cold war is likely to lead to greater international instability.

The cold war is *not* a period of unbounded peace and prosperity. There were many wars in the Third World, a few of which involved the superpowers in serious combat. Afghanistan, Korea, and Vietnam are the most prominent examples. Virtually all Third World conflicts indirectly involved the superpowers, since they both worked hard to gain client states in the Third World. These wars produced modest casualties for the superpowers, but large casualties for Third World nations. Furthermore, the cold war inflicted oppressive political regimes on the peoples of Eastern Europe, who were denied basic human rights by their forced membership in the Soviet empire. It also consumed national wealth by giving rise to large and costly defense establishments in both East and West.

On the other hand, there has been no great power war since 1945. Europe, which has been plagued by war throughout its history, and was the scene of two extremely costly world wars in the first half of this century, enjoyed its longest period of peace in the cold war. The early years of the cold war (1945–63) were marked by a handful of crises, although none brought Europe to the brink of war. Since 1963, however, there have been no East-West crises in Europe. It has been difficult—if not impossible—for the last two decades to find serious national security analysts who have thought there was a real chance the Soviets would attack Western Europe. Northeast Asia is the other scene of great power war in the first forty-five years of this century. Except for the Korean conflict, this region too has been remarkably stable during the cold war.

Given the vast violence and suffering that attends great power wars, the chief criterion for assessing the stability of different world orders must be whether they make such conflicts more or less likely. On that score, the cold war looks remarkably attractive, and one can safely conclude that the net human and economic costs of the cold war order have been far lower than the costs of the disorder that marked the period between 1900–1945. What about the future?

The next decades in a world without the superpowers will probably not be as violent as the first forty-five years of this century, but will probably be substantially more prone to violence than the past forty-five years. First, the prospects for great power crises and war are likely to increase markedly in the wake of the cold war. Second, there is not likely to be any abatement in either the number or the ferocity of Third World conflicts. Third, nuclear proliferation, which has been contained reasonably well in the cold war, is likely to become a significant problem in the decades ahead, increasing the chances of nuclear war.

Great Power Conflict

This pessimistic assessment about great power conflict rests on the argument that the distribution and character of military power are the root causes of peace and war. Specifically, the comparative peacefulness of the postwar era flowed from the bipolar distribution of power in the international system, and the rough equality of military strength attained by those two polar states—as well as from a third cause, the appearance of nuclear weapons, which vastly expanded the potential violence of war, and so made deterrence exceedingly robust.

Bipolarity made both Europe and Northeast Asia a simpler place in which only one point of friction—the East-West conflict—needed to be managed to avoid war. The two blocs encompassed most of the states in these crucial regions, leaving few unprotected weak states for the Soviets to conquer.[12] As a result the Soviets have had few targets to bully in one-on-one encounters. They have also been unable to gang up with another major power against the few states that are unprotected, because their West bloc adversary has been their only potential ganging-up partner.

Bipolarity also left less room for miscalculation of both resolve and capability. During the first fifteen years of the cold war the rules of the road for the conflict were not yet established, giving rise to several serious crises. However, over time both sides gained a clear sense of how far they could push the other, and what the other would not tolerate. A set of rules came to be agreed upon: an understanding on the division of rights in Austria, Berlin, and elsewhere; a proscription on secret unilateral redeployment of large nuclear forces to areas contiguous to the opponent; mutual toleration of reconnaissance satellites; agreement on rules of peacetime engagement between naval forces; and so forth. The absence of serious crises during 1963–91 was due in part to the growth of these agreements on the rights of both sides, and the rules of conduct. These could develop in large part because the system was bipolar in character. Bipolarity meant that the same two states remained adversaries for a long period, giving them time to learn how to manage their conflict without war. By contrast, a multipolar world of shifting coalitions would have forced adversaries to frequently relearn how their opponents' defined their interests, to reach new accords on the division of rights, and to reestablish rules of competitive conduct.

Bipolarity also left less room to miscalculate the relative strength of the opposing coalitions. The composition of possible war coalitions has been clear because only two blocs have existed, both led by an overwhelmingly dominant power that could discipline its members. Either side could have miscalculated its relative military strength, but bipolarity removed ambiguity about relative strength arising from uncertainty about diplomacy.

The East-West military balance has been roughly equal throughout the cold war, which has further bolstered stability. This approximate parity strengthened deterrence by ensuring that no state was tempted to use force to exploit its power advantage. Parity, in turn, resulted partly from bipolarity. Because the two blocs already encompassed all the states of Europe and Northeast Asia, both sides have balanced mainly by internal means (military build-up), rather than external means (diplomacy and alliances); these more efficient means have produced a more nearly equal balance.

Nuclear weapons also played a key role in preventing great power war in the decades after World War II.

Western elites on both sides of the Atlantic quickly recognized that nuclear weapons were vastly destructive and that their widespread use in Europe would cause unprecedented devastation. Soviet leaders also recognized the horrendous results that a nuclear war would produce. Some Soviet military officers have asserted that victory is possible in nuclear war, but even they have acknowledged that such a victory would be Pyrrhic. Soviet civilians have generally argued that victory is impossible. Official rhetoric aside, the actual behavior of policy makers on both sides has been very cautious in the presence of nuclear weapons. There is not a single case of a leader brandishing nuclear weapons during a crisis or behaving as if nuclear war might be a viable option for solving important political problems. On the contrary, policy makers have never gone beyond nuclear threats of a very subtle sort, and have shown great caution when the possibility of nuclear confrontation has emerged.[13] This cautious conduct has lowered the risk of war.

Nuclear weapons also imposed an equality and clarity on the power relations between the superpowers. This equality and clarity represented a marked change from the earlier non-nuclear world in which sharp power inequalities and miscalculations of relative power were common.

Bipolarity will disappear with the passing of the cold war, and multipolarity will emerge in the new international order. Germany, France, Britain, and perhaps Italy will assume major power status in Europe. The Soviet Union will decline from superpower status but will remain a major European power, and probably be a force to reckon with in Asia as well. China, India, Japan, and perhaps Pakistan will be major powers in Asia. The United States will surely remain a great power, with the capability to influence events in both Europe and Asia. The other two dimensions of the new order—the distribution of power among these great powers, and the distribution of nuclear weapons among them—are not predetermined, and several possible arrangements could develop.

This new international system would suffer the problems general to multipolar systems, and would therefore be more prone to instability. There would be many possible conflict dyads across which war might break out. Power imbalances would be commonplace as a result of the opportunities this system would present for bullying and ganging up. There would also be considerable opportunity for miscalculation, since the new order might well witness shifting patterns of conflict, leaving insufficient time for adversaries to develop agreed divisions of rights and agreed rules of the road, or constantly forcing them to reestablish new agreements and rules as old antagonisms fade and new ones arise. The problem of containing German and Japanese power will emerge once again, but the multipolar configuration of power in Europe and Asia will make it difficult to form effective counterbalancing coalitions, for much the same reason that effective counterbalancing coalitions failed to form in the 1930s. Eventually the problem of containing the Soviet Union could also reemerge. Finally, conflicts may erupt in Eastern Europe, providing the vortex that could pull others into a wider confrontation.

It is difficult to predict the precise balance of military power that will emerge among the great powers, although there is potential for unstable power imbalances among them. Consider the balance of power in post–cold war Europe, where the future of Soviet power is hard to forecast. The Soviet Union might recover its strength soon after withdrawing from Central Europe. In this case Soviet power would outmatch German power. Conversely, centrifugal national forces may pull the Soviet Union apart, leaving no remnant state that is the equal of a united Germany. Finally, and most likely, Germany and the Soviet Union might emerge as powers of roughly equal strength. The first two scenarios, with their marked inequality between the two leading powers, would be especially worrisome, although there is still cause for concern even if Soviet and German power is balanced.

The end of the cold war also complicates the matter of nuclear deterrence. For example, the departure of the superpowers from Central Europe would remove the large nuclear arsenals they now maintain in that potentially dangerous region. This would thereby remove the pacifying effect that these weapons have had on European politics. Of course, the Germans do not have their own nuclear weapons, a situation likely to make them feel insecure and create powerful incentives to acquire them. The Japanese also have no nuclear weapons, and there too it is likely that as the American nuclear umbrella is removed from over their head, pressure will build to acquire nuclear weapons.

There are essentially three broad nuclear futures, none of which is likely to serve as the basis of a stable new international order.

Many Europeans and some Americans seek to eliminate nuclear weapons from the international system. Fashioning a nuclear-free world would require Britain, China, France, India, Israel, the Soviet Union, the United States, and presumably Pakistan and South Africa to rid themselves of these talismans of their sovereignty—an improbable event, to say the least. Those who wish for it nevertheless believe it would be the most peaceful arrangement possible. In fact, a nuclear-free world has the distinction of being the most dangerous among the envisionable post–cold war orders. The pacifying effects of nuclear weapons—the caution they generate, the security they provide, the rough equality they impose, and the clarity of relative power they create—would be lost. Peace would then depend on the other dimensions of the new order—the number of poles, and the distribution of power among them. The geometry of world power would probably look much like it did between the world wars—a design for tension, crisis, and possibly war.

A more plausible order for the post–cold war world is one in which the existing nuclear powers keep their nuclear weapons, but no new nuclear powers emerge. This scenario sees a nuclear-free zone in Central Europe, but leaves nuclear weapons on the European flanks. Neither Germany nor Japan acquire nuclear weapons in this scenario. This also seems unlikely, since many non-nuclear states will have substantial incentives to acquire their own nuclear weapons. Germany and Japan, for example, are likely to want nuclear weapons to protect themselves from blackmail by other nuclear powers. Moreover, Germany and Japan would have greater economic strength than either Britain or France, and therefore may well desire nuclear weapons to raise their military status to a level commensurate with their economic status. The minor powers of Eastern Europe will also have strong incentives to acquire nuclear weapons. Without them, the East European states would be open to nuclear blackmail from the Soviet Union and Germany (if the latter acquired its own nuclear arsenal), and the fact that no East European state could match their conventional strength gives these minor powers an additional incentive to acquire a nuclear deterrent. In short, a continuation of the current pattern of ownership without proliferation seems unlikely.

How stable would this order based on nonproliferation be? The continued presence of nuclear weapons in the hands of a few major powers would have some pacifying effects. Specifically, nuclear weapons would induce greater caution on their owners, would give the nuclear powers greater security, would work to equalize the relative power of states that possess them, and would reduce the risk of miscalculation. However, these benefits would be limited if nuclear weapons did not proliferate beyond their current owners, to include the other great powers in the system. There are four main reasons for this conclusion.

First, the caution and the security that nuclear weapons impose would be missing from the center of Europe. The entire region between France and the Soviet Union, extending from the Arctic in the north to the Mediterranean in the south, and comprising some eighteen significant states, would become a large zone of "safety" for conventional war. Second, asymmetrical power relations would be bound to develop, between nuclear and non-nuclear states and among non-nuclear states, raising the dangers that attend such asymmetries. Third, the risk of miscalculation would arise, reflecting the multipolar character of this system and the absence of nuclear weapons from a large portion of it. A durable agreed political order would be hard to build because political coalitions would tend to shift over time, causing miscalculations of resolve between adversaries; and the relative strength of potential war coalitions would be hard to calculate because coaltion strength would depend heavily on the vagaries of diplomacy. Such uncertainties about relative capabilities would be mitigated in conflicts that arose among nuclear powers: nuclear weapons tend to equalize power even among states or coalitions of widely disparate resources, and thus diminish the importance of additions or defections from each coalition. However, uncertainty would still be acute among the many states that would remain non-nuclear. Fourth, Japan and the conventionally armed states of Central Europe would depend for their security in mass armies, giving them an incentive to infuse their societies with hypernationalism in order to maintain public support for national defense efforts.

The most probable scenario in the wake of the cold war is further nuclear proliferation. This outcome is laden with dangers, but it also provides the best hope for maintaining stability among the great powers. Everything depends on how proliferation is managed. Mismanaged proliferation could produce disaster, while well-managed proliferation could produce an order nearly as stable as that of the cold war. Unfortunately, a mismanaged proliferation process is the more likely outcome.

The dangers that could arise from mismanaged proliferation are both profound and numerous. There is the danger that the proliferation process itself could give one of the existing nuclear powers a strong incentive to stop its non-nuclear neighbor from joining the club, much as Israel used force to halt Iraq's nuclear program in 1981. There is also the danger that an unstable nuclear competition will emerge among the new nuclear states. They may lack the resources to make their nuclear forces invulnerable, which could create first-strike fears and incentives—a recipe for disaster in a tense crisis. Finally, there is the danger that proliferation, by increasing the number of fingers on the nuclear trigger, would increase the risk of nuclear weapons being fired by accident, or captured by terrorists, or used by madmen.

These and other dangers of proliferation can be lessened if the current nuclear powers take the right steps. To forestall preventive attacks, they can extend security guarantees. To help the new nuclear powers secure their deterrents, they can provide technical assistance. And they can help to socialize nascent nuclear societies to understand the lethal character of the forces they are acquiring. This kind of well-managed proliferation can help bolster peace.

Ideally proliferation should stop with Germany and Japan. Each has a large economic base, and thus can afford to build a secure nuclear retaliatory force. Moreover, Germany and Japan will no doubt feel insecure without nuclear weapons, and if they feel insecure their impressive conventional strength will give them a significant capacity to cause trouble. Different states in Asia and Eastern Europe may also come to want their own nuclear weapons. Since these states may be unable, even with superpower help, to build a secure deterrent, it would be best if they did not go nuclear. However, if the broader spread of nuclear weapons proves impossible to prevent without taking extreme steps, the current nuclear powers should let proliferation in Asia and Eastern Europe go on, while doing all they can to channel it in safe directions.

I am pessimistic that proliferation can be well-managed. The current members of the nuclear club are likely to resist proliferation, but they cannot easily work to manage this tricky process while at the same time resisting it. There is a natural tension between the two goals. There will be several motives to resist. The established nuclear powers will be exceedingly chary of helping the new nuclear powers build secure deterrents, simply because it runs against the grain of state behavior to share military secrets with other states. After all, knowledge of sensitive military technology could be turned against the donor state if that technology were further passed on to adversaries. Furthermore, proliferation in Asia and Europe would undermine the legitimacy of the 1968 Nuclear Non-Proliferation Treaty, and this could open the floodgates of proliferation worldwide. The nuclear powers would not want that to happen, and so they will probably spend their energy trying to thwart proliferation, rather than seeking to manage it.

The best time for proliferation to occur would be during a period of relative international calm. Proliferation in the midst of a crisis would be especially dangerous, since states in conflict with the emerging nuclear powers would then have a powerful incentive to interrupt the process by force. However, proliferation may not begin until the outbreak of crisis, because the opposition to it within potential nuclear powers would be so vociferous, and the external resistance from the nuclear club would be so great. Thus it may take a crisis to make potential nuclear powers willing to pay the domestic and international costs of building a nuclear force. All of which means that proliferation is likely to occur under international conditions that virtually insure it will be mismanaged.

Third World Conflict

There is a popular belief that most wars in the Third World were caused by the superpowers, which competed with each other across the entire globe. The United States and the Soviet Union, after all, fought battles with proxies on different continents, and they destabilized Third World governments, which led to greater regional instability. With the demise of the cold war, and the shrinking of the superpowers' power projection capabilities, some students of international politics expect that there will be a significant reduction of Third World conflict.

There was an intense superpower competition in the Third World that contributed to the instability that plagued the less de-

veloped regions of the world. However, this is not the whole story
about the origins of Third World conflict. There are two other
dimensions to this phenomenon, which point toward a more pessimistic conclusion about the post–cold war prospects for peace in
the Third World.

First, the *root* cause of Third World conflict has been intense
hostility between and within the regional states themselves. The
traditional sources of great power conflict—balance-of-power
logic, ideological antagonism, nationalism, territorial disputes—
are also the main source of war in the Third World. This situation
is hardly surprising since states are the principal actors in the industrialized world as well as the Third World, and there is little
reason to expect, at either the domestic or the international level,
fundamental differences in how these two categories of states behave. Although the superpowers often exacerbate tensions between Third World states, the root causes of trouble are invariably
local. A simple rhetorical question illustrates this point. Is it likely
that the Arab-Israeli conflict, the India-Pakistan conflict, or the
Iraq-Iran conflict would not have occurred, or even been less intense, if the superpowers had confined their competition solely to
Europe? I think not. In short, Third World feuds were not caused
by the superpowers, and therefore they are not likely to disappear
in the wake of the cold war.

Second, although the superpowers often made a bad situation
worse in the Third World by exploiting it for selfish purposes, they
sometimes worked to keep a crisis between Third World states
from escalating into a war. The Soviets, for example, tried to
discourage the Egyptians from going to war against Israel in 1973.
After the war broke out, the Soviets and the Americans stopped it
before Israel could destroy the Egyptian army. There was concern
at the time that the superpowers might come to blows over this
war. The fact is that the superpower competition sometimes had a
dampening effect on Third World conflict because both the Americans and the Soviets feared that a regional war might escalate to a
world war that neither wanted.

The bottom line is that while superpower involvement in the
Third World often led to instability, it was not the root cause of
regional trouble, and, in fact, it could work as a stabilizing as well

as destabilizing force. Thus there is no good reason to expect the demise of the cold war to lead to a more stable Third World.

There are two additional reasons for pessimism about peace in the Third World.

It is likely that the great powers that dominate the new multipolar world will intervene in the Third World. A cursory glance at the history of imperialism makes clear that Third World intervention did not start with the superpowers, but was a refined practice long before the cold war. The United States, for example, intervened in Latin America on numerous occasions before 1945. The great powers will surely find reasons—good and bad—for military intervention. Protecting resources like oil will be a rationale. After all, the Persian Gulf war was a post–cold war crisis, and it was driven in part by concern about the control of oil. Border disputes like the one between China and Vietnam will also be a problem in the post–cold war world. The power projection capabilities of the great powers will not reach superpower levels, but that limit in reach will be compensated for by the increase in the number of major powers that will be active in the Third World.

Finally, there is the issue of nuclear proliferation. It is likely to accelerate. The growing technical capacities of Third World states will boost proliferation, but the crucial driving forces will be political not technical. Specifically, the cold war order had an important dampening effect on proliferation, which is about to be lost.[14]

The two superpowers opposed nuclear proliferation, preferring instead that they alone had nuclear weapons. The superpowers had such a clear-cut preponderance of military power that they were able to place smaller states with acute security problems under their nuclear umbrellas. The Soviets, for example, assuaged Syrian concerns about the Israeli nuclear threat, and also provided nuclear deterrence for European allies like Poland. The United States extended nuclear deterrence to worried allies like Germany, Japan, South Korea, and Taiwan. These superpower guarantees reduced the incentives for smaller states to acquire their own nuclear weapons. The superpowers also derived good old-fashioned bargaining leverage from their many alliances with smaller powers that enabled the superpowers to pressure their allies not to go nuclear.

These barriers to proliferation are coming down with the demise of the cold war order. First, none of the great powers in the new multipolar world is likely to have the preponderance of military power necessary to extend its nuclear shield far and wide, like the Americans and Soviets did in the cold war. Second, great powers will face credibility problems if they attempt to extend nuclear deterrence. Alliance patterns are typically much more fluid in multipolarity than in bipolarity, where rigid alliance structures are the rule. The reason is: there are more potential alliance partners in a multipolar system to pick and choose among, which allows states to change partners over time. Consequently, "fair weather" friends are more commonplace in a multipolar than a bipolar system, a situation that will work to reduce the credibility of nuclear commitments proffered by great powers. Third, future great powers will not have as much bargaining leverage vis-à-vis Third World states as the superpowers did in the cold war. The new great powers, after all, will not have the military might of the Americans and the Soviets, and they will be plagued by the credibility problems described above.

Widespread nuclear proliferation is laden with dangers for the Third World. Not only will there be powerful incentives for nuclear powers to strike against non-nuclear powers about to acquire nuclear weapons, but resource-poor Third World states are not likely to build survivable retaliatory forces, the *sine qua non* of nuclear stability. Furthermore, it is possible that some Third World leaders might not fully appreciate the destructiveness of nuclear weapons. Finally, the precarious state of most political systems in the Third World increases the risks that nuclear weapons might be fired by accident, captured by terrorists, or used by madmen.

Conclusion

The passing of the cold war does not spell the end of the state system, nor does it mean that states will have to worry less about security than they did during the cold war. International politics will remain a fundamentally competitive activity involving states that have the capacity to inflict massive harm on each other. States invariably understand that they are involved in a competition that can have deadly consequences if they adopt flawed security policies. The problem states face, however, is that in a world of imperfect information, where only those with the benefit of hindsight have 20-20 vision, it is often difficult to figure out the best military policy for dealing with potential threats.

This problem will be especially acute for the United States, as it moves from the simplicity and stability of the cold war's bipolar order to the complexity and instability that is likely to attend the coming multipolar world. What should be the guiding principles of American national security policy in the decades ahead?

The main goal should be to prevent great power war by quickly and forcefully balancing against potential aggressors. Great power wars are very dangerous because the United States usually gets drawn into them, as happened in both world wars, and because of the threat of great power nuclear war, which would probably have terrible consequences for the United States, even if it was not a direct participant in the conflict. Support for such a commitment will be difficult to mobilize, because its principal purpose would be to preserve peace, rather than to prevent an imminent hegemony in Europe or Asia, and the prevention of hegemony is a simpler goal to explain publicly. Moreover, it is the basic nature of states to focus on maximizing relative power, not on bolstering stability, so this prescription asks them to take on an unaccustomed task. Nevertheless, the American stake in peace is real, and thus it should be possible to lead the American public to recognize its interest and support policies that protect it.

The other goal of American security policy should be to avoid Third World military intervention. The Third World is strategically unimportant, not only because Third World states cannot threaten the security of the United States, but also because it is largely a myth that great power rivals can gain important strategic advantages over the United States through expansion in the Third World. This was true during the cold war, when there was a Soviet threat that could plausibly be used to justify American involvement in the Third World, and it is certainly the case now that the Soviets have lost their superpower standing.[15] Furthermore, American military involvement in the Third World is more likely than not to exacerbate regional conflicts, causing greater casualties and prolonging the war.

In short, the United States should maintain robust military forces to help keep peace among the great powers, while going to great lengths to resist the temptation to get dragged into Third World conflicts.

Notes

[1] Optimists offer a third key line of argument: ever-increasing numbers of states are becoming democratic, and democracies do not fight wars against each other. I have challenged this "theory of peace-loving democracies" in Mearsheimer (1990a) and (1990b).

[2] See Gellner (1983).

[3] See Evans (1989) and Maier (1988).

[4] See Mueller (1989). Also see Kaysen (1990.

[5] See Caidin (1960), especially pp. 159–160, for a graphic description of the effects of the strategic bombing campaign on the Japanese homeland.

[6] Among the best overviews on the German killing machine are Kershaw (1989), chapters 5, 8, 9; Mason (1981), pp. 90–113; and Mason (1988), pp. 542–569.

[7] See Levy (1983).

[8] See Mearsheimer (1983).

[9] See Posen (1991).

[10] See Lukas (1986).

[11] See Waltz (1979).

[12] The one exception to this rule was the blossoming of the Sino-Soviet competition in the 1960s.

[13] See Adomeit (1982); Betts (1987); and Bundy (1988).

[14] For a more elaborate discussion of the themes discussed below, see Benjamin Frankel, "The Brooding Shadow: Nuclear Proliferation in the 1990s," unpublished manuscript.

[15] See Van Evera (1990) and Walt (1989).

8B

Balance of Power Sustained

HENRY A. KISSINGER

I n his speech of January 16, 1991 announcing hostilities with Iraq, President Bush described the opportunity for building a new world order "where the rule of law . . . governs the conduct of nations," and "in which a credible United Nations can use its peacekeeping role to fulfill the promise and the vision of the UN's founders." I greatly admired President Bush's skill and fortitude in building the coalition to oppose Iraq's aggression. But the new world order cannot possibly fulfill the idealistic expectations expressed by the president; I doubt indeed whether they accurately

HENRY A. KISSINGER is former U.S. secretary of state and former assistant to the president for national security affairs. He is the author of many books and articles, and contributes frequently to newspapers and journals. Dr. Kissinger was awarded the Nobel Peace Prize in 1973. He is now chairman of Kissinger Associates, an international consulting company. This chapter is assembled from "It's Back to Czarist Russia—and Western Policy-Makers Aren't Ready," "The Delicate Balance," and "The Soviet Union Searches For Its Own New Order," all *Los Angeles Times*, respectively, January 20, 1991, February 24, 1991 and March 31, 1991. All material is copyrighted Henry A. Kissinger 1991.

describe what happened during the Gulf crisis.

Today, conventional American thinking about foreign policy translates into the notion of "a new world order," which would emerge from a set of legal arrangements and be safeguarded by collective security. The problem with such an approach is that it assumes that every nation perceives every challenge to the international order in the same way, and is prepared to run the same risks to preserve it. In fact, the new international order will see many centers of power, both within regions and among them. These power centers reflect different histories and perceptions.

In such a world, the deepest challenge to America will be philosophical: how to define order. History so far has shown us only two roads to international stability: domination or equilibrium. We do not have the resources for domination, nor is such a course compatible with our values. So we are brought back to a concept maligned in much of America's intellectual history—the balance of power. Of course, it is possible to define the problem away by postulating the absence of clashing interests. I would welcome such an outcome, but find little support for it either in history or in the circumstances we have recently confronted—in the Gulf or in Europe.

The Need for a Balancer

Despite the near unanimity of UN decisions, historians will in all likelihood treat the Gulf crisis as a special case rather than as a watershed. An unusual set of circumstances combined to foster consensus. The Soviet Union, wracked by domestic crises and needing foreign economic assistance, had no stomach for conflict with the United States and had already curtailed their interests in the Middle East. But this does not mean that postwar Soviet objectives in the Middle East will necessarily be identical or even compatible with those of the United States. China, though wary of superpower military action, sought to demonstrate the advantages of practical cooperation despite Tiananmen Square and ideological conflict. For Beijing considers Washington an important partner in China's determination to resist either Soviet or Japanese hegemony in Asia.

The Gulf states and Saudi Arabia saw their very survival at stake and were not much concerned with the principle involved to safeguard their existence. Syria's President Hafez Assad had been in mortal conflict with Saddam Hussein for ten years preceding the Gulf crisis. As for Egypt, the rulers of the Nile competed with the rulers of Mesopotamia for 4,000 years before the doctrine of collective security was invented. The Persian-Arab conflict is of more recent vintage as history is measured in the Middle East; it is only 2,000 years old. This is why after Iraq is sufficiently weakened, Iran will probably continue its historical quest for dominance in the Gulf by pressuring America to leave.

Finally, two special nonrecurring circumstances facilitated the creation of the global alliance. The first was the noxious character of Saddam Hussein. Another aggressor is unlikely to present so unambiguous a challenge.

The second key element was American leadership—symbolized by the extraordinary set of personal relations between President Bush and world leaders. Poignantly, though, American preeminence cannot last. Had Kuwait been invaded two years later, the American defense budget would have declined so as to preclude a massive overseas deployment. Nor can the American economy indefinitely sustain a policy of essentially unilateral global intervention—indeed, we had to seek a subsidy of at least $50 billion to sustain this crisis. Therefore, neither the United States nor foreign nations should treat the concept of a new world order as an institutionalization of recent practices.

The world into which we are moving will be infinitely more complex than cold war. Then, the ideological conflict led to a more or less uniform perception of the threat, at least among the industrial democracies that produce 72 percent of the world's GNP. The military and—for the greater period of those years—technological predominance of the United States also shaped a common military policy. Economically, interdependence moved from slogan to reality.

In the world ahead, ideological challenges will be fewer; the danger of nuclear war with the Soviet Union will be sharply reduced. On the other hand, no one can know how well Soviet command and control arrangements for nuclear weapons will withstand domestic upheaval. Elsewhere, local conflicts will be both more likely and, given modern technology, more lethal. The collapse of the Soviet empire in Eastern Europe and the loosening bonds of the Western Alliance have unleashed nationalist rivalries not seen since World War I. The postcolonial period has spawned fanatical fundamentalist forces very hard for the comfortable, if not smug, industrial democracies to comprehend, much less to master. Economic rivalry among Japan, which is growing into superpower status, the European Community, which is becoming increasingly assertive, and the United States will no longer be restrained by overriding security concerns. The confluence of these elements will characterize the new era as one of turmoil, and will require major adjustments in how we think about international relations.

In the world before us, United States policy makers face a number of imperatives.

• They must recognize that it is not possible to deal with every issue simultaneously. America must be selective, husbanding its resources as well as its credibility. Three levels of threat must be distinguished: those we must be prepared to deal with alone if necessary, those we will deal with only in association with other nations, and those threats that do not sufficiently challenge American interests to justify any military intervention.

• They need to reexamine alliance policy and reallocate responsibility. Countries associated with us must be brought to understand that the United States' armed forces are not a mercenary force-for-hire. The special circumstance of the Persian Gulf left President Bush no choice except a disproportionate assumption of risk by the United States. As a general rule in the future, however, American military forces should be employed only for causes for which we are prepared to pay ourselves. That, in fact, is a good working definition of American national interest.

United States policy makers must recognize that the new world order cannot be built to American specifications. America cannot force-feed a global sense of community where none exists. But it has an opportunity for creating more limited communities based on a genuine sense of shared purpose. This is why perhaps the most creative—if least well known—foreign policy initiative of the

Bush administration is its effort to create a Western Hemispheric
Free Trade Area, beginning with Mexico, Canada, and the
United States.

There is no escaping the irony that our triumph in the cold war
has projected us into a world where we must operate by maxima
that historically have made Americans uncomfortable. To many
Americans, the most objectionable feature of the balance of power
is its apparent moral neutrality. For the balance of power is concerned above all with preventing one power or group of powers
from achieving hegemony. Winston Churchill described it:

> The policy of England takes no account of which nation it is that seeks the
> overlordship of Europe. It is concerned solely with whoever is the stron-
> gest or the potentially dominating tyrant. It is a law of public policy which
> we are following, and not a mere expedient dictated by accidental cir-
> cumstances of likes or dislikes. . . .

Restoring Balance in the Gulf

To that end, ironically, maintaining equilibrium in the Gulf
requires us to navigate between a solution that leaves Iraq too
strong and an outcome that would leave Iraq too weak. The tragedy of the Kurds demonstrates just how hard it is to so navigate.
But, after all, one of the causes of the present crisis is the one-sided
way the Western nations rushed to the defense of Iraq in its war
against Iran, forgetting that if Iran was excessively weakened Iraq
might become the next aggressor.

It would be ironic if another bout of tunnel vision produced an
Iraq so weak that its neighbors, especially Iran, sought to refill the
vacuum.

As the UN peace terms stipulate, we should take care that Scud
missiles are not reintroduced. We should prevent Iraq from im-
porting high-technology equipment, including high-performance
aircraft with long ranges, and from reacquiring the means to manufacture biological and nuclear weapons. However, Iraq's capacity to defend itself with conventional weapons against ground attack from its neighbors would in the long run not be a threat to
stability but a contribution to it.

In the Gulf, the new balance of power cannot be based on the permanent presence of American ground forces. This was the weakness of diplomatic solutions that would have kept Iraq's military preponderance intact. The cultural gap between even the best-behaved American troops and the local population is unbridgeable. A major Western ground force in the area would inevitably become the target of radical and nationalist agitation. After a brief period, American ground forces would be considered foreign intruders. There would be a repetition of our experience in Lebanon, including terrorism and sabotage. American ground forces in the area should be withdrawn after victory; residual forces should be stationed beyond the horizon—at sea or perhaps at a few remote air bases.

Military equilibrium, however, cannot be the sole aim of American policy in the Gulf. It is essential that America learn to become less dependent on oil and generate a viable energy program. We cannot suffer through an energy crisis every decade. We should stress conservation and develop alternative sources of energy, avoiding the self-indulgent attitudes of the 1980s, when plentiful oil caused the search for alternative energy sources to be largely abandoned.

We must also remember the possibility of renewed Soviet designs on the region. For the time being, domestic problems keep the Soviets from running any significant foreign risks. But 200 years of Russian expansionism toward the Gulf indicate a certain proclivity. And this drive may be compounded as Moscow's preoccupation with its more than 50 million Muslim citizens grows. After some domestic equilibrium is restored, the Kremlin might become more active in the Middle East—especially in Iran, Iraq, Pakistan, and Turkey, which border the Soviet Union. The intensity of that thrust will depend on internal developments within the Soviet Union. If the Muslim republics remain Soviet, Moscow will be wary of Muslim radicalism lest it inflame its own Muslim population. But if the Muslim republics break off and become independent, Moscow may seek favor in the breakaway states by embracing Islamic radicalism—especially if the Muslim world turns more extremist.

Finally, and perhaps most importantly, a new balance of power will revive prospects for progress on the Arab-Israeli conflict. A peace process dominated by Saddam Hussein, or heavily influenced by him, would have been a debacle. For it would have taught the lesson that radicalism, terrorism, and force are the road to diplomatic progress in the Middle East. This is why President Bush was right in resisting the linkage of the Kuwait and Palestinian problems.

Yet the peace process as currently conceived is likely to lead to a dead end. The Arab-Israeli problem is usually stated as a negotiating issue: how to convene an international conference that returns Israel to the 1967 border, defines a new status for Jerusalem, induces the Arabs to "accept" Israel, and provides international guarantees for the resulting arrangements. I have grave doubts about every one of these propositions.

The United States would be totally isolated at such an international forum; instead of being a mediator, it would be maneuvered into the role of Israel's lawyer. Worse, the formula would force each side to accept something they find unbearably difficult: for the Israelis, it is a Palestinian state; and for the Arabs, it is the Israeli state. How, then, does one define "credible guarantees"? Even in the case of Kuwait, where there was unanimous international support for the victim (something that would be inconceivable for Israel), it took six months to organize resistance while the country was looted and pillaged and the population expelled.

I know of no conflict between Arab nations—let alone between the Arabs and Israel—that has ever been resolved by the method suggested for the Palestinian issue: namely, with one conclusive negotiation resulting in a legal document intended to last for all time.

A revived peace process should begin by redefining the objectives. A final settlement at this moment seems a legalistic mirage. On the other hand, the status quo will sooner or later sound the death knell for moderates on all sides. As it is, too many Israelis consider the peace process a one-sided means to gain acceptance without sacrifice. They are unwilling to give up any occupied territory, or will do so only if de facto Israeli control is maintained. Too many Arabs, especially in the PLO (Palestine Liberation Organization), see in the Middle East a replay of Vietnam, where peace talks were used to soften up the opponent for escalating pressures leading to his ultimate collapse.

An interim solution might seek to introduce the moderate Arab governments, fresh from the victory over Iraq, as a buffer between Israel and the PLO. It might reduce the amount of territory Israel is asked to give up in return for something less than formal peace.

The aftermath of the allied victory over Iraq offers a perhaps never-to-recur opportunity. Moderate Arab states are disillusioned with the PLO, which in effect has backed Iraq. They are also dismayed by the fact that the PLO has never unambiguously dissociated itself even from terrorism aimed at the moderate Arabs. As a result, these governments may no longer be prepared to give the PLO a veto over their actions.

As for Israel, it must avoid two possible nightmares. If it insists on holding onto every square inch of occupied territory, it could suffer the fate of South Africa and find itself ostracized, and even ultimately under UN sanctions. On the other hand, if it follows the maxims of conventional wisdom and gives up all the occupied territories, it runs the risk of winding up like Lebanon, gradually squeezed to the point of obliteration. For its own sake, Israel must find a middle way. And there is no better moment to do that than when its most dangerous enemy has been defeated.

Dealing with the Soviet Union

The end of the cold war permitted the West to stop treating the Soviet Union as a permanent adversary; the recent return to autocracy in the Soviet Union should cause us to abandon the illusion of considering it a permanent partner. The task now is to find a method for dealing with it as a major power with sometimes compatible and occasionally clashing interests, promoting our basic values and giving new impetus to reconstructing the historic Europe.

No outcome of the current conflict in the Soviet Union is likely to be clear-cut, and the country will probably experience all three possibilities in succession—disintegration followed by attempted repression and, failing that, a gradual drift toward confederation of at least some of the key republics.

Since the eighteenth century, the Russian monolithic state has been pressing against its border as Russian armies have invaded Europe at least a dozen times in pursuit of a variety of causes. Now, all foreseeable Soviet outcomes will reduce for a considerable time that threat that has been hanging over the heads of all of Russia's neighbors since the time of Peter the Great.

The weakening of the central authority of America's principal strategic rival is certainly a short-term geopolitical advantage. At the same time, a collapse of the Soviet Union would produce dangers of its own. Almost all the Soviet republics contain large, unhappy minorities. Civil war could trigger mass migration into the fragile new democracies of Eastern Europe or into adjoining countries of the Middle East. Repression could spill over into military actions against neighboring territories. And who in the end will control the Soviet military forces, especially the nuclear forces? What will be the legal status of existing agreements with the Soviet Union?

Moreover, Russia's historical role in preventing hegemony in Europe (even while, at times, itself seeking it) must also be recognized. The defeats of Napoleon, of Imperial Germany, and of Hitler would have been impossible without Russian help. Thus Russia faces us with a paradox. When monolithic, it threatens domination; but if impotent, it threatens disequilibrium.

That paradox imposes on us the need to safeguard essential national interests even in relations with states that do not share our fundamental values. But there need to be criteria distinguishing the legitimate and moral pursuit of the national interest from opportunistic collaboration with tyranny and encouragement of it.

The following principles seem to me crucial:

(1) We must stop basing policy on Soviet personalities. We know too little of Soviet dynamics and even less about how to affect them to make strengthening any leader a cardinal principle of Western policy. Focusing relations on balancing fundamental interests rather than on psychological speculation will in fact bring greater stability to the relationship.

(2) The Western security interest in the Soviet Union is its peaceful conduct outside its borders. The moral objective of the West is compatible domestic institutions. What we need is a defi-

nition of coexistence and an agenda for its achievement even as we disapprove of some Soviet domestic actions. Coexistence should not be lightly abandoned. But we should recognize that it is based on self-interest and not delude ourselves into believing that it is a means to help Gorbachev promote democracy inside the Soviet Union.

(3) An analysis must be made of those areas of common action that are necessary for a structure of peace and those that are undertaken to promote democratic values. The latter—including economic aid—are subject to modifications if Soviet internal conduct becomes too offensive. In any event economic aid should generally be given for political and economic, not psychological, reasons except in periods of humanitarian emergency. It is sure to be wasted without appropriate economic reforms.

(4) On the issue of self-determination, the United States needs to stick to its historic position with respect to the independence of the Baltic states. The situation is more complex with respect to the other republics, especially in the Caucasus, where different ethnic populations have been mixed over centuries and intercommunal violence is a permanent threat. On the other hand, Soviet leaders must understand that even when we continue to deal with them on the security agenda, other areas of cooperation are narrowed by the convictions of our people should Moscow's conduct offend America's deepest values.

(5) The changes in Moscow should recall to the West the importance of strengthening the ties within the Atlantic area and above all between Eastern and Western Europe. While the Soviet Union is dealing with its internal problems, the West should give the highest priority to reestablishing as rapidly as possible the historic Europe. Eastern Europe—especially Hungary, Poland, and Czechoslovakia—should be given the opportunity to join the West European political and economic system on an urgent basis.

The West is presently in danger of neglecting the countries of Eastern Europe whose successful struggle for freedom inspired us only yesterday. Two steps are needed. First, the West—and especially Western Europe—must move quickly to integrate Eastern Europe into the European Community and other Atlantic institutions (with the exception of NATO). Second, we must give Eastern

Europe an economic breathing space. As a step in that direction, the European Community should take immediate steps to open its markets to East European agricultural products.

Soviet turmoil casts doubt on the expectation that democracy and market economics produce peaceful Soviet conduct. Nevertheless, if the Soviet Union transforms itself from a cause to a nation, and if the United States learns to deal with it on a nonideological basis, prudence may bring about what idealism precludes at the moment—a Soviet Union strong enough to defend itself but not so centralized as to be able to conduct geopolitical offensives; sufficiently cohesive to fulfill aspiration truly common to all its peoples but not subject to absolutist rulers manipulating foreign dangers and embarking on international proselytizing missions.

A policy based on balancing power knows few permanent enemies and few permanent friends. In the current Gulf crisis it would avoid branding Iraq as forever beyond the pale. Rather, it would seek to balance rivalries as old as history by striving for an equilibrium between Iraq, Iran, Syria, and other regional powers. In Northeast Asia it would seek to maintain equilibrium between China, Japan, and the Soviet Union. In Europe, where the old balance has collapsed, the shape of its successor will depend on the outcome of the Soviet Union's internal struggles, especially on the Soviet capacity to continue its historic role in Europe.

These balances all need a balancer—a role the United States can no longer play entirely by itself and in some circumstances may not choose to exercise at all. But it needs criteria to establish priorities.

It is a paradox that no nation is in a better position to contribute to a new world order than the United States: it is domestically cohesive, its economy is less vulnerable to outside forces, its military capacity for the foreseeable future is still the world's largest and most effective. Our challenge is the price of success: triumph in the cold war has produced a world requiring adjustment of traditional concepts. But the price of success is one for which most other nations would envy us.

8C

A New Concert for Europe

CHARLES A. KUPCHAN AND
CLIFFORD A. KUPCHAN

This chapter argues that erecting a collective security structure in the new Europe is both viable and desirable.[1] The conditions necessary for a collective security organization to form and function successfully are now present. Such a transition is not only possible, but also preferable; it would provide a more stable—that is, less war-prone—international environment. We propose that a new concert based collective security organization for Europe be erected. Concert based collective security relies on a small group of major powers to guide the operation of a region-wide security structure. In laying out our design for a concert based organization, we draw on the nineteenth-century Concert of Europe.

CHARLES A. KUPCHAN is assistant professor of politics at Princeton University. He is the author of *The Persian Gulf and the West—The Dilemmas of Security*, *The Vulnerability of Empire*, and numerous articles and reviews. In 1990 Professor Kupchan was a visiting scholar at the Institute of War and Peace Studies, Columbia University.
CLIFFORD A. KUPCHAN, A Ph.D. candidate at Columbia University, is currently a policy analyst in Washington, D.C. He is the author of articles and reviews on security affairs.

We begin by defining collective security, and then show that the conditions necessary for a collective security organization to function successfully are present in today's Europe. The chapter next examines the different types of structures that fall within the collective security family and argues that a concert is the most practicable form of collective security given current international conditions. The chapter then describes how a new concert of Europe would work today. We argue that the Conference on Security and Cooperation in Europe (CSCE) should be recast to function as a concert based collective security organization. A security group of major powers—the United States, the Soviet Union, France, Britain, and Germany—would guide the operation of a pan-European security structure. Finally, the chapter examines the implications of our proposal for U.S. foreign policy.

Why Collective Security Can Work in the New Europe

Collective security rests on the single notion of all against one. Participation in a collective security organization entails a commitment by each member to join a coalition to confront any aggressor with opposing preponderant strength. The underlying logic of collective security is twofold. First, the balancing mechanisms that operate under collective security should prevent war and stop aggression far more effectively than the balancing mechanisms that operate in a balance-of-power setting. In a balance-of-power setting, deterrence operates because states confront each other with relatively equal military capability. At least in theory, collective security makes for more robust deterrence by ensuring that aggressors will be met with an opposing coalition that has preponderant rather than merely equivalent strength. Second, a collective security organization, by institutionalizing the notion of all against one, contributes to the creation of an international setting in which stability emerges through cooperation rather than through competition. Because states believe that they will be met with overwhelming force if they aggress, and because they believe that other states will cooperate with them in resisting aggression, collective security mitigates the rivalry and hostility of a self-help world.

Three conditions must be present if a collective security organization is to take shape and function effectively.[2] The first condition is that no single state can be so powerful that even the most robust opposing coalition would be unable to marshal preponderant force against it. This condition is clearly met in today's Europe. No single European power is so militarily strong that an opposing coalition of all other states would fail to present a formidable obstacle to aggression. In addition, nuclear weapons enhance the deterrent effect associated with the notion of all against one. An aggressor would face the prospect not only of conventional defeat, but also of nuclear devastation.

The second condition is that the major powers of the day must have fundamentally compatible views of what constitutes a stable and acceptable international order. There can be no revisionist power, no state intent on overturning the international order for either ideological or power related reasons. The radical change in Soviet foreign policy orchestrated by Mikhail Gorbachev means that all major powers are coming to hold a common view of what constitutes an acceptable status quo. Despite some backsliding, the broad contours of Soviet foreign policy remain compatible with the Western vision of a stable international order. The Soviets have unilaterally withdrawn troops from Eastern Europe, agreed to allow a unified Germany to enter the North Atlantic Treaty Organization (NATO), effectively renounced their support for "liberation movements" in the Third World, and stood firmly behind the international coalition that drove Iraq from Kuwait. They have strongly endorsed international institutions: the Soviets have become firm supporters of the United Nations, obtained observer status in the General Agreement on Tariffs and Trade, and expressed interest in participating in the World Bank and the International Monetary Fund.

Change in Soviet thinking about an acceptable international order is not only profound, but also unlikely to be reversed. Market reform and stabilization of the economy require a peaceful international environment: the Soviet economic crisis is so dire that the commitment to lowering defense spending and attracting foreign capital is unlikely to change regardless of the fate of Gorbachev. The range of policy options before the Soviet leadership makes highly unlikely, at least in the near term, a return to an aggressive and ideologically driven foreign policy. While the Soviets and the Western powers still need to resolve outstanding issues, profound change in the Soviet Union suggests that the major powers now agree on the essential features of a desirable international order.

The (third) condition is that the major powers must "enjoy a minimum of political solidarity and moral community."[3] Elites must share awareness of an international community, the preservation of which furthers long-term national interests. In this sense, national self-interest becomes equated with, but not subjugated to, the welfare and stability of that international community. It is this minimum level of trust that allows states to pass up opportunities for short-term gain and to exercise restraint under the assumption that others will do the same. This condition is becoming increasingly present in today's Europe, as exemplified by the growing practice of reciprocity—the making of mutual concessions. Mutual concessions have emerged on a broad range of issues. The Soviets have made deep cuts in conventional forces and have begun to withdraw troops from Eastern Europe. Although these actions initially occurred on a unilateral basis, the Western powers eventually reciprocated by proposing further mutual cuts in force levels and exercising restraint in reacting to ethnic crises within the Soviet Union. Washington and European capitals have deliberately avoided pressuring Moscow over its treatment of ethnic uprisings in the Baltic republics, Azerbaijan, and Georgia. Soviet approval of NATO membership for a unified Germany was clearly linked to Western offers of economic aid to the Soviet Union. In December 1990 the United States approved a billion dollars in loans to the Soviet Union, explicitly linking U.S. assistance to a relaxation in Moscow's emigration policy. This increasing reciprocity has furthered the process of ending the cold war and fostering an international community conducive to collective security.

The Case for Concert Based
Collective Security

Collective security organizations can take many different institutional forms along a continuum ranging from ideal collective security to concerts. These organizations vary as to number of members, geographic scope, and the nature of the commitment to collective action. What Inis Claude calls ideal collective security entails participation of all states of the world, covers all regions of the world, and involves a legally binding and codified commitment on the part of all members to respond to aggression whenever and wherever it might occur.[4] An ideal collective security organization assumes a very high degree of congruent interest among its members. Interstate rivalry and power politics are effectively eliminated. Balancing behavior occurs only in response to aggression.

A concert lies at the other end of the continuum; it represents the most attenuated form of collective security. Though predicated on the notion of all against one, membership in a concert is restricted to the great powers of the day. A small group of major powers agrees to work together to resist aggression; they meet on a regular basis to monitor events and, if necessary, to orchestrate collective initiatives. A concert's geographic scope is flexible. Members can choose to focus on a specific region or regions, or to combat aggression on a global basis. Finally, a concert entails no binding or codified commitments to collective action. Rather, decisions are taken through informal negotiations, through the emergence of a consensus. The flexibility and informality of a concert allow the structure to retain an ongoing undercurrent of balancing behavior among the major powers. Though a concert is predicated upon the assumption that its members share compatible views of a stable international order, it allows for subtle jockeying and competition to take place among them. Power politics is not completely eliminated; members may turn to internal mobilization and coalition formation to pursue divergent interests. But the cooperative framework of a concert, and its members' concern about preserving peace, prevent such balancing from escalating to overt hostility and conflict.

Our preference for a concert based system rests on both historical and pragmatic considerations. In historical terms, the Concert of Europe enjoyed far more success in preserving peace than did either the League of Nations or the United Nations, organizations that more closely approximate ideal collective security. The concert kept the peace for forty years in the absence of bipolarity and nuclear weapons—the two factors that conventional wisdom credits with preserving stability since 1945. It was established by Europe's major powers at the close of the Napoleonic Wars (1815) and lasted until the outbreak of the Crimean War in 1854. The concert was predicated upon the understanding that each of the members—Britain, France, Prussia, Russia, and Austria—would honor the territorial settlement reached at the Congress of Vienna in 1815. Members agreed to defend the territorial status quo, or to allow change only when they reached a consensus to do so. Decisions to engage in collective action were taken through informal negotiations. Furthermore, mechanisms for implementing collective action were left unstipulated. Despite, or, more accurately, *because* of its informality, members were able to resort regularly to diplomatic initiatives, military threats, and military action to preserve peace in Europe.

Our assertion that a concert is the most practicable form of collective security stems from three considerations. First, as the difficulties involved in drafting the League Covenant and the UN Charter demonstrated, states are very reluctant to join organizations that entail binding commitments to collective action; simply put, they fear such commitments entail an unacceptable loss of sovereignty. The United States in fact refused to participate in the League of Nations largely because of congressional concern about taking on the obligations specified in the covenant. A concert's flexibility and informality circumvent these problems and thus ensure wide participation. Second, a concert, because it endows the major powers with prime responsibility for managing security affairs, more realistically reflects power realities than other types of collective security organizations. Europe's major powers are not about to devolve to an unwieldy body of thirty-four nations responsibility for core-level security issues. Third, because a concert retains an undercurrent of subtle jockeying and competition among its members, it is better suited to a strategic landscape that

is still very much in flux. While Gorbachev's dramatic reorientation of Soviet foreign policy is unlikely to be reversed, the Western
powers must remain on guard for a resurgence of aggressive behavior on the part of the Soviet Union.

A concert has one clear disadvantage: its exclusivity. As it operated during the nineteenth century, the concert acted as a great
power club, effectively ignoring, and at times violating, the concerns of Europe's smaller powers. In a normative sense, this attribute compromises the collective nature of the enterprise of collective security. While a concert's exclusivity may have been
politically acceptable—or, perhaps, tolerable—in the nineteenth
century, it would not be so today. While major powers still have
more influence than minor powers in shaping events, international
relations have, at least to some extent, been democratized.

Our solution to this political obstacle is to create a hybrid structure—one that combines the representative breadth of ideal collective security with the effectiveness and practicality of a concert.
We call such a structure a concert based collective security organization. An inner group of Europe's major powers would guide the
operation of a region-wide security structure. A concert based collective security organization would capitalize upon the cooperative potential of today's international setting without violating
power realities or entailing undue risks.

A New Concert for Europe

Four criteria shape our proposal for a new European collective
security organization. First, the structure of the organization
should allow effective leadership and reflect current power realities. Effectively, this means that the body should be guided by
Europe's major powers. Second, the body should develop mechanisms, based on the notion of all against one, for deterring and
resisting aggression. It should also develop long-term prophylactic
measures for dampening the domestic sources of expansionist behavior. Militarism, autocratic rule, and hypernationalism have
played a key role in creating states intent on pursuing policies of
forceful expansion. Third, the body should avoid codified commitments to collective action and allow members the flexibility to

tailor their responses to specific challenges as they arise. Fourth, the body should include all European states and thus serve as a vehicle for building a pan-European consensus and promoting cooperation.

What might a new collective security structure for Europe look like? A framework for this structure already exists: the Conference on Security and Cooperation in Europe. Founded in 1975 with all European countries (except Albania) plus the United States and Canada as members, CSCE has dealt with a host of issues: political-military confidence-building measures; human rights; and scientific, cultural, and educational cooperation.[5] Because CSCE enjoys legitimacy and popularity, especially in Eastern Europe and the Soviet Union where a new institution is most needed, it is the ideal venue for a new security structure. In its present form, however, CSCE is too unwieldy to serve as an effective security structure. Each of its thirty-four members has an equal vote and any action requires unanimity. It is wholly unrealistic to assume that the major powers would devolve to such a body responsibility for managing a new European security order. To adhere to the unanimity rule would ensure CSCE only a marginal role in shaping a new Europe. By recasting CSCE along the lines of a concert, however, the body can be turned into a viable collective security structure.

A new security system must find a way of balancing the need to reflect power realities with the need to foster consensus among the states of Europe. We therefore propose a two-tiered design for CSCE: a security group consisting principally of Europe's major powers, with jurisdiction over core-level security issues; and the full thirty-four-member body, with jurisdiction over a host of other security-relevant matters. The security group would deal with issues that have direct and immediate bearing on national security, such as arms control, territorial boundaries, and peace-keeping. The strong, efficient leadership that only a small group can provide is essential in these core areas if the efforts to build a collective security organization for Europe are to come to fruition. In dealing with these core-level issues, the security group would take into consideration, but not be bound by, the interests expressed by each of CSCE's members. The full body, while it would indeed have input into core-level security matters, would have exclusive jurisdiction over the following types of issues: enhancing confidence and security-building measures (CSBMs), suppressing hypernationalism, promoting democratic institutions, and monitoring human rights. On these matters, CSCE would retain its unanimity rule; CSCE's traditional role as a consensus builder would continue.

The Security Group

The new organization should evolve around a concert of five major powers: the United States, the Soviet Union, Britain, France, and Germany. The big five would serve as a core security group within CSCE, bringing the body more into line with current power realities and facilitating its ability to act in a timely and coordinated fashion. A limited number of other CSCE members should join the security group on a rotating basis to ensure input from Europe's smaller countries. We envisage three such members, selection occurring on a regional basis so that the concerns of countries in northern, eastern, and southern Europe are represented. As in any concert, the security group would have no explicit decision-making rules or binding contracts of collective action to enforce commitments to the notion of all against one.

During its initial phase of five to ten years, the security group and NATO should coexist. NATO has certainly served well and should remain in place until a workable alternative exists. The near-term strategy would thus be two-track: relying on NATO while nurturing a new pan-European institution. Should all go well and the Soviet Union maintain nonthreatening and cooperative foreign policies, NATO would cede increasing responsibility to the security group. The Warsaw Pact already having disappeared, the security group would become the natural forum to oversee continent-wide security issues. This arrangement presents minimal risk to NATO members because if this new security structure fails to develop, NATO can reassert control over European security; the NATO command structure would remain ready to provide collective defense to its members. Furthermore, because the security group would operate as a concert, retaining an undercurrent of balancing behavior, NATO members would remain watchful for signs of renewed aggressive intent in the Soviet Union. Weapons procurement and operational planning would remain tied, to an appropriate extent, to Soviet behavior and capabilities; concerts do not breed naiveté. The security group should develop the following mechanisms to preserve stability in Europe:

Arms Control Negotiation and Verification. Given the demise of the Warsaw Pact, the security group would serve as a natural body to oversee the process of arms control in Europe. Its concert-like structure would allow the United States and the Soviet Union to remain the central parties in negotiations on both nuclear and conventional reductions, but the process would be more open to other European powers. The security group should also establish a permanent verification center. The Treaty on Conventional Armed Forces in Europe (CFE) provides for the creation of a Joint Consultative Group (JCG) to serve as a forum in which participating nations could file complaints regarding compliance. The JCG could be turned into a permanent verification and monitoring center for Europe, pooling information that would be available to all CSCE members. Devolving responsibility for verification and monitoring of arms control agreements to a multinational body would depoliticize the process and make it far less susceptible to the vicissitudes of domestic political change.

Prevention of Nuclear Proliferation. The security group should strengthen mechanisms for preventing nuclear proliferation. The presence of nuclear weapons in Europe, provided they continue to be based in an invulnerable manner, would serve to increase the peaceful effects of a concert. These weapons work with, not against, the underlying logic of a concert: they induce caution, minimize the chance that misperception of military capability will lead to deterrence failures, and reinforce the deterrent effects associated with the notion of all against one. A concert based structure would not, however, rely on nuclear weapons to preserve peace in Europe. It would preserve stability primarily through the stabilizing effects of collective security. Furthermore, a collective security structure, by dampening the insecurity that many non-nuclear states may feel in the new Europe, would diminish the incentives of these states to acquire nuclear weapons. The reduced demand for nuclear weapons, current political opposition to proliferation, and the extreme dangers inherent in the spread of nuclear capability make the prevention of proliferation an important task for the security group.

Peacekeeping/Joint Action. Under a peacekeeping mandate, the security group would undertake joint diplomatic and military initiatives. Such actions could range from joint declarations of policy to joint recognition of newly independent states to coordinated peacekeeping activities. The establishment of joint criteria for diplomatic recognition of new states could be crucial, given the growing momentum of independence movements in the Soviet Union and Yugoslavia. Similarly, the demand for peacekeeping in Europe is likely to be related to border conflicts arising from national and ethnic rivalries. Forces might be needed to prevent hostilities, to circumscribe fighting, or to enforce a ceasefire.

Areas of Special Interest. Despite the waning of the cold war, the major powers continue to view certain regions, for geopolitical and historical reasons, as of special importance. The security group should recognize that certain powers will retain areas of special interest and it should delineate states' rights and obligations in contested areas. Such rights and obligations will exist whether explicitly recognized or not; explicit recognition decreases the chances of misunderstanding. Michael Howard, for example, has argued that the Western powers must accept that the Soviet Union has "a certain *droit de regard* in Eastern Europe.[6] The major powers should similarly recognize Germany's prominent interests in Central Europe.

Fencing Off Regional Conflict. The end of the cold war will by no means lead to the end of conflict in the Third World. The security group should ensure that peripheral conflicts are fenced off or resolved and not allowed to jeopardize cooperative efforts in Europe. The United States and the Soviet Union already have taken steps in this direction. In Nicaragua, the superpowers cooperated to encourage free elections, and similar arrangements may soon be extended to other areas in Central America. In areas where the legacy of the cold war remains more prominent—such as Angola, Ethiopia, and Afghanistan—tensions are more fenced off than during the 1980s. The powers could further dampen rivalry in the periphery by agreeing to strict "rules of the game" governing engagement in third areas.

The Full Body

While the security group would be able to act on core-level security issues without the approval of each CSCE member, it would continuously consult with the full body in reaching decisions. Matters other than core-level security issues would fall under the jurisdiction of the full body. CSCE's traditional mandate would remain fully intact. The thirty-four would continue to strengthen CSBMs through the existing Conflict Prevention Center (CPC) and would protect human rights in member states. In addition, the full body should oversee the task of developing and implementing prophylactic measures to prevent the emergence of aggressor states. In dealing with these matters, CSCE would maintain its current unanimity rule.

Some may object that this division of labor—and a concert based structure more generally—tramples on the rights of Europe's smaller powers. Establishing a CSCE security group that functions as a concert indeed endows the major powers with predominant influence in Europe. Yet these states have such influence de facto from their dominant economic and military capability. In effect, concert-like behavior has characterized European diplomacy for much of the postwar era. Germany, France, and Britain dominate the European Community (EC). The United States, Germany, and Britain effectively call the shots in NATO. A concert structure only formalizes these relationships. Furthermore, the creation of a security group would in fact broaden European input into the formation of policy; the two countries that have dominated the shaping of Europe's strategic landscape—the United States and the Soviet Union—would have to make more room for France, Britain, and Germany. Our proposal leaves to the full body jurisdiction over all security-relevant issues covered by CSCE's current mandate. It also gives the thirty-four member countries input into the full range of core-level security issues that now lie outside CSCE's purview. In addition, by transforming CSCE into an effective pan-European security organization, a concert based structure strengthens the voices of East European countries, which are currently unattached to any meaningful security organization.

The full body should fulfill its tasks through the following mechanisms:

Conflict Management. CSCE should continue to develop two procedures for conflict management: examination of unusual military activity and arbitration through third parties. Current procedures within the CPC give all CSCE members the right to request explanation of unusual military activities within forty-eight hours of observation. If the party is unsatisfied with the response, it can refer the matter to a meeting of concerned states. Current proposals for third-party arbitration call for a group of experts to serve as fact finders and to make recommendations for resolving disputes. Many CSCE members also favor the identification of a typology of disputes, certain classes of which would be subject to mandatory binding arbitration.

Sharing of Military Information. The full body should oversee and expand the CPC's efforts to increase transparency and encourage contact between national military establishments. The widespread and symmetrical provision of military information is crucial to the operation of a collective security organization and underlies many of its advantages. The CPC is currently working on improving the dissemination of information on forces-in-being, new weapons deployments, and defense budgets. It is also constructing a new communications network, strengthening provisions for foreign observers to be present at national military maneuvers, and developing plans for new exchanges between military establishments.

The Suppression of Hypernationalism and the Promotion of Democracy. The full body should establish two permanent commissions to oversee the task of developing and implementing prophylactic measures to prevent aggression. The Commission on Political Development (CPD) would focus on the suppression of hypernationalism. History provides ample demonstration of the potentially disastrous consequences associated with unchecked nationalism. The Commission on Democracy (COD) would concentrate on promoting democratic institutions and values. As we mention above, the spread of democracy will contribute to the preservation of peace in Europe; democracies tend not to go to war with each other.[7] It is no coincidence that the three principal aggressor states of the twentieth century were ruled by essentially autocratic governments.

The Commission on Political Development can contribute to the suppression of hypernationalism through three principal mechanisms. First, the CPD can watch carefully to ensure that national elites do not use hypernationalist propaganda as a domestic tool. It should expose those caught doing so, single them out for censure, and pressure them to cease by widely circulating a "blacklist" of irresponsible leaders. Second, efforts to protect the rights of foreign journalists would play an important role in making local elites more accountable for their actions and rhetoric. At the same time, CPD should take steps to ensure that a free domestic press thrives in all member states. The CPD should also become involved in local radio and television programing, in terms of both monitoring broadcasts and countering nationalistic propaganda through its own broadcasts. Third, the CPD can monitor the education system in member states. It is critical that the textbooks used in primary and secondary education present an accurate account of national history. CSCE should also continue to encourage freedom of access to national archives for all scholars, both foreign and national. CSCE should set forth guidelines in each of these three areas, and access to European development funds should be made contingent upon compliance with these guidelines.

The Commission on Democracy, which would incorporate the existing Office of Free Elections (OFE), can take several steps to promote the spread of democracy. In addition to fulfilling the OFE's current tasks of ensuring that national elections are open to foreign observers and disseminating results, the COD could open branches in all member countries to support representative institutions and democratic values. Based on the notion that the free flow of ideas undermines authoritarian regimes, the COD should fan the spread of the information revolution. It should help to ensure that all political groups have access to photocopiers, fax machines, and computers. The College of Europe in Bruges would be a natural location for COD activities in the education field. Students from leading national universities could come to Bruges to study democratic theory and pan-European political processes.

Implications for U.S. Policy

U.S. participation is crucial to the successful functioning of a collective security organization in the new Europe. The United States remains the world's leading military power. The ability to deploy this military capability in Europe in relatively short order is still needed to balance against Soviet strength and to make credible the notion that any aggressor will be met with an opposing coalition of preponderant strength. As the crisis in the Persian Gulf demonstrated, U.S. political leadership is also needed to facilitate policy coordination among the major powers. The Soviet Union cannot provide such leadership in Europe; it is too preoccupied with domestic problems and its future is too uncertain. Germany, too, must address a pressing domestic agenda—consolidating unification—before it can play a leading role in shaping European security affairs. Britain is still tentative about full participation in pan-European processes, and France arguably lacks the military and political clout to take the lead in forging a new security structure.

Though U.S. leadership may be needed by default, it is also in the interests of the United States to continue to play a very prominent role in European security. The basic tenets of containment still ring true: should any single power come to dominate the power centers of Eurasia, U.S. national security would be gravely threatened. The United States must therefore continue to ensure that Eurasia's centers of industrial and military capability remain independent. Even a relatively small U.S. presence would be adequate to serve as a tripwire and provide extended deterrence in

Europe. A U.S. presence also offers Washington continued political influence on the continent. Because the United States is a member of CSCE and is not a member of the European Community or the Western European Union—other candidates for a pan-European security structure—only CSCE offers the opportunity for continued American involvement. The complete withdrawal of U.S. troops and the formation of a Europe-only security structure would indeed lead to a sharp decline in U.S. influence in European affairs.

Concert based collective security provides a structure through which the United States can stay directly involved in Europe, but at the same time reduce the political and economic costs that accompany such involvement. A more equal sharing of political responsibilities under the auspices of CSCE will reduce opposition within Europe to a continued U.S. presence. A more equal sharing of defense burdens will help to disarm opposition within the United States to the continued deployment of U.S. troops in Europe. Furthermore, deterrence based on collective security would allow all parties to make major reductions in defense spending.

U.S. force requirements would be predicated upon the assumption that a self-sustaining fighting force—roughly 100,000 troops—needs to be permanently deployed in Europe. In order to make credible the commitment to defend third parties against aggression, this force would have to retain some offensive capability, including intratheater lift. But U.S. forces would be structured and sized primarily for defensive missions. Troops and equipment stationed in Europe would be devoted primarily to air defense, close-air support, and antitank operations. Offensive capabilities—tanks, deep-strike aircraft, and heavy mobile artillery—could be substantially reduced. Nevertheless, the United States would have to retain the capability to bring significant force to bear on the European continent on relatively short notice. Light and heavy divisions—and the lift needed to transport them to Europe—should remain readily available. Leaving a sizable U.S. presence of troops and equipment on the continent even after the devolution of NATO's functions to CSCE would be crucial to the successful operation of a new collective security structure. Members must remain willing and able to uphold their commitment to resist aggression.

Conclusions

We have developed two main arguments to show that concert based collective security can best preserve peace in the post–cold war Europe. First, we have shown that the conditions necessary for a collective security organization to form and function successfully are present. Second, we have shown that concert based collective security is the most appropriate and practicable form of collective security for today's Europe. Accordingly, we have argued that CSCE should be recast to function as a concert based collective security organization. We have laid out mechanisms through which this body can preserve peace in Europe and shown why it is in the interests of the United States to help bring this vision to fruition.

In order to minimize the risk that our proposal presents to the Western alliance, we recommend that NATO and a recast CSCE coexist until political and economic conditions in the Soviet Union stabilize. Should the Soviet Union again pursue an aggressive for-eign policy, collective security would become unfeasible and NATO would reassert control over European security. On the other hand, if Soviet foreign policy continues on its current trajec-tory, NATO would gradually cede more security functions to CSCE. The eventual endpoint would involve the dismantling of NATO and the transformation of CSCE into an effective and viable collective security structure built around a small and work-able concert of the big five.

This proposal is grounded in historical precedent, would suc-ceed in bringing the European order more into line with the changing strategic landscape, and would provide a more stable and peaceful international environment. Because the world is at a unique historical juncture, it is necessary to rely on the past to think creatively about the future, and to take the initiative in forg-ing a new European order.

ideal col sec → Concert col sec ← alliance

Notes

[1] For a more detailed exposition of the arguments presented in this chapter, see Kupchan and Kupchan (1991).

[2] Thompson (1953), pp. 758–762.

[3] Thompson (1953), p. 761.

[4] Claude (1962), pp. 110, 168.

[5] For a historical overview of CSCE, see Maresca (1985). For a description of CSCE's current institutional structure, see CSCE "Charter of Paris" (1990).

[6] Howard (1990), p. 103.

[7] Doyle (1986).

8D

Practical Internationalism

RICHARD N. GARDNER

We are all groping for a unifying concept to define what American foreign policy should be in the post–cold war, post–Gulf War world. This is no easy task, given the multiplicity of the problems we face in this new world situation and the difficulty of predicting what the future holds in store. The best that this writer can come up with is the concept of "practical internationalism."

"Practical internationalism" is a concept that seeks to avoid the extremes of "come home America" isolationism, global unilateral-

RICHARD N. GARDNER is the Henry L. Moses Professor of Law and International Organization at Columbia University Law School and of counsel to the law firm of Coudert Brothers. He served as deputy assistant secretary of state for international organization affairs from 1961 to 1965 and as U.S. ambassador to Italy from 1977 to 1981. He is the U.S. cochair of the U.S.–Soviet Working Group on Multilateral Cooperation under the auspices of the United Nations Association of the two countries. His books include *Sterling-Dollar Diplomacy: The Origins and the Prospects of Our International Economic Order* and *In Pursuit of World Order: U.S. Foreign Policy and International Organizations*.

ism, and utopian multilateralism. It envisages a leadership role by the United States in working with other nations to build a peaceful world order through effective international organizations. It recognizes that the most effective instruments of foreign policy may not always be found in the United Nations and global organizations—that bilateral, regional, and "plurilateral" approaches not involving every member of the world community may often be better designed to serve our interests—and that unilateral action (such as the bombing of Tripoli in response to Libyan terrorism) may sometimes be necessary.

"Practical internationalism" does, however, recognize the U.S. interest in encouraging respect for international law. This means that when acting outside the United Nations, we should try to act "inside the charter," in Senator Arthur Vandenberg's felicitous phrase, conforming our behavior to internationally accepted standards and encouraging the use of third-party mechanisms to resolve international disputes.

Almost everywhere we look in the new international situation that confronts us we find a strong objective case for promoting both our own national interests and the general welfare of nations through cooperative action in international agencies. The United Nations and its family of agencies are likely to be much more effective as a result of the new and constructive emphasis on the UN in Soviet foreign policy, the liberation from communism of the East European countries, and the growing political and economic moderation in the Third World.

The United Nations has already proved its effectiveness as a forum for mobilizing a coalition to defeat Iraq's aggression against Kuwait and is proving to be no less valuable in dealing with the aftermath of the conflict. Under the provisions of Resolution 687 of April 2, 1991, it deployed an observer group on the Iraq-Kuwait border, assured the elimination of Iraq's weapons of mass destruction and the means for their delivery, provided the legal framework for a continued embargo on arms sales and for a modified embargo on other trade, and organized the system by which Iraq will pay compensation for the damage it caused. The UN also provided humanitarian assistance to the Kurds and other displaced persons and refugees inside and outside Iraq.

The World Bank group, the International Monetary Fund, and the Regional Development Banks for Latin America, Asia, and Africa are vitally important instruments for the economic development of the less developed countries. If a reasonably successful outcome can be achieved in the Uruguay Round, the General Agreement on Tariffs and Trade will be a central instrument for maintaining an open and multilateral world trading system and of applying commonly accepted principles to previously uncovered areas like agriculture, services, investment, and the protection of intellectual property. As we move toward the next century, we will be relying more and more on the World Health Organization to deal with the global AIDS epidemic, on the International Atomic Energy Agency to assist with nuclear safety and nonproliferation, and on an upgraded UN Environment Program to help us with global warming and with other threats to the habitability of our planet.

On the continent of Europe, the new European Bank for Reconstruction and Development, working with the other international financial institutions, will help former Communist countries to preserve their fragile democratic institutions as they adjust to free market economies. The newly strengthened Conference on Security and Cooperation in Europe (CSCE) will continue to promote the freedoms of speech, press, assembly, and religion, the right to periodic free elections, and the rights of minorities, which are valuable not only in and of themselves but which are important for the maintenance of peace. Dozens of other examples could be cited on the utility of international agencies for our unfolding foreign policy agenda in Europe and throughout the world.

But what, more precisely, should be the role of international organizations in dealing with the most direct and fundamental threats to American security? Let us focus on two of these threats—(1) the aggressive use of armed force and (2) the spread of weapons of mass destruction and the means to deliver them to unfriendly or unstable countries.

Aggressive Use of Armed Force

For the first of these security threats, NATO will remain, for the next decade at least, an indispensable instrument of American policy. Despite the demise of the Warsaw Pact and the withdrawal of Soviet troops from Eastern Europe, the Soviet Union is still a formidable military power. Its future political evolution is quite unpredictable. Were power to be seized by hard-line Communists or Great Russian Nationalists (or a coalition of both)—a contingency that cannot entirely be excluded—European security could be at risk once again. NATO is also needed to keep the military potential of a united Germany locked into an integrated military structure. And perhaps, despite the reservations of France and others, NATO could play a role in coping with threats to the NATO countries coming from the Middle East or Africa. The Rapid Reaction Corps of up to 70,000 troops now being created for use within NATO's borders might be developed into a force that could operate outside the NATO area as well; if necessary, it could undertake out-of-area activities under the authority of the Western European Union. To deal with the residual Soviet threat and the out-of-area contingencies, we will need to maintain about 100,000 U.S. air, sea, and ground forces in Europe for the foreseeable future. NATO provides the only politically acceptable way for us to maintain this presence with the necessary basing and facilities. We should beware of anything that would weaken it.

After the year 2000, we may need to begin exploring institutions that might replace NATO and make the presence of American troops in Europe unnecessary in the event that the Soviet threat recedes entirely. It will be difficult to persuade the American people to keep U.S. troops in Europe indefinitely—even at the reduced level of 100,000. As European unity proceeds, either the Western European Union or the European Community could take on responsibility for establishing and directing a joint European force with sufficient capabilities to cope with security challenges arising within Europe or from neighboring areas. If such an alternative to NATO should develop in the security area, NATO's political functions could be absorbed by the Organization for Economic Cooperation and Development (OECD), which would have the advantage of bringing Japan more fully into the political decision-making system of the industrialized democracies.

The Conference on Security and Cooperation in Europe, with its new small Secretariat and Center for Conflict Prevention, could become the main instrument for pan-European political cooperation and for the settlement of intra-European disputes, including disputes arising over the rights of minorities, as well as for pan-European cooperation on economics and on human rights. To avoid duplication in these last two areas, it may be necessary for CSCE to absorb the work of the Economic Commission for Europe and the Council of Europe. If CSCE is to discharge its new responsibilities well, however, it will need to supplement the plenary meetings of thirty-four countries with smaller councils similar to the UN Security Council with some permanent members and with rotating membership for smaller countries.

In the post–cold war world, the main threats to the security of the United States and its allies will most likely come, as the Gulf crisis demonstrated, from conflicts arising in the Third World. It is in the U.S. national interest to develop, if possible, new institutions for collective security to prevent or contain such conflicts, and to deter and if necessary defeat acts of aggression. A 1991 *Time* poll showed that Americans by a margin of 75 percent to 20 percent reject the idea of the U.S. as world policeman. There are not many situations like Iraq's invasion of Kuwait where considerations of legal principle, economic interest, and international security would join to persuade the United States to send half a million men and women to fight in the Third World far from our own borders. No other country is currently proposing to play the role of global policeman; we would be unlikely to welcome it if one volunteered.

It is true, of course, that most conflicts in the Third World do not threaten U.S. security directly. It can be argued that it is of no concern to the United States if Libya attacks Chad, if Tanzania attacks Uganda, if India attacks Nepal, or if Indonesia attacks Papua New Guinea. Yet with few exceptions, American presidents from Roosevelt to Bush have all pledged our country to seek international arrangements that would provide all countries with security against aggression. In his Four Freedom's speech, President

Franklin D. Roosevelt called for a postwar order that would assure "freedom from fear"—"everywhere in the world." John F. Kennedy, in his Inaugural Address, called for "a new world of law, where the strong are just and the weak secure and the peace preserved." And President George Bush committed his administration to "a new world order." The president was quite explicit about its content in his address to the United Nations General Assembly on October 1, 1990:

We have a vision of a new partnership of nations that transcends the cold war; a partnership based on consultation, cooperation and collective action, especially through international and regional organizations; a partnership united by principle and the rule of law and supported by an equitable sharing of both cost and commitment; a partnership whose goals are to increase democracy, increase prosperity, increase the peace and reduce arms.

If statements like these by American presidents are more than meaningless historical flourishes, it must be because we consider that the construction of a global security system that protects all nations is something that serves the interest of the United States. But why should we care if Ruanda attacks Burundi and no immediate vital interest of the U.S. or an ally is evidently at risk? It must be because (1) we feel a moral concern for the rights of the Burundians, (2) we believe that aggression if unpunished there will encourage aggression elsewhere, and (3) the United States will not be politically successful in mobilizing coalitions to defeat aggressions that threaten our vital interests if we show indifference to aggressions that threaten the vital interests of others.

Up to this point, the United Nations has not developed any institutionalized system to deter and defeat international aggression. On two occasions—Korea in 1950 and the Gulf in 1990—it authorized an ad hoc coalition of forces led by the United States to act in its name. Otherwise its principal contributions to international peace and security have been in nonenforcement or peacekeeping operations in places like Cyprus, Lebanon, the Golan Heights, or Namibia. It is currently helping to bring about settlements in El Salvador, Western Sahara, Angola, and Cambodia that may require, particularly in the latter case, significant UN peacekeeping forces.

The question we now need to consider is whether the UN can build on its success in the Gulf and develop a new capacity that goes beyond peacekeeping to deterring and resisting aggression. Two specific ideas should be seriously explored.

First, the UN secretary-general could be given the means that he presently lacks to carry out his authority under Article 99 of the UN Charter to "bring to the attention of the Security Council any matter which in his opinion may threaten the maintenance of international peace and security." He could be given four or five high-level representatives responsible for the main regions of the world who could monitor incipient conflict situations and engage in missions of preventive diplomacy. In addition, the five permanent members of the Security Council could be asked to share intelligence information with the secretary-general on a regular basis, including information from satellites, that would help him identify possible threats to the peace. With these two new instruments at their disposal, the secretary-general and the Security Council could engage in a continuing "global peace watch" that might anticipate and possibly head off conflicts like Iraq's invasion of Kuwait or the Falklands War.

Second, the UN could establish a Rapid Deployment Force under Article 43 of the charter that would be available in three types of situations: (1) to be stationed preemptively on the border of any UN member that was threatened by aggression; (2) to defeat aggression when it occurred; and (3) in exceptional situations, such as with the Kurdish minority in Iraq, to put an end to mass repression against a civilian population constituting a threat to international peace and security.

Between twenty to thirty UN members could be encouraged to pledge and set aside a brigade (2,000 troops) or in exceptional cases a battalion (600 troops) for use in such operations, so that the secretary-general could call up the particular mix of forces that was most appropriate for each crisis in terms of geography and nationality. The different national forces would receive common training for UN service in advance of a crisis and would engage in joint training exercises under a UN commander. Of course, the Rapid Deployment Force would clearly be insufficient to defeat an army of the size that Iraq sent into Kuwait in August of 1990; for aggressions on this scale we will still have to rely on U.S.–led coalitions. It should be made clear that an Article 43 force would not exclude the use of such ad hoc coalitions where they were required to do the job.

Under Article 43 of the UN Charter, whose implementation was frustrated until now by the cold war, members of the UN are to make units of their armed forces available for UN enforcement action in accordance with special agreements between themselves and the Security Council. The Military Staff Committee, consisting of the chiefs of staff of the five permanent members of the council or their representatives, is to be responsible under the authority of the council for the "strategic direction" of these units and for advance preparation of their employment. The Military Staff Committee is authorized to invite the military representatives of other UN members to join it when this is required for the "efficient discharge" of the committee's responsibilities. Moreover, the Security Council itself can invite a member not represented on it to participate in decisions concerning the employment of that member's military contingents. Use of these provisions would make it possible to give a role in decision making on the preparation and employment of UN armed forces to important countries like Germany and Japan who are not regularly represented on the Security Council, helping to encourage such countries to participate in UN military operations.

The Article 43 system for UN collective security actions, if it could be implemented, would have a number of advantages. It would provide an assured means of providing troops for UN enforcement actions—and this would help deter as well as defeat some kinds of aggression. It would put the troops of other countries on the front lines instead of American forces in a number of crisis situations, thus meeting the desire of the American people for a more equitable sharing of international responsibility for peace enforcement. It would constitute a true UN military force, with a UN commander responsible to direction by the Security Council with the advice of the Military Staff Committee, thus avoiding the charge faced in the Gulf War that the operation was really an American one under virtually exclusive U.S. control. Moreover, the Soviet Union has already said it favors implementing this system and would earmark forces for it. In addition, under the UN Participation Act, once an Article 43 agreement between the

United States and the Security Council is concluded and approved by the Senate, U.S. forces designated under the agreement can be sent into hostilities without further action by the Congress. If the Senate is still willing to live with this arrangement, it would avoid divisive arguments about presidential war powers.

On the other hand, the Article 43 system for UN collective security actions is a very ambitious one—perhaps too ambitious for the present state of international politics. Once an agreement is made between a UN member and the Security Council, the member is committed to supply earmarked units of its armed forces whenever the council so requires. The five permanent members are protected by the veto, but the other 154 members of the UN may not be willing to sign a blank check to make their forces available for enforcement actions they might consider contrary to their interests. It may be necessary to incorporate a provision in agreements with the council permitting a member to "opt out" of supplying its troops for exceptional reasons involving supreme national interest. The question is whether such a provision would fatally compromise the effectiveness and deterrent value of the proposed collective security system.

If the Article 43 approach to collective security is considered too ambitious, we could follow the approach envisaged in the Uniting for Peace Resolution adopted in 1950, which merely invited members to maintain units of their armed forces that could be made available to the UN, without any commitment to do so in a particular case. Such forces would not need to be placed under a UN commander, but could simply be called on to help carry out a Security Council decision to suppress an act of aggression, as was done in Korea and the Gulf. The units could in that event be placed under the command of the UN member supplying the largest share of the fighting forces. While this approach would provide for greater flexibility, it would also entail the disadvantages complained of in Korea and the Gulf of identifying a UN operation with a single member and of depriving the UN of control over the conduct of the military campaign. A hybrid arrangement is also conceivable, using the Uniting for Peace approach but with forces serving under a UN commander and responsible to the Security Council advised by the Military Staff Committee.

Spread of Weapons
of Mass Destruction

A second area where greater resort to international organizations will be necessary to serve the security interests of the United States and other UN members is that of the proliferation of weapons of mass destruction, of the missiles for their delivery, and of high-tech conventional arms. Secretary of Defense Dick Cheney has said that by the year 2000 "more than two dozen developing nations will have ballistic missiles, 15 of those countries will have the scientific skills to make their own and half of them either have or are near to getting nuclear capability as well." He added that "30 countries will have chemical weapons and 10 will be able to deploy biological weapons." Among the countries that either have or soon will have missiles and mass destruction warheads are North Korea, Libya, Iran, Syria, Saudi Arabia, Egypt, Israel, India, Pakistan, and South Africa.

One of the most important achievements in Security Council Resolution 687 was to require that Iraq be deprived of all chemical, biological, and nuclear weapons and all missile capabilities. These requirements will be enforced by on-site inspection by a UN Special Commission and by the International Atomic Energy Agency.

Paragraph 14 of Resolution 687 states that these measures "represent steps toward the goal of establishing in the Middle East a zone free from weapons of mass destruction and all missiles for their delivery. . . ." When we consider the prospect that another war in the Middle East would probably be fought with missiles much more accurate than the Scuds fired randomly by Iraq against population centers in Israel and Saudi Arabia, that those missiles could be fitted with chemical, biological, or even nuclear warheads, and that potential victim states with little warning time would be under enormous political pressure to launch preventive strikes, we can see that the goal stated in this paragraph should not await a final settlement of the Middle East conflicts but should be pursued with extreme urgency.

Here again, the role of the UN and its family of agencies will be enormously important. For example, Hans Blix, the able director-general of the International Atomic Energy Agency (IAEA), stated in a speech on February 26, 1991, that to implement a nuclear-free zone in the Middle East the following measures going far beyond the agency's current safeguards system would need to be considered:

- Inspection by the IAEA would need to be supplemented by regional or mutual inspection by the parties to the nuclear weapons-free zone to provide added confidence.
- Inspection should not be limited to nuclear material as at present, but should apply to all nuclear installations as well, and the right of access, both in terms of frequency and location, would need to be more extensive.
- The IAEA would need to be authorized to make special inspections when requested and when the agency considered it necessary.
- Information and consultation would be required well in advance of any construction of any installations for the production of fissionable material. Renewed consideration would need to be given to placing all nuclear installations under regional or international management.

If we want a nuclear nonproliferation regime in which we have full confidence, these ideas will have to be considered for application not only in the Middle East but on a worldwide basis as well. With respect to chemical weapons, the treaty now under negotiation in Geneva envisages an equally ambitious role for the new international agency that will be charged with its implementation.

Finally, our agenda in the area of proliferation will need to include the strengthening of the seven-nation regime established some years ago for the control of the proliferation of missile capabilities. The Soviet Union, China, Brazil, Argentina, and other missile suppliers will need to be associated with the regime; the list of prohibited export items will need to be tightened; and enforcement measures will need seriously to be examined. Probably some new international institution will be needed to make the regime effective. We should also explore the possibility of negotiating a worldwide ban on intermediate-range missiles, in effect generalizing to the world the main provisions of the Intermediate-

Range Nuclear Forces Treaty concluded between the U.S. and the Soviet Union.

In his second and last speech to the UN General Assembly in September 1963, President Kennedy declared that "the United Nations, building on its successes and learning from its failures, must be developed into a genuine world security system." Clearly not *the* system—but certainly *part* of one.

President Kennedy's statement looked utopian at the time. It does not look so utopian today.

8E

The Uneven, but Growing, Role of International Law

JOHN H. BARTON AND
BARRY E. CARTER

I nternational law and institutions took on new significance after
World War II, with the United States in the forefront of efforts

---

JOHN H. BARTON is George E. Osborne Professor of Law at Stanford University, where he teaches international business transactions, international environmental law, international human rights, and law and technology. He is coprincipal investigator on a study, funded by the Hitachi Foundation, of the evolution of law in the Pacific Basin high-technology community, and is consultant to a variety of international organizations on legal issues associated with technology. Among his publications are *International Trade and Investment* (with B. Fisher), *Law in Radically Different Cultures* (with J. Gibbs, V. Li, and J. Merryman), and *The Politics of Peace*.
BARRY E. CARTER is a professor of law at Georgetown University and chair of its Committee on International Law Programs. He teaches a variety of international law courses and European Community law. He was a senior counsel on the Senate Select Committee on Intelligence Activities in 1973 and was a member of Dr. Henry Kissinger's National Security Council staff from 1970–72, where he worked especially on U.S.–Soviet and European issues. His book on *International Economic Sanctions: Improving the Haphazard U.S. Legal Regime* (1988) received the annual award from the American Society on International Law for the outstanding new book on international law subjects. Recently published is his *International Law* (with P. Trimble).

to create an international legal order. Although the law and institutions have continued to evolve rapidly since then, they have failed to keep pace with the changes in the world.

Today could well be a time of extraordinary opportunity for updating the world order. Most of the nations in the world—including all the major industrialized ones—appear refreshingly open to discussion, negotiation, and agreement. Yet, in some areas, the United States is lagging rather than leading, even though it has an important stake in world stability and development. Specifically, by encouraging the growth of international law and influencing its content, the United States could help protect its broadly defined security interests. Potential friction and conflicts in future years over a number of issues could be channeled and moderated. Such issues include restrictive trade barriers and other trading relations; measures to protect the world's environment from ozone depletion, the greenhouse effect, and other dangers; and ethnic strife.

The Changes in International Law

The most visible evolutionary changes in the international legal system since the late 1940s have been in the institutions—from the fluctuating role of the United Nations to the metamorphoses in the General Agreement on Tariffs and Trade (GATT) to the emergence of important new entities such as the European Community.[1] These are discussed elsewhere in this book.

Paralleling the changes in institutions have been equally important, though often less visible, changes in international law. Most notably, (a) the international system is no longer confined to relations among nations, and the individual person has emerged as an independent actor, and (b) national and international tribunals are offering new—and much more effective—means for enforcing international law.

The Emergence of the Person

The traditional concept of international law was of law between nations. As late as 1963 a very respected English treatise defined public international law as "the body of rules and principles of action which are binding upon civilized states in their relations with one another."[2]

Reciprocity was the critical element in ensuring that international rules and norms were observed. Formal rules about the treatment of ambassadors or about respect for a state's territorial sea, for example, were usually followed because the potential offender was also a potential victim. For reasons discussed below, only rarely would states resort to the International Court of Justice (or its predecessor, the Permanent Court of International Justice) or to formal arbitration.

In the immediate postwar era, international law's restriction of its scope to nation states expanded to encompass the new international and regional institutions. For example, UN organs and agencies were allowed to seek advisory opinions from the International Court of Justice, which was otherwise restricted to disputes among states.

Since then, the person (whether an individual or corporation) has been increasingly accepted as an independent actor, subject to and benefiting from international law. This has been an inevitable result of the increasing global interactions and shared interests of persons across frontiers.

Among the early steps were efforts by foreign investors and businesses to protect themselves from expropriation or other mistreatment by a host country. Under traditional international law, the investor would rely on its home country to protect its interests through diplomatic arguments and pressure. The investor, however, also wanted independent protection. Moreover, host countries wished to attract investment and all parties sought to resolve disputes quickly and reasonably. As a result, a trend developed toward arbitration between the investor and the host government by a panel that applies international principles that directly affect the investor as well as the host government.

This is part of a much larger phenomenon in which the traditional barriers between so-called public and private international
law have come tumbling down. In contrast to the public international law of rules between states, there has long been a private
international law dealing with the activities of individuals, corporations, and other private entities when their activities crossed national borders. This was particularly important in the laws of ad-
miralty governing the maritime sector and in choice-of-law rules
determining which country's domestic law would apply to transnational transactions between the nationals of two different countries.

The distinctions between public and private international law
have become increasingly artificial as many states and their in-
strumentalities have entered the marketplace in a major way, either as traders themselves or as guardians of industrial policy, and
as commerce and foreign policy have become more intertwined.
For example, the Iraqi invasion of Kuwait and the resulting UN
economic sanctions involved traditional issues of public international law; yet the implementation of the sanctions very much
affected a U.S. or European bank with Iraqi or Kuwaiti deposits.
At much less dramatic levels, the same kinds of mixed public-
private issues are posed daily by satellites broadcasting across national boundaries, by fishers in international waters, and by investors trading on foreign stock exchanges. Courts, national
governments, and international organizations struggle with such
issues every day. Thus when the European Community developed
its judicial system, it realized that individuals would have to be
able to appeal to or against community action just as much as
governments.

The independent role of individuals has probably advanced fur-
thest in the human rights area. The tragic experience of Nazi
Germany caused many to believe that citizens of a state should
have some form of international protection against even their own
state, a view reinforced by the recent tragic plight of the Iraqi
Kurds. There is no question that international law now defines a
number of such rights, such as against official torture. Many treaties go much further in defining rights. As will be seen below, these
rights can sometimes be enforced in a nation's domestic courts. In
Europe, they also can be enforced before the European Court of

Human Rights, which has provided a mechanism of judicial review for even nations like Great Britain that reject judicial review by their national courts. (The technical litigants before this European court are the nation and the European Commission of Human Rights, but in many respects, the proceeding is really one between a nation and the individual affected by the alleged human rights violation.)

Enforcing International Law

Paralleling this increased role of the individual is an equally dramatic change in the mechanisms available to enforce international law.

The traditional—and still important—mechanism is reciprocity. After invading Panama in December 1989, what basically kept the United States from storming the Vatican nunciature to capture General Manuel Noriega was the possibility that this would be a precedent that would endanger U.S. embassies everywhere. It would also have been a clear violation of the Vienna Convention on Diplomatic Relations of 1961, to which the United States, Panama, the Vatican, and about 150 other states are now parties. That convention strengthens reciprocity by providing a reasonably clear definition of the rights of ambassadors and embassies.

For traditional international law, the best-known adjudicatory body was, and probably still is, the International Court of Justice (ICJ). The court will probably remain as the principal forum for resolving general legal issues between two or more states, especially boundary disputes.

An expanded role for the court, however, has been hampered by a perceived lack of bite. Under the UN Charter, a member "undertakes to comply with the decision" of the court if "it is a party" to the case, and the UN Security Council may "decide upon measures to be taken to give effect to the [court's] judgement" (Article 94). Although states have complied with the court's judgments in many of the cases where the judgment required an action, recalcitrant states have on occasion refused to comply, and the Security Council has yet to decide upon any enforcement measures in those situations.

For instance, the ICJ's first decision in a contentious case was against Albania for mining the Corfu Channel and causing damage to British warships. In 1949 the ICJ determined that Albania should pay monetary damages. Over forty years later, Albania has yet to do so. In 1980 Iran refused to comply with the court's judgment to release the U.S. hostages. Most recently, the United States did not stop its support of the Nicaraguan contras in spite of the court's 1986 decision that the extensive U.S. involvement with the contras violated international law.[3]

This uncertain enforceability of the ICJ's judgments is one of several reasons why the court has not emerged as an important institution for resolving legal disputes as its founders wished. The court has also been burdened by the politicized nature of selecting its fifteen judges, by reactions to its early decisions, and by its relatively rigid procedures. Although most judicial selection procedures are political, the election of an ICJ judge requires a majority vote in the UN General Assembly and Security Council, votes that in recent years have been characterized by intense political lobbying. Add to that the ICJ's past record that has often seemed to lean toward indecision or to be interpreted as favoring one group of countries over another. Of the eighty-four cases that have been brought to the ICJ, the court has dismissed over fifteen for lack of jurisdiction, and a few prominent cases long caused the developing countries to question whether the court was biased in favor of the developed countries.

The court's formal procedures have also discouraged its use. Its procedures do not yet recognize the emergence of the person in international law; only states can be parties in contentious cases although UN entities can also seek advisory opinions. Moreover, a state that wants a dispute resolved promptly finds uninviting this court's procedures that are not well adapted for fact finding and the fact that a long time usually passes before the court renders a decision, even with its light caseload. Although there has been a recent surge in the number of cases brought to the court, its eighty-four cases in nearly forty-six years averages out to less than two new cases per year, hardly a heavy caseload—and much below that of its League of Nations predecessor.

The court has recently shown a willingness to reform itself. It adopted revised rules in 1978 to enable a state to bring cases before three- or five-judge panels, in which each country would have one of its nationals as a judge and a voice regarding the other judges. The court's decision in 1984 to take jurisdiction in Nicaragua's case against the United States could also be seen as reflecting a new aggressiveness toward finding jurisdiction.

But the court's changes are minor compared with the wide variety of attractive alternative arrangements that have emerged for formal enforcement of international rules and norms. These alternatives include international arbitration, regional and specialized courts, and transnational use of domestic courts. They amount to a revolution in international law.

Arbitration. The 1958 New York Convention on the Recognition and Enforcement of Foreign Arbitral Awards has been ratified by over eighty countries, including the United States and all the other major industrialized countries. According to this treaty, subject to very narrow exceptions,[4] a decision by an international arbitral panel sitting in a contracting state will be enforced by the domestic courts of any other contracting country as if the decision were by that domestic court. As a result, a winning party in an international arbitration can usually be assured of collecting against a recalcitrant losing party, if the loser has assets—bank accounts, real estate, goods—in any one of the N.Y. Convention countries. It is only necessary to take the arbitral award to the local court for authority to have the assets seized and sold off under local law.

Libya's Colonel Mu'ammar al-Qadhafi learned first-hand of this convention in the 1970s. After his coup, Qadhafi nationalized valuable interests of foreign oil companies operating in Libya. These oil companies had entered into long-term agreements with the prior Libyan government, under which the companies were entitled to submit any dispute to arbitration and the principles of international law. Qadhafi claimed that the nationalization decree invalidated these contract provisions and that the companies had to seek redress in Libya's domestic courts. The oil companies disagreed and sought arbitration. Sole arbitrators were appointed in three separate cases. Each decided that he had jurisdiction and each ultimately entered awards against Libya. Qadhafi apparently refused initially to pay, but eventually settled for tens of millions of dollars. Had Libya not paid, the successful companies could have moved to enforce their arbitral awards against Libya in, say, Italy, Germany, Switzerland, or any of the other N.Y. Convention countries by moving to attach Libyan oil, bank accounts, airplanes, or other assets.

The N.Y. Convention gave a powerful boost to arbitration, but it is not the only reason why arbitration has grown. Arbitration already had the advantages of flexibility. The parties can choose the place of arbitration and the number, specialization, and even identity of arbitrators; they can select the procedural rules (including those governing confidentiality and the amount of discovery allowed); and they can specify the substantive rules (e.g., general principles of international law, an individual country's laws, or even specially drafted provisions). This flexibility makes arbitration particularly useful in disputes between nations and investors or between economic interests in different nations. Arbitration also has been strongly supported in a variety of U.S. Supreme Court decisions.

As a result, arbitration has been a growth industry in the last twenty to thirty years. For example, 365 new requests for arbitration were filed in 1990 with the International Chamber of Commerce (ICC). Although the ICC handles commercial disputes, 20 percent of its cases involved governmental or parastatal entities, such as government owned utilities or airlines. Similarly, the American Arbitration Association (AAA) had 205 new international arbitration cases in 1990.

The World Bank created the International Centre for the Settlement of Investment Disputes (ICSID) for resolving disputes between foreign investors and the host country through conciliation and arbitration. ICSID's own multilateral convention has enforcement provisions similar to those in the N.Y. Convention. ICSID has gotten off to a relatively slow start, with only about twenty-six arbitration cases since 1971.

The Iran–U.S. Claims Tribunal, however, has been a pacesetting institution. It was created in 1981 as part of the arrangement for freeing the U.S. hostages and resolving a number of outstanding claims between the two countries. In spite of initial delays and wrangling, the tribunal has issued awards regarding over 300 large U.S. private claims (more than $250,000 each) and 3,000 small U.S. private claims, as well as over 110 private Iranian claims. The awards in favor of U.S. claimants have totaled over $2 billion; the Iranian awards about $130 million. Some government-to-government claims are still pending. The awards in favor of U.S. claimants have been paid out of an escrow account set up with Iranian funds transferred from those frozen by the U.S. government in 1979–81. Iranians, however, can count on collecting on awards in their favor because of the availability of the N.Y. Convention.

The United States and Canada provided for arbitration as the binding method for dispute resolution in the Canada–U.S. Free Trade Agreement. In the short period since the agreement came into effect in January 1989, there have already been at least fifteen requests for arbitration panels. They deal with challenges to administrative decisions by U.S. or Canadian government agencies about the respective country's trade laws. The decisions that are already being reached are published along with judicial decisions on similar issues and will probably become part of the common law of international trade.

Regional and Specialized Courts. The new regional courts of Europe—whose decisions are as effective as those of any domestic court—are among the most dramatic examples of the new mechanisms of international law. The European Community's Court of Justice had 390 new cases brought to it in 1990; its own court of first instance, or trial court, had to be organized in September 1989 to meet the press of the court's business. The European Court of Human Rights has received about thirty new cases each year for the past several years.

The Court of Justice handles a variety of appeals regarding community actions, and it can also be called on to interpret community law for the benefit of national courts. It is open to individuals as well as national governments. Among its decisions are landmark opinions that community law has precedence over national law, opinions very similar to the federalism decisions of the U.S. Supreme Court.

The European Court of Human Rights enforces an international bill of rights drawn in part on the U.S. Bill of Rights—the European Convention for the Protection of Human Rights and Fundamental Freedoms. All of the nineteen European states that have submitted to the compulsory jurisdiction of the court have agreed to abide by its decisions, which have normally been accepted and implemented. These have covered areas as sensitive as freedom of the press, wiretapping, and the regulation of homosexuality. In addition, some of the member states, like France and Italy, have incorporated the European Convention's bill of rights into domestic law. Interestingly, because the United Kingdom has no formal written constitution or formal domestic guarantee of individual rights, U.K. nationals are among the most frequent petitioners seeking the protection of the European Convention and the European Court.

The success of these European courts is in large part a result of Europe's overall political moves toward integration. The European Community is obviously of vital interest to its member states. The European Court of Human Rights and the related Council of Europe enjoy widespread popular support and prestige in Europe. (Hungary and Czechoslovakia have recently joined the Council of Europe, and other Eastern European nations are now seeking admission, in part to stabilize their new democratic governments.) The courts have a focused jurisdiction and relatively easy access, unlike the ICJ. Perhaps most important, it is very difficult to build the type of federalism being sought in Europe without a judicial institution to draw the lines between central and local authority. Judicial review, an American invention, has largely taken over in Europe, even in France, which had historically looked to a popularly elected legislature as a defense against aristocratic judges.

A sign of the recent times is the dispute resolution system in the proposed 1982 Convention on the Law of the Sea. This convention, drafted under UN auspices, is likely to come into force within a few years, perhaps with minor changes to respond to U.S. concerns.[5] Disputes under this convention may be referred not only to the ICJ, but also to a new International Tribunal for the Law of the Sea and two different arbitration arrangements. The choices reflect the developing countries' unhappiness with ICJ judgments at the time of drafting the convention, and the drafters' hope of achieving enforceability under the N.Y. Convention. The arrangement also reflects efforts to rely more on specialized courts or on arbitration. Each country is to select the dispute resolution institution it prefers when it ratifies the convention. If the two or more parties who are later involved in a dispute did not agree on the institutions in their ratification documents, then the convention directs that the parties are to use arbitration. Arbitration is implicitly the preferred lowest common denominator.

Domestic Courts. As international trade, finance, investment, and travel have mushroomed, the domestic courts of most countries have naturally found themselves considering more and more cases that have an international impact. These courts have sometimes declined to hear such cases because of concerns about the extraterritorial impact of their decisions, and they have developed a variety of doctrines for that purpose.

The overall trend, however, is to hear more such cases and effectively to develop what amounts to an international common law that lies between traditional domestic and traditional international law. This includes a country's domestic statutes and court decisions that affect international matters, as well as international treaties and the other international legal rules generally called customary international law. (These international common law doctrines are often developed further by international and regional courts and by international arbitrations. Tribunals and scholars are often looking to one another's work to develop the harmony needed to make the system work.)

This international flow of legal ideas is especially important in human rights issues, in international economic issues, and in resolving jurisdictional conflicts. Thus domestic courts will often entertain claims that foreign corporate conduct violated domestic antitrust law, that a foreign government violated the rights of a domestic business that had contracted with it, or that a corporation should be liable for work hazards affecting foreign workers. The courts will develop rules as to when and how a foreign subsidiary is bound by the employment discrimination law or banking law of the parent corporation's home nation.

This developing role of domestic courts is evident in the human rights area. For example, the U.S. federal courts allowed a suit by relatives of a Paraguayan citizen against a former Paraguayan police official who was accused of torturing and murdering the citizen in Paraguay.[6] The U.S. courts decided the case on the basis of a U.S. law that allows injury suits by an alien for a violation of "the law of nations or a treaty of the United States." In this case, the court was enforcing a domestic law that incorporates international practices that it found binding as well as international treaties.

Judgments by these domestic courts are, of course, enforceable within their own country, just like any other judgment by the domestic court. As for foreign enforcement, such judgments are usually given considerable respect in other countries, but practices differ among nations and even among the fifty states of the United States.

The domestic courts also have an influence beyond their specific judgments—their decisions are often cited in other national courts and in the regional courts just discussed. Thus there is the further development of an international common law, although, discouragingly, U.S. courts tend to consider foreign decisions much less than the foreign courts consider U.S. decisions.

Where to Go from Here?

In short, the international legal regime is very different from that envisioned after World War II. There is now a complex mix of international and domestic law, administered and enforced by a variety of entities and often invoked by individuals. This new law builds on a variety of shared interests, well beyond traditional international reciprocity. It forms an international legal network complementing other networks—e.g., economic, communications, and family—that are increasingly integrating the world.

Although the legal network is far too weak to guarantee security, it can contribute to the security of the world and of the United States. An improved international legal regime would probably be most beneficial in areas that fit under a broad definition of national security—e.g., international trade and business relations, environmental protection, ethnic and religious disputes. The legal network, for instance, could provide even more than it does today generally accepted rules as well as the means of adjudicating and even enforcing these rules. The volume and complexity of international trade and economic relations call out for a stronger international arrangement than the present rules under the General Agreement on Tariffs and Trade; the rapidly growing need to protect the world's environment requires much more than the present collection of ad hoc treaties and a very limited international entity such as the United Nations Environmental Program (UNEP); and the impressive human rights protections developed regionally in Western Europe are unmatched in any other region of the world.

An improved legal regime is less likely to provide as substantial benefits in the near term in the traditional areas of national security concerns, such as arms control and the use of military force. These issues are often so fundamental to a nation's existence that its leaders are chary of accepting rules—much less any effective adjudicatory system and enforcement mechanisms—that might limit their action. Nevertheless, progress is occurring. Recent arms control agreements between the United States and the Soviet Union involve much more detailed restrictions and standards, plus means for verifying adherence to the agreements. (The agreements, however, still fall far short of including any binding third-party dispute resolution, such as arbitration.) And in response to the Iraqi invasion of Kuwait, most of the nations of the world supported the UN Security Council not only condemning the Iraqi actions, but also taking positive steps to reverse that action.

The ideas underlying an improved legal network are, in many cases, U.S. ideas. The nation has been a leader in international arbitration, and it invented judicial review. More recently, however, the United States has been relatively lukewarm toward taking the lead in further developing the international legal system.

The United States can usefully play a much greater role in improving international law. It has much more to gain than to lose by strengthening and more fully participating in this emerging legal order.

The dramatic trends in international law, noted earlier, toward the emergence of the person as an actor and the enforceability of international law must be encouraged to continue, if not accelerate. Individuals and corporations can play an indispensable role in helping to call nations to account. International norms and rules will obviously mean much more if there are effective mechanisms for enforcing them.

When the United States acts to reform or create international entities or when it enters into international agreements, it should take the lead in ensuring that the resulting rules are enforceable and can be invoked by persons as well as states. In this vein, the United States is to be commended for having already done what we now recommend when it agreed to the Iran–U.S. Claims Tribunal in 1981 and to the Canada–U.S. Free Trade Agreement in 1988. Current U.S. support of improved procedures for the GATT dispute system also reflects progress, although more needs to be done to allow persons to invoke the GATT rules within the GATT or in U.S. courts. Likewise, we recommend that binding dispute mechanisms that allow persons to bring actions—probably before an arbitral panel or a specialized court—should also be incorporated in any Mexico–U.S. free trade arrangement.

These recommendations lead us to a painful observation. Too many international lawyers have for too long placed too much hope on the International Court of Justice. As discussed earlier, the court is seriously flawed—by the relative difficulty in enforcing its judgments, by the heavily politicized selection of judges, by access limited to states and UN entities, and by relatively rigid procedures. The United States and other countries, therefore, should push for substantial changes in the court. One important step would be to make any monetary judgment of the court enforceable through domestic courts, much as arbitral awards are enforceable under the N.Y. Convention. Other reforms are suggested by the more open access and flexible procedures of the European regional courts and the various international arbitral tribunals. At least until such reforms are made in the ICJ, we must respectfully urge the United States to continue to give greater support to binding international arbitration and, if they are created, to regional or specialized courts.[7]

Indeed, the U.S. support for binding international arbitration or for the new GATT dispute system does not go far enough. As we noted above, the current worldwide trend toward stronger judicial review and enforcement has created a significant new body of law between traditional international and domestic laws. This international common law is the heart of European integration and human rights protection. It is the context within which international trade and environmental disputes will regularly be settled in the future.

The United States has been one of the slowest nations to accept international judicial penetration of its legal system. Until the 1981 Algiers Accords with Iran and the Canada–U.S. Free Trade Agreement, the United States had accepted none of the treaties that were likely to permit private suits against the U.S. government. Furthermore, when the United States enters into a treaty or executive agreement, it usually seeks to retain the authority to interpret these documents in the executive branch or through implementing U.S. legislation, rather than to entrust interpretation to the courts. The United States must instead be willing to accept—and take the leadership in accepting—the full implications of effective and enhanced international institutions and international law. For instance, the United States must be even more ready than at present to accept international arbitration when one party is the U.S. government. It must be willing to accept international treaties and executive agreements that can be interpreted and enforced by U.S. domestic courts, thus allowing the U.S. courts to participate fully in the development of international treaty and common law.

The United States must also accept that certain of the individual rights protected in the Constitution or in international human rights conventions govern the U.S. government even when it acts abroad. In a recent case involving U.S. officials' search of residences in Mexico, a plurality of the justices suggested that there were no U.S. constitutional restraints on U.S. actions when they were taken abroad against foreigners.[8] Such a narrow, territorial based approach fails to reflect the U.S. role in setting norms for the rest of the world.

The United States should play both a judicial and a political role in shaping this new law as well as in shaping international

institutions. Our recommendations are designed to allow this. The
United States would benefit, as would the rest of the world. The
alternatives are much less attractive.

Notes

[1] It is also known as the "European Communities." The distinction is semantic
only, because the institutions of each of the three communities—the European
Coal and Steel Community (ECSC), the European Atomic Energy Community
(Euratom), and the European Economic Community (EEC)—were merged under
the Merger Treaty in 1967, and there was further integration in the community
under the Single European Act.

[2] Brierly (1963).

[3] *Military and Paramilitary Activities in and against Nicaragua (Nicar. v. U.S.)*, 1986 ICJ
14 (Merits: Judgment of 27 June). Although the court determined that it had
jurisdiction to hear the case, the United States contested the court's jurisdiction
and then did not participate in the proceedings on the merits of the Nicaraguan
claim.

The court has still pending Nicaragua's claim for damages for over $12 billion.
If the court were to rule that the U.S. government owes even a fraction of that
amount, it is uncertain that the Bush administration would seek the necessary
funds from Congress. Some observers believe that the court might have delayed
ruling on the damage amount in hopes that the matter will be resolved between
the two governments, rather than having another judgment of the court be ignored. At this writing, there are news reports that the Bush administration is trying
to get the Nicaraguan government of President Violeta Barrios de Chamarro to
drop the damage claim. Some negotiated arrangement would seem likely.

[4] These exceptions include, among others, the situation where the losing party
had not been given proper notice of the arbitration, or if the award dealt with a
matter beyond the scope of the submission to the arbitrator, or if recognition or
enforcement of the award would be contrary to the public policy of the country
where the court is sitting. In practice, in the United States for example, courts
rarely find these exceptions to apply and almost all international arbitral awards
are recognized and enforced.

[5] The convention itself would provide a comprehensive treaty regime for the
use of the seas, including rules for drawing the boundaries for each country's
territorial sea and other areas where the country has special rights, rules for
freedom of passage and for use of the high seas, and rules for mining materials
found in the bottom of the ocean. The convention was signed in 1982, but it is not
yet in force, due in large part to opposition over the deep seabed mining provisions
led by the Reagan administration and continued by the Bush administration.
However, forty-three states have already ratified the convention. Only sixty states
are required to bring the convention into force, at least among the contracting
states.

[6] *Filartiga v. Pena-Irala*, 630 F2d 876 (2d Cir. 1980).

[7] We hasten to note that the United States should not further desert the court
or even halt its present efforts with the Soviet Union and a few other countries to
accept the court's jurisdiction on additional specific matters.

[8] *United States v. Verdugo-Urguidez*, 110 S.Ct. 1056.

8F

The Unipolar Moment

CHARLES KRAUTHAMMER

E ver since it became clear that an exhausted Soviet Union was calling off the cold war, the quest has been on for a new American role in the world. Roles, however, are not invented in the abstract. They are a response to a perceived world structure. Accordingly, thinking about post–cold war American foreign policy has been framed by several conventionally accepted assumptions about the shape of the post–cold war environment.

First, that the old bipolar world would beget a multipolar world with power dispersed to new centers in Japan, Germany (and/or "Europe"), China, and a diminished Soviet Union/Russia. Second, that the domestic American consensus for an internationalist foreign policy, a consensus radically weakened by Vietnam, would substantially be restored now that policies and debates inspired by "an inordinate fear of communism" could be safely retired. Third, that in the new post-Soviet strategic environment the threat of war would be dramatically diminished.

CHARLES KRAUTHAMMER is a syndicated columnist for *The Washington Post* and a contributing essayist for *Time* magazine. He is a recipient of the Pulitzer Prize for Distinguished Commentary.

All three of these assumptions are mistaken. The immediate post–cold war world is not multipolar. It is unipolar. The center of world power is the unchallenged superpower, the United States, attended by its Western allies. Second, the internationalist consensus is under renewed assault. The assault this time comes not only from the usual pockets of post-Vietnam liberal isolationism (e.g., the churches) but from a resurgence of 1930s-style conservative isolationism. And third, the emergence of a new strategic environment marked by the rise of small aggressive states armed with weapons of mass destruction and the means to deliver them makes the coming decades a time of heightened, not diminished, threat of war.

The Unipolar Moment

The most striking feature of the post–cold war world is its unipolarity. No doubt, multipolarity will come in time. In perhaps another generation or so there will be great powers coequal with the United States, and the world will in structure resemble the pre–World War I era. But we are not there yet, nor will we be for decades. Now is the unipolar moment.

There is today no lack of second-rank powers. Germany and Japan are economic dynamos. Britain and France can deploy diplomatic and to some extent military assets. The Soviet Union possesses several elements of power—military, diplomatic, and political—but all in rapid decline. There is but one first-rate power and no prospect in the immediate future of any power to rival it.

In late 1990 it was conventional wisdom that the new rivals, the great pillars of the new multipolar world, would be Japan and Germany (and/or Europe). How quickly a myth can explode. The notion that economic power inevitably translates into geopolitical influence is a materialist illusion. Economic power is a necessary condition for great power status. But it certainly is not sufficient, as was made clear by the behavior of Germany and Japan, which pretty much hid under the table when the first shots rang out in Kuwait. And while a unified Europe may sometime in the next century act as a single power, its initial disarray and disjointed national responses to the Gulf crisis again illustrate that "Europe" does not yet qualify even as a player on the world stage.

American preeminence is based on the fact that it is the only country with the military, diplomatic, political, and economic assets to be a decisive player in any conflict in whatever part of the world it chooses to involve itself. This became blindingly clear when the United States, with a prodigious act of will, turned history in the Arabian peninsula. But the new structure of the international system has nothing at all to do with the Gulf War. It is the direct result of the collapse of the Soviet empire. The unipolar world was born in Stavropol in July of 1990 when, at the Kohl-Gorbachev summit, the Soviet Union ceded the jewel of its European empire, East Germany, to NATO. It is the end of the cold war that changed the structure of the world. The Gulf War simply revealed it.

Iraq, having inadvertently revealed the unipolar structure of today's world, cannot stop complaining about it. It looks at allied and Soviet support for American action in the Gulf and speaks of a conspiracy of North against South. Although it is perverse for Saddam Hussein to claim to represent the South, his analysis does contain some truth. The unipolar moment means that with the close of the century's three great northern civil wars (World War I, World War II, and the cold war), an ideologically pacified North seeks security and order by aligning its foreign policy behind that of the United States.

The Iraqis are equally acute in demystifying the much celebrated multilateralism of this new world order. They charge that the entire multilateral apparatus (UN resolutions, Arab troops, EC [European Community] pronouncements, etc.) established in the Gulf by the U.S. is but a transparent cover for what is essentially an American challenge to Iraqi regional hegemony.

But of course. There is much pious talk about a new multilateral world and the promise of the UN as guarantor of a new post–cold war order. But this is to mistake cause and effect, the U.S. and the UN. The UN is guarantor of nothing. Except in a formal sense, it can hardly be said to exist. Collective security? In the Gulf, without the United States leading and prodding, bribing and blackmailing, no one would have stirred. Nothing would have been done: no embargo, no threat of force, no war. The world would have written off Kuwait the way the last body pledged to collective security, the League of Nations, wrote off Abyssinia.

There is a sharp distinction to be drawn between real and apparent multilateralism. True multilateralism involves a genuine coalition of coequal partners of comparable strength and stature—the Big Three wartime anti-Nazi coalition, for example. What we have today is pseudomultilateralism: a dominant great power acts essentially alone, but, embarrassed at the idea and still worshiping at the shrine of collective security, recruits a ship here, a brigade there, and blessings all around to give its unilateral actions a multilateral sheen. The Gulf is no more a collective operation than was Korea, still the classic case study in pseudomultilateralism.

Why the pretense? Because a large segment of American opinion doubts the legitimacy of unilateral American action but accepts quite readily actions undertaken by the "world community" acting in concert. Why it should matter to Americans that their actions get a Security Council nod from, say, Deng Xiaoping and the butchers of Tiananmen Square is beyond me. But to many Americans it matters. It is largely for domestic reasons, therefore, that American political leaders make sure to dress unilateral action in multilateral clothing. The danger, of course, is that they might come to believe their own pretense.

But can America long sustain its unipolar preeminence? Is not America in decline? Indeed, before the Gulf, American "declinists" were in full voice lamenting America's fall from its perch at the top of the world in—their favorite benchmark year of the golden age—1950. Well, in 1950 the U.S. engaged in a war with North Korea: it lasted three years, cost 54,000 American lives, and ended in a draw. Forty-one years later, the U.S. engaged in a war with Iraq: it lasted six weeks, cost 196 American lives, and ended in a rout. If the Roman Empire had declined at this rate, you would be reading this in Latin.

Aha, you say, but in Korea the U.S. had to contend not just with North Korea but with China. You cannot compare the two wars.

But that, of course, is precisely the point. In 1950 America's adversaries had strategic depth. They had the whole Communist world behind them. That is why the U.S. was not able to win in Korea and Vietnam. In 1991, with the cold war won, the great adversary that provided strategic depth to America's adversaries is in retreat. Whatever enemies the U.S. does encounter, like Saddam, now have to face America on their own. Which is why they do not stand a chance. The very difference between Korea and Iraq—victory in the cold war, the neutralization of America's great geopolitical adversaries, a resulting American preeminence—is precisely what defines the unipolar moment.

But what of America's economic difficulties? The sight of a secretary of state and secretary of the treasury flying around the world rattling a tin cup to support America's Persian Gulf deployment exposed the imbalance between America's geopolitical reach and its resources. Does that not imply that the theorists of American decline and "imperial overstretch" are right and that unipolarity is unsustainable?

It is, of course, true that if America succeeds in running its economy into the ground, it will not be able to retain its unipolar role for long. But if the economy is run into the ground it will not be because of imperial overstretch, i.e., because America has overreached abroad and drained itself with geopolitical entanglements. The United States today spends 5.4 percent of GNP on defense. Under John F. Kennedy, when the United States was at its economic and political apogee, it spent almost twice as much. Administration plans have U.S. defense spending on a trajectory down to 4 percent by 1995, the lowest since Pearl Harbor.

An American collapse to second-rank status will be not for foreign but for domestic reasons. America's low savings rate, poor educational system, stagnant productivity, declining work habits, rising demand for welfare-state entitlements, and new taste for ecological luxuries have nothing at all to do with engagement in Europe, Central America, or the Middle East. Over the last thirty years, while taxes remained almost fixed (rising from 18.3 percent to 19.6 percent) and defense spending declined, domestic entitlements nearly doubled. What created an economy of debt unrivaled in American history is not foreign adventures but the low-tax ideology of the 1980s, coupled with America's insatiable desire for yet higher standards of living without paying any of the cost.

One can debate whether America is in true economic decline. Its percentage of world GNP is roughly where it has been throughout the twentieth century (between 22 and 26 percent), excepting the aberration of the immediate post–World War II era when its competitors were digging out from the rubble of world war. But even if one does argue that America is in economic decline, it is simply absurd to imply that the road to solvency is to, say, abandon El Salvador, evacuate the Philippines, or get out of the Gulf. There may be other good reasons for doing all of these. But it is nonsense to suggest doing them as a way to get at the root of America's economic problems.

It is, moreover, a mistake to view America's exertions abroad as nothing but a drain on its economy. As can be seen in the Gulf, America's involvement abroad is in many ways an essential pillar of the American economy. The United States is, like Britain before it, a commercial, maritime, trading nation that needs an open, stable world environment in which to thrive. In a world of Saddams, if the United States were to shed its unique superpower role, its economy would be gravely wounded. Insecure sea lanes, impoverished trading partners, exorbitant oil, explosive regional instability are only the more obvious risks of an American abdication. Foreign entanglements are indeed a burden. But they are also a necessity. The cost of ensuring an open and safe world for American commerce—5.4 percent of GNP and falling—is hardly exorbitant.

Isolationism

Can America support its unipolar status? Yes. But *will* Americans support such unipolar status? That is a more problematic question. For a small but growing chorus of Americans this vision of a unipolar world led by a dynamic America is a nightmare. Hence the second major element of the post–cold war reality: the revival of American isolationism.

I have great respect for American isolationism. First, because of its popular appeal and, second, because of its natural appeal. On the face of it, isolationism seems the logical, God-given foreign policy for the United States. It is not just geography that inclines us to it—we are an island continent protected by two vast oceans, bordered by two neighbors that could hardly be friendlier—but history. America was founded on the idea of cleansing itself of the intrigues and irrationalities, the dynastic squabbles and religious wars, of the Old World. One must have respect for a strain of American thinking so powerful that four months before Pearl Harbor the vote to extend draft enlistments passed the House of Representatives by a single vote.

Isolationists say rather unobjectionably that America should confine its attentions in the world to defending vital national interests. But the more extreme isolationists define vital national interests to mean the physical security of the United States, and the more elusive isolationists take care never to define them at all.

Isolationists will, of course, say that I am being unfair, that they do believe in defending vital national interests beyond the physical security of the United States. Well, we have just had a test case. Iraq's invasion of Kuwait and hegemonic designs on Arabia posed as clear a threat to American interests as one can imagine—a threat to America's oil based economy, to its close allies in the region, and ultimately to American security itself. The rise of a hostile power fueled by endless oil income building weapons of mass destruction and the means to deliver them regionally and eventually intercontinentally (Saddam has already tested a three-stage rocket) can hardly be a matter of indifference to the United States.

If under these conditions a cadre of influential liberals and conservatives found that upon reflection (and in contradiction to the doctrine enunciated by the most dovish president of the postwar era, Jimmy Carter) the Persian Gulf is not, after all, a vital American interest, then it is hard to see what "vital interest" can mean. If the Persian Gulf is not a vital interest, then nothing is. All that is left is preventing an invasion of the Florida Keys. And for that you need a Coast Guard. You don't need a Pentagon, and you certainly don't need a State Department.

Isolationists dream of a return to normality, meaning (for them) a time—say, nineteenth-century America—when the world sorts itself out on its own, leaving America unmolested. But the world does not sort itself out on its own. In the nineteenth century, for example, international stability was not achieved on its own but, in large part, as the product of Britain's unrelenting exertions on behalf of the balance of power. America tended her vineyards, but only behind two great ocean walls patrolled by the British navy. Alas, the British navy is gone.

International stability is never a given. It is never the norm. When achieved, it is the product of self-conscious action by the great powers, and most particularly of the greatest power, which for now and for the foreseeable future is the United States. If America wants stability, it will have to create it. Communism is indeed finished; the last of the messianic creeds that have haunted this century is quite dead. But there will constantly be new threats disturbing our peace.

The New Strategic Environment

What threats? Everyone recognizes one great change in the international environment, the collapse of communism. If that were the only change, then this might be a normal time and the unipolar vision I have outlined would seem at once unnecessary and dangerous.

But there is another great change in international relations. And here we come to the third and most crucial new element in the post–cold war world: the emergence of a new strategic environment marked by the proliferation of weapons of mass destruction. It is a certainty that in the near future there will be a dramatic increase in the number of states armed with biological, chemical, and nuclear weapons and the means to deliver them anywhere on earth. "By the year 2000," estimates Defense Secretary Dick Cheney,

more than two dozen developing nations will have ballistic missiles, 15 of those countries will have the scientific skills to make their own, and half of them either have or are near to getting nuclear capability, as well. Thirty countries will have chemical weapons and ten will be able to deploy biological weapons.

It is, of course, banal to say that modern technology has shrunk the world. But the obvious corollary, that in a shrunken world the divide between regional superpowers and great powers is radically narrowed, is rarely drawn. Missiles shrink distance. Nuclear (or chemical or biological) devices multiply power. Both can be bought at market. Consequently, the geopolitical map is irrevocably altered. Fifty years ago Germany—centrally located, highly industrial, and heavily populated—could pose a threat to world security and to the other great powers. It was inconceivable that, say, a relatively small Middle Eastern state with an almost entirely imported industrial base could do anything more than threaten its neighbors. The central truth of the coming era is that this is no longer the case: relatively small, peripheral, and backward states will be able to emerge rapidly as threats not only to regional but to world security.

Saddam's (prewar) Iraq was the prototype of this new strategic threat. North Korea, hard at work on nuclear technology, is the next candidate. Then, perhaps Libya. Windfall wealth allows oil states, like Iraq and Libya, to import high-technology weapons in the absence of a mature industrial base. However, it is not hard to imagine maturer states—say, Argentina, Pakistan, Iran, South Africa—reaching the same level of weapons development by means of ordinary industrialization. (Today most of these countries are friendly, but some are unstable and potentially hostile.)

The post–cold war era is thus perhaps better called the era of weapons of mass destruction. The proliferation of weapons of mass destruction and their means of delivery will constitute the greatest single threat to world security for the rest of our lives. That is what makes a new international order not an imperial dream or a Wilsonian fantasy but a matter of the sheerest prudence. It is slowly dawning on the West that there is a need to establish some new regime to police these weapons and those who brandish them.

How? There is no definitive answer, but any solution will have to include three elements: denying, disarming, and defending. First, we will have to develop a new regime similar to COCOM (Coordinating Committee on Export Controls) to deny yet more high technology to such states. Second, those states that acquire such weapons anyway will have to submit to strict outside control or risk being physically disarmed. A final element must be the development of antiballistic missile and air defense systems to defend against those weapons that do escape Western control or preemption.

There might be better tactics. But the overall strategy is clear. With the rise of revolutionary new technology, there is no alternative to confronting, deterring, and, if necessary, disarming states that brandish and use weapons of mass destruction. And there is no one to do that but the United States backed by as many of its allies as will join the endeavor.

I do not mean to imply that weapons of mass destruction are the only threat facing the post–cold war world. They are only the most obvious. Other threats exist, but they are more speculative and can be seen today only in outline: the rise, for example, of intolerant aggressive nationalism in a disintegrating Communist bloc (in one extreme formulation, the emergence of a reduced but resurgent, xenophobic and resentful "Weimar" Russia). And some threats to the peace of the twenty-first century are as invisible today as was, say, Nazism in 1920. They will make themselves known soon enough. Only a hopeless utopian can believe otherwise.

Nor do I mean to imply that the unipolarity of the world structure is license for the unilateral pursuit of American self-interest, simply because the U.S. has the power to pursue such a policy. On the contrary. Preeminence imposes heavy burdens on the U.S.

One of those burdens is to make the connection between America's moral and geopolitical standing. The Gulf War marks the official beginning of an era of Pax Americana. Now, historically, the world recoils at the thought of a single dominant power for fear of what it will do with its power. Much of the world fought against Germany (World War II) and resisted the Soviet Union (the cold war) for just that reason. America is an exception to this rule. Most people who live under our influence welcome it. They look at the three controlled experiments in Pax Americana—Korea, Germany, and China—and see the result: that part of the country assigned to America's sphere of influence became infinitely more prosperous and free than the other. For every country demanding that Soviet troops leave their territory, there are two begging American forces to stay. When the people shut out of Pax Americana are offered entry, as the East Germans were, they vote overwhelmingly to join.

The world acquiesces to American hegemony because the

world generally sees it as benign. The war for Kuwait has bolstered the sense that America acts not just out of self-interest but a
sense of right. America's retreat from Iraq after the war not only
tainted the whole Kuwaiti adventure, it put the benignity of Pax
Americana in question. Friends, allies, and neutrals will be more
reluctant to fall in behind a superpower that is driven by cold
calculation of its own self-interest.

The "new world order" cannot be all power, which we now
have. It cannot be all will, which we have just demonstrated. If it is
not to be ruinously difficult to impose, it requires acquiescence.
Otherwise we encounter the kind of sullen, then active resistance
that the Soviet empire engendered when it extended itself west
into Europe and south into Asia.

Which is why the U.S. must be careful how it expresses its
unipolar predominance. The U.S. may find itself acting unilaterally. When doing so is necessary, the U.S. should be unembar-
rassed about it, but also polite. Where multilateralism is possible,
where we can consult and act in concert with others, we should of
course do that, as we did in Kuwait.

But where it is not possible, we may have to act regardless. That
is what happened in Kurdistan. After Saddam's victory over the
Kurdish rebels, President Bush decided that something had to be
done. He consulted with the British and the French and Turks and
decided to intervene. There is little international legal basis for
what he did. Yet it is hard to see how the president could have
done otherwise.

Now, we will, of course, round up the usual international lawyers who will, in turn, round up the usual necessary Security
Council resolutions to retrospectively justify our actions in Kurdistan under international law. That is what international lawyers are
for. But let us be honest. We acted unilaterally in Kurdistan because it was the right thing to do. We got a couple of allies to join
us, but it is truly stretching things to say that this was done in
accord with international legality. Too bad. This will not be the
last time the U.S., with or without its allies, will be called upon to
intervene unilaterally, if necessary.

The alternative to such a robust interventionism, the alternative
to unipolarity, is not a stable, static multipolar world. It is not an

eighteenth-century world in which mature powers like Europe, Russia, China, America, and Japan jockey for position in the game of nations. The alternative to unipolarity is not multipolarity but chaos.

We are in for abnormal times. Our best hope for safety in such times, as in difficult times past, is in American strength and will— the strength and will to lead a unipolar world, unashamedly laying down the rules of world order and being prepared to enforce them. Compared to the task of defeating fascism and communism, averting chaos is a rather subtle call to greatness. It is not a task we are any more eager to undertake than the great twilight struggle just concluded. But it is just as noble and just as necessary.

8G

An International
Liberal Community

MICHAEL W. DOYLE

A mericans have always wanted to stand for something in the world. As liberals, we have wanted to stand for freedom, when we could. In recent times, both Republicans and Democrats have joined in this cause. In 1982 President Ronald Reagan announced a "crusade for freedom" and "a campaign for democratic development." In the 1988 presidential campaign, Vice President George Bush endorsed the "Reagan Doctrine." Governor Michael Dukakis repeated President John F. Kennedy's pledge to "pay any price, bear any burden, meet any hardship, support any friend, [and] oppose any foe to assure the survival and

MICHAEL W. DOYLE is professor of politics and international affairs in the Politics Department and Woodrow Wilson School, and faculty associate of the Center of International Studies, Princeton University. He was an SSRC/MacArthur Foundation Fellow in International Peace and Security Studies from 1985–89. He is the author of *Empires*, coeditor with Arthur Day of *Escalation and Intervention: Multilateral Security and Its Alternatives*, and coauthor with Fred Hirsch and Edward Morse of *Alternatives to Monetary Disorder*. Prof. Doyle would like to thank Peter Gellman and Hongying Wang for their thoughtful criticisms of this chapter.

success of liberty." Since then, President Bush has ordered an invasion of Panama and announced as a "plain truth: the day of the dictator is over. The people's right to democracy must not be denied."[1] He then justified the invasion as a way to protect U.S. citizens, arrest Manuel Noriega, and bestow democratic freedom to the people of Panama.

Realist skeptics, however, have denounced the pursuit of liberal ideas in foreign affairs as a dangerous illusion that threatens our security. Instead, they say we should focus on employing our national resources to promote our power in a world where nothing but self-help and the balancing of power against power will assure our security.[2] Radical skeptics, on the other hand, have portrayed liberal foreign affairs as little more than a cloak for imperialism.[3] Both sets of critics have identified actual dangers in liberal foreign policy.

What the skeptics miss, however, is the successful establishment of a liberal community of nations, and in missing the liberal community, they miss what appears to be the single best hope for the growth of a stable, just, and secure international order.

In this chapter, I want to examine the legacies of liberalism on foreign affairs and explore their foundations in the liberal community of democratic republican states. After tracing the mixed record of liberal influences on U.S. foreign policy, I will suggest ways in which the United States and its allies in the liberal community can preserve, manage, defend, expand, and (where needed) rescue the community from the threats it now faces.

A Liberal Community of Peace

For almost two centuries liberal countries have tended and, now, liberal democratic countries do tend, to maintain peaceful relations with each other. This is the community's first legacy. Other democracies are our natural allies. We tend to respect and accommodate democratic countries. We negotiate rather than escalate disputes.

During the nineteenth century, the United States and Great Britain engaged in nearly continual strife. But after the Reform Bill of 1832 defined actual representation as the formal source of the sovereignty of the British Parliament, Britain and the United

States negotiated their disputes despite, for example, severe British grievances against the Northern blockade of the South, with which Britain had close economic ties. Despite severe Anglo-French colonial rivalry, liberal France and liberal Britain formed an entente against illiberal Germany before World War I, and in 1914–15, Italy, the liberal member of the Triple Alliance with Germany and Austria, chose not to fulfill its treaty obligations under the Triple Alliance to support its allies. Instead, Italy joined in an alliance with Britain and France that had the effect of preventing it from having to fight other liberal states, and declared war on Germany and Austria. Despite generations of Anglo-American tension and Britain's wartime restrictions on American trade with Germany, the United States leaned toward Britain and France from 1914 to 1917, before entering World War I on their side.

Liberal states thus appear to exercise peaceful restraint, and a separate peace exists among them. This separate peace provides a political foundation that defines common strategic interests for the United States' crucial alliances with the liberal powers—NATO (North Atlantic Treaty Organization), our Japanese alliance, ANZUS (Australia, New Zealand, United States Treaty Alliance). This foundation resists the corrosive effects of the quarrels with our allies that bedeviled the Carter and Reagan administrations. It also offers the promise of a continuing peace among liberal states and, as the number of liberal states increases, it announces the possibility of global peace this side of the grave and short of a single world empire.

Of course, the outbreak of war, in any given year, between any two given states, is a low-probability event. But the occurrence of a war between any two adjacent states, considered over a long period of time, would be more probable. The apparent absence of war between liberal states, whether adjacent or not, for almost 200 years thus may have significance. Similar claims cannot be made for feudal, Fascist, Communist, authoritarian, or totalitarian forms of rule; nor for pluralistic, or merely similar societies. More significant, perhaps, is that when states are forced to decide on which side of an impending world war they will fight, liberal states wind up all on the same side, despite the complexity of the paths that take them there.

A liberal community of peace has become established among

liberal states. (More than forty liberal states currently compose their informal union. Most are in Europe and North America, but they can be found on every continent.) The firm maintenance of their separate peace since the eighteenth century offers the promise of a continuing peace, and a continuation of the unsteady but overall increase in the number of liberal states since that time announces the possibility of an eventual world peace (see Table 1 at the end of this chapter).

Although this banner has recently been waved before President Reagan's Republican "crusade for freedom," under President Woodrow Wilson's effort to make the world "safe for democracy" it formed the core vision of the foreign policy of the Democratic party. Wilson's war message of April 2, 1917 expressed this liberal commitment well: "Our object now, as then, is to vindicate the principles of peace and justice in the life of the world as against selfish and autocratic power and to set up amongst the really free and self-governed people of the world such concert of purpose and of action as will henceforth ensure the observance of those principles."

These characteristics do not prove that the peace among liberals is statistically significant, nor that liberalism is the peace's sole valid explanation.[4] But they do suggest that we consider the possibility that liberals have indeed established a separate peace—but only among themselves.

Liberal Imprudence

Liberalism, as the critics note, also carries with it other legacies. Peaceful restraint only seems to work in the liberals' relations with other liberals. Liberal states have fought numerous wars with non-liberal states.

Many of these wars have been defensive, and thus prudent by necessity. Liberal states have been attacked and threatened by nonliberal states that do not exercise any special restraint in their dealings with liberal states. Authoritarian rulers both stimulate and respond to an international political environment in which conflicts of prestige, of interest, and of pure fear of what other states might do all lead states toward war. War and conquest have thus characterized the careers of many authoritarian rulers and ruling parties, from Louis XIV and Napoleon to Mussolini's Fascists, Hitler's Nazis, and Stalin's Communists.

But we cannot simply blame warfare on the authoritarians or totalitarians, as many of our more enthusiastic politicians would have us do.[5] Although most wars arise out of calculations and miscalculations of interest, misunderstandings, and mutual suspicions, such as those that characterized the origins of World War I, aggression by the liberal state has also characterized a large number of wars. Both France and Britain fought expansionist colonial wars throughout the nineteenth century. The United States fought a similar war with Mexico in 1846–48, waged a war of annihilation against the American Indians, and intervened militarily against sovereign states many times before and after World War II. Liberal states invade weak nonliberal states and display striking distrust in dealings with powerful nonliberal states.

We need therefore to remind ourselves that a "freer world" does not automatically mean "a more peaceful world." Trying to make the world safe for democracy does not necessarily make democracies safe for the world.

On the one hand, democracies are prone to being tempted into aggressive crusades to expand overseas the "free world" of mutual security, civil liberties, private property, and democratic rule, and this has led in the past to enormous suffering and only infrequently to successful transplants of democratic rule to previously nondemocratic countries. Furthermore, we distrust nondemocratic countries, sometimes excessively. We regard their domestic oppression as an inherent sign of aggressive intent and downplay the role of error. In the KAL (Korean Airlines) 007 disaster, according to journalist Seymour Hersh, our government pronounced horrible error as evil intent, and we were all too ready to accept that verdict.

On the other hand, democratic majorities sometimes succumb to bouts of isolationism and appeasement, tempting aggressive states to employ strategies of piecemeal conquest (salami tactics). Self-indulgent majorities thus undermine what can be vital collective security interests.

Foundations

Neither realist nor Marxist theory accounts well for these two legacies. They can account for aspects of certain periods of international stability.[6] But neither the logic of the balance of power nor of international hegemony explains the separate peace maintained for more than 150 years among states sharing one particular form of governance—liberal principles and institutions. Balance-of-power theory expects, indeed is premised upon, flexible arrangements of geostrategic rivalry that regard foreign capabilities (whether democratically governed or not) as inherently threatening. Realist balancing theory therefore expects rational states to balance against proximate power. It also includes preventive war. But liberal neighbors, such as the United States and Canada, have maintained a long undefended border for over a century. Hegemonic states can police the lesser powers but, as hegemonies wax and wane, the liberal peace still holds. Marxist "ultraimperialists" (Kautsky-ists) expect a form of peaceful rivalry among capitalists, but only liberal capitalists maintain peace. Leninists do expect liberal capitalists to be aggressive toward nonliberal states, but they also (and especially) expect them to be imperialistic toward fellow advanced capitalists, whether liberal or not.

Perpetual Peace, an essay by the eighteenth-century German philosopher Immanuel Kant, helps us understand the effects of democratic republicanism on foreign affairs. In that essay, Kant shows how liberal republics lead to dichotomous international politics: peaceful relations—a "pacific union" among similarly liberal states—and a "state of war" between liberals and nonliberals.

First, Kant argues, republican governments tame the aggressive interests of absolutist monarchies by making government decisions subject to the control of majority representation. They also ingrain the habit of respect for individual rights. Wars then appear as the direct charges on the people's welfare that he and the other liberals thought them to be. Yet these domestic republican restraints do not end war. If they did, liberal states would not be warlike, which is far from the case. They do introduce republican caution, Kant's "hesitation," in place of monarchical caprice. Liberal wars are only fought for popular, liberal purposes. The historical liberal legacy is laden with popular wars fought to promote freedom, protect private property, or support liberal allies against nonliberal enemies.[7]

Second, in order to see how the pacific union removes the occasion of wars among liberal states and not wars between liberal and nonliberal states, we need to shift our attention from constitutional law to international law. Complementing the constitutional guarantee of caution, international law, according to Kant, adds a second source—a guarantee of respect. The separation of nations is reinforced by the development of separate languages and religions. These further guarantee a world of separate states—an essential condition needed to avoid a "global, soul-less despotism." Yet at the same time, they also morally integrate liberal states: "as culture grows and men gradually move towards greater agreement over their principles, they lead to mutual understanding and peace." As republics emerge (the first source) and as culture progresses, an understanding of the legitimate rights of all citizens and of all republics comes into play, and this, now that caution characterizes policy, sets up the moral foundations for the liberal peace.

Correspondingly, international law highlights the importance of Kantian publicity. Domestically, publicity helps ensure that the officials of republics act according to the principles they profess to hold just and according to the interests of the electors they claim to represent. Internationally, free speech and the effective communication of accurate conceptions of the political life of foreign peoples are essential to establish and preserve the understanding on which the guarantee of respect depends.

Domestically just republics, which rest on consent, presume foreign republics to be also consensual, just, and therefore deserving of accommodation. The experience of cooperation helps engender further cooperative behavior when the consequences of state policy are unclear but (potentially) mutually beneficial. At the same time, liberal states assume that nonliberal states, which do not rest on free consent, are not just. Because nonliberal governments are perceived to be in a state of aggression with their own people, their foreign relations become for liberal governments deeply suspect. Wilhelm II of Imperial Germany may or may not have been aggressive (he was certainly idiosyncratic); liberal democracies such as England, France, and the United States, however, assumed that whatever was driving German policy, reliable democratic, constitutional government was not restraining it. They regarded Germany and its actions with severe suspicion—to which the Reich reacted with corresponding distrust. In short, fellow liberals benefit from a presumption of amity; nonliberals suffer from a presumption of enmity. Both presumptions may be accurate. Each, however, may also be self-fulfilling.

Democratic liberals do not need to assume either that public opinion directly rules foreign policy or that the entire governmental elite is liberal. They can also assume a third possibility: that the elite typically manages public affairs but that potentially nonliberal members of the elite have reason to doubt that antiliberal policies would be electorally sustained and endorsed by the majority of the democratic public.

Lastly, "cosmopolitan law" adds material incentives to moral commitments. The cosmopolitan right to hospitality permits the "spirit of commerce" sooner or later to take hold of every nation, thus creating incentives for states to promote peace and to try to avert war. Liberal economic theory holds that these cosmopolitan ties derive from a cooperative international division of labor and free trade according to comparative advantage. Each economy is said to be better off than it would have been under autarky; each thus acquires an incentive to avoid policies that would lead the other to break these economic ties. Since keeping open markets rests upon the assumption that the next set of transactions will also be determined by prices rather than coercion, a sense of mutual security is vital to avoid security motivated searches for economic autarky. Thus, avoiding a challenge to another liberal state's security or even enhancing each other's security by means of alliance naturally follows economic interdependence.

A further cosmopolitan source of liberal peace is that the international market removes difficult decisions of production and distribution from the direct sphere of state policy. A foreign state thus does not appear directly responsible for these outcomes; states can stand aside from, and to some degree above, these inevitably contentious market rivalries and be ready to step in to resolve crises. The interdependence of commerce and the international contacts of state officials also help create crosscutting transnational ties that serve as lobbies for mutual accommodation. According to modern liberal scholars, international financiers and transnational and transgovernmental organizations create interests in favor of accommodation. Moreover, their variety has ensured that no single conflict sours an entire relationship by setting off a spiral of reciprocated retaliation. Conversely, a sense of suspicion, like that characterizing relations between liberal and nonliberal governments, makes transnational contacts appear subversive. Liberal and nonliberal states then mutually restrict the range of contacts between societies, and this can further increase the prospect that a single conflict will determine an entire relationship.

No single constitutional, international, or cosmopolitan source is alone sufficient. Kantian theory is neither solely institutional nor solely ideological, nor solely economic. But together (and only together) the three specific strands of liberal institutions, liberal ideas, and the transnational ties that follow from them, plausibly connect the characteristics of liberal polities and economies with sustained liberal peace.[8] But in their relations with nonliberal states, liberal states have not escaped from the insecurity caused by anarchy in the world political system considered as a whole.[9] Moreover, the very constitutional restraint, international respect for individual rights, and shared commercial interests that establish grounds for peace among liberal states establish grounds for additional conflict in relations between liberal and nonliberal societies.

A Need for New Thinking

In our recent past we have often failed to appreciate the significance of the liberal community. So, like the Russians, we stand in need of "new thinking." Our record fits the liberal community, but our debates have failed to understand it. Our failure to understand the opportunities of the liberal community may indeed be an important source of our frequent experience of the imprudent appeasement and crusading imperialism of which conservative and radical skeptics have warned us.

Before our rise to world power in the 1890s, American principles seemed to take a back seat to a series of pressing necessities. Securing our effective independence from England called for a strategy of limited involvement (enunciated in Washington's Farewell Address).[10] Acquiring a secure hold on the preponderance of North America stimulated a doctrine of spheres of influence (the Monroe Doctrine) and a policy of frontier colonialism (Manifest Destiny). Avoiding, succumbing to, then repairing the ravages of civil war reinforced the drive for continental hegemony and isolation from foreign entanglements. None of these dominant strategies was uncontested. Few of our foreign policy debates have been as spirited as the disputes over how best to achieve those goals of national security and economic development, as we can see in the domestic fights over the Jay Treaty (1794), the Tariff (1828), or the Mexican War (1848).

But the principle of freedom followed behind our national strategy. The United States was too weak to export freedom either through force or foreign aid as democratic internationalists such as Thomas Paine had urged and as France and later Britain did. Americans settled upon an international identity as a secularized republican version of the Puritan "City upon a Hill."[11] America would be a model for democratic republicanism, a laboratory of democratic experiment, and a refuge for oppressed liberals from around the world. The American democrats chose "democracy in one country." Defending our existence preempted exporting our essence.

The recent post-1945 cold war period is no better guide to our challenges. Our commitment to freedom was not subordinated to our security or our prosperity; it was, as we then saw it, indistinguishable from them. In 1947 President Truman declared that nearly every nation had to chose between two alternative ways of life: democratic freedom or autocratic oppression. He defined our purposes by announcing that "I believe it must be the policy of the United States to support free peoples who are resisting attempted subjugation by armed minorities or by outside pressures." Following the defeat of the Axis powers, the Communist Soviet Union posed the greatest threat to democratic freedom on a worldwide basis. But in those years national security and economic prosperity pointed in very much the same direction. George Kennan's geopolitical analysis of the five centers of potential global industrial power suggested that as long as the United States prevented any rival from acquiring control over Eurasia, the U.S. would remain secure. Containing the USSR, preventing it from dominating Western Europe and Japan, effectively satisfied this geostrategic imperative.[12] Equally, preserving our prosperity seemed to mean avoiding the spiraling escalation of tariff and investment restrictions, competitive monetary depreciation, and financial expropriation that had accompanied the worldwide economic crisis of the Great Depression. Protectionism, of course, was widespread as the industrial and agrarian economies attempted to readjust to peacetime conditions, but the most serious threat of total restrictions again came from the spread of communism. Having rejected isolationism, we were spared other hard choices. Our principles, our national security, our economic interests all pointed the same way, toward containment of the Communist bloc.

Our last age of intellectually difficult strategic choice was thus the age of our rise to world power, between 1890 and 1940. But it too serves as a poor model for today. Even if we could allow for the significant differences in political and economic environment, the choices made then represent not a positive but a negative model, what we must try to avoid rather than to repeat. We first chose liberal imperialism toward our weaker neighbors in Latin America and the Pacific. Then we chose isolationism in the face of growing demand for our participation in the international organization of international security.

In 1899 President McKinley grandiloquently proclaimed that "our priceless principles undergo no change under the tropical sun. They go with the flag." But from our perspective today, the racism and arrogance that also shaped those policies render them unacceptable, even if the imperial variety of international paternalism were affordable.

The isolationist response to dealings with other powerful states created equally costly results. The United States Senate rejected our participation in the League of Nations, leaving a fatal gap in its membership. As importantly, our reluctance to play a direct and active role in European security complicated the management of the European debt problem (despite the active role played by New

York bankers) and in the 1930s raised anew the problem of who or
what would contain a reviving Germany. Today, even more
clearly, the integration of the world trading system, United States
and Third World international debts and deficits, the resource
dependence of the major industrial nations of Europe and Japan
make an isolationist strategy reckless in the extreme.

We need to go beyond those two historic alternatives in United
States national strategy—moralistic isolationism and liberal imperialism.[13] We lack the simple constraints of pre-1898 weakness and
post-1945 cold war. Today our economic interests are ambiguous.
Can we best revive our sagging productivity through nationalism
or multilateralism?[14] President Mikhail Gorbachev's steps toward
detente and democratic reform are depriving the original cold war
of its purpose.[15] Looming shifts in the balance of resources and
productivity suggest to some an increase in Japanese, Chinese, and
(if united) European power. But do we really want to regard them
as potential enemies and therefore to play multipolar balancing
against them?

Securing and Expanding
the Liberal Community

An important alternative to the balancing of enemies is thus the
cultivation of friends. If the actual history of the liberal community
is reliable, a better strategy for our foreign relations lies in the
development of the liberal community.

If a concern for protecting and expanding the range of international freedom is to shape our strategic aims, then policy toward
the liberal and the nonliberal world should be guided by general
liberal principles. At the minimum, this means rejecting the realist
balance of power as a general strategy by trusting the liberal community and therefore refusing to balance against the capabilities of
fellow democratic liberals. At its fullest, this also means going
beyond the standard provisions of international law. Membership
in the liberal community implies accepting a positive duty to defend other members of the liberal community, to discriminate in
certain instances in their favor, and to override in some (hopefully

rare) circumstances the domestic sovereignty of states in order to
rescue fellow human beings from intolerable oppression. Authentically liberal policies should, furthermore, attempt to secure personal and civil rights, to foster democratic government, and to
expand the scope and effectiveness of the world market economy
as well as to meet those basic human needs that make the exercise
of human rights possible.

In order to avoid the extremist possibilities of its abstract univer-
salism, however, U.S. liberal policy should be constrained by a
geopolitical budget. Strategy involves matching what we are prepared to spend to what we want to achieve. It identifies our aims,
resources, threats, and allies. While liberal democracy thus can
identify our natural allies abroad, we must let our actual enemies
identify themselves.

One reason for this is that we cannot embark upon the "crusades" for democracy that have been so frequent within the liberal
tradition. In a world armed with nuclear weapons, crusading is
suicidal. In a world where changes in regional balances of power
could be extremely destabilizing for ourselves and our allies, indiscriminate provocations of hostility (such as against the People's
Republic of China) could create increased insecurity (for Japan
and ourselves). In a world of global interdependence, common
problems require multilateral solutions. We simply do not have the
excess strength that would free us from a need to economize on
dangers or to squander opportunities for negotiated solutions.

A second reason why we should let our enemies identify themselves is that our liberal values require that we should reject an
indiscriminate "crusade for democracy." If we seek to promote
democracy because it reflects the rights of all to be treated with
equal respect, irrespective of race, religion, class, or nationality,
then equal respect must guide both our aims and our means. A
strategy of geopolitical superiority and liberal imperialism, for example, would both require increased arms expenditures and international subversion and have little or (more likely) a retrogressive
effect on human rights in the countries that are our targets.

Instead, our strategy should lean toward the defensive. It should
strive to protect the liberal community, foster the conditions that

might allow the liberal community to grow, and save the use of force for clear emergencies that severely threaten the survival of the community or core liberal values.

Preserving the Community. Above all, liberal policy should strive to preserve the pacific union of similarly liberal societies. It is not only currently of immense strategic value (being the political foundation of both NATO and the Japanese alliance); it is also the single best hope for the evolution of a peaceful world. Liberals should be prepared, therefore, to defend and formally ally with authentically liberal, democratic states that are subject to threats or actual instances of external attack or internal subversion. We must continue to have no liberal enemies and no unconditional alliances with nonliberal states.

We have underestimated the importance of the democratic alliance. Our alliances in NATO, with Japan, ANZUS, and our alignments with other democratic states are not only crucial to our present security, they are our best hopes for long-term peace and the realization of our ideals. We should not treat them as once useful but now purposeless cold war strategic alignments against the power of the USSR.

They deserve our careful investment. Spending $200 million to improve the prospects of President Corazon Aquino's efforts to achieve a transition to stable democracy in the Philippines cannot be considered too large an investment. Placing a special priority on helping the Argentineans and Mexicans manage their international debts is a valuable form of discrimination, if we take into account that financial decompression in those countries might undermine their democratic governance. With the help of West European and Japanese allies, a similar political investment in the economic transition of the fledgling democracies of Eastern Europe merits equivalent attention.

Managing the Community. Much of our success in alliance management has to be achieved on a multilateral basis. The current need to redefine NATO and the increasing importance of the U.S. relationship with Japan offer us an opportunity to broaden the organization of liberal security. Joining all the democratic states together in a single democratic security organization would secure an important forum for the definition and coordination of common interests that stretch beyond the regional concerns of Europe and the Far East. As the cold war fades, pressures toward regionalism are likely to become increasingly strong. In order to avoid the desperate responses that might follow regional reactions to regional crises such as those of the 1920s and 1930s, a wider alliance of liberal democracies seems necessary. It could reduce pressures on Japan and Germany to arm themselves with nuclear weapons, mitigate the strategic vulnerabilities of isolated liberal states such as Israel, and allow for the complementary pooling of strategic resources (combining, for example, Japanese and German financial clout with American nuclear deterrence and American, British, and French expeditionary thrust).

Much of the success of multilateral management will rest, however, on shoring up economic supports. Reducing the U.S. budget and trade deficits will especially require multilateral solutions. Unilateral solutions (exchange rate depreciation, increased taxation) are necessary but not sufficient, and some (protectionism) are neither. Avoiding a costly economic recession calls for trade liberalization and the expansion of demand abroad to match the contraction of governmental and private spending in the United States. But we will also need to create a diplomatic atmosphere conducive to multilateral problem solving. A national strategy that conveys a commitment to collective responsibility in United States diplomacy will go far in this direction.

Discovering ways to manage global interdependence will call for difficult economic adjustments at home and institutional innovations in the world economy. Under these circumstances, liberals will need to ensure that those suffering losses, such as from market disruption or restriction, do not suffer a permanent loss of income or exclusion from world markets. Furthermore, to prevent these emergency measures from escalating into a spiral of isolationism, liberal states should undertake these innovations only by international negotiation and only when the resulting agreements are subject to a regular review by all the parties.[16]

Protecting the Community. The liberal community needs
to be protected. Two models could fit liberal national strategy
designed to protect against the international power of nonliberal
states.[17]

If faced with severe threats from the nonliberal world, the liberal community might simply balance the power of nonliberal
states by playing divide and rule within the nonliberal camp, trian-
gulating, for example, between Russia and China as the United
States did during the 1970s.

If, on the other hand, the liberal community becomes increasingly predominant (or collectively unipolar) as it now appears to be
becoming, the liberal community could adopt a more ambitious
grand strategy. Arms exports, trade, and aid could reflect the relative degrees of liberal principle that nonliberal domestic and foreign policies incorporate. Liberal foreign policy could be designed
to create a ladder of rewards and punishments—a set of balanced
incentives, rewarding liberalization and punishing oppression, rewarding accommodation and punishing aggression. This strategy
would both satisfy liberal demands for publicity—consistent public
legitimation—and create incentives for the progressive liberalization of nonliberal states.

Expanding the Community. There are few direct measures
that the liberal world can take to foster the stability, development,
and spread of liberal democratic regimes. Many direct efforts,
including military intervention and overt or covert funding for
democratic movements in other countries, discredit those movements as the foreign interference backfires through the force of
local nationalism. (The democratic movement in Panama denounced U.S. political aid before the invasion and today suffers at
home and abroad from its overt dependence on the United States.)

Much of the potential success of a policy designed to foster
democracy rests therefore on an ability to shape an economic and
political environment that indirectly supports democratic governance and creates pressures for the democratic reform of authoritarian rule.

Politically, there are few measures more valuable than an active
human rights diplomacy, which enjoys global legitimacy and (if

successful) can assure a political environment that tolerates the sort of dissent that can nourish an indigenous democratic movement. There is reason to pay special attention to those countries entering what Samuel Huntington has called the socioeconomic "transition zone"—countries having the economic development that has typically been associated with democracy.[18] For them, more direct support in the form of electoral infrastructure (from voting machines to battalions of international observers) can provide the essential margin persuading contentious domestic groups to accept the fairness of the crucial first election.

Economically, judging from the historical evidence of the 1920s and 1930s, democratic regimes seem to be more vulnerable to economic depression than authoritarian regimes. (This is why economic aid should be targeted at the margin toward fledgling democracies.) But in periods of stable economic growth, democratic regimes seem to accommodate those social groups that are newly mobilized by economic growth better over the long run than do authoritarian regimes. Democracies expand participation better. They also allow for the expression of nonmaterial goals more easily, it seems, than do the more functionally legitimated authoritarian regimes. Economic growth thus may be the liberals' best long-run strategy.

Following World War II, the allied occupation and remaking of Germany and Japan and the Marshall Plan's successful coordination and funding of the revival of Europe's prewar industrial economies and democratic regimes offer a model of how much can be achieved with an extraordinary commitment of resources and the most favorable possible environment. Practically, today, short of those very special circumstances, there are few direct means to stimulate economic growth and democratic development from abroad. But liberals should persevere in attempts to keep the world economy free from destabilizing protectionist intrusions. Although intense economic interdependence generates conflicts, it also helps to sustain the material well-being underpinning liberal societies and to promise avenues of development to Third World states with markets that are currently limited by low income.[19] To this should be added mutually beneficial measures designed to improve Third World economic performance. Export earnings insurance, international debt management assistance, export diversification assistance, and technical aid are some of these. In the case of the truly desperate poor, the condition of some of the populations of Africa, more direct measures of international aid and relief from famine are required, both as a matter of political prudence and of moral duty.

Rescuing the Community.

Rescuing the Community. Liberal principles can also help us think about whether liberal states should attempt to rescue individuals oppressed by their own governments. Should a respect for the rights of individuals elicit our help or even military rescue? Historically, liberals have been divided on these issues,[20] and the U. S. public today has no clear answer to these questions. It supported the "rescue" of Grenada and the purge in Panama, but as many rejected "another Vietnam" in Nicaragua.[21]

Traditionally, and in accord with current international law, states have the right to defend themselves, come to the aid of other states aggressed against, and, where necessary, take forcible measures to protect their citizens from wrongful injury and release them from wrongful imprisonment.[22] But modern international law condemns sanctions designed to redress the domestic oppression of states. The United Nations Charter is ambiguous on this issue, since it finds human rights to be international concerns and permits the Security Council to intervene to prevent "threats" to "international peace and security." Given the ambiguity of the charter and the political stalemate of the Security Council, difficult moral considerations thus must become a decisive factor in considering policy toward domestic oppression in foreign countries.[23]

Nonintervention also has important moral foundations. It helps encourage order—stable expectations—in a confusing world without international government. It rests on a respect for the rights of individuals to establish their own way of life free from foreign interference.

The basic moral presumption of liberal thought is that states should not be subject to foreign intervention, by military or other means. Lacking a global scheme of order or global definition of community, foreign states have no standing to question the legitimacy of other states other than in the name and "voice" of the individuals who inhabit those other states. States therefore should be taken as representing the moral rights of individuals unless there is clear evidence to the contrary. Although liberals and democrats have often succumbed to the temptation to intervene to bring "civilization," metropolitan standards of law and order, and democratic government to foreign peoples expressing no demand for them, these interventions find no justification in a conception of equal respect for individuals. This is simply because it is to their sense of their own self-respect and not our sense of what they should respect that we must accord equal consideration.

What it means to respect their own sense of self-determination is not always self-evident. Ascertaining what it might mean can best be considered as an attempt at both subjective and objective interpretation.

One criterion is subjective. We should credit the voice of their majority. Obviously, this means not intervening against states with apparent majority support. In authoritarian states, however, determining what are the wishes of the majority is particularly difficult. Some states will have divided political communities with a considerable but less than a majority of the population supporting the government, a large minority opposing, and many indifferent. Some will be able to suppress dissent completely. Others will not. Widespread armed resistance sustained by local resources and massive street demonstrations against the state (and not just against specific policies) therefore can provide evidence of a people standing against their own government. Still, one will want to find clear evidence that the dissenters actually want a foreign intervention to solve their oppression.

The other criterion is objective. No group of individuals, even if apparently silent, can be expected to consent to having their basic rights to life, food, shelter, and freedom from torture systematically violated. These sorts of rights clearly crosscut wide cultural differences.

Whenever either or both of these violations take place, one has (1) a prima facie consideration favoring foreign intervention.[24] But even rescuing majorities suffering severe oppression or individuals suffering massive and systematic violations of human rights is not sufficient grounds to justify military intervention. We must also have (2) some reasonable expectation that the intervention will actually end the oppression. We need to expect that it will end the

massacre or address starvation (as did India's intervention in East
Pakistan and Tanzania's in Uganda). Or, if prodemocratic, it
should have a reasonable chance of establishing authentic self-
determination, rather than (as J. S. Mill warned) merely introducing new rulers who, dependent on outside support, soon begin to
replicate the oppressive behavior of the previous rulers. (The U.S.
invasion of Grenada and the covert push in the Philippines seem
to qualify; the jury is still out on Haiti and Panama.)

Moreover, (3) the intervention must be a proportional response
to the suffering now endured and likely to be endured without an
intervention. Countries cannot, any more than villages, be destroyed in order to be saved. We must consider whether means
other than military intervention could achieve the liberation from
oppression, and we must ensure that the intervention, if necessary,
is conducted in a way that minimizes casualties, most particularly
noncombatant casualties. In short, we must be able morally to
account for the expected casualties of an invasion both to our own
soldiers and to the noncombatant victims.

And (4) a normal sense of fallibility, together with a decent
respect for the opinions of the entire community of nations,
recommends a resort wherever feasible to multilateral organizations to guide and legally legitimate a decision to violate the autonomy of another state.

A Liberal Future

If, as is likely, liberal principles and institutions continue to influence the formulation of United States foreign policy in the
1990s, what opportunities and dangers might arise?

Where liberal internationalism among liberal states has been
deficient is in preserving its basic preconditions under changing
international circumstances, and particularly in supporting the liberal character of its constituent states. It has failed on occasion, as
it did in regard to Germany in the 1920s, to provide international
economic support for liberal regimes whose market foundations
were in crisis. It failed in the 1930s to provide military aid or
political mediation to Spain, which was challenged by an armed
minority, or to Czechoslovakia, which was caught in a dilemma of
preserving national security or acknowledging the claims (fostered

by Hitler's Germany) of the Sudeten minority to self-determination. Farsighted and constitutive measures have only been provided by the liberal international order when one liberal state stood preeminent among the rest, prepared and able to take measures, as did the United States following World War II, to sustain economically and politically the foundations of liberal society beyond its borders. Then measures such as the British Loan, the Marshall Plan, NATO, the General Agreement on Tariffs and Trade, the International Monetary Fund, and the liberalization of Germany and Japan helped construct buttresses for the international liberal order.[25]

Thus the decline of U.S. hegemonic leadership in the 1990s may pose dangers for the liberal world. The danger is not that today's liberal states will permit their economic competition to spiral into war, nor that a world economic crisis is now likely, but that the societies of the liberal world will no longer be able to provide the mutual assistance they might require to sustain liberal domestic orders if they were to be faced with mounting economic crises.

Yet liberals may have escaped from the single greatest traditional danger of international change—the transition between hegemonic leaders. Historically, when one great power begins to lose its preeminence and to slip into mere equality, a warlike resolution of the international pecking order became exceptionally likely. New power challenges old prestige, excessive commitments face new demands; so Sparta felt compelled to attack Athens, France warred Spain, England and Holland fought with France (and with each other), and Germany and England struggled for the mastery of Europe in World War I.[26] But here liberals may again be an exception, for despite the fact that the United States constituted Britain's greatest challenger along all the dimensions most central to the British maritime hegemony, Britain and the United States accommodated their differences. After the defeat of Germany, Britain eventually, though not without regret, accepted its replacement by the United States as the commercial and maritime hegemon of the liberal world. The promise of a peaceable transition from one liberal hegemon to the next liberal hegemon thus may be one of the factors helping to moderate economic and political rivalries among Europe, Japan, and the United States.

Choices in Liberal
Foreign Policy

In the years ahead we will need to chart our own national strategy as a liberal democracy faced with threats, but now also with opportunities for new thinking. In order to fulfill the promise of liberal internationalism, we must ensure a foreign policy that tries to reconcile our interests with our principles.

We will need to address the hard choices that no government truly committed to the promotion of human rights can avoid. Acknowledging that there may arise circumstances where international action—even force—is needed, we need strategic thinking that curbs the violent moods of the moment.

We will also need to keep our larger purposes in view. Those committed to freedom have made a bargain with their governments. We need only to live up to it. The major costs of a liberal strategy are borne at home. Not merely are its military costs at the taxpayers' expense, but a liberal foreign policy requires adjustment to a less controlled international political environment—a rejection of the status quo in favor of democratic choice. Tolerating more foreign change requires more domestic change. Avoiding an imperial presence in the Persian Gulf may require a move toward energy independence. Allowing for the economic development of the world's poor calls for an acceptance of international trade adjustment. The home front thus becomes the front line of liberal strategy.

The promises of successful liberal internationalism, however, are large and can benefit all. The pursuit of freedom does not guarantee the maintenance of peace. Indeed, the very invocation of "crusade" as a label for President Reagan's democratic initiative of the 1980s warns us otherwise. But the peaceful intent and restraint to which liberal institutions, principles, and interests have led in relations among liberal democracies suggest the possibility of world peace this side of the grave. They offer the promise of a world peace established by the expansion of the separate peace among liberal societies.

**TABLE 1. The Liberal Community
(By date "liberal")[a]**

Period		Total Number
18th century	Swiss Cantons[b]	3
	French Republic 1790–1795	
	United States[b] 1776–	
1800–1850	Swiss Confederation,	8
	United States	
	France 1830–1849	
	Belgium 1830–	
	Great Britain 1932–	
	Netherlands 1848–	
	Piedmont 1848–	
	Denmark 1849–	
1850–1900	Switzerland,	13
	United States,	
	Belgium, Great Britain,	
	Netherlands	
	Piedmont–1861, Italy 1861–	
	Denmark–1866	
	Sweden 1864–	
	Greece 1864–	
	Canada 1867–[c]	
	France 1871–	
	Argentina 1880–	
	Chile 1891–	
1900–1945	Switzerland,	29
	United States,	
	Great Britain,	
	Sweden, Canada	
	Greece–1911,	
1928–1936	Italy–1922	
	Belgium–1940;	
	Netherlands–1940;	
	Argentina–1943	
	France–1940	
	Chile–1924, 1932	
	Australia 1901	
	Norway 1905–1940	
	New Zealand 1907–	
	Colombia 1910–1949	
	Denmark 1914–1940	
	Poland 1917–1935	

TABLE 1. *(Continued)*

Period		Total Number
	Latvia 1922–1934	
	Germany 1918–1932	
	Austria 1918–1934	
	Estonia 1919–1934	
	Finland 1919–	
	Uruguay 1919–	
	Costa Rica 1919–	
	Czechoslovakia 1920–1939	
	Ireland 1920–	
	Mexico 1928–	
	Lebanon 1944–	
1945[d]–	Switzerland, the United States,	
	Great Britain, Sweden	
	Canada, Australia, New Zealand,	
	Finland, Ireland, Mexico	
	Uruguay–1973; 1985–	
	Chile–1973;	
	Lebanon–1975	
	Costa Rica–1948, 1953–	
	Iceland 1944–	
	France 1945–	
	Denmark 1945–	
	Norway 1945–	
	Austria 1945–	
	Brazil 1945–1954, 1955–1964; 1985–	
	Belgium 1946–	
	Luxemburg 1946–	
	Netherlands 1946–	
	Italy 1946–	
	Philippines 1946–1972; 1987–	
	India 1947–1975, 1977–	
	Sri Lanka 1948–1961, 1963–1971, 1978–1983	
	Ecuador 1948–1963, 1979–	
	Israel 1949–	
	West Germany 1949–	
	Greece 1950–1967, 1975–	
	Peru 1950–1962, 1963–1968, 1980–	
	El Salvador 1950–1961	
	Turkey 1950–1960, 1966–1971; 1984–	
	Japan 1951–	
	Bolivia 1956–1969, 1982–	

TABLE 1. *(Continued)*

Period	Total Number
Colombia 1958–	54
Venezuela 1959–	
Nigeria 1961–1964, 1979–1984	
Jamaica 1962–	
Trinidad and Tobago 1962–	
Senegal 1963–	
Malaysia 1963–	
Botswana 1966–	
Singapore 1965–	
Portugal 1976–	
Spain 1978–	
Dominican Republic 1978–	
Honduras 1981–	
Papua New Guinea 1982–	
Argentina 1983–	
South Korea 1988–	
Taiwan 1988–	

[a]I have drawn up this approximate list of "liberal regimes" (through 1982) according to the four "Kantian" institutions described as essential: market and private property economies; polities that are externally sovereign; citizens who possess juridical rights; and "republican" (whether republican or parliamentary monarchy), representative government. This latter includes the requirement that the legislative branch have an effective role in public policy and be formally and competitively (either inter- or intraparty) elected. Furthermore, I have taken into account whether male suffrage is wide (that is, 30 percent) or, as Kant would have had it, open to "achievement" by inhabitants (for example, to poll tax payers or householders) of the national or metropolitan territory. (This list of liberal regimes is thus more inclusive than a list of democratic regimes, or polyarchies. Female suffrage is granted within a generation of its being demanded by an extensive female suffrage movement; and representative government is internally sovereign (for example, including and especially over military and foreign affairs) as well as stable (in existence for at least three years). (Banks and Overstreet [1983]; U.K. Foreign and Commonwealth Office [1980]; *The Europa Yearbook, 1985;* Langer [1968]; U.S. Department of State [1981]; Gastil [1985]; Freedom House [1991].

[b] There are domestic variations within these liberal regimes. For example, Switzerland was liberal only in certain cantons; the United States was liberal only north of the Mason-Dixon line until 1865, when it became liberal throughout. These lists also exclude ancient "republics," since none appear to fit Kant's criteria (Holmes [1979]).

[c]Canada, as a commonwealth within the British empire, did not have formal control of its foreign policy during this period.

[d]Selected list, excludes liberal regimes with populations less than 1 million. These include all states categorized as "Free" by Freedom House and those "Partly Free" (45 or more free) states with a more pronounced capitalist orientation.

Notes

[1] *Department of State Bulletin*, June 1989.

[2] For an eloquent polemic defending this view, see the fine essay by Mear-sheimer (1990a). For a thoughtful and thorough critique of the position and pre-scription, see Ullman (1991), chapter 7.

[3] An important account of the many ways in which liberal ideology has served as a cloak for imperialism in U.S. foreign policy can be found in Williams (1962).

[4] See the discussion of Kant's international politics and the evidence for the liberal peace in Doyle (1986). Babst (1972) did make a preliminary test of the significance of the distribution of alliance partners in World War I. He found that the possibility that the actual distribution of alliance partners could have occurred by chance was less than 1 percent (p. 56), but this assumes that there was an equal possibility that any two nations could have gone to war with each other; and this is a strong assumption. Rummel (1983) has a further discussion of significance as it applies to his libertarian thesis.

[5] There are, however, serious studies that show that Marxist regimes have higher military spending per capita than non-Marxist regimes. But this should not be interpreted as a sign of the inherent aggressiveness of authoritarian or totalitar-ian governments or—with even greater enthusiasm—the inherent and global peacefulness of liberal regimes. Marxist regimes, in particular, represent a minor-ity in the current international system; they are strategically encircled, and, due to their lack of domestic legitimacy, they might be said to "suffer" the twin burden of needing defenses against both external and internal enemies.

[6] See Aron (1986), pp. 151–54, and Russett (1985).

[7] Kant regards these wars as unjust and warns liberals of their susceptibility to them. At the same time, he argues that each nation "can and ought to" demand that its neighboring nations enter into the pacific union of liberal states.

[8] For a more extensive description and analysis of the liberal community, see Doyle (1983a). Streit (1939), pp. 88, 90–92, seems to have been the first to point out (in contemporary foreign relations) the empirical tendency of democracies to maintain peace among themselves, and he made this the foundation of his pro-posal for a (non-Kantian) federal union of the fifteen leading democracies of the 1930s. Recent work by Russett, Maoz, Ray, and Modelski has extended this field into considerations of wider strategies of international reform and the evolution of the international system.

[9] For evidence, see Doyle (1983b).

[10] Neo-Washingtonians (to coin a label) such as John Gaddis propose a similar strategy for the 1990s. See his "Toward the Post–Cold War World: Structure, Strategy, and Security" (forthcoming in *Foreign Affairs*).

[11] See Baritz (1964) and discussion in Davis and Lynn-Jones (1987), p. 22.

[12] See the evidence and argument in Gaddis (1982) and (1977).

[13] Our record indicates a tendency to succumb to these alternatives, as has been well demonstrated in Ullman (1975–76).

[14] See the informative debate between Laura Tyson and Robert Reich in *The American Prospect* (Winter 1991), and for a thorough background to the issues, see Gilpin (1987).

[15] George Kennan, America's premier Sovietologist, told the Senate Foreign Relations Committee on April 4, 1989, that the break-up of the system of power

through which the Soviet Union has been ruled since 1917 indicates that the time "has clearly passed for regarding the Soviet Union primarily as a possible, if not probable, military opponent."

[16] These and similar policies are developed by Bergsten et al. (1978) and Cooper et al. (1978).

[17] For a discussion of strategy toward once-enemies now in a transition zone toward potential friends, see Allison (1988).

[18] See the comments of Larry Diamond on some suggestions made by Juan Linz in Diamond (1989).

[19] Liberal democrats should consider that two serious rival democratic political economies might emerge. The East Asian national corporatist strategy is immensely successful (e.g., Singapore). It is a crucial minor key in Japanese development, it is the major key in Taiwan and South Korea, and it is spreading as a developmental ideal. Another is social democracy. Social insurance and egalitarianism are too deeply rooted in Eastern Europe (witness Walesa's trouncing of Mazowiecki and Yeltsin's defeat in the Russian legislature on land ownership) to allow a happy accommodation with the heavily capitalist element in Western democracy. Furthermore, there are the not as yet very democratic Third World variants, such as Islamic fundamentalism.

[20] Liberals also give mixed advice on these matters. Kant argued that the "preliminary articles" from this treaty of perpetual peace required extending nonintervention by force in internal affairs of other states to nonliberal governments and maintaining a scrupulous respect for the laws of war. Yet he thought that liberal states could demand that other states become liberal. J.S. Mill said that intervention was impermissible except to support states threatened by external aggression and by foreign intervention in civil wars. Yet he justified British imperialism in India.

[21] See the *ABC/Washington Post* poll reported in *Time*, November 21, 1983, and the *Washington Post*, October 24, 1984.

[22] Cutler (1985).

[23] Reisman (1984) suggests a legal devolution of Security Council responsibilities to individual states. Schachter (1984) argues that such rights to intervene would be abused by becoming self-serving. For a carefully reasoned revival of moral arguments for just war criteria, see Walzer (1977). The policy of sanctions against South Africa, designed to undermine the domestic system of apartheid, is an earlier instance of these efforts.

[24] Lesser violations of human rights (various lesser forms of majority tyranny, for example) can warrant foreign diplomatic interference. The two severe abuses of liberal respect call for something more. The two severe abuses, of course, also tend to go together. Democratic resistance to authoritarian or totalitarian governments tends to result in the government inflicting severe abuses of human rights on the democratic resistance. Governments that systematically abuse the rights of their citizens rarely have widespread popular support. But they need not go together, hence their independence as criteria. There is one further constraint. Although the only popular movements for which one might justly intervene need not be democratically liberal, it would by these standards clearly be wrong to intervene in favor of a popular movement committed to a political program that would involve the systematic abuse of basic, "objective" human rights.

[25] Kindleberger (1973), Gilpin (1975), and Hirsch and Doyle (1977).

[26] The popular classic making these arguments is Kennedy (1987).

THINKING BEYOND
THE GULF WAR

9A

Military Lessons and U.S. Forces

WILLIAM E. ODOM

I t will require years of analysis to work through the lessons of Operation Desert Storm for modern warfare and future planning, but some conclusions are unambiguous. Clearly, there has been a qualitative change in warfare, one that has enormous implications for designing future American forces.

The Changing Nature of War

First, the U.S. military has traditionally thought of interstate wars in the Third World as "limited" or "low-intensity conflicts." Many of them have and will increasingly exceed those characteri- ꜜ

Lieutenant General WILLIAM E. ODOM, USA (Ret.) is director of national security studies for Hudson Institute and an adjunct professor at Yale University. At the time of his retirement from the Army, General Odom was director of the National Security Agency and chief, Central Security Service, and had served as a senior member of the National Security Council staff during the Carter administration. General Odom has written widely on Soviet political and military affairs, including his recent book, *The Soviet Volunteers*.

zations. Industrialization in some parts of the Third World and vast transfers of modern arms mean that many Third World states have fairly modern military arsenals and rather large ones.

Second, notwithstanding the character of some Third World armies, even their best efforts cannot bring forces to the conflict that begin to rival the American forces used in Desert Storm. That fact will not deter all Third World leaders from risking interstate war, but it will deter most of them if U.S. forces are available and deployable to the area of the conflict.

Third, though, this large U.S. military advantage will not necessarily deter insurgencies and internal wars. On the contrary, it could make them more attractive as ways to avoid a direct collision with American military might. Declining Soviet support to insurgencies has created the impression that the end of the cold war will also mark a decline in internal wars in the Third World. One consequence of Desert Storm could be to prompt dissatisfied Third World states more frequently to resort to support for insurgency and internal war rather than risk an external war—that is, a direct interstate military conflict. The end of the cold war, therefore, may not be marked by fewer internal wars in the Third World.

Fourth, strategic lift is a major factor for future warfare. It can both limit participation and expand it, depending on the lift capabilities of the states that want to be involved. Projecting forces is also constrained by diplomacy. En route basing and support are required even for the United States, and diplomacy must succeed to make them available. Thus coalition warfare is likely to be the case if the United States or its allies are to be involved. The same is true for the Soviet Union, and given its changed foreign policy and its changing relations with client states, Soviet force projection potential—never very great—has declined.

Fifth, the role of nuclear weapons in future war is changing. Strategic defense will clearly acquire a new importance. That is so because while large "bolt out of the blue" nuclear attacks seem most improbable after the end of the cold war, limited strikes, especially by some Third World states, are perhaps somewhat more probable. In the long run, nuclear weapons could lose much of their military importance in the same way that chemical weapons have, primarily among the major powers.

Implications for
American Force Structure

Designing a proper force structure, of course, requires a clear view of both U.S. commitments and threats to U.S. interests, a topic far beyond what can be comprehensively treated here. As a kind of shorthand, we can sketch three U.S. strategy options for the post–cold war era.

The first option is isolationism, which in principle cannot be ruled out, but a number of strong factors make it unlikely. Forces for this strategy could be quite small. Second, America can take on the role of global policeman, creating a Pax Americana in which U.S. military dominance in the key strategic regions keeps the peace. The forces required for this strategy, to be sure, would be very large, above our present levels in some categories. A third intermediate option is a strategy of maintaining regional balances of power. The United States need not out-match all the forces in a region. Rather, through diplomacy and alliances it would act at the margins, preventing destabilizations that adversely affect our interests. The forces for this strategy could be much smaller than those for the Pax Americana strategy because we would expect to have allies in each region, and our objectives for both military and diplomatic purposes would be to check the aggressive actions of mischief makers, deterring them, and containing them, not necessarily destroying them wholly as adversaries in military conflicts.

In choosing to expel Iraq from Kuwait by military action, the United States came close to shifting from a regional balance-of-power strategy to Pax American. Now it seems intent on getting back to the balancing pattern initiated by President Carter in 1980 and followed throughout the Reagan administration. It seems, therefore, that Soviet strategy is most likely to follow the regional power balance scheme after all the debate and discussion has subsided. Its first instrument is obviously diplomacy, but what kinds and sizes of forces will the United States need to back diplomacy in implementing such a strategy?

Strategic Forces. Sustaining nuclear deterrence vis-à-vis the Soviet Union, or even a residual large Russian state or confederation of Slavic republics that retain the present Soviet nuclear arsenal, will remain a central military mission. It should not, however, require the same level of strategic forces as during the cold war. How could they be prudently reduced?

First, keeping present forces ready for instant response to an attack is expensive, and reducing readiness would produce savings that might not be large but could be significant for a declining defense budget.

Second, the bomber leg of the triad could be reduced, perhaps eliminated. Mobile land and submarine based missiles would still provide a formidable retaliatory force. Defending against them will remain much harder than upgrading air defenses against bombers. Taking bombers out of strategic nuclear forces does not, however, mean eliminating bombers. Long-range bombers were used in the Gulf War and against Libya; their utility in naval warfare has been neglected, and it should be given new attention.

Some savings, however, should be realized by dropping the requirement to penetrate Soviet air defenses, a requirement that has plagued the B-1 bomber. The B-2 or Stealth bomber inherently solves the penetration problem, but that bomber is very expensive, and it might make sense to scale back the program if defense funds are short. Both the B-1 and the B-2, to be sure, are readily employable in a general purpose long-range bombing force.

Any savings should be shifted to defensive systems. The Strategic Defense Initiative (SDI) was timely but wrongly conceived and wrongly implemented. By shifting *away* from ground based point defense against incoming warheads—where the United States had been making progress—and *toward* the launch phase of ballistic missiles, SDI put the new emphasis on immature technologies and operational schemes of dubious practicality. It left the United States without any operational defense capability.

The changing strategic environment, however, is making the need for some defense more urgent, certainly against tactical ballistic missiles. This is where the emphasis should now be put. Using point defense, the United States could deploy a ground based system within the limits of the Anti-Ballistic Missile (ABM) Treaty. Although such a defense would hardly meet all the threats we might like to defend against, it would provide some operational experience in preparation for the changing strategic environment—without forcing an immediate decision about whether to seek change in the ABM treaty.

Naval Forces. The only navy in the world that can challenge the American belongs to the Soviet Union, and it is hardly a match. Its submarine force, however, is powerful, and the capability to destroy it will remain a requirement.

From the look at the nature of future war, it should be clear that large carriers need skeptical review. The fourteen carrier battle groups in the U.S. Navy require most of the surface fleet for protection. And a carrier has less airpower than is sometimes thought—only about forty ground attack aircraft in its wing. The four carriers that sailed to the Persian Gulf and Red Sea affected the military balance on the ground only marginally. They could only provide a total of 160 ground attack aircraft, and until two of them sailed into the Persian Gulf, those aircraft required air refueling to reach Iraq and Kuwait. Still they were limited in range.

Land based tactical air is much cheaper. In most parts of the world where the United States is likely to become militarily engaged, land based air can be deployed. That was the case in the Gulf. If land bases are not available or cannot be captured, the United States simply cannot be effectively engaged.

Thus in the 1990s the U.S. Navy should rethink its future and perhaps begin the long-term restructuring of its fleet for the twenty-first century. The lessened prospect of a war with the Soviet Union provides the time interval needed for this kind of major redesign. The decade should be used to cut the fleet, particularly the number of carriers, perhaps by a third or a half. New diversity in types of submarines may be desirable, as may different kinds of surface ships. Land based naval air should be considered. And naval targeting for cruise missiles and other "smart" weapons remains to be solved.

One naval program needs urgent attention: sealift, which the Navy has sorely neglected, only purchasing eight fast SL-7 ships in 1980 under specific direction from the president. Yet those ships were the only available means to get a few heavy ground forces to Saudi Arabia quickly in August 1990. Except for one, which was so poorly maintained that its boilers blew, these ships proved their worth many times. Sadly, there were not enough of them to move many of the waiting Army forces on the docks. America's next adversary may not be as obliging as Saddam Hussein in providing time to cobble together lift.

The sealift shortage was so severe that the first heavy Army units arrived in Saudi Arabia only two months after Iraq's invasion of Kuwait. Had Iraqi forces continued southward into Saudi Arabia as late as the beginning of October, they could have pushed the U.S. forces into the Persian Gulf. In November, when it was decided to move the VII Corps from Europe, commercial sealift had to be contracted from foreign carriers.

The SL-7 roll-on/roll-off ship can sail from the East Coast of the United States through the Suez Canal in twelve or thirteen days. Eight of these ships, if they are ready, can move one heavy Army division. Thirty can move an entire heavy corps. Had they been available, a heavy corps might well have been deployed in Saudi Arabia by the end of August. The sealift problem desperately needs to be pulled out of the closet.

Air Forces. With the decline of the Soviet threat in Europe, the Air Force can afford to cut back its interceptor and long-range bombing fleets. By contrast, the Gulf War demonstrated clearly the need for modernizing the Air Force's capability for close air support of ground forces. The A-10 "Warthog," an ugly stepchild in the tactical Air Force, was on its way to extinction before the war. It may still have to be phased out, but it has to be replaced.

The Air Force's approach has been to try to make air-to-air fighters, like the F-16, double as close air support aircraft. Close air support inevitably gets shortchanged in the process. Recognizing this failing, Congress offered to transfer the close air support mission to the Army, but the Army refused to take it. Giving it to the Army, however, remains a possible solution, and if the Air Force does not take the mission seriously, it may be the required solution.

As the Gulf crisis also demonstrated, the Air Force has woefully neglected airlift, just as the Navy has neglected sealift. The Air Force put considerable R & D money into the C-17 transport, then failed to procure it. At the same time, its C-141 fleet, the workhorse for transoceanic lift, is so old that many of those aircraft are no longer safe to fly. Nor has the C-5A fleet been increased. It should be. And finally, the intratheater C-130 fleet is slowly decaying without replacement.

Given the urgency of strategic lift for future contingencies in the key regions of the world—Europe, East Asia, the Middle East, and Central America—it badly needs a higher priority by both the Air Force and Navy. If the United States has forces based in forward areas, that of course eases the requirement for lift. In the new strategic environment, however, forward basing is likely to decline, making strategic lift all the more critical.

Marine Forces. The Marines are something of a national monument with a large popular constituency. Unlike all other services, they have gotten the Congress to write into the law the size of their forces—four divisions. At the same time, Marine amphibious forces are less and less relevant to modern warfare. There simply are better ways to get ashore in hostile circumstances. Landing on the beach may still leave forces so far from the critical point of action that the landing has no real military impact. Marine divisions have neither the proper armor nor adequate logistics to fight inland. When they were used to invade Kuwait, they were wholly dependent on Army logistics units, and the Army's Tiger Brigade of the 2d Armored Division had to reinforce them to face Iraqi T-72 tanks.

If the United States keeps four divisions of Marine forces, it ought at least to realize that they are an antique luxury. The resources devoted to them could be used far more effectively elsewhere. *Some* amphibious capability should be retained as a hedge against uncertain future contingencies. Four divisions, however, are hardly necessary for that purpose. One would be adequate to maintain a training base and a small ready capability.

Army Forces. Forward deployments in Europe and Korea during the cold war probably kept the Army from being almost wholly demobilized. In order to provide a rotation base for the Army personnel serving in them, a fairly large Army force structure had to be maintained in the continental United States. When units have been withdrawn from Europe and Korea, as a rule they have been put into the reserves or disbanded. The prospect of large withdrawals from Europe today, and possibly from Korea, means that Army divisions can be expected to decrease dramatically. Before Desert Storm, the plan was for reduction from the present eighteen divisions to twelve.

As active duty Army units have been cut back, the National Guard and the Army Reserve have been able to accept some of those units into their own structure, backed by its powerful lobby, especially the National Guard Association. After Vietnam, the Army tried to make a virtue of necessity through the "Total Army" concept—raising the level of equipment, staffing, and training for the reserves and including them in contingency war plans for Europe and Asia. And so the 1980s witnessed the creation of "roundout" brigades, National Guard brigades assigned as the third of the three brigades in U.S. based active duty divisions. Combat support and service support units in the reserves also took a bigger role, especially for the NATO contingency.

When the Iraqi crisis arose in August 1990, the Army found itself woefully short of heavy combat forces. The 24th Mechanized Division could not take its National Guard "roundout" brigade to Saudi Arabia because it was not ready. It was eventually mobilized, however, but readiness training kept it unable to deploy until about the time the war was over. The point was clear: for post–cold war emergencies, National Guard maneuver units contribute virtually nothing.

The same was not true of support units. Their military specialties tend to have civilian counterparts; medical, transportation, engineer, ordnance, and quartermaster skills overlap with many civilian job skills. These units were able to achieve adequate readiness fairly quickly, unlike the armor and infantry units that have no real civilian counterpart specialties. The National Guard and reserves also work well for several Air Force needs. Air defense interceptor pilots, A-10 pilots, and transport pilots were also able to get up to scratch quickly.

The lesson for Army force design in the decade ahead is that contingency combat units—armored, infantry, and artillery— need to be in the active component and highly trained. In other

Army branches, a considerable part of the force structure can be in the reserves and yet available for deployment with only a few weeks delay. The National Guard has ten divisions—one light division (about 10,000 personnel, very little tactical mobility, and little antiarmor capability), five infantry divisions (organized and equipped on the pattern of 1950s and early 1960s regular divisions, with very little tactical mobility or antiarmor capability), and four heavy divisions (organized on the latest heavy division pattern).

This structure perhaps had some utility for a NATO contingency with several months of warning time. For the Gulf War it had none. Even for a NATO contingency only the four heavy divisions were really of importance. A strong military case for the other six divisions is difficult to make. In reality, they are an expression of the strength of the National Guard lobby, not a military need.

Yet the cost of procuring and maintaining a National Guard heavy division over a ten-year life cycle is two-thirds of the cost of a regular active heavy division. In other words, three of the heavy National Guard divisions cost what two active duty heavy divisions would cost. All four National Guard heavy divisions could probably be transferred to the active Army for the price of six or seven of the National Guard divisions—all without increasing the "Total Army" budget.

Several peculiarities of the Army force structure are important for future planning. One is the XVIII Airborne Corps. It includes one airborne division (the 82d), one air mobile division with a large helicopter component (the 101st), and one heavy division (the 24th). The support elements directly under the corps are designed for light forces and had to be beefed up for the Gulf War where they supported more heavy forces.

Large airborne units are as much an anachronism as the Marine amphibious divisions. A couple of separate airborne brigades and the three extant Ranger battalions are wholly adequate for forced entry by airborne assault. It is difficult to justify an airborne corps headquarters and an airborne division, but, like its Marine and National Guard counterparts, the airborne lobby within the Army has remained powerful, and this antique force structure reflects its strength.

Another peculiarity of Army force structure is the four new light divisions formed in the 1980s. They are strategically very mobile because they are lightly equipped and small (10,000 personnel), but they possess very little tactical mobility or antiarmor capability. Although one of them, the 7th Division, was used in the operation in Panama, the heavy fighting was done by units of the 5th Mechanized Division.

Had these light divisions been mechanized with light armor vehicles and strong antiarmor firepower, they would have some utility as air-deployable contingency forces. With adequate combat engineer support, they could dig in, compensating for their light armor protection, and stand off or delay an attacking heavy armor force. They would have been worth a lot in August in Saudi Arabia had they been mechanized, but they are not. Where they might be useful as light foot infantry, other such forces—the Rangers and airborne brigades—are already available.

The Future

What do these comments suggest for an Army of the 1990s and early 2000s?

First, assuming American ground forces remain in Germany at reduced levels, a corps is the smallest unit that can really operate independently far from the United States. Any smaller force would tend to be only of symbolic significance. Thus one heavy corps for NATO would seem to be the lowest prudent force level.

Second, assume U.S. forces remain in Korea for the duration of the 1990s. The 2d Division, now in Korea, is only partially heavy, and it depends largely on its Korean host for its operational significance. It is backed by strong tactical air support, part of the Fifth Air Force.

Third, to deal with another Desert Storm–type contingency in the Middle East, two heavy corps of three heavy divisions each would be required. They would be based in the United States and deployable by air and sealift. Each of the corps will also need an armored cavalry regiment, a heavy screening and reconnaissance force. These three regiments make roughly one more heavy division equivalent.

That totals to ten heavy divisions. During another Gulf War contingency, are we to leave the continental United States wholly without heavy forces? Are we willing to risk that there will never be another threat at the same time? It would seem highly prudent to have two or three additional divisions. When the airborne brigades, the Rangers, and the 101st Airmobile Division are included, the total number of division equivalents is fourteen or fifteen. And less than two division equivalents are "light" forces, that is, the airborne brigades and the Rangers.

Summing Up the Force

This tally is not the nostalgia of a retired Army officer. Rather, my point in detailing a future Army active duty force structure is to note that it considerably exceeds the planned twelve-division force. Nor can it depend on National Guard "roundout" brigades. An adequate heavy Army force could be created from the present "Total Army" structure, but it will not be possible if the Army moves toward that planned target. Curiously, after seeing what post–cold war contingencies require in one of the four critical regions of the world, the present defense budget is designed to push Army heavy forces considerably below that requirement.

In light of the new strategic realities, is it wise or prudent to demobilize precisely the forces that made Desert Storm possible? The answer is more than just "no." Victory in the Gulf War not only fails to make such future contingencies improbable, it so destabilized the Persian Gulf area that American ground forces are not likely to be fully withdrawn. Before a new regional balance of power can be established, President Bush may have to reverse his commitment not to station ground forces there. Instead he will have to plan for a long-term presence at a reduced level backed by a capability to regenerate the present level in a few days or weeks.

We have set an example in the liberation of Kuwait for future aggressors, but the historical record suggests that historical examples seldom deter. Aggressors make their decisions to go to war based on the forces they must meet in battle. (See the analysis by Paul Huth and Bruce Russett, "Testing Deterrence Theory: Rigor Makes a Difference," *World Politics*, July 1990.) The lesson from

Desert Storm will be as lasting as the readiness of American forces to repeat the operation.

A global strategy of regional power balancing cannot be implemented by diplomacy and past demonstrations of military power alone. It will require military force in being and the capacity to project it quickly into areas of conflict. The "projection" component will be as important as the "force" component. As forward basing shrinks in the 1990s, therefore, strategic lift will grow in importance as a critical part of our military power.

[handwritten marginalia, partially legible:] contradiction: he emphasizes power projection but would ... but naval, army's & Marine power ... forces. Despite his advocacy of Army power projection, his heavy ... proposal would inherently not be timely, which is a hallmark of power projection

9B

The Hard Realities
of the
Arab-Israeli Conflict

GEORGE BALL

O ne obvious lesson of the Gulf War is that the Arab-Israeli
dispute is not the only source of conflict in the turbulent
Middle East. Yet because Arab nations fight one another only
sporadically, inter-Arab quarrels are far less dangerous to world
peace than the seemingly endless conflict between the Arabs and
Israelis.

The current main focus of the Arab-Israeli dispute is on the fate
of the Palestinians in the occupied territories. It has threatened the
peace of the area ever since Israel's armies overran the West Bank
and Gaza Strip in the 1967 war. After the war Israel failed to
withdraw its armies, but instead installed its military authorities to
subject the present 1.75 million Palestinian residents of those areas
to a progressively brutal repression.

GEORGE BALL began his career in public service in the general counsel's office, Department of the Treasury, in 1933. He served as under
secretary of state from 1961–66, and as U.S. permanent representative to
the United Nations in 1968. Mr. Ball is the author of numerous books and
articles, including *The Past Has Another Pattern* and *Error and Betrayal in
Lebanon*.

To resolve that problem is now the indispensable first step toward avoiding further escalation and expansion of the violence and ultimately another war. In the words of General Norman Schwarzkopf, it is "the most important factor to stability and peace in the Middle East . . . it is a major impediment to peace."

Why has the Palestinian problem remained still unsettled after a quarter century of half-hearted and failed diplomacy? By their obstinacy immediately after the war, the Arabs no doubt contributed to the jelling of the situation in its currently unacceptable configuration. But the principal blame must rest on the Israelis who insisted on a deliberately deceptive formulation of Resolution 242. Had that resolution not been written in language so equivocal as to invite its nullification through self-serving, perverted, Israeli misinterpretation, it could have been self-executing.

The resolution called for "withdrawal from territories of recent conflict." The deliberate omission of the definite article was insisted upon by the Israelis quite obviously to enable them to argue that it did not require more than a token withdrawal from a portion of the lands seized in battle. No matter that such a bizarre interpretation directly contradicted the assurances given to the Arab negotiators both by the American secretary of state and the president or that it was explicitly repudiated by the man who personally drafted the language, Lord Caradon, the British permanent representative to the United Nations. Caradon said:

It was from occupied territories that the Resolution called for withdrawal. The test was which territories were occupied. That was a test not possibly subject to doubt. As a matter of plain fact East Jerusalem, the West Bank, Gaza, the Golan and Sinai were occupied in the 1967 conflict; it was on withdrawal from occupied territories that the Resolution insisted.

Had anything like the Israeli position been advanced as the real meaning of that resolution, the Arabs would never have agreed to it and the Security Council would not have approved it.

Today, the Arab states are justifiably adamant that the territorial assurances given them in 1967 be adhered to, a position to which the United States government at least gives lip service. Israel, on the other hand, totally rejects this interpretation, insisting that it has the right to maintain military control of the occupied

areas. In fact, by settling its own people in the area it is systematically following the American cow bird–like practice of gradually
forcing out of their homes the native Palestinian residents.

Israel has carried out this illegal program of de facto absorption
with the undisguised objective that what it coyly refers to as "creating new facts" will effectively sabotage the fundamental principle
of Resolution 242, the exchange of territory for peace. Up to this
point it has by its settlements program managed to preempt more
than 70 percent of the land area and 93 percent of the water supply
of the West Bank. In the Gaza Strip Israel has taken over one-third
of the land and 80 percent of the water for the exclusive use of
2,500 Israeli settlers to the deprivation of nearly 700,000 Palestinian residents.

Meron Benvenisti, a widely known and highly respected Israeli
sociologist who has been charged with studying the area for
decades, sadly concluded in 1987 even prior to the *Intifada* that the
Arabs were insufficiently united to dislodge Israel by force and that
the United States would never compel Israel to leave. Thus the
situation, he concluded, had by now become irreversible—merely
an internal issue for Israel, though he expressed little hope that
Israel would find a humane solution.

Benvenisti was indubitably right when he noted that any Israeli
government that tried to comply with Resolution 242 by evicting
already established Israeli settlers would encounter armed resistance. He further implied the practical impossibility of an Israeli
government emerging with the political guts to initiate such an
undertaking. Nor, as I see it, is any American government ever
likely to take effective action to dissuade Israel from continuing its
currently ongoing program of expanding its de facto annexation of
the area. Its promises to desist have so far had the half-life of a June
bug.

That Israel's settlements practice is clearly a violation of the
Fourth Geneva Convention to which Israel is a signatory was the
view of a succession of legal advisors to the secretary of state—and
it was almost without exception accepted by international law experts until the presidency of Ronald Reagan, whose qualifications
as an authority on international law still remain one of the White
House's most closely guarded secrets. In spite of—or because of—

his ignorance, Reagan cavalierly dismissed the authoritative opinions of his government's most highly qualified legal experts with
the unsupported declaration that the settlements were *not* illegal—
although, when pressed, he conceded that they might be "an obstacle to peace." His position has not been reversed by President
Bush.

Meanwhile, over 1.75 million Palestinians in the occupied areas
live under the increasingly stern repression of the Israeli military,
which has closed the schools and universities for the past three
years and imposed every kind of indignity and hardship, responding brutally to the yearning for freedom of unarmed Palestinian
children and adolescents, when they express their desperate aspirations for freedom by throwing stones at Israelis. That practice
has proved costly for a whole young generation of Palestinians;
Israeli soldiers have in return killed over 800 of them.

At the moment Palestinian residents of the so-called occupied
areas not only live in misery but must helplessly watch as Israeli
soldiers steadily thrust them out of their ancestral lands. Their
anxieties are increased by the growing influx of immigrant Soviet
Jews expanding the Israeli population by more than 180,000 in
1990 alone. Soviet Jews are forced to go to Israel rather than to
America or Europe as they would like because some American
pro-Israeli organizations in collaboration with Israel's government
deliberately sought to stop the well-established practice of Soviet
Jewish emigrants leaving the Soviet Union with Israeli visas, then
switching planes and emigrating to America.

Israel's American friends used their political muscle to persuade
Washington to impose a 40,000-person American admission
quota on Soviet Jewish refugees, on the grounds that the costs of
resettling them in America would be an excessive burden on
strained American finances. But that is absurd on its face. America
is saving no money by this action; it is merely paying Israel to
perform a task that could be more cheaply done here, since the
United States would at least gain well-educated immigrants. The
American government, under pro-Israeli pressure, has already
provided Israel with a loan guarantee of $400 million to build
housing for the Soviet immigrants—and the Israeli ambassador to
Washington announced in 1991 that in addition to its annual sub-

sidy that approaches $4 billion and other supplementals, Israel will shortly ask for an additional $10 billion over the next five years for that same purpose. The Israeli radio announced on January 22, 1991 that the Israeli foreign minister had requested $13 billion in supplemental assistance; $3 billion for expenses Israel suffered during the Gulf War and $10 billion over five years for settling Soviet Jews in Israel, while the newspaper *Hadashot* reported on February 8, 1991 that the figure requested for settling Soviet Jews would be $17 billion over five years.

President Bush denied Israel's request for a loan guarantee for new housing until he had received a letter from Prime Minister Yitzhak Shamir assuring him that Israel had no plans to build housing for Soviet Jews in the occupied territories.

Although Shamir gave a nominally affirmative answer, it was sufficiently ambiguous to be a negation of Bush's demands. At the same time, the Israeli government's Housing Ministry, headed by General Ariel Sharon, openly seeking to frustrate Secretary of State James Baker's peace mission, promptly issued a report announcing its plans to set up 13,000 new housing units in the occupied areas. That action was quite consistent with a sentiment frequently expressed by members of the Shamir government that if Israel could obtain peace only by giving up some portion of the occupied territories, they would prefer a continued state of war.

One might think this whole situation of repression and openly avowed annexation would be so offensive to America's declared principles that the government would no longer tolerate it. But, on the contrary, the United States still continues to provide Israel with an endless stream of money and military equipment in response to the slightest whim of whatever Israeli government happens to be in power.

Yet even though it plays feebly, America still talks a good game. In his speech to Congress on March 6, 1991, President Bush asserted that peace between Israel and the Arabs could bring "real benefits to everyone" and that he would, at the conclusion of the Gulf War, "go forward with new vigor and determination" to try to "close the gap between Israel and the Arab states—and between Israelis and Palestinians." Peace between them, he asserted, must be "grounded in United Nations Security Council Resolutions 242 and 338 and the principle of territory for peace."

These words were uttered at a time when the president who spoke them had achieved a historic high level of domestic political approval. They were noted with particular care in the Middle East because, in referring to Resolution 242 and its principle of exchanging territory for peace, the president was directly challenging Prime Minister Shamir and members of Shamir's government who have repeatedly stated that Israel's control of the occupied territories is not negotiable. To this defiance, however, our government has not replied, for many members of the American Congress are scared to death of organized pro-Israeli opinion. If, as Lloyd George charged in 1909, the House of Lords was "Mr. Balfour's poodle," the American Congress today is Israel's well-trained performing seal, leaping through hoops and applauding Israel on cue.

President Bush began his promised search for a solution by sending Secretary of State Baker on one more succession of ritualistic tours of the Middle East—a familiar modern-day phenomenon that, in the current cynical world, passes for diplomacy. That Baker's view of the situation is essentially defeatist is reflected by his answer to a press inquiry in Amman in April 1991 as to why he had dropped the proposal for an international peace conference:

The primary reason is because we want to develop and create a process that will work. No one can impose peace in this situation. Peace will only come if the parties are determined to make it happen. It can't be imposed by the United Nations. It can't be imposed by the United States. It can't be imposed by the Soviet Union. It can't be imposed by a collection of all of those entities, organizations, and countries, and a whole lot more.

This statement is, of course, palpable nonsense. Almost every peace is imposed—the only question is whether it is imposed by another nation in a shooting war or by an international body applying established international principles. Baker's defeatist sentiments totally ignore the settlements imposed on Japan and Germany at the end of the Second World War or the recent success of a coalition of nations in compelling Iraq to leave Kuwait.

It is quite remarkable for the United States to say that no one can impose peace on Israel—a nation that can maintain its standard of living only by continued and increasingly lavish American handouts.

In spite of its own conspicuous failure as a peacemaker, the United States has sought to monopolize the "peace process" in the Middle East by excluding, at Israel's behest, the European Community, the UN, and the Soviet Union. But the United States is by no means an objective mediator, and the world does not regard it as such; it is only America that does not recognize its disqualifications.

As a result America's efforts at bringing the parties together have resembled somnambulism more than diplomacy. Ever since Camp David, American envoys have first tried to determine what the then existing Israeli government wanted, then sought to sell its demands to the Arabs with a foreordained lack of success. The Arabs, for their part, have understandably refused to take less than what they understand Resolution 242 offered them.

As long as neither side sees that a conference offers any reasonable expectation of achieving its goals, each will immerse itself in endless procedural controversies, trying to tie up the negotiations and shift the blame for a lack of progress upon the other. As Thomas L. Friedman of the *New York Times* put it on April 14, 1991:

> Since all of the parties are going to fight over a small procedural issue with the same vigor as though they were fighting over the actual substance, some Middle East analysts say, "Why not go to the substance now, with an American plan both for a long-term settlement and the lengthy transition process needed to get it there."

Significance of the Middle East's Arms Race

Equally urgent for Middle East peace as settling the Palestinian question is the need to check the escalating arms race. That race has already resulted in piling up military equipment in Middle Eastern arsenals approaching both in quality and quantity the totality of that assigned to NATO.

The primary engine driving the Middle East's frenzied desire for new weapons is a perpetual motion machine created in 1967 by

President Lyndon Johnson. He assured Israel that the United States would at all times guarantee it a clear advantage in military equipment over that procured by any conceivable combination of its Arab neighbors. As might have been expected, that promise initiated an irreversible competitive process. As soon as America gives Israel a new weapon, its Arab neighbors hasten to buy either an improved version of that weapon or an effective defense against it. That spurs other Arab nations to buy more weapons to maintain their positions in the race, which, in turn, stimulates the Israelis to demand gifts of more weapons from America. Since there is no limit to the amount of weaponry the United States is prepared to provide free to Israel in line with its promise to keep Israel in the lead, this is an endless process. Israel has long taken America's ever-flowing cornucopia for granted.

But even were our president so inclined, he would have to expend much of his political capital trying to deliver the necessary congressional approval for cash sales of arms to Arab nations against the constant vigilance of the pro-Israeli organizations. They try—with almost invariable success—to block America's arms sales to any Arab purchasing countries. When that proves infeasible, they effectively nullify such sales by arranging stifling restrictions on the use of the weapons for which the Arab purchasers have paid hard cash.

But that does not mean that America's refusal to sell arms to the Arab nations in any way curtails the arms flow into the Middle East. It merely diverts such sales to other arms-supplying countries—at great losses to American industry and the American balance of payments.

One might have thought that, in view of our coalition with the Saudis in stopping the Iraqi advance, Israel's American supporters would now take a more moderate position; yet the chief pro-Israeli lobby, AIPAC, continues to play the same militant recording. On March 19, 1991, at a meeting called by AIPAC for its 2,000 delegates attended significantly by forty-eight of America's one hundred senators, the delegates approved a lobbying agenda that put special emphasis on blocking arms sales to Arab nations. Meanwhile, Israel demanded that it be compensated dollar for dollar in gifts from America for each dollar of Arab sales.

If the efforts of AIPAC are costly to America's arms makers they wonderfully benefit the competition, and substantially keep it alive for future competition with America. AIPAC's actions have, at different times, helped the arms industries of France, Britain, China, and the Soviet Union. The most famous example of this phenomenon involved two successive sales to the Saudis of Tornado airplanes made by Britain, one in 1986, the other in 1988. These sales were made only after the White House had made clear that it would not undertake to overcome the opposition of the Israeli lobby to the sale of F-15s, and had even provided Saudi Arabia a letter stating that the administration would not object if the Saudis chose to buy elsewhere. Saudi Arabia's purchase of Tornadoes was referred to by the trade as the "arms sale of the century." British Aerospace's 1988 financial statement placed a value on both contracts for their twenty-five-year life at 150 billion pounds or, at the then value of $1.70 per pound, $255 billion.

These sales will keep the British, Italian, and German military aircraft consortium afloat for the next decade. The profits from these sales will help finance the next generation of high-performance European aircraft in competition with American industry and will dissuade European nations from participating in any common effort to reduce the dangerous flow of arms into the Middle East.

On this whole issue of reducing arms exports to the Middle East the United States is currently behaving with unseemly hypocrisy. Although it preaches restraint to other supplier nations, it is at this writing (if not blocked by AIPAC) preparing to make huge Middle East arms transfers of its own, not merely as gifts to Israel but sales in hard currencies to Kuwait, the United Arab Emirates, Bahrain, and Turkey.

But the biggest potential arms purchaser is Saudi Arabia, which is hoping to buy a package costing $15 billion, consisting of U.S. weapons of the kind that helped win the Gulf War.

Meanwhile, though piously urging restrictions on foreign producers, the administration is suggesting the use of Export-Import Bank credits to promote U.S. arms exports and thus maintain our smaller arms producers at a time when the military budget is being cut. I doubt that, short of a new catastrophe, we shall ever achieve an effective slowdown of the Middle East arms race; more likely our continued reckless practices will intensify it.

Let us not ignore the fact that the need to stop this nonsense transcends the mere encouragement of war through excessive armaments. America is wasting precious resources to fuel this race. Meanwhile, the revenues of the Arab states are being squandered on arms at a time when the poorer Middle East states urgently need investment capital to provide jobs and food for their burgeoning populations. All are impoverished by the process. So long as our policies encourage this stupid misallocation of resources, poverty and political instability will remain an increasingly bitter reality.

Meantime, the *Intifada* will continue so long as Israel persists in its ruthless use of excessive force against a whole generation of young Palestinians. Stimulated by the sanctions imposed by the European Economic Community (EEC) on imports of flowers from Israel, the Israeli military has just announced the reopening of Hebron University. But we should greet this news with caution, for the other three universities in the West Bank remain closed as they have been for three years. One can only conclude that Israel shares the exploitative colonialist view that the best way to keep the natives docile is to keep them ignorant.

The probable evolution of Israeli politics seems unlikely to improve the cause of world peace. The polls show an increasing number of Israelis favoring the extreme right-wing policy of expelling the Palestinian population from the West Bank and Gaza Strip, and the best political predictions are that the influx of Soviet Jews will incrementally strengthen the hard-line position. Many believe, in fact, that it is only a question of time until Shamir may be replaced by Sharon, who not only favors the expulsion of the Palestinians but also a military attack on Jordan designed to depose the Hashemite monarchy, annex the Jordan Valley, and install a puppet regime in Amman.

How to Achieve a Settlement of the Palestinian Issue

What then should be done about it?

America makes a tactical error in acting as though it were commissioned by divine right to exclude other major nations from an effective role in seeking a Palestinian solution. Although constantly declaring our intention not to be the policeman or nanny for the world, our country continues to talk as though it presided over a Pax Americana. The reality is very different, particularly in the Middle East. One is reminded of Robert Cecil, Viscount Chalwood's comment on Britain's brutal policies in Ireland before 1921: "With so much dishonor, you [Lloyd George] might have brought us a little peace."

It is a fair comment on America's conduct in the Middle East. What we have proved so far is our disqualification to act as peacemaker, and we should now let the United Nations take over.

The Gulf War has refocused attention on the availability of the United Nations machinery for dealing with intractable conflicts. Thus America might be well advised to try to persuade some friendly nation, such as France, to return the issue to the United Nations Security Council, which took jurisdiction when it adopted Resolution 242.

The preamble to the resolution should recite the confusion that has been caused by the failure of the parties to agree on a common interpretation of the language, and it should then explicitly and unequivocally set forth the conditions for a settlement in accordance with the principles of the UN Charter and of established international law.

The charter would appear to sanction such a course of action. Article 33 provides that parties to any dispute should first of all seek a solution by negotiation—a process that has now been thoroughly exhausted. Then under Article 35 if they are unable to settle it by negotiation, they shall refer it to the Security Council. And Article 37 provides that if the Security Council deems that the continuance of a dispute is "likely to endanger the maintenance of international peace and security" it may recommend "such terms of settlement as it may consider appropriate."

One might hope that a Security Council resolution recommending the terms of a principled settlement would provide effective pressure on the contestant parties without need to invoke the enforcement machinery of Chapter VII, but that could be used if necessary.

The terms of the clarifying resolution should include, among other things, the following:

- The return of the West Bank and the Gaza Strip to such entity as the Palestinians might choose to establish through an exercise of their right of self-determination.
- A condominium administration of Jerusalem, which is a holy city equally for Islam, Christianity, and Judaism, with the understanding that it may contain the capitals of both Israel and the new Palestinian state.
- Palestinians living outside the new state of Palestine should be offered the option either for taking local or Palestinian citizenship.
- The Golan Heights should be demilitarized and returned to Syria while a United Nations force (not subject to removal without both parties' consent) is posted to enforce its demilitarization.
- The boycotts and the various states of war on the part of the Arab states against Israel must be terminated.
- Arrangements for the control of conventional arms should be included, and the U.N. should put renewed impetus behind the proposal to make the area a nuclear-free zone sufficiently broad to include both chemical and biological weapons and the ballistic missiles to deliver them.

This is an urgent agenda, for now if ever is a propitious moment to break the momentum that seems likely to result, if unchecked, in a cataclysmic world conflict. As noted in the spring 1991 *Foreign Affairs* by Ze'ev Schiff, one of the most respected of Israel's military commentators:

If the effort to arrive at broad-based political settlements in the Middle East—which must include arms-control arrangements—should fail, it will no longer be possible to speak of conventional deterrence. For this will have been the last major war in the Middle East to be fought with conventional weapons.

At this writing, President Bush is at what seems likely to be a high point in his popularity. An epoch has ended. The cold war is fading. A crisis in the Gulf has been at least temporarily terminated. The Western powers have shown their ability to mobilize vast forces and act together at a time of crisis. The Soviets are eager for a peaceful settlement in the Middle East. So if we do not act now, God knows when we shall ever act. There is an old axiom as true in diplomacy as in gastronomy: a souffle can never be made to rise twice.

9C

U.S.–Japan Relations in a Changing Strategic Environment

ALAN D. ROMBERG

The drama of developments in Eastern Europe, the Soviet Union, and the Middle East has dominated the headlines, but significant—if less revolutionary—but nonetheless significant—changes are taking place in East Asia as well. As a result, beyond the well-publicized economic frictions with the United States, America's security role in the Pacific is being increasingly called into question in an atmosphere of intensifying budgetary pressures in the U.S. and growing nationalism and economic strength of many Asian countries.

Most important among the American treaty relationships in Asia is that with Japan. That treaty has broad regional and even

ALAN D. ROMBERG is the senior fellow for Asia at the Council on Foreign Relations. Formerly, he served in various positions dealing with East and Southeast Asia at the State Department, including the staff of the National Security Council and the State Department's policy planning staff, and as director of the State Department's Office of Japanese Affairs. Mr. Romberg has written and edited many books and articles including his most recent volume, *Same Bed, Different Dreams: America and Japan—Societies in Transition.*

global significance, and together with the other alliances—and the basing arrangements for U.S. forces—the U.S.–Japan relationship is a vital political and military anchor for the United States in Asia. Now the alliance is coming under increasing pressure from domestic forces in both countries, which challenge its importance in the post–cold war world and which are unhappy with its division of financial and military responsibilities. Unless the alliance is "updated"—at least in the way it is implemented if not in terms of its formal provisions—maintaining the alliance over the long run could become increasingly difficult.

The Changing Region

Many of the same economic and political pressures that are forcing changes in Soviet and American policies in Europe are also operating in Asia, but there are obvious and critical differences. In Asia, for example, both American and Soviet alliances have been, generally speaking, bilateral rather than multilateral. In part this is because the Soviet Union never created among its Asian Communist allies the same kind of external empire that it created in Eastern Europe. But the trend toward bilateral pacts also reflected the complicated relationships and the competition among the non-Communist states of the region. There was no single, unifying threat such as the one that existed in Europe.

Moscow's alliances in East Asia have undergone important changes, influenced in part by developments in Eastern Europe but largely the result of evolutionary shifts in the strategic picture over a period of several years. Beijing terminated the 1950 Sino-Soviet Treaty of Friendship, Alliance, and Mutual Security at the end of its fixed thirty-year term, and a less intimate but more stable relationship between equals has replaced that pact.

Because of this easing of Sino-Soviet hostility, along with the normalization of Sino-Mongolian ties, the need for the USSR to defend the Mongolian People's Republic (MPR) against possible conflict with China has essentially evaporated. As a result, Moscow is in the process of withdrawing all of its forces from the MPR.

The Soviet military commitments to Vietnam are also much less important now. Moscow has severely reduced its economic and military assistance, and the USSR is no longer so interested in using Vietnamese military and naval facilities, the principal benefit it received in return for its 1978 commitments. The need to help Vietnam against a potential Chinese threat has disappeared with the easing—though not yet settlement—of the situation in Cambodia; and Moscow has no intention of taking sides in the disputes among China, Vietnam, and other regional claimants to small islands in the South China Sea.

Even the Kremlin's alliance with North Korea has evolved—especially since the establishment of USSR–ROK diplomatic relations in September 1990—to function more as a lever to restrain Pyongyang from engaging in reckless adventurism than as a deterrent against a theoretical attack by the South.

Despite these developments, Mikhail Gorbachev's "new political thinking" and his proposals for arms reductions have not had the same dramatic impact in Asia that they have had in Europe and the United States. In large part this is because, although it has reduced its ground forces along the border with China and is withdrawing most combat forces from Vietnam, Moscow has done little to reduce its strategic deployments in the North Pacific. The Kremlin is withdrawing 120,000 forces from the Far East, and is eliminating a significant number of obsolete ships, tanks, and planes. The number of days it is keeping ships at sea has also been greatly reduced. But Moscow has continued to modernize its air and naval forces in Asia that are targeted against the United States and Japan. And although it has removed the SS-20 missiles in Asia as it promised to do in the 1987 U.S.–Soviet Intermediate-Range Nuclear Forces (INF) agreement, it is deploying newer, longer-range missiles.[1] All in all, its mobility and firepower continue to grow.

The continuing confrontation between North and South Korea has a crucial effect on the strategic environment in East Asia, and on U.S. security interests there. Although the DPRK occasionally shows an interest in the reduction of tensions with the South, Pyongyang continues to launch vicious propaganda attacks against both Seoul and Washington, and two-thirds or more of its 1 million-troop force[2] remains poised in offensive positions just north of the Demilitarized Zone (DMZ), only twenty-five miles from Seoul. Of particular concern has been the continued construction of unsafeguarded nuclear facilities believed by many to be part of a clandestine DPRK nuclear weapons program.[3]

South Korea's development in both political and economic terms is one of the world's most impressive performances. The ROK political system has made a significant transition in recent years from military dominated authoritarianism to an increasingly stable, pluralistic society. On the other side, not only is North Korea's political system rigidly ideological and its economy stagnating, but Pyongyang has suffered enormous diplomatic setbacks including the establishment of Soviet–South Korean relations, the collapse of Eastern Europe, and China's signals that it might well not block the South's application for independent UN membership, thus forcing the North to reverse course and apply for simultaneous, separate entry into the world body. It is clear that North Korea has become increasingly apprehensive about its international isolation and is beginning to grapple with the reality of the South as reflected in Pyongyang's acceptance of North-South prime ministerial talks, the opening of negotiations to normalize relations with Japan, and most recently its request for admission to the United Nations. It has also made clear it seeks official or even full diplomatic relations with the United States. In addition, though still unacceptable to either the United States or South Korea, the North's recent arms control proposals have displayed somewhat more flexibility than in the past. How realistic they will eventually become remains to be determined.

U.S. Alliances in Asia

For over thirty-five years, the United States has been committed to the defense of both Japan and the Republic of Korea;[4] since the Korean War, it has stationed large numbers of forces in both countries. These two alliances, and the American deployments, have faced many challenges in the past, but today they have the strong support of large majorities of people in all three countries. Indeed, despite the more positive view of Soviet intentions that exist in Asia as well as in Europe, and although most Asians no longer fear the People's Republic of China (PRC) as a security threat in the near future, many nations in East Asia are still concerned both about Moscow's and Beijing's long-term ambitions and about the long-term foreign policy goals of other regional powers such as Vietnam and Japan. Especially in the context of the general agreement that North Korea remains unpredictable and dangerous, few East Asian governments want major changes in American military deployments or in the "balancing" role the United States continues to play in the area. On the contrary, these nations welcome Washington's alliances with Tokyo and Seoul—and the Philippines—as positive contributions to keeping peace in Asia.

Meanwhile, however, both Japanese and South Koreans are exhibiting more confidence and national pride, and they are increasingly frustrated over their countries' continuing dependence on the United States and American insistence that they yield to Washington's views on a wide variety of issues. These attitudes are now matched by growing pressure in the United States to reduce defense expenditures, and there are rising calls in the American Congress and public to reduce U.S. forces stationed overseas and to demand more support ("burden sharing") from those countries where U.S. forces remain. More and more frequently, mutual frustration gets mixed up with resentments over trade disputes, and as a result, economic issues are beginning to create problems for America's defense relations with both countries.

In an attempt to reduce this growing negativism on both sides—and yet maintain U.S. forces in the region—in April 1990 the Pentagon announced plans to reduce the 135,000 American forces in East Asia by 10 to 12 percent over the next three years. By 1993 the United States will withdraw 2,000 Air Force personnel and 5,000 Army personnel from Korea, and another 5,000 to 6,000 troops from Japan. (It will also withdraw approximately 2,000 to 3,000 Air Force and Navy personnel from the Philippines.) Washington will consider further reductions in later years, but only after considering any changes in the security situation in the region. The Pentagon's plan is to make steady but slow reductions of American forces, with any major withdrawals tied to a substantially improved security environment.[5] But even under this plan, the changes over the next five to ten years could be very large. And

Congress may want to draw down forces faster yet.

Thus, although there have been no dramatic shifts in East Asia recently, it is clear that, against a background of evolving Soviet commitments and an expectation that Gorbachev's new thinking will also eventually be reflected in reduced Soviet deployments in Asia, there is growing pressure on some aspects of America's alliance structure in the region. Until now, the basic purposes and strength of these alliances have not been seriously challenged; but this could happen.

U.S.–Japan Relations

The U.S. alliance with Japan relates importantly to the maintenance of peace and stability in Korea, as well as to the defense of Japan itself, and to the effective projection of American economic and political interests as well as military power throughout the region. More than simply a military pact, the alliance is essential to the overall U.S. relationship with Japan, enhancing the sense of security that Japanese themselves, as well as other Asians, feel. It makes manifest the U.S. determination to remain an active player in Asia, preventing any sense of a "vacuum" that Japan or others might fill. The reassurance this provides also facilitates an active and constructive Japanese economic and political role throughout the region.

This is not the place to review in detail the sometimes difficult history of U.S.–Japan security relations since the end of World War II. Suffice it to say that, following the revision of the Treaty of Mutual Cooperation and Security in 1960 and the massive Japanese protest demonstrations at that time, Washington and Tokyo have developed perhaps the closest and most constructive alliance relationship that the United States has had with any single country. For Tokyo, too, this relationship has been essential, providing Japan with its principal security anchor—in fact its only alliance and its only nuclear deterrent. Of critical importance for both nations, the 1960 treaty is the political foundation underlying the most dynamic economic relationship in the world.

Since 1978 the two nations have deepened their cooperation in joint military planning, training, and information sharing. This has taken place within the context of the Japanese constitutional prohibition against the development of offensive forces and of Tokyo's three non-nuclear principles—no production, no possession, and no introduction of nuclear weapons into Japan. Beginning in 1976 Japan had maintained a policy of holding defense expenditures to less than 1 percent of gross national product (GNP). Although this limit was formally eliminated in 1986, the five-year defense program that was adopted in its place did not, in fact, require defense expenditures much above the 1 percent level. In some years since 1986, it has remained below 1 percent. No qualitative change in this regard is likely in the foreseeable future.

Although U.S.–Japan trade relations have become more contentious during the past decade, American attitudes toward the defense relationship with Tokyo have generally been very positive, especially among those Pentagon officials and members of Congress who are familiar with the extent of the cooperation. Some people have occasionally spoken against a Japanese "free ride," and in 1987 Congress even passed a resolution demanding that Tokyo spend 3 percent of GNP on defense. But when Japanese defense specialists pointed out that this level of spending could finance ten aircraft carrier task forces, even the strongest congressional critics of Japan calmed down.

Today the Japanese people strongly support both the U.S. treaty relationship and their own self-defense forces: over 70 percent of the Japanese public approve of these two principal elements of Tokyo's security policy. In part, this support is due to a broader Japanese vision of its own security role. Primarily, however, it reflects the value that the Japanese attach to the alliance as the key link with the United States. That link, once seen as dangerous, became more attractive in the second half of the 1970s with the end of the Vietnam War, the normalization of U.S. and Japanese relations with China, the growth of Soviet military deployments in Asia (including in the Japanese claimed but Soviet occupied Northern Territories, off the coast of Hokkaido), the Soviet role in supporting Vietnamese aggression against Cambodia, the beginning of Soviet air and naval deployments in Vietnam, and the Soviet invasion of Afghanistan.

As a result, Japan has made more contributions to the cost of maintaining U.S. forces in Japan, Tokyo now financing 40 percent of the costs of stationing U.S. forces in Japan (approximately $2.8 billion yearly) and having agreed to finance fully half of the costs over the next few years, which would encompass virtually all yen based expenditures. However justified American concerns with economic problems may be, the Japanese contribution to the alliance and to the promotion of mutual interests—both financially and in terms of joint activities—remains of great significance. It would be foolish in the extreme to allow emotions to generate unreasonable demands that Tokyo adopt qualitatively different defense policies. By the same token, one should not yield to the dangerous lure of a "balance of power," seeking to maintain good relations with China, for example, for the sake of countering Japan.

Many U.S. economic officials and business leaders believe that the U.S. government has pushed aside trade problems in order to preserve the security relationship. This is not really true. It is true, however, that the United States has generally designed policy to keep those problems in proper perspective and to maintain a distance between contentious economic disputes and the highly satisfactory security relationship. But, during the years 1986–90, as the bilateral trade imbalance remained at close to $50 billion per year (which was 45 percent of the U.S. global trade deficit in 1989 and almost 40 percent in 1990), American emotions rose, and there was some effect on defense issues. This was demonstrated through a variety of incidents in recent years, such as the angry congressional reaction to the illegal sale by a Japanese company to the Soviet Union of sophisticated equipment that was useful in building quieter submarines; in the controversy over coproduction of the next-generation Japanese fighter aircraft, the FSX; in congressional demands for Japan to send naval forces to help protect oil supplies from the Persian Gulf during the Iran-Iraq war; and in the pressure—from Congress and from the administration—for a significant Japanese financial and even noncombat personnel contribution toward the Gulf War.

Despite these problems and difficult questions, the Mutual Security Treaty remains of immense value to both Tokyo and Washington, especially, as already noted, when considering the essentially undiminished Soviet strategic power in Asia.

Soviet-Japan Relations

Although Japan's relations with the Soviet Union are improving, they are still not normal. Moscow and Tokyo restored diplomatic relations in 1956, but they never signed a peace treaty after World War II, and the Kremlin's policies toward Japan have not undergone the same transformation that has been seen in Moscow's new thinking toward Europe, the United States, and China.

The USSR now formally acknowledges that Japan "disputes" the Soviet claim to sovereignty over the Northern Territories. And Moscow is now willing to listen to Tokyo's arguments on that subject. In addition, the Soviets now seem ready to give Japan a degree of respect that was missing in earlier periods. Nonetheless, many Japanese complain that Moscow still does not take their views seriously. The "halfway" proposals Moscow has made so far to resolve the Northern Territories issue reveal a fundamental Soviet unwillingness—or inability—to deal seriously with Tokyo's deep desire to regain sovereignty over all four islands.

Japan is maintaining its policy of linking economics to politics by refusing to provide government credits or guarantees for major trade and investment deals in the Soviet Union until there is a peace treaty and full normalization of relations. But Japanese do worry that because of this hard line, Japan will become the only exception in a new era of detente. So the Japanese government is taking steps to deal with domestic criticism that it is becoming isolated. For example, in addition to major political, investment, and aid initiatives in Eastern Europe, Tokyo has agreed to various cultural and educational exchanges with the USSR, more frequent official consultations, technical support for *perestroika* as the USSR shifts to a market economy, and promotion of normal trade and other relations. It has agreed to emergency food aid to the USSR, as well. But Japanese authorities do not intend to change their demand for the return of all the Northern Territories as a precondition for the full normalization of relations. And they feel no serious domestic political pressure to do so.

In any case, since most Japanese do not believe that the Soviet military threat in East Asia has been greatly reduced, and since their desire to participate in major investment projects in the Soviet Union has decreased over the last decade or two, few of them want to change existing security arrangements with the United States, even if a peace treaty with the USSR is eventually signed.

In fact, many Japanese are worried by what they see as too much American enthusiasm over recent reforms in Soviet domestic and foreign policy. If the United States were to consider the alliance less vital in global strategic terms, this could create genuine security risks for Japan, they believe; it could also lead to reduced concern in Washington policy-making circles about the political impact of highly confrontational U.S. economic measures. They are very aware of public opinion polls that show Americans far more worried about the Japanese economic "threat" than about Moscow's relatively undiminished military might.

In fact, there is no strong movement in Washington to make fundamental changes in the alliance with Japan. To the contrary, there is widespread recognition that the alliance is the cornerstone of the U.S. Asian security policy, and the general consensus in the Bush administration and in Congress is that with the future of American basing arrangements in the Philippines now up in the air, and with the mission of U.S. forces based in Korea limited to a defensive role on the peninsula, both reliable American access to bases in Japan and continuing—and expanded—cooperation with Japanese defense forces in the Western Pacific are essential to protect broad U.S. security interests in Asia.

Redefining the Alliance

The American alliance with Japan represents more than shared military purposes, structures, and operations; it is the political "glue" that binds the nations together in ways that go well beyond traditional strategic concerns. It is useful to recall that this was not the case even a few years ago; public reference to the very idea of an "alliance" with the U.S. forced the resignation of the Japanese foreign minister in the early 1980s. Since then, the situation has changed dramatically, and today Japanese leaders routinely identify the alliance with the United States as the cornerstone of the overall relationship.

At the same time, American and Japanese views about the exact

purposes of the treaty and the way it is implemented will also need
to keep pace with domestic developments in Japan as well as in the
United States. Mutual security interests will remain an important
core of the alliance. Nonetheless, Washington and Tokyo will need
to shift the focus of their working partnership, applying their joint
economic and political power constructively to a broader range of
shared concerns. To make this approach work, however, they will
also need to reduce the mutual harsh criticism over narrow trade
issues and adopt more respectful methods of resolving disputes.

Together the United States and Japan produce about 40 percent of the world's total output of goods and services (GNP). In
addition, they have over $140 billion in bilateral trade each year,
and at the end of 1989 they had $83 billion invested in each other's
economy. As a result, the two economies have already become so
interdependent that either one would be seriously hurt if the other
suffered a recession or adopted protectionist policies.

Still, if the political bonds were torn—and this would almost
certainly happen if the alliance were abandoned—this extraordinary economic relationship would be exposed to enormous strains.
The very concept of an alliance relationship involves a sense of
mutual reliance and closeness not only of security relations but
even of trade and investment ties that a "purely" economic relationship would not. To loosen that connection would not free the
United States to pursue its economic interests with fewer constraints, as some people have argued, but it would, instead, destroy
much of the incentive that both sides have to resolve trade issues in
mutually satisfactory ways.

Because of America's size and global responsibilities, U.S. political leadership will still be necessary. But American leaders face a
dilemma in having—for the first time since World War II—to
share decision-making power over key international issues with
their allies, including Japan, rather than simply asserting their will.

Moreover, the Japanese must now confront the reality of the
outside world's rising expectations that they will assume greater
global responsibilities, taking risks for purposes going beyond
Japan's immediate concerns rather than pursuing policies calculated purely for their national benefit. It is essential that Japan
"stand for" something larger than itself if it is to gain a respected

voice in world councils. However, when it does so, the rest of the world needs to pay attention to what it says. Indeed, no issue will be more crucial to the health of the U.S.–Japan relationship over the coming decade than Japan's willingness to stand up and be counted, and America's willingness to allow—and even encourage—it to do so regardless of differences on specifics.

Whether this means that Tokyo should actively seek, and Washington should support, a permanent seat for Japan on the UN Security Council is a complicated question that will take time to address. Even removal of the so-called enemy states clauses in the UN Charter risks opening a Pandora's box. But the principal international organizations must find ways to bring Japan more centrally into the decision-making process—not only with respect to economic questions, and not only on those affecting Asia, but on global political and security issues, as well. In this regard, active Japanese participation in UN peacekeeping operations would be an appropriate and positive development.

In sum, in the new era of East-West detente, the continuing vitality of American alliances in Asia, as elsewhere, will depend critically upon American boldness and vision in helping to transform them from instruments of U.S. military power into partnerships with shared responsibilities. This will require that Americans think beyond tomorrow, or even next month. It will also require that they accept that changes are taking place in East Asia and that they should act to help shape them, rather than thinking they can prevent them.

Notes

[1] Informed Soviet observers attribute Moscow's reluctance to draw down its Far Eastern forces radically at least partially to an inadequate U.S. response thus far, which, they say, has caused the Soviets to feel they are being "regarded unfairly," and to the continuing growth of Japan's military potential. According to these observers, the slow pace of U.S. force reductions in the Far East "plays into the hands" of the Soviet Ministry of Defense, which prefers to limit its own reductions in the region.

[2] Pyongyang claims its forces number only 420,000, many of whom are engaged in large-scale civilian construction projects.

[3] North Korea has not concluded a full-scope safeguards agreement with the International Atomic Energy Agency despite its obligations to do so under the

nonproliferation treaty that it signed in 1985. Though not foolproof, IAEA inspections—especially if they could be conducted on a "challenge" as well as routine basis—would provide at least some level of assurance against a weapons program. If Pyongyang actually "went nuclear," it would create a very unstable situation on the peninsula and throughout the region. In late May/early June 1991, North Korea, which denies it has a nuclear weapons program, dropped broad hints about accepting IAEA inspections. Should Pyongyang proceed along that line, it could well facilitate withdrawal of any American nuclear weapons that are based in South Korea. For a discussion of U.S. military options in Korea see Crowe and Romberg (1991).

[4] It has also had treaty commitments elsewhere in the region, the only vestiges of which are the 1951 Mutual Defense Treaty with the Philippines and a commitment to Thailand under the Manila Pact of 1954. The U.S. commitment to Australia under the 1952 ANZUS Treaty also remains in effect; defense commitments to New Zealand were suspended in 1986 due to that country's legislative restrictions on nuclear ship visits.

[5] This plan is presented in the Pentagon's extensive response to the Nunn-Warner amendment to the FY 1990 Defense Authorization Act. It outlines the rationale for a continued military presence in the Asian-Pacific region over the coming decade. See U.S. Department of Defense (1990).

9D

The Grand Bargain: The West and the Future of the Soviet Union

GRAHAM ALLISON AND ROBERT BLACKWILL

The United States and the West have profound stakes in the future of the "Second Russian Revolution" now occurring in the Soviet Union. When completed, its consequences for politics, economics, ownership, and the character of the Soviet gov-

---

ROBERT BLACKWILL is on the faculty of the Kennedy School of Government at Harvard University. In 1989–90 he was special assistant to President Bush for European and Soviet Affairs on the staff of the National Security Council. A career diplomat, from 1985–87 he was U.S. ambassador and chief negotiator at the negotiations with the Warsaw Pact on conventional forces in Europe. Ambassador Blackwill is a member of the International Institute for Strategic Studies and the Council on Foreign Relations. He is on the board of the American Council on Germany and on the steering committee of the U.S.–EC Association. In December 1990 Ambassador Blackwill was awarded the Commander's Cross of the Order of Merit by the Federal Republic of Germany for his contribution while at the White House to German unification. He is the author of many articles on European security and East-West relations and coeditor of *Conventional Arms Control and East-West Security* and *A Primer for the Nuclear Age*. This chapter builds on "America's Stake in the Soviet Future," *Foreign Affairs*, Summer 1991.

ernment may be no less profound than those of 1917. Voltaire observed that the Holy Roman Empire was neither holy nor Roman nor an empire. What we have known as the Union of Soviet Socialist Republics will increasingly be neither soviet nor socialist nor a union. The U.S. stakes in the Soviet Union's future merit a Grand Bargain between the United States and the other industrial democracies and the Soviet Union and its republics, a U.S. strategy of step-by-step and conditional engagement as robust and refined as America's victorious cold war strategy. The joint program would consist of initiatives that the Soviet governments—the center and the republics—would take to move rapidly to democratic pluralism and the market economy, and actions the West would take to motivate, enable, and facilitate these Soviet initiatives.

We begin with U.S. stakes. The preeminent American interest in the Soviet Union continues to be to avoid a nuclear war between the two countries. Although the likelihood of a nuclear exchange has mercifully declined, the consequences of a failure of deterrence are so great that the nuclear issue must continue to top any list of U.S. interests vis-à-vis the Soviet Union. Moreover, with the possibility of widespread Soviet internal disorder, it is easy to imagine a tragic intersection between civil violence and a civil nuclear facility. The bloody disintegration of the Soviet Union would also raise an almost unimaginable specter of transcending interest to the United States. Under conditions of chaos and civil wars, what would happen to the Soviet arsenal of 30,000 nuclear weapons? Can we expect that such weapons would remain under centralized command and control? No single event in the postwar period would pose such high and uncontrollable risks of nuclear war as the violent collapse of the Soviet Union into chaos and civil wars.

The size, capabilities, and location of Soviet conventional forces will also continue to matter to the United States and its European allies. Even under the 1990 Treaty on Conventional Armed Forces in Europe (CFE), Soviet armed forces will be the largest and most capable in Europe. These factors are important because of the risks they present, their impact on U.S. defense spending, and the size of the American forces that should prudently remain in

Europe. The United States has a profound interest in whether the Soviet Union, even with its severe economic problems, eventually begins a new round of force modernization or pursues force reductions, either unilaterally or through arms control agreements. A breakup of the Soviet Union and a fragmenting of its enormous military force into war among its components would pose unprecedented defense policy challenges for Washington.

Many of Moscow's policies in the political and diplomatic area will affect important U.S. interests. Will Moscow be a partner with the West in trying to help manage the emergence of an independent and relatively peaceful Eastern Europe, or will Soviet actions add to the inherent instability in that region? Will Soviet new thinking extend to Asia, and particularly to Soviet-Japanese relations? Will the Soviet government continue its cooperation with Washington to ameliorate internal and regional conflicts, to build a more stable Middle East after the Gulf War? And will Moscow support Western efforts to slow the flow of nuclear, chemical, biological, and ballistic missile technology to unstable parts of the world, in particular, to the Middle East and South Asia?

But U.S. interests do not end there. The broad U.S. public responded to Mikhail Gorbachev's reforms not because they promised a slowdown in Soviet tank production, however welcomed that was. Rather, *glasnost* and democratization touched the broad public because these reforms reflected American values. The prospect, however distant, of nearly 300 million more human beings enjoying freedom's benefits and the market's prosperity must gladden the spirit of America and must be fundamentally in this nation's enduring interests.

But what of America's policies, in light of the continuing tensions within the Soviet Union between order and reform, between power at the center and its devolution to the republics, and between the preservation of the union and outright independence or self-determination? Here are some guidelines.

The violence against the Baltic people must stop, and, because of their special history, these three republics must have the opportunity to regain their independence. As for the other twelve Soviet republics, any consensual arrangement acceptable to any republic and the Soviet central government should be acceptable to the

United States. But universal self-determination is not an American constitutional principle, as amply demonstrated by our own Civil War. There is no end to boundless self-determination or to the progressively smaller ethnic groups that will demand it. Why should the United States support endless and automatic self-determination based on nationality—and at whatever price—in the Soviet Union, including Russia and the Ukraine, more vigorously than in Serbia, Transylvania, Slovakia, or for Quebec? The United States should refuse to be intimidated by invocations of this principle—both as a matter of priorities and because of its destructive effect on the territorial integrity of the Soviet Union and, therefore, on the U.S. interests that would surely be threatened by the Soviet Union's violent disintegration.

Finally, America's interests clearly require that it support and speak out on behalf of democratic change. This is consistent with both its values and its best traditions. The best long-term prospect for cooperative Soviet behavior abroad is the sustained development of Soviet democratic institutions at home.

Many believe there is little the United States can do to affect the outcome of the Soviet domestic struggle: there is too much turmoil to be influenced positively from the outside; Gorbachev's *perestroika* may wind down anyway; the United States has no money; America has to tend to its own problems. The West therefore must simply watch events in the Soviet Union unfold, hoping for the best but expecting much worse.

Such passivity is curious, if not dangerous, on a matter that has such profound implications for the future security of the United States. Having spent some $5 trillion to meet the military challenge of the Soviet Union around the globe, are the United States and its allies to opt out now when the Soviet future is being formed?

It may well be that a large and coordinated Western effort to encourage the formation of a market economy and democratic institutions would fail because of Soviet bureaucratic resistance or incompetence, opposition of the Soviet people, or Gorbachev's (or his successor's) unwillingness to make the necessary reforms. The odds of failure indeed appear higher than those of success. But with so much at stake, Western delay in engaging deeply to do what we can to limit the risks of catastrophic outcomes and make more probable Soviet futures compatible with our interests is myopic.

What, then, should the West do, and do urgently, to try to promote a positive Soviet future, to avoid the return of dangerous and destabilizing Soviet external policies or the violent disintegration of the Soviet state?

First, we should recognize that events in the Soviet Union present a historic opportunity. People in the Soviet Union have concluded that their society has failed. They believe that the economic and political democracies of the West have succeeded. They thus stand at a "learning moment," eagerly receptive to the lessons of Western experience in what they call "normal" and "civilized" societies. The West must not abandon the brave Soviets fighting for reform. If it gives up, many of them will prudently do the same. The West should make a major effort to distill and communicate these core truths to Soviet citizens whose entire lives have been confined to a prison of distorting mirrors. The conversion of a military-industrial society must occur most importantly in the minds of key people: one by one.

The Soviet Union is today open to printing presses, copying machines, personal computers, fax machines, and satellite dishes. Specific assistance can make the opening of the Soviet consciousness irreversible. Western support, however, must be differentiated. Help should be given to those whose actions bring democracy and a market economy, not to opponents or those who wish to dismember, violently if necessary, the USSR. Reform, yes. Repression, no. Encourage devolution to a new federation or confederation. Discourage anarchy surrounding the disintegration of the Soviet state.

Second, the United States should continue active attempts to engage the Soviet Union in the management of what will remain a dangerous and frequently unstable international environment. This means rapid implementation of CFE and the Strategic Arms Reduction Treaty (START); sharp reductions in military forces and budgets; cessation of aid for nations and forces promoting regional conflicts; and accelerated cooperation in international problem solving including regional disputes, the spread of weapons of mass destruction, and terrorism.

Third, in an effort to forestall Soviet futures that would most deeply threaten Western interests and global stability, a coalition of Western governments led by the United States should immediately design and offer to the Soviet Union a *Grand Bargain* of Marshall Plan proportions. The terms: substantial financial assistance to Soviet reforms *conditional* upon continuing political pluralization and a coherent economic program for moving rapidly to a market economy. The strategy: create incentives for leaders at the center and in the republics to choose a future consistent with our mutual best interest by promising real assistance for real reform.

Here is the outline of such a historic bargain between the Soviet Union and the West. This concept is not one of a "cosmic contract" that spells out in every detail every step every government would take for life or even the next few years. We envision mutually agreed commitments, principles, and parameters that would shape a relationship of engagement in pursuit of common goals. Lord Acton wrote of the "remote and ideal objective" that by the splendor of its conception captures the mind and motivates. In such strategic engagement, some agreements would be implicit or understood. In other areas, however, commitments would be explicit, detailed, verifiable, and monitored.

On the Soviet side, a major step toward meeting the terms of the West was taken in the April 23rd power-sharing "Statement of the Ten" (signed by President Gorbachev and the leaders of the nine major republics, but not six others). The terms include:

- Recognition of the depth of the crisis and the real risk of violent disintegration.
- Acceptance of the republics as "sovereign states," each of which has the specific right to decide independently whether to join the new union or to be separate and independent.
- For those who join the union, agreement on a common economic space among them, protection of human rights of all individuals, restoration of constitutional order, and strict compliance with current law.
- Immediate preparation of a new Union Treaty, followed by a new constitution of the USSR and new elections for national office.

The draft of the new Union Treaty embodying these principles had been completed at this writing. What more should the West require? Essentially two things.

First, consistent with the "Statement of Ten" and earlier commitments by the USSR to the Conference on Security and Cooperation in Europe (CSCE) Treaty, Soviet authorities at all levels would reaffirm their international commitment to respect human rights of individuals within the Soviet Union whatever their national, ethnic, or religious identification.

Second, the states who join the new union would commit themselves to focus in the next stage of development on a rapid transition to a market economy as the essential foundation for sustaining democracy. Experts designated by the ten would devise a realistic program for moving rapidly to a free market economy with substantial Western cooperation and assistance. The Marshall Plan offers an instructive precedent. The United States promised financial aid only if the European parties could agree on a joint plan for reconstruction. The major steps in the Soviet program must include: (a) stabilization: sharp reductions in fiscal and monetary deficits by cutting defense spending and subsidies to state enterprises; (b) legalization of enterprise: beginning with ownership, legalizing economic initiative including much of what remains gray or black in the present Soviet economy; (c) liberalization of prices: moving in stages to total decontrol in which prices will reflect scarcity values, first within the Soviet Union and soon thereafter in the world economy; and (d) demonopolization and privatization transferring productive economic activity to private hands in an environment in which many enterprises compete.

The U.S./Western side of the Grand Bargain should entail a well-designed, step-by-step, strictly conditional program of assistance provided both to the center and to the republics. The core elements of the Western program of major incentives would include:

1. A clear signal of the West's commitment to help the Soviet Union in this peaceful transformation in any way Western assistance can make a significant difference in the probability of success.

2. Forthrightness that this means major financial assistance only if and as the Soviet Union is committed to a realistic plan for the transition to the market economy—a plan to which Western assistance can make a difference. Unconditional aid, no. Aid contingent upon actions that increase the probability of success, yes. Real aid for real reform.

3. Special associate status in the International Monetary Fund (IMF) and World Bank. As the Soviet government, in conjunction with Western assistance, undertakes the necessary structural changes in its economic and financial institutions and policies, it should become eligible for billions of dollars of aid from these institutions as well.

4. Massive technical assistance distilling lessons of international experience and providing those lessons in an array of appropriate training programs for essential activities in the transition.

5. To create the conditions for private investment on which Soviet economic health will ultimately depend, Western financial assistance, if Soviet reform takes off, on the order of $15–20 billion per year for each of the next three years in grants, not loans, the cost to be shared by the U.S., Europe, and Japan. The grants should be allocated appropriately between the center and the republics. Funds would go for general balance of payments support, project support for key items of infrastructure (like transportation and communication), and the maintenance of an adequate safety net as part of a general "conditionality program" following basic IMF–World Bank guidelines. This is a notional level of Western assistance, notional because there is no magic number in this regard. Instead, in the final analysis Soviet financial needs would emerge in the design and implementation of the program after lengthy negotiations between Soviet central government and republic officials and Western experts, especially from the IMF.

The need for external aid to assist the Soviet reform program has sometimes been questioned on the grounds that the Soviet Union is a rich country that should be able to transform its economy without outside help. Technically, and over a very long time period, that could be possible. However, radical economic reorganization in a situation like that of the Soviet Union, where output is already declining very rapidly, would produce massive economic dislocation, a collapse of investment and output, and extremely sharp declines in consumption. Under these conditions, the reform program would probably not be politically sustainable, and economic and political chaos could well follow. Thus the steepness of the reform path that Soviet leaders can choose and realistically follow, the speed of the journey, the odds on success, the pain involved, and the risks—including those of cataclysmic failure—depend critically on the extent of Western engagement.

Thus the West should state clearly and ahead of time what it is prepared to do *if* the Soviet Union is ready and able to undertake a realistic and rapid transition to the market economy. Most theories of bargaining and diplomacy recognize the power of a credible promise of substantial assistance rather than distant admonitions. Particularly in the current worsening conditions within the Soviet Union, the knowledge of specific Western readiness to extend a strong helping hand would provide crucial incentives for Soviet politicians and citizens.

But the Grand Bargain is not, most importantly, about economics. Rather, it depends on a conceptual breakthrough in the interaction among the Soviet Union, its republics, and the West. This new strategic engagement ultimately must be centered on shared values, the democratic values that have evolved over centuries. This is the essence of the relationship between the Soviet Union and the West that could lie beyond containment.

It should be clear from the above what the Grand Bargain is not.

It is not a one-time "big bang" to use Secretary of State James Baker's apt phrase, not billions up front to the Soviet Union on the basis of fervent hope and vague promises of reform. Indeed, money is neither the first requirement nor the last. If the West were now to put a bag of billions on the table in advance of fundamental Soviet economic reform, failure would be ensured and the money would be lost. Rather, the West would provide large-scale assistance on a step-by-step basis only if the Soviet leadership pursued a detailed and tangible program of political and economic transformation. If it did not, or if reform failed, then this highly conditioned aid would not be disbursed.

It is not a means to prop up a tottering and rotten Communist regime. That system and its policies have brought the Soviet Union to disaster and the edge of political, economic, and moral collapse. Communism is not the future. It does not work. It cannot be saved through tinkering. It must be replaced by democratic and free market institutions, with to be sure a Soviet (and Russian, Ukrainian, Georgian, etc.) stamp on them.

It is not a program to rescue Mr. Gorbachev and buttress the autocratic center at the expense of reformist forces in the republics. The peaceful transformation of the Soviet Union to democracy and the market cannot occur without close and enduring cooperation between the central government and the emerging popularly supported politicians of the republics. The right wing views of the Soyuz movement notwithstanding, the center is unlikely to hold unless it strikes devolutionary deals over the long run with the republics. And despite feverish local proclamations to the contrary, the republics are unlikely to go it alone successfully. These two levels of government, power, and reform need one another to save themselves. Establishing this fragile coalition through the "9 + 1" agreement has been no easy task. Maintaining it through uncertainty and pain will be much, much harder. But failing to do so will surely accelerate the Soviet downward spiral.

And the Grand Bargain *is not* a Western effort to bail out, bribe, or blackmail the Soviet Union. The Soviet Union is and will remain a great power. In the transformation to democratic institutions and the market economy, Soviet resources, Soviet courage, Soviet determination, and Soviet endurance will be the decisive factors. Soviets have to want to transform their political and economic systems—for their own reasons, not because the West believes it is good for them. We can encourage and assist. They must make it happen.

Would Gorbachev and the leaders of the republics strike such a Grand Bargain? The answer is unclear as this is written. But as conditions worsen, the beacon of substantial Western assistance could indeed come to concentrate the minds not only of reformers, but of straddlers as well. Even if the offer and its incentives should ultimately be refused, the West could take some comfort in knowing that the Soviet reform effort did not fail for want of something it could have provided.

Recall that it was not until three years after the end of World War II that George Marshall called for a massive coordinated program to assist the reconstruction of Europe. The founding fathers of the transatlantic relationship on this side of the ocean persevered against what many at the time believed were very long odds, knowing that to do otherwise would be to consign the next generation and beyond to a world less stable and less safe. As a result of this seminal American leadership and vision, we now have a Europe close to whole and free. A U.S.–led effort to help transform the Soviet Union would certainly be significantly more difficult than the challenge undertaken by the United States through the Marshall Plan. It would at best take many years to accomplish. Nevertheless, there are more than enough reasons of self-interest and values to try.

9E

The End of American History: American Security, the National Purpose, and the New World Order

DAVID C. HENDRICKSON

The principal assumption of this paper is that the lineaments of President Bush's "new world order" may be understood best against the background of past conceptions of American security and the national purpose. The president's vision of the new world order and of the American role in that order has incorporated ideas that have formed part of the classic debate over American security and the national purpose from the beginning of the nation's history; at the same time, the president has given these old themes a novel and in crucial respects unprecedented expression. His vision of a "new world order," I shall argue, entails an inflated conception of American security requirements; it also threatens a

DAVID C. HENDRICKSON is associate professor of political science at Colorado College. He is the author of *The Future of American Strategy* (1987) and *Reforming Defense: The State of American Civil-Military Relations* (1988). He has written two books with Robert W. Tucker: *The Fall of the First British Empire: Origins of the War of American Independence* (1982) and *Empire of Liberty: The Statecraft of Thomas Jefferson* (1990). Prof. Hendrickson would like to thank Robert W. Tucker for advice and counsel in the course of writing this chapter.

fundamental betrayal of the national purpose.

It may seem peculiar to assume, as I do, that the classic expressions given by American statesmen of our national purpose and of the criteria under which the nation might make war remain of relevance in our own day. Two hundred years is a long time in the life of a nation. At the outset, the United States existed on the periphery of world politics. The European powers who constituted the core of that system often conducted their diplomacy and fought their wars with scarcely a glance at the power and principles of the United States. Today the United States stands at the center of the international system, or rather it sits at the top of one of the more impressive hegemonial orders in history. It appears to invite parallels not with the nation we once were but with the great empires of the past.

It may be conceded that these vast disparities in power and position make it impossible to go back in toto to the doctrines and principles that once animated American diplomacy. The last fifty years, during which the United States emerged as the dominant power in the world, have altered American commitments and responsibilities in such a way that the political separation from the rest of the world for which Americans once yearned is no longer possible or desirable. Still, it remains useful to recall these older doctrines today, if only to regain our moorings after the extraordinary events that surrounded the beginning of the 1990s, including both the collapse of the Soviet empire in Eastern Europe and America's military victory over Iraq in the Gulf War. Nations, Edmund Burke said, were partnerships of the dead, the living, and the yet unborn, and for no state is this observation more true than for our own. If we are to fulfill our role in this compact among the generations, it will be through the constructive use of memory and imagination—memory to allow us to recall the nature of the old doctrine and the old faith, imagination to apply it creatively to the predicaments and opportunities facing the United States today.

American Security and
the National Purpose:
The Original Understanding

It is part of the natural history of great powers that their security requirements grow apace with their power. Certainly this is true of the United States. For the first eighty years of the nation's existence (from the end of the War of American Independence until the Civil War), the primary security problem faced by the country was internal. The overwhelming specter, to which every generation gave voice, was that of a breakup of the Union, which carried with it the danger of a state system in North America that would breed wars and threaten republican government. The need to avoid "entangling alliances," expressed by both Washington and Jefferson, was closely related to the fear of dissolution, for only in circumstances of disunity might foreign security threats prove truly alarming. In the absence of disunion, Americans felt increasingly confident that their geographical isolation from Europe provided them with a greater measure of security than that enjoyed by any European state.

If security might be achieved through the perpetuation of the Union, so too might the country's purpose. From the beginning of the nation's existence, the American purpose was seen in terms of the achievement at home of a condition of ordered liberty. The establishment of representative institutions and courts to resolve disputes according to a written constitution was considered a great advance on the old European method, in which force was employed on behalf of principles of religious or political despotism, shedding oceans of needless blood in the process. The rule of law and the peaceful resolution of disputes were the two main hallmarks of a *novus ordo seclorum* that would show the world the error of its ways, and demonstrate the superiority of free institutions and free markets.

The nation's purpose or mission was both inward and outward looking. If Americans believed that they were part of a form of civilization higher than the polished societies of Europe, they also thought that their purpose imposed an obligation to adhere to the highest standards of conduct in their own internal and external policy. The reputation of republican government was at stake. Understood in this sense, the idea of a national purpose lent itself not only to displays of self-righteousness but also to sober introspection. It directed a reproach not only against the characteristic delusions of despotic governments but also against the potential betrayal of national ideals by Americans themselves. African slavery and Indian removal were attacked on these grounds; so, too, were the wars with Mexico and Spain in 1846 and 1898.

Among the Founders, force was generally looked upon with thoroughgoing skepticism. Though most Americans came to understand, in Daniel Webster's phrase, that "the last logic of kings is also our last logic," and that force might sometimes be necessary "to preserve our honor in some unequivocal point, or to avoid the sacrifice of some right or interest of material and permanent importance," primary emphasis was placed by Jeffersonians and Hamiltonians alike on the dangers that force would entail. Force, they thought, had a logic that was ultimately inimical to liberty. The early generation of American statesmen had reflected long and hard on the imperial experience of Rome, Great Britain, and France. "From whatever there was of good in the systems of former centuries [America] drew her nourishment; the wrecks of the past were her warning." Jeffersonians saw at work in past history a dynamic by which force begot the expansion of an executive or consolidated power inevitably hostile to liberty, whereas Hamiltonians professed astonishment "with how much precipitance and levity nations still rush to arms against each other . . . after the experience of its having deluged the world with calamities for so many ages." Both sides sought to devise institutional bulwarks, prudential maxims, and moral barriers against the easy resort to war. Experience seemed to show only too clearly that nations and empires became corrupted at home and weakened abroad unless the easy resort to force were somehow tamed or suppressed.

It was a customary feature of American statecraft in the nineteenth century to invoke the law of nations on behalf of American rights and interests, but outside the confines of the Union itself the idea of collective action was considered an infringement on the independence of action to which the nation aspired. Even the Monroe Doctrine of 1823, which warned against European encroachments in this hemisphere, implied no commitment to the security or freedom of any other state. If we went to war it would be for our own reasons and for our own security. We would neither expect nor rely on the cooperation of other states.

With but few exceptions, these attributes characterized the outlook of American diplomatists from the founding up until the early years of the twentieth century. Only with America's intervention in World War I in 1917 did intimations appear—and they were as yet but intimations—of a seismic shift in the permanent bases of American foreign policy. Though Woodrow Wilson entered the war as an associated power and thereby advertised the distinction between American and allied war aims, he also came increasingly to see the meaning of the war as a crusade to make the world safe for democracy and to establish a world organization devoted to the collective realization of universal ideals. It was no narrow partisan feeling that led Senator Henry Cabot Lodge to reject Wilson's vision of collective security as a betrayal of American diplomatic traditions, of "the policy of Washington and Monroe"; yet Wilson's ideal lived on in American diplomacy in the twentieth century. Like a seed buried deep in the ground that awaited water and sunshine, it would burst forth whenever the international climate became more benign (only later to wither under a cold blast from the East).

With the First World War there also appeared indications that threats to American security might arise from the wars of other continents—an idea that had been common currency during the wars of the French Revolution and Napoleon but that had been progressively forgotten during the long peace that followed from 1815 to 1914. The proximate cause of America's intervention in World War I—certainly the cause felt most deeply by public opinion—was Germany's decision to launch unrestricted submarine warfare in early 1917 and the unmistakable challenge that decision posed to American neutral rights and honor. But an articulate minority of Americans had also become increasingly fearful that a German victory would imperil either American security or republican institutions. Neo-Hamiltonians warned that a German victory would break the sea lines of communication across the Atlantic and derange the European balance of power, inevitably posing a threat to American security; neo-Jeffersonians feared that such a victory might force the United States to build armaments to counter the threat of German militarism. To a nation that had prided itself on the doctrine that its influence would spread peaceably and by example, such an outcome appeared ominous. As Colonel Edward Mandell House wrote in 1914, it would "change the course of our civilization and make the United States a military nation."

America's involvement in World War I, however, signified no lasting change of policy. In the aftermath of the war, Americans attempted to revert, as best they could, to the original understanding. They wisely rejected the indefinite commitment to the territorial integrity and political independence of other states thought to be entailed by membership in the League of Nations. Less wisely, they came to believe that American intervention had not been necessary to avert a German victory and the dangers to security and republican institutions that such a victory would have brought. The nation reverted to its former conviction that all the European powers were animated by selfish ambitions (and as such were morally equivalent), and hence it refused the alliance with England and France that was necessary to preserve the peace settlement. American involvement in the world war was increasingly seen as an aberration, and it was thought that a reversion to America's traditional policy of no entangling alliances would pose no danger to American security. The country was secure and prosperous. Calvin Coolidge, who was a far more acute theorist of the old American order than is generally realized, summarized the security position of the nation in 1926 with his customary economy: "The American people," he observed in his State of the Union message,

are altogether lacking in an appreciation of the tremendous good fortune that surrounds their international position. We have no traditional enemies. We are not embarrassed over any disputed territory. We have no possessions that are coveted by others; they have none that are coveted by us. Our borders are unfortified. We fear no one; no one fears us.

The Cold War Consensus

It was American participation in the Second World War, the occasion for which was a direct attack on American territory by Japan, that led to several decisive changes in the way in which American leaders defined the diplomatic objectives of this nation. No sooner had the Axis powers of Germany and Japan been destroyed than another threat arose from the Soviet Union. In each instance, a justification for repelling aggression that fell back on the criteria of international law (order) came to be paired with a certain diagnosis of the conditions in which peace might be secured (the spread of free institutions). Neither of these ideas would have been foreign to the outlook of the Founding Fathers, who had made the law of nations part of our supreme law and who also equated (with one or two exceptions) international peace with free institutions. What *was* novel was the degree to which the United States was now thought obligated to assume responsibility for ensuring compliance by aggressor states with the law of nations and for establishing a protective umbrella over selected areas of the world under which free institutions would prosper.

These departures from traditional policy were accompanied by a reversal of the nation's longstanding attitude toward "entangling alliances." Having previously abjured commitments in peacetime to the security of any other state, the United States entered into a wide range of multilateral security pacts, beginning with the North Atlantic Treaty Organization (NATO) in 1949, for the purpose of containing the expansion of a Communist movement led and supported by the Soviet Union. These alliances with democratic states with which we had endured the vicissitudes of two total wars reflected the view that they were in fact our permanent allies. The nation entered the compacts creating these security communities with a conviction that our fate and theirs were indissolubly tied together and with a belief in close cooperation among democratic states. Both the conviction in a common fate and the belief in cooperative action among republican regimes harkened back to the motives that had led to the establishment of the American union in 1787. Both dates, it may be observed, signified the creation of an empire of liberty.

America's new world role might have provoked far greater domestic dissension than it did—and in fact might not have been taken up at all—were it not for the fact that the threat posed by the Axis powers and the Soviet Union to free institutions and to international law was simultaneously a threat to American security. Whatever else they were, Nazi Germany and the Soviet Union were great powers, and the threat they posed could be expressed in terms of a realist concern with American security just as much as an idealist defense of legal principle or free institutions. For different reasons, Americans arrived at a common conclusion: the Soviet Union had to be contained. During the cold war, Americans debated whether containment should be particularist or universalist, and whether the primary danger stemmed from the great power threat emanating from the Soviet Union or from communism as such. Nevertheless, a rough equation was readily established between ensuring order and protecting freedom, on the one hand, and providing for security on the other. The equation was capable of uniting otherwise disparate outlooks, of holding under its capacious roof Republicans and Democrats, realists and idealists, and all varieties of the tough-minded and woolly-headed. It formed the solid foundation of the cold war consensus, which the party squabbles and partisan divisions of the day barely disturbed.

The war in Vietnam badly shook, but did not break, the cold war consensus. Each of the elements that had made up the consensus was drawn into serious question by critics of the war. The Johnson administration's insistence that the United States was protecting South Vietnam against North Vietnamese aggression was met by the criticism that the war in Vietnam was above all a civil war and could not be properly classified as a case of counterintervention (which was the only basis for the legality of the American presence under international law). The hope that free institutions would take root in South Vietnam came to be regarded as a quixotic aspiration that bore little relation to Vietnamese history or to current realities. Finally, and perhaps most crucially, the link between establishing a condition of ordered liberty in Southeast Asia and ensuring American security came to seem less and less plausible. It was indicative of the difficulty of making this equation that so much of the justification for staying

the course in Vietnam came to rest on the fact, which was indis-
putable, that America had staked its prestige on the outcome. At
the beginning, the justification (the equation between order, liberty, and security) had provided the basis for the commitment. At
the end, the commitment itself had become the justification.

Despite the doubts and anguish that it produced, Vietnam had
a lesser effect on American foreign policy than many observers
had feared (or hoped) at the time. Though there occurred, particularly in the 1970s, a general reassessment of American interests in
the Third World, America's core alliances in Europe and Japan
survived intact. Nor did Americans draw the conclusion from
Vietnam that freedom was an ideal from which the nation should
now turn away. Indeed, the promotion of freedom became the
centerpiece of efforts under both Carter ("human rights") and
Reagan ("the democratic revolution") to restore the domestic consensus on foreign policy.

It was the effect of Vietnam on American attitudes toward the
use of force that was perhaps most problematic. One segment of
domestic opinion drew the conclusion that American blood and
treasure might be ventured in war only under circumstances
where a direct threat to security was present. This skeptical attitude toward the use of force revived older conceptions of the circumstances under which the nation might make war. Though
often labeled the "Vietnam syndrome," it in fact had much deeper
roots in the nation's history. It was challenged, however, by a view
that saw the failure in Vietnam not as a function of misguided ends
but of incoherent means. Rechristened as a noble cause and as an
attempt to both promote freedom and ensure order, Vietnam
demonstrated that the American people would support wars only
if our objective was to win. Domestic support for war, in this view,
did not rest on the demonstration of a compelling link to American
security; it rested instead on the adoption of a war plan in which
victory was sought as rapidly as possible and through the use of
overwhelming force.

The End of the Cold War

It was not defeat in Vietnam that forced a change in the foundations of American foreign policy, but rather victory in the cold war. The fundamental reorientation of Soviet foreign policy introduced by Mikhail Gorbachev, together with the breakdown of the economic mechanism in the Soviet Union, made the Soviet threat appear far less formidable than it had once done. When the old guard was thrown out of office throughout the traditional Soviet *glacis* in Eastern Europe, it constituted an epochal development that undermined the assumptions that had guided American foreign policy for nearly half a century.

The collapse of the Soviet empire in Eastern Europe, together with the symptoms of internal disorganization and breakdown the Soviet system manifested, led to a dramatic improvement in the American security position, which in the twentieth century had been threatened by states that were militaristic, totalitarian, and powerful. It also vindicated the American purpose, which had always been to show the peoples of the world through peaceful example that free institutions and free markets constituted the key by which their political oppression and economic misery might be lifted.

The internal disarray of the Communist powers (for the Soviet Union was not alone in suffering from the internal contradictions of Communist rule) contributed to circumstances in international relations for which it is difficult to find a true parallel in the history of the modern states system that grew up in Europe in the seventeenth and eighteenth centuries and that finally encompassed the globe in the twentieth. Save for one or two unusual moments in international history (the prime example being the collaboration among the victors after the Napoleonic wars), antagonism had always existed among the great powers at the core of the system. For the Soviet Union to give up its empire in Eastern Europe by default was so contrary to the normal behavior of great powers that its verbal professions ("the Sinatra Doctrine") could hardly be believed until they were acted upon.

The implications of this change for American foreign policy were highly paradoxical. The novel situation that came to exist in relations among the superpowers made the connection that was drawn during the cold war between world order and American security more tenuous than ever. Without a great power base behind them, the threat posed to American security by what minor despots remained was sharply diminished in significance. At the same time, the enhanced cooperation among the superpowers made it possible for the United States to entertain objectives in the world (and particularly on the periphery) that had previously been stymied by antagonism at the center.

The favorable circumstances in international relations that allowed the United States to entertain a renewed vision of world order thus also made it less necessary for purposes of security to do so. It appeared to break the equation that had been established during the cold war between freedom, order, and security. The nation's freedom to turn inward and to devote attention to domestic purposes was greater than it had been since the 1930s; but it also had, by virtue of the very same development, a greater opportunity to exercise leadership on behalf of world order since the ill-fated Grand Coalition of World War II.

How the nation would use its newly found freedom of action needed only a great crisis to reveal, which was duly provided by Saddam Hussein's invasion of Kuwait on August 2, 1990 and the decision of the Bush administration to restore Kuwaiti sovereignty through military force.

The Gulf War and the New World Order

America's victory in the Persian Gulf War was widely hailed as propelling the country into a new era. The sense of patriotism the victory excited and the boldness with which President Bush led the country into war were widely seen as having finally put to rest "the Vietnam syndrome." For the American people, victory in the Gulf War was as euphoric as defeat in Vietnam had been debilitating. It appeared to resolve the debate over foreign policy that had sprung up with the end of the cold war. Declinists, we were told, had been routed; isolationists (if any were so bold as to accept the term) had been relegated to the outer reaches of the lunatic fringe.

Of equal importance to a restored domestic base for an activist foreign policy led by the president was the justification that Mr. Bush employed in marshalling his forces. From the outset of the crisis in August 1990, when the administration cobbled together diplomatic support at the United Nations for Draconian economic sanctions against Iraq, the president said repeatedly that the response given to Iraqi aggression would be a crucial test of a new world order. The same idea figured prominently in the administration's case when it announced on November 8, 1990 a doubling of American forces in Saudi Arabia with the purpose of providing an offensive option. The president again appealed to the new world order after victory had been won and the Iraqi forces were expelled from Kuwait.

Two ideas were associated with the new world order from the beginning. One was that aggression against the territorial integrity of other states would not be allowed to stand. The president repeatedly invoked the traditional principle of international law that every state, however defenseless, was entitled to its own independent existence. The principle of international law to which the president appealed was closely related to the second idea he attributed to the new world order—that states ought to join together in collective action to repel wrongdoing. In its whirlwind tours and near-constant communications with other states, the administration attempted to secure the widest possible consensus in international society. In this it was remarkably successful, far more so than either its friends or critics might have anticipated before the crisis broke out. Not only longstanding allies but also former adversaries were brought around to support (or at least not to oppose) U.S. aims in the crisis. The administration continually appealed to the authority granted by the twelve U.N. resolutions, the last of which authorized the use of "all necessary means" to expel the Iraqis from Kuwait.

On the basis of these considerations, it might be thought that the new world order will be characterized by increasing respect for the traditional principles of international law and by multilateral efforts to secure recognition of these principles. Yet there were other aspects of the crisis that pointed in a much different direction. As the crisis developed, the administration clearly placed increasing weight on the need to destroy Iraq's military machine, including its incipient capabilities in weapons of mass destruction. It may be stretching matters to call this the real though unavowed motive for the war (recalling Thucydides's explanation of the origins of the Peloponnesian War); yet it clearly was of considerable moment.

The argument for doing so was quite similar to the classic justification for preventive war. Yet no consensus within international society exists for the proposition that preventive war is justified to stop other states from either acquiring weapons of mass destruction or maintaining what is regarded as a disproportionately large military establishment. Preemptive war may in some circumstances be thought legitimate, but preventive war has generally been condemned, particularly in the twentieth century (and particularly by the United States). If the United States were to view its action against Iraq as a precedent for future military strikes against states developing weapons of mass destruction (as some commentators are now urging), it would probably have to do so on a largely unilateral basis and in opposition to traditional principles of international law.

Similarly, the American effort to achieve a consensus at the United Nations is unlikely to harken the birth of an era of true multilateralism. It was clear from the beginning that the whole sustained effort would not have been carried through without the iron-like determination of the president to achieve his objective. The president worked hard to achieve this consensus, but in the end acknowledged that he would not have acted differently had he faced determined opposition at the United Nations. Apart from Great Britain, which saw eye to eye with the United States throughout the crisis, and the Arab coalition states of Saudi Arabia, Egypt, and Syria, who wished along with Israel to see Saddam Hussein destroyed, many other states (the Soviet Union, China, Japan, France, Iran, India, and even Germany) had serious reservations over the course chosen by the United States. But their doubts were ignored in Washington and their protests, such as they were, were ineffectual. Perhaps the most impressive feature of the Gulf War is not that other states entertained these doubts but that they were either unwilling or unable to deflect the course chosen by the president. Nor, as it turned out, was Congress, whose support, like that of the United Nations, was also deemed valuable but not indispensable.

The victory won by President Bush and U.S. armed forces was extraordinarily impressive in military terms. The victory, however, was attended by serious political and moral liabilities. In the Gulf War, a strategy of keeping American casualties to a minimum could only be pursued by the expenditure of massive amounts of firepower against the enemy, resulting in the wholesale slaughter of front-line Iraqi troops and the creation of near-apocalyptic conditions within Iraq itself. The United States rigorously distinguished between military and civilian objectives, but defined its military objectives so widely as to include the whole infrastructure of modern services that supported civilian life in the country. The president invoked St. Thomas Aquinas and his theory of the just war; but somehow the result bore an uncanny resemblance to "Hama rules."[1]

Even worse from a moral point of view was that the war did not create the conditions for a better peace. Though both order and liberty were invoked by the administration in the days leading up to the war, neither order nor liberty was established in Iraq in its aftermath. The Shi'ite and Kurdish peoples within Iraq, who mistook the president's call for uprisings to overthrow Saddam Hussein as a pledge of support and protection and who rose up in response, were then left alone to suffer the might of Saddam Hussein's fury. The result was to make a mockery of American idealism.

The consequences that ensued from the decision to unleash the dogs of war raised the question of whether it was right to have made war in the first place. The judgment that it was rested on the view that there was no alternative to going to war if Saddam Hussein were to be made to get out of Kuwait. Yet this view in itself was a curious one. It rested on the assumption that the legal objective of restoring Kuwaiti sovereignty was identical to the strategic objective of ensuring American security. Those two objectives, however, were quite distinct.

Security of access to Saudi oil might have been provided indefinitely by the maintenance of relatively small military forces in

Saudi Arabia. (Air power, it seems clear, would have been almost sufficient by itself for this task.) The danger that Iraq might grow in power and even achieve regional hegemony was amply guarded by the indefinite denial to Saddam Hussein of his oil revenues, resources that were the necessary though not sufficient condition of any further adventures on his part (and which the United States had the power to maintain unilaterally even if, as was unlikely, the coalition opposing Iraq were to fracture). The threat posed by Saddam Hussein's quest for nuclear weapons, exaggerated though it certainly was, might have been contained through measures short of war. Even had such measures been deemed insufficient, the United States would have retained the ability to severely retard these capabilities through a hundred air sorties (as opposed to a hundred thousand).

That war was chosen despite the strength of the forces boxing in Saddam Hussein owed above all to the domestic pressures facing President Bush. The administration, fearing Carterization, viewed the prospect of a protracted engagement with Saddam Hussein with alarm. This impatience with a strategy of long-term containment accounts for the readiness with which the United States went to war in the first place; the fear of American casualties accounts for the extraordinarily destructive character of the ensuing conflict. These two fears—of protracted engagements and of large casualties—were also of critical importance in the decision to stop short in American war aims and to refuse (behind the shield of a disfigured doctrine of "nonintervention") the arduous burdens of a pacification.

The outcome fostered by the United States contrasts badly with the experience of the Roman, French, and British empires, which in the wake of war normally brought, for all their other faults, peace and civil order. Conquered populations, cowed or beaten into submission, at least found themselves at the end of the day in a civil state, not in a state of nature.

That the United States has undertaken an imperial role without discharging the classic duties of imperial rule reflects an extraordinary disjunction between power and responsibility. This disjunction throws into grave doubt the proposition that the American nation is really well suited for its new calling as the primary military enforcer of the new world order. The difficulty is not that our purpose of ordered liberty can never be vindicated through the use of force; the experience of World War II and of the successful occupation imposed upon Germany and Japan demonstrates otherwise. But unless war is the only way to vindicate compelling security interests—as it was in World War II but was not in the Gulf War—it is highly unlikely that we will be willing to complete the circle and accept the responsibilities that the use of power imposes on us. Faced with these domestic constraints, an imperial power whose central *raison d'être* is the maintenance of order cannot help but act as an agent of disorder. A nation whose central purpose is the promotion of ordered liberty thus acts to achieve neither when it resorts to arms.

Lessons of the Gulf War

What lessons should be drawn from this episode? The principal lesson is that the United States must learn to exercise far greater caution and restraint than it has recently displayed in the use of its military power. It must resist the corrupt moral reasoning by which the evil attributes of an enemy afford a license for the progressive removal of restraints on our own conduct. And it must accept the basic ethical principle that the large-scale use of force carries with it moral responsibilities for pacification and reconstruction—responsibilities that the nation can refuse only at grave danger to its reputation for justice and humanity.

It will be said that these warnings erect a straw man, or that the Gulf War was *sui generis* and that we are in no danger of repeating the experience. Let us hope that this is the case. The reasons for thinking that it may not be the case, however, deserve consideration. The United States is now the world's preeminent military power, with a global reach far surpassing that of any great empire in the past; it went to war on the basis of a doctrine that held that aggression anywhere in the world constituted a threat to the international legal order that it was the duty of the United States to repel; and its way of war was enormously popular at home, allowing the American people to insulate themselves from the suffering normally attendant on war while also rescuing the president from the precipitous fall in popularity that he suffered in October 1990. If to these factors are added the highly unusual circumstances that now prevail in international society—which make both former adversaries and traditional allies either unable or unwilling to oppose us—it hardly seems excessive to warn that the United States may yet again face powerful temptations to use its force for nonvital purposes.

We hardly see these temptations today, because we have persuaded ourselves that we are different, that American power will not be misused, that we are exempt from the weaknesses and imperfections of human nature. The cruel and bitter irony is that, in thus celebrating our exceptionalism, we have forgotten some of the very elements of our political order that were to make us exceptional. Those elements consisted of limits on the circumstances in which we might make war and self-imposed restrictions on the fulfillment of our mission that are now regarded as feeble and unbecoming the conduct of the world's preeminent military power.

A case in point is the renewed interest in doctrines of preventive war. In spite of the manifest improvement in the American security position that ensued from the ideological bankruptcy and internal disorganization of the Soviet Union, many argue today that security threats to the United States have not diminished, that the proliferation of nuclear, chemical, and biological weapons in the hands of the "weapons states" poses a threat to security that is as direct and ominous as any we have known. "The proliferation of weapons of mass destruction and their means of delivery," Charles Krauthammer argues, "will constitute the greatest single threat to world security for the rest of our lives. That is what makes a new international order not an imperial dream or a Wilsonian fantasy but a matter of the sheerest prudence." Strategies for dealing with the threat, Krauthammer contends, should include "denying, disarming, and defending. . . . There is no alternative to confronting, deterring and, if necessary disarming states that brandish and use weapons of mass destruction."[2]

It would be unwise to rule out on a priori grounds a preventive war that had the purpose of denying another state with which we are locked in mortal rivalry access to weapons of mass destruction.

"Never say never," as President Reagan once said. But we should realize that the threat to security posed by proliferation is not a novel one; that states seeking weapons of mass destruction face formidable operational obstacles in achieving their objectives; that lesser measures of precaution (deterrence) have in the past always proved adequate; and that diplomatic efforts to achieve multilateral embargoes on weapons components and military efforts to provide ground based defense against missile attack both promise considerable success. Nor is it irrelevant to remember that preventive war was urged as the appropriate response to the danger of proliferation on several occasions during "the long peace" from 1945 to the present—against Russia in the late 1940s and early 1950s, against China in the early 1960s, against Cuba in 1962. It would be difficult to conclude today that American leaders were wrong when they rejected that advice at the time, viewing it as highly imprudent and indeed a violation of American traditions (reminiscent of the infamous attack at Pearl Harbor). Those who call for such actions today qualify the undertaking in language that lacks any test of immediacy or imminence, of clear and present danger. Their anticipations are a mile long.

American Security and the National Purpose: The Future

We have reached a peculiar stage in the debate over American foreign policy. The customary antinomies that have long played a central role in America's self-understanding—between interventionism and isolationism, or empire and liberty, or "leadership" and "disengagement"—no longer seem an adequate guide to current circumstances. It is hard to speak, for instance, of the relative primacy of foreign and domestic policy without noting the immediate qualification that many domestic problems (such as economic competitiveness, financial indebtedness, environmental degradation, or migratory pressures stemming from explosive population growth in poor countries) have a vital international component. It seems obvious that solutions must be found for these problems on both the domestic and the foreign level, or they will not be found at all.

A similar observation may be made with regard to the old contrast between "isolationism" and "interventionism." As a consequence of its victory in World War II and the subsequent global rivalry with the Soviet Union, the United States entered into a series of security commitments with foreign states—preeminently in Western Europe and East Asia—that it should not walk away from. Large military arsenals are still in place in Europe; to reduce them without endangering stability or encouraging nuclear proliferation (which might yet pose a danger to American security) seems a prudent and realizable objective. In undertaking this task, there is no reason to abandon the North Atlantic Treaty Organization, which was entered into at a time, in 1949, when the expectation was that virtually no American military forces would need to be stationed permanently on the continent. The kind of disengagement in which the United States abandoned its commitment to the security of our traditional allies would be foolish and rash, especially at a moment when that security is achievable at far less cost than was paid during the years of the cold war. (It would also be inconsistent with one of the fundamental principles in the American diplomatic tradition: Washington's Farewell Address, it is well to recall, advised fidelity to existing engagements.)

If, however, by disengagement or isolationism is meant a refusal to enter into new security commitments, or an unwillingness to employ American military power to vindicate a supposed universal commitment to the territorial integrity and political independence of all states, then the nation should embrace it unreservedly. It is undoubtedly the case that, having violated both injunctions by going to war for the liberation of Kuwait, and having set in motion events (the rising and subsequent repression of the Kurds) for which the United States is partially responsible, the United States cannot simply wash its hands of the duty to afford protection and humanitarian aid to the Kurds of northern Iraq. Against our will, and even with a conscious realization that such a course of action will give rise to policy dilemmas for which there is no painless solution, the commitment appears unavoidable. This fact may certainly be taken to mean that cautionary rules against new or universal security commitments may afford no meaningful guide to action once they have been broached and the decision to use force on a massive scale has been made. But the unavoidability of commitments stemming from the use of force also underlines the wisdom of observing restrictions on the use of force in the first place.

A return to a more stricted view of the circumstances in which the nation might make war would carry with it many advantages. It would allow for greater reductions in military expenditures than those now contemplated by the Bush administration. It would help free up resources that the nation might use to address a range of pressing economic and environmental problems, for which American leadership is indeed indispensable. And it would constitute a barrier against the inflated conception of American security and the pervasive corruption of national purpose sanctioned by President Bush and his "new world order."

In the original understanding of American diplomacy, one that became deeply ingrained in the nation's outlook for 150 years, conceptions of American security and the national purpose were closely linked. If sharp restrictions were placed on the objectives for which the nation would use force, it was because of the belief that our real purpose as a nation lay elsewhere. The American creed was thought to have universal significance, in that the philosophical assumptions underlying the institutions of civil freedom were in principle open to all humanity, if humanity would have the wit to see them. But the nation went not abroad, in search of monsters to destroy. It understood that to do so would entail an insensible change in the fundamental maxims of American policy "from *liberty* to *force.*"[3]

History, one imagines, will never come to an end, but particular histories end all the time. The momentary achievements of men and nations may live on in the memory for a while, but in the normal course of events they are forgotten or survive only as objects of curiosity to antiquarians. The proud boast of American civilization has always been that we were different in this respect; that we would not forget the admonitions of the Founding Fathers and their epigones, nor suffer the basic principles of the American experiment to undergo corruption. American history will come to an end when these sentiments no longer animate our national life.

Notes

[1] "Hama rules" is a term of Middle Eastern political art named after Syrian President Assad's ruthless killing of 20,000 rebels in Hama, Syria, in 1982.

[2] See chapter 8F of this volume.

[3] John Quincy Adams, "An address delivered at the request of a committee of the citizens of Washington, on the occasion of reading the Declaration of Independence," Washington, D.C., 1821.

10

Conclusion: Getting from Here to Where?

GREGORY F. TREVERTON
AND BARBARA A. BICKSLER

T he world has changed. So must America's definition of its
security. The preceding chapters have laid out perspectives
on a new definition of "national security." But like the period
following World War II, the change will not be quick. It will be a
process—an iterative, public, and political process, not a closed or
purely analytic one.

That process will both reflect and affect how Americans think
about their security, and ultimately it will touch how the nation
does its public policy business. For forty years, "containment"
commanded broad acceptance as the polestar of American foreign
policy. Or so it seems in retrospect. No new polestar is evident;
and indeed, it took ten years from 1945 to 1955 for containment to
be elaborated and accepted. And so the question now is less what

BARBARA A. BICKSLER is a member of the research staff of the Institute for Defense Analyses. She has been engaged in several Council on
Foreign Relations projects in recent years. Previously she worked in the
Office of the Secretary of Defense on the Defense Guidance Staff and in
the Office of Program Analysis and Evaluation.

can replace containment than how to think about public attitudes toward America's security in its absence.

The cold war, coming on the heels of World War II, shaped the American "national security establishment" as we have come to know it: the National Security Council, the Department of Defense, and the Central Intelligence Agency. Since 1948 these institutions have been tinkered with, giving more or less power to various players, but on the whole not fundamentally changed. It would seem surprising if the end of the cold war did not eventually drive changes, perhaps dramatic ones, in this structure. What might a new structure look like, and how might it come about?

This chapter hardly proposes a definitive answer to these questions. Only as the debate over a "new" definition of security unfolds will such answers be possible. Instead, it seeks to contribute to the debate by examining the institutional legacy and the shape of public opinion during the cold war and by drawing lessons from this experience for the future.

National Security as Military

That America defined its security over the last forty years primarily in military terms is plain. Thus, not surprisingly, the institutions at the center of the "national security establishment" were military as well. So, too, "coordination" meant first, integrating the perspectives and operations of the military services and, second, blending military means with diplomacy. The forty-year history of trying to accomplish the former is a cautionary tale if the future definition of American security will be broader, thus implying the need to integrate across a broader set of considerations and institutions.

The arrangements ratified in the National Security Act of 1947 were argued about in terms of preventing surprise attack and improving cooperation among the military services. While the players were rather clear—the president, the National Security Council (NSC), the secretary of defense, the military services, the Joint Chiefs of Staff (JCS), the intelligence community, and Congress—their roles, missions, and authorities continued to be debated.[1]

The act established a loose federation of the military departments—the Army, Navy, and Air Force—with their separate secretaries and staffs. The new secretary of defense was charged with *coordinating* the services; interservice relations were to be dealt with by the Joint Chiefs of Staff, which then lacked a formal chair. The act ratified the president's role in setting national security policy, supported by the National Security Council.

Yet this new arrangement did little to delimit the roles of the individual services, so scarcely diminished interservice rivalry over missions. As "coordinator" of the services, the secretary had scant staff, few tools, and little control. The first secretary of defense, James Forrestal, twice attempted to force closure on this service rivalry. First in Key West, Florida, the service chiefs met with Forrestal to work through the problem of dividing responsibility. The resulting agreement assigned one service primary responsibility for each major mission area.

The Key West agreement left many questions unanswered, particularly in the nuclear realm where services competed for the new mission. So again Forrestal met with the chiefs, this time in Newport, Rhode Island, in August 1948. After three days, the chiefs amended the Key West agreement, assigning planning and budgeting responsibility for major missions to the service with primary responsibility while recognizing that actual operations would be the responsibility of all.[2] Yet still the secretary and the services battled over roles, missions, organizations, and budget levels. The imminent Soviet threat did not elicit a cohesive strategy for military programs, and the government went from one crisis to the next, one budget battle to another.

In 1949 the National Security Act was amended in order to strengthen the powers of the secretary of defense by converting the nation's military establishment from a federation into a single Department of Defense atop the three military departments. The amendment began a trend that continued through the next decade, centralizing defense policy planning in the office of the secretary of defense (OSD). At the same time and for the same reason—curbing interservice rivalry—the JCS was given a formal chair.

However, the incoming Eisenhower administration still identified interservice rivalry as the greatest obstacle to efficient defense planning. The new administration believed it could organize away these problems and achieve "security with solvency." Twice, in 1953 and 1958, the National Security Act was amended in the attempt to provide more central control, within the Pentagon and the national security establishment as a whole. The 1953 reforms institutionalized the National Security Council as the focal point for coordinating the Pentagon and the State Department. The 1958 reforms were the first in a long series that sought to enhance the power of the JCS chair at the expense of the service chiefs.

But these reorganizations did not realize the goal of saving money; they neither dampened service budget requests nor brought greater rigor to weapons procurement and materiel management. The Pentagon then faced a problem familiar to today's defense establishment—too many programs chasing too little money. Nor could institutional reform solve the central problem the military confronted: how could increasingly nuclearized military forces make credible the commitment to "forward defense" of allies in Europe and Asia?

The 1960s began a new chapter for national security institutions, though formal structure remained unchanged. John Kennedy campaigned on the theme of military reform—centralizing defense decision making and increasing civilian control. The vehicle was a strong OSD under Defense Secretary Robert McNamara. McNamara's instruments were the planning, programming, and budgeting system (PPBS) and the five-year defense plan (FYDP), tools designed to tighten the connection between military spending and national purposes and to improve "coordination" among the military departments in defense planning and budgeting.

The Kennedy administration had sought to enhance executive control, but the other development of the 1960s was the sharply increased role of Congress in defense matters. Defense budgets were a casualty of Vietnam—military spending declined 37 percent between 1968 and 1974—and so was the public's commitment to defense and its faith in the federal government, particularly the president and executive branch. Congress moved into the void created by public disillusionment over Vietnam. Committee staffs grew with the role of committees, adding new cooks tending the national security kettle. Congress has since been a pivotal player in debates over not just the size but also the shape of the defense budget; and it has levied more and more legislative requirements on the Pentagon.

By the end of the Carter administration the defense establishment had begun to recover from the damage of Vietnam, and it did so even more during Ronald Reagan's first term when defense spending increased to over 7 percent of gross national product (GNP). President Reagan's defense secretary, Caspar Weinberger, gave the military departments substantial freedom in determining how to spend their rapidly increasing budgets—a clear reversal from the McNamara days. Decision making seeped away from OSD and toward the services themselves.

By 1983, however, newspaper reports of $600 toilet seats and of serious technical problems emerging in a number of major weapons programs shifted the public focus to waste, fraud, and abuse. They also put defense reformers back in business.

In 1986 two major efforts at defense reorganization came to fruition. First, the Blue Ribbon Commission on Defense Management, chaired by former Deputy Secretary of Defense David Packard, proposed a package of reforms that has become the benchmark for Pentagon performance. The Packard Commission concentrated on the weapons procurement process—calling for centralized decisions but decentralized execution—and it proposed a stronger "independent" (that is, of the services' biases) military voice in defense decision making.

Second, after years of hearings and debates, Congress passed the Goldwater-Nichols Defense Reorganization Act of 1986 that formally established the chair of the JCS as the principal military advisor to the president—the culmination of three decades of strengthening the chair by comparison to his service colleagues. The bill also enhanced the role of joint institutions in planning forces and conducting military operations, to match the greater authority of the chair.

Despite all these efforts at centralizing, for most of the last forty years the military departments largely ruled, dominating the choices of programs and weapons according to individual missions and interests. "Pentagon-wide" planning remained elusive despite the series of enhancements to the roles of the secretary of defense and the chair of the JCS. Whatever the evaluations of national security policy as defined at the highest levels, those broad policies were not well connected to decisions about weapons, forces, and budgets. That gap persisted despite the fact that national security was rather narrowly defined—largely in military terms, its polestar containment.

The Economic Dimension

The 1980s were a heyday for military reformers in and out of Congress. Yet reform then, as throughout the cold war, focused on getting more independent military advice and on centralizing planning in the Pentagon. It did not much address how to integrate economics or trade or energy policy into "national security" decision making. The arrangements created in the National Security Act of 1947 have worked reasonably well at connecting military and diplomatic instruments. The NSC is, by membership, tradition, and staffing, politico-military, and through it the military has acquired regular access to diplomacy bearing on it—arms control, for instance.

Economics has been genuflected to in the security debate but usually has been regarded as a separate element of national security, dealt with on a parallel track. To be sure, some economic instruments, export controls in particular, have been conceived in tight relation to America's military purposes, however the resulting policies are judged. Others, like sanctions, have been used in pursuit of national security purposes. And foreign economic policies—decisions to apply penalties to particular countries for unfair trading, for instance—have been influenced by whether there was bilateral "national security" business being done at the same time.

But most such linkages have been haphazard, more the result of specific choices by presidents or Congress than of any coherent strategy, let alone mechanisms for fashioning it. The Marshall Plan seems a clear example of an economic instrument used for security concerns: rebuilding Western Europe's economy after World War II would protect Europe from the Soviet threat. Yet it was initially conceived primarily as an economic response to an economic problem, Europe's devastation; only later did the security imperative seem overwhelming. And since the Marshall Plan, there have been few examples of so clear a linkage.

America's relationships with allies and trading partners in Europe and Asia have for the most part been pursued on two tracks—one security, one economic. In some cases the two have crossed, but examples are few. The 1969 deal with Japan that apparently, but tacitly, struck a link between reversion of Okinawa to Japan and Japanese forbearance in textile exports is striking because it is so singular.[3]

More characteristic is the Soviet gas pipeline case of 1981–82.[4] In the end the United States retreated from its economic sanctions against its European allies for their participation in the pipeline. It did so in part because of a link to pressing security business—the Europeans were in the process of working through the politics of accepting new American Pershing and cruise missiles. But Washington relented only after an open transatlantic row and only after a year in which U.S. pressure against the pipeline had proceeded simultaneously with U.S. urging to take the new missiles.

Usually the economic task is seen primarily as domestic, ensuring a healthy economy and thus a strong base for creative foreign policy. Eisenhower placed real emphasis on economics, but his was preeminently the reminder that the nation's security rested on a strong domestic economy. John Foster Dulles's speech that is now remembered for nuclear "massive retaliation" began with the admonition that "it is not sound to become permanently committed to military expenditures so vast that they lead to 'practical bankruptcy.' "[5]

Eisenhower did establish a Council on Foreign Economic Policy (CFEP) in 1954, roughly in parallel to the NSC.[6] It was composed of the heads of "economic" departments, plus the secretary of state. It never managed much coordination of those economic departments, and its relation to the NSC was haphazard; moreover, it suffered in stature by comparison to the NSC, which the president himself frequently chaired.

Kennedy relied on ad hocracy across the board in foreign policy rather than formal structure, and international economics was no exception. The Eisenhower CFEP was abolished and replaced by the designation of a deputy national security advisor with special responsibility for economics, an arrangement that obtained throughout the Kennedy and Johnson administrations. It worked relatively well, in part because Vietnam was consuming and so the deputy became the focal point for "everything else." It also demonstrated the importance of personal attributes, for the arrangement required a deputy who had the stature to deal with the treasury secretary as a peer, a national security advisor who was tolerably interested in economics, and a president who could be made to be.

The Nixon administration returned to reliance on the formal structure, establishing a council of international economic policy—a sort of "economic NSC"—as a mechanism to better link international economics to international security. It did not live long. The Ford and later the Reagan administrations effectively used an economic policy board (called council in the Reagan years), but its primary purpose was connecting domestic economic choices to their international economic implications. Connections to military matters, if they were made, occurred through the overlapping mandates of key senior officials.

The secretary of the treasury was not made an NSC member by the original act, and while virtually every administration has sought from time to time to bring economic choices into the NSC system, none has done so often or systematically. Some economic choices, like trade, are so deeply political as to defy the politico-military structure and relative detachment from domestic politics that characterize the NSC. For others, like international money, the relevant technicians resist the intrusion of anyone, and surely not a body dominated by politico-military considerations. In that sense, the U.S. Treasury is special and specially self-contained; it makes the Pentagon look open, a pushover by comparison.

As it dawned on Americans in the 1970s that domestic economics could not be separated from international—"interdependence" in jargon then and now—proposals for reorganizing the government became a modest cottage industry. The proposals differed most visibly in whether they sought to create something else in parallel to the NSC for economics or would subsume the NSC in a broader coordinating structure. Of the former, for instance, Bayless Manning recommended an executive branch council on international and domestic affairs and a congressional committee of the same name. His proposal was avowedly narrow and thus, he hoped, feasible and flexible; the NSC would continue to exist.[7]

The most cited broader proposal was that by Graham Allison and Peter Szanton.[8] Theirs was a less sweeping version of one made by Nelson Rockefeller to Senator Henry Jackson's famous subcommittee on government organization in 1960. Rockefeller had called for a "first secretary of government" as "executive chairman" of the NSC but with a broad mandate to coordinate across international activities from culture to defense.[9] Allison and Szanton recommended an "executive committee of the cabinet" or ExCab, reminiscent of President Kennedy's vehicle for managing the Cuban Missile Crisis, the ExCom.

ExCab was to be composed of the secretaries of state; defense; treasury; (then) health, education and welfare (HEW); and a new U.S. economic department formed by merging commerce and labor. Its mandate would be all major policy issues, domestic, foreign, and economic.

In essence, though, Allison and Szanton's motivation was not so different from Manning's; both reflected the worry that economic issues would be posed too narrowly, through their foreign or, more often, their domestic face. And that worry, in turn, derived from the other theme of these 1970s proposals—that, by temperament but encouraged by the NSC structure, presidents had engaged themselves in politico-military choices to a degree they rarely did in economics. And so the agenda of these proposals was to raise the profile of economics, either separately or in connection with "traditional" NSC issues.

Containment as Polestar

Surely all postwar presidents were drawn toward traditional national security policy, for it was more elegant than the grubbiness of domestic and economic issues: in diplomacy, words alone mattered, and military bureaucracies were responsive to their commander in chief, certainly by comparison to their domestic counterparts. At the same time, containment, defined primarily in

military terms, provided presidents with an overriding argument.
While it is easy in retrospect to cover the past with a misleading
gauze of bipartisanship or consensus, there was a certain stability
to the framework of public opinion. The threat was reasonably
well defined, and the priority of military security broadly accepted.
Americans wanted both to be strong and at peace—indeed connected the two—but which face of that twin preference predominated at any given moment depended on the circumstances.

The onset of the cold war brought with it public concern over
America's military security—defined principally in relation to the
Soviet Union. Hostility toward the Soviet Union was particularly
intense during the 1950s, with some 90 percent of those polled
reporting negative attitudes. During this early postwar period, the
public strongly supported increasing the nation's military strength.
In a May 1946 Roper poll, 38 percent of those surveyed believed
that the United States had sufficient military strength; 52 percent
felt it needed more. Gallup polls from 1947 to 1950 recorded two-
thirds or more of the public in favor of increasing the size of the
military services (see Table 1).[10]

This public support was the backdrop for the Truman administration's famous policy review, NSC-68, and for the ensuing trip-
ling of defense spending between 1950 and 1953, triggered by the
Korean War. Public support for a strong military endured
throughout the 1950s. In April 1953, when the armistice ending the

TABLE 1. Public Views Toward the Military, 1948–1950

		Increase Army	Increase Navy	Increase Air Force
February 1948	Yes	61%	63%	74%
	No	29	26	17
	No Opinion	10	11	9
February 1949	Yes	56%	57%	70%
	No	29	27	17
	No Opinion	15	16	13
July 1950	Yes	85%	85%	89%
	No	9	9	6
	No Opinion	6	6	5

Korean War was at hand, 71 percent of the public thought that the United States should maintain its military strength—at that time nearly 3.5 million people served in the nation's armed forces. In September 1955, 72 percent surveyed by Gallup favored defense spending that remained at current levels—support that was repeated in 1957 despite a budget-cutting wave in the Defense Department and Congress.[11]

As the cold war slackened after the Cuban Missile Crisis and then the United States became embroiled in Vietnam, public support for defense began to erode. The nuclear threat began to subside and the public saw the Soviet Union more as a competitive rival than a mortal threat. At the height of detente in the 1970s, only 36 percent of the American public had an unfavorable view of the Soviets. Peace, not strength, was the public's primary concern from 1964 to 1974.[12]

Vietnam also destroyed, at least for a time, the consensus in support of containment defined in military terms. If a third of the public remained committed to containment, almost half showed little interest in foreign affairs; moreover, the concerns of those who labeled themselves interested were economic and humanitarian, not military.[13]

By the mid-1970s, polls indicated that the American public believed defense spending was adequate and that the armed forces could perform their missions despite post-Vietnam spending cuts. The increasing military capacity of the Soviet Union did not seem likely to be used for coercive purposes. Nuclear deterrence and the defense of NATO justified military spending but at lower levels than in the past.[14]

However, within a few years the public mood shifted again—evidently a reaction to the takeover of the American embassy in Iran and the Soviet invasion of Afghanistan, both in late 1979. Public opinion returned to a more hostile view of Soviet intentions, a feeling that the Russians had betrayed detente. The public was increasingly insecure about Moscow's military strength and its propensity for adventurism. Ronald Reagan's campaign theme of rearming America to regain military superiority over the "evil empire" commanded strong public support—strength had replaced peace as the paramount public concern.

Yet while the public strongly supported increasing military strength, attitudes toward intervention still betrayed the shadow of Vietnam. The public, sensitive to the risks of foreign entanglement, seemed to remain so even after the overwhelming American success in the 1991 Gulf War. At this short distance, the war has not fundamentally altered the public's relatively cautious view of the military as a policy instrument. If the United States should remain engaged in military terms, that engagement should be cautious. Indeed, it can be argued that America's reluctance over overseas military operations has historical roots much deeper than Vietnam.

By the mid-1980s, Americans were both wary of detente and skeptical of the postwar containment policy. A Public Agenda Foundation poll, conducted in 1984, indicated that 67 percent of the public believed that the Soviet Union had used detente to lull the United States into a false sense of security while building up their own military capability. At the same time, however, 76 percent of those surveyed agreed that the United States had to accept some of the blame for the tensions in U.S.–Soviet relations.[15]

This combination of views produced a majority of Americans who took an attitude of "pragmatic rejection" toward communism: communism could be tolerated without endorsing it, and the peace face again predominated. The time was right for cooperative problem solving between the superpowers as a means to reduce the risk of war.[16] This pragmatic attitude became even stronger by 1987–88 as Mikhail Gorbachev's policies of *glasnost* and *perestroika* began to influence public perceptions of the Soviet Union.

Accordingly, public support for high military spending began to wane in the mid-1980s, and by 1985 the defense budget itself began to decline. Satisfied with the success of the Reagan military buildup and what seemed to be a greatly reduced chance of nuclear war, the concerns of Americans began to shift. In a 1987–88 poll, 59 percent of the public agreed that economic competitiveness posed a greater threat to national security than military adversaries.[17] For the first time since World War II, economic concerns were viewed as a vital threat to national security. Nearly two-thirds of the public believed that excess military spending was sapping the economy.

Even so, the polls still indicated a wariness on the part of the American public about going too far in the opposite direction, no doubt reflecting fears of being burned as America had been during the first detente. In early 1988, 42 percent of the public still viewed Soviet aggression as the greatest threat to American security, while 48 percent thought it was time to turn attention to global concerns such as terrorism and economic competition. An attitude of "proceed with caution" seemed to prevail.

Caution notwithstanding, the shift in public attitudes toward the Soviet Union represents "new thinking" among Americans.[18] No longer does the Soviet threat, or any military threat for that matter, dominate American national security concerns. Improved relations with the Soviet Union and a reduced concern about the risk of nuclear war have made room for other foreign policy issues to rise to the top of the security agenda. In a September 1988 Americans Talk Security (ATS) survey, more than half the respondents agreed that

threats to U.S. national security are changing. Whereas our military adversaries used to be the greatest danger, new threats like international drug trafficking and international economic competition now pose the greatest danger, and these new threats require different kinds of national security policies than we've used in the past.

A March 1990 ATS survey identified drug trafficking as the top national security threat (Table 2). This survey highlights several striking changes in public attitude in only a few years. The nature of the Soviet threat had declined dramatically. In October 1987 Soviet nuclear weapons and Soviet aggression ranked fifth and seventh, respectively, among the top threats to national security.[19] Two years later, after the fall of the Berlin wall, they came in last in a list of fourteen top threats.

Strikingly, the only military threat viewed as a very serious threat to national security was the proliferation of nuclear weapons in the Third World. The emergence of nonmilitary threats as preeminent threats to national security is plain. Such threats were named among the top two threats 90 percent of the time, as compared with 51 percent for military threats.[20] Americans believe that threats to national security are changing—a change that shifts the boundaries within which national security policy can be set.

TABLE 2. Threats to U.S. National Security

Drug trafficking	84*
Third World nuclear weapons	74
Air/Water pollution	74
Violent crime	72
Cost of health care	69
Federal budget deficit	64
International economic competition	61
Terrorist activities	61
Man-made climate change	53
Radiation/nuclear reactors	52
Mideast conflicts	51
Central American conflicts	44
Soviet nuclear weapons	43
Soviet aggression/world	24

*percentage citing as an extremely or very serious threat

Reconfiguring the Establishment: Lessons from the Past

As the military threat from the Soviet Union continues to wane, designing a national security strategy will become more complex. During the past forty years, national strategy was largely indistinguishable from military strategy, and the latter frequently was criticized as little more than the combination of what the separate services desired. The gap persisted between official rhetoric—what Paul Nitze called "aspiration policy"—and actual military plans.

Whether the Desert Storm War against Iraq is testimony to success in four decades of wrestling with the gap is an open question. At this short distance from events the answer seems "yes." How deeply the culture of jointness has pervaded the Pentagon remains to be seen, but the Gulf War was an impressive demonstration of joint operations on the battlefield. The separate service chiefs were all but invisible in comparison to the JCS chair and the unified operational commander, General Norman Schwarzkopf. The chiefs' role in constructing military options was healthy, but Schwarzkopf, as the regional commander, could pick and choose among those options instead of being constrained by their choices.

Moreover, the recent Pentagon budget process was dominated, so many say, by the secretary and the chair. Thirteen major weapon systems were cut, comprising $80 billion over six years; this marks a real change from the Pentagon's proposals during the past five years of declining defense budgets, when weapons programs were more often stretched out rather than eliminated. But the budget debate only begins in the Pentagon; in past years, interests at both ends of Pennsylvania Avenue have collided to produce near gridlock.[21] And while the Goldwater-Nichols reforms seem to be taking hold, at least in terms of joint operations, the data points are still too few to draw long-term conclusions in the planning and budgeting arena.

In broader terms, the United States was better at defining military strategies than national strategies. As Samuel Huntington put it:

The record of these efforts at strategy-making demonstrates that, whatever the intent of those leading the process, the U.S. government cannot and has not defined national strategy in any meaningful sense. It can and has, on occasion, defined military strategy, and if it starts out to do the former, it ends up doing the latter. A national strategy is impossible because the interests, institutions, and purposes involved are simply too diverse and complex to be brought together and integrated into any sort of coherent pattern.[22]

As the military threat is reduced, nonmilitary aspects of security will become relatively more important. Decisions will no longer be primarily "military," force structure no longer the primary measure. Comparing the past with the future points to tough problems and uncertain solutions. In one sense, the problems of the past seem easy: making decisions about force structure based on a "military" threat, and coordinating roles and missions of three military departments.

As we look ahead, the threat is more diffuse, the institutions more varied, and the roles and missions of the players more diverse, while the consensus in the American public over what the primary issues really are, at least for the near term, will be much looser. The end of the cold war stands as the ultimate "success" of containment. But if America was not always as successful as it might have been in fighting that war, what hope is there for doing as well, let alone better, in the period to come? The lessons of the last forty years suggest several watchwords as America thinks about reshaping its national security business.

Money Matters. For the near term and beyond, most of the "national security" budget will still belong to the Pentagon; hence continuing forty years of efforts to better connect military outputs to strategic choices is warranted. Old definitions of security will not change overnight. Despite the recognition by recent Pentagon statements of the declining Soviet threat, it will take time before these views filter down through the defense organization to the point where they influence planning, programming, training, and doctrine—where they become part of the "culture" of the institution. Thus it makes sense to work where the money is by continuing to improve decision making in the military establishment.

Past efforts at reform suggest the importance of presidential leadership in setting national security strategy, supported by the National Security Council; of more centralized management of the Defense Department; and of giving Congress a central role in broad guidance while limiting its "micromanaging" of the Pentagon. So, too, there is a remarkable consensus among analysts about next steps. For instance, while the experience with trying to authorize major weapons, or even fund them, for more than one year has been mixed, there is broad agreement on stretching the funding horizons over which the services can reliably plan.

Or, a more "flexible" system of weapons acquisition is widely seen as the right response to meet the more varied but less demanding threats of the new world. Such a system would maintain a rich base of research and development while emphasizing incremental improvements in weapons systems, such as replacing components and subsystems. It would downplay, though surely not eliminate, the role of major advances in weapons capabilities— qualitative changes like that represented by Stealth technology.[23]

Whether or not broad new mechanisms for integrating military and economics are constructed, the overlap is increasing in fact and cries out for at least limited new arrangements. For instance, as chapters 4 and 5 in this volume underscore, the cold war logic of weapons technology "spinning off" commercial applications is being reversed: commercial technology now leads the Pentagon's in many areas, and so weapons development will have to be reshaped to use that technology, not try to develop its own from the ground up. That surely implies new forms of cooperation between managers of civilian and military technology, public and private. It perhaps signals the need to shift a portion of the Pentagon's research and development resources toward adapting commercial technology or even away from exclusive Pentagon control.

Caution Is Called For. The institutional history of integrating the economic and military dimensions of national security, like that of integrating the military services, says the task is hard. Moreover, while Desert Storm seems to indicate that the latter integration was worth the effort, the history does not settle whether the former would also be wise. There have been benefits to the "separate-tracking" of economic and military questions. The two kinds of issues have been argued about separately, mostly on their respective merits. It was thus possible for the Reagan administration and the French government of François Mitterrand to disagree sharply over fiscal policy in the early 1980s while cooperating closely on European security questions.

Integrating the two more tightly in the structure of the American government might permit a more strategic view. The sporadic debate over America's role in Japan's next generation military aircraft, the FSX, sometimes touched, but never sharply posed, long-term questions about the military and economic components of U.S.–Japanese relations; most of the time, separate departments managed the issue to fit their specific interests, military or economic. A more integrated structure might have done better.

It might also have done worse. It might merely have made the relevant choices more accessible to particular short-run economic interests. "Integration" of economics and security might, for instance, have meant using the FSX as a lever for yet more "Japan bashing," another marginal opening of the Japanese market to some particular American commodity. Indeed, that might have been all the more likely in the absence of an overriding security argument like that imposed by the Soviet threat.

Major organizational changes always have second-order effects; sometimes those diminish, or even undercut, their avowed purpose. With the world in such flux, now is the time to think about radical change in the way America does its national security business but probably not to implement it. It is also time to draw another lesson from history, also apparent but often overlooked.

Purposes Are Paramount. The definition of national security purposes should determine organizational structure, not some quest for administrative tidiness. For instance, the current debate often suggests that the purpose is tightening the connection between the economic and military dimensions of security. Although what "tightening" means is usually vague, the purpose implies a mechanism to consider the two sets of issues more systematically side-by-side at levels of government beneath the very top. If this is the purpose, history brings immediately to mind three alternatives for change:

- A broadened National Security Council, adding to the current membership (president, vice president, secretaries of state and defense) the secretary of the treasury, the trade representative, and perhaps other "domestic" department heads. The NSC staff would have to be broadened accordingly. No recent national security advisor, for instance, has been comfortable with economics, let alone the domestic constituencies of economic issues.
- An economic security council, a "sister" council instead of expanding the NSC. This implies that the future problem is the one identified in the 1970s—making sure that the long-run and international aspects of economic issues are not overwhelmed by their short-run and domestic faces. Connecting this new council to the NSC would still be needed.
- Lodging responsibility for integration in a particular official. Notice that the NSC has been, if anything, even more politico-military in recent years: several national security advisors have been retired military officers, as have several deputies, occasionally at the same time. The Kennedy-Johnson experience suggests that if coordination is the aim, an NSC deputy—one with

a broad brief but a special background in economics or energy or the environment—probably makes more sense than creating a new post with lofty title but no connection to the rest of officialdom.

Yet "coordination" is often loose language covering a different intent—reshuffling priorities to give less dominance to, say, the military dimension and more to another. Some of this change will happen naturally, without a formal change in organization, as the nation's attention shifts. If the U.S. defense budget shrinks by a third or even a half over a decade, the change in emphasis will be gradual but its cumulative effect dramatic. Already the environmental protection administrator is more often in the news than his predecessors, reflecting the nation's growing concerns over the environment. As Ernest May reminds us in chapter 3, no one would have thought Defense or State the premier department of the American government in the 1920s or 1930s; then they were Commerce or Agriculture.

Innovations in organization might reflect, or enhance, the shift in priorities. Presidentially appointed "czars" for energy or the environment or drugs find it hard to actually get control of the relevant government actions, for usually they are symbolic monarchs disconnected from the operating agencies. But they can serve as a focal point for public debate: witness William Bennett as President Bush's drug czar. By the same token, an environmental deputy on the NSC staff, for instance, would be isolated in the absence of internal interest or external pressure; present one or the other, however, the post might serve a useful function.

Congress Is Central. The debate over defense reform for most of the last forty years was preoccupied with the executive branch. But the history of those years argues compellingly that reform at one end of Pennsylvania Avenue alone will not suffice. No weapons acquisition process reform will make much difference unless it touches the existing incentives for the Pentagon to site, and members of Congress to defend, weapons production in as many districts as possible.

The possibilities for institutional reform in Congress begin with the modest but still hard, like several-year budgeting to provide stability to defense planning. The base closure commission is another example. Because members wanted bases closed to save money but provided the savings came from some *other* congressional district, they in effect tied their hands by using a commission to decide which bases would be closed (and then chafed at the bounds).

If integrating across the dimensions of security becomes the goal, a congressional security committee would be the analogy to an expanded NSC. It might subsume the functions of Foreign Relations, Armed Services, and the international aspects of Banking and Finance.[24] If such an idea seems far-fetched now, perhaps the experience of the budget committees is suggestive: they began their integrating roles with little effective power but grew over a decade or more. By analogy, new security committees might begin with a loose mandate to connect existing committees but gradually come to dominate them.

In the interim, other mechanisms might build some points of responsibility in Congress. The congressional "reforms" of the last generation, which disbursed power so widely across the houses that committee chairs were eviscerated and accountability drained away, are not likely to be reversed soon. Now, however, the committees themselves are often overshadowed by less formal working groups of interested and informed members.

In Congress as in the executive, shifting priorities will affect structure. The Foreign Affairs Committees have lost influence, particularly in the Senate, for a number of reasons—weak leadership, the absence of tangible gains for one's district, Vietnam, and the like—but surely one reason was the primacy of the military even as subjects of international negotiation, especially arms control. Accordingly, the Foreign Affairs Committees lost ground to the Armed Services and later to the Intelligence Committees. Declining defense budgets may not restore luster to Foreign Affairs but might diminish that of Armed Services.

Or budgetary scarcity might impel the Armed Services Committees to take a broader view of security, perhaps not a bad second-best if formal organizational change proves impossible. So far, those committees seem to have taken the congressional lead in thinking about how to integrate new dimensions of security.

Searching for a Polestar:
The Need for Leadership

As a baseline, the safest assumption for the next decade or so is that the public debate surrounding America's national security business will be more volatile than during the last forty years when containment served as the polestar. While the elements of new thinking in public opinion have persisted for several years, it remains to be seen whether they will turn into an enduring public focus or are better seen simply as concerns that came to the fore because the overarching rivalry with the Soviet Union went away. After all, it is not as though cold war American foreign policy was unconcerned with values such as democracy or free trade or economic integration; much of the debate over Vietnam, for instance, or over human rights was about whether the policy was an element of or in conflict with the overriding interest in containing the Soviet Union.

This volatility suggests a number of possibilities, not all of them happy ones:

• *Policy could become the "crusade of the month,"* at least in terms of public attitudes. Drugs now, terrorism next, and so on: these might be the priorities discovered by poll readers. Notice that terrorism ranked among the top ten security concerns in the 1990 poll; yet judged in terms of real risk, terrorism has not been much of a threat to America. More Americans are killed each year on German autobahns or by lightning than by terrorists. But with the deadening hand of the Soviet threat lifted, the search for new "threats" could lead to considerable volatility, and perhaps to mischief.

• *The demands of the post–cold war era might increase volatility.* Americans are often regarded as uncomfortable with *realpolitik*, with shifting friends and enemies, with moral values that sometimes can be pursued but sometimes have to be suppressed. If that is true, the future seems likely to throw up more such ambiguities; it will hold more gray hats, fewer black and whites ones. During the Gulf War the Bush administration was quite successful in incorporating Syria, a country it had branded a supporter of terrorism, into the anti-Saddam coalition; most Americans seemed to accept that immediate enmity justified holding old scores in abeyance. Yet almost before the war was over the search began for who was guilty of tilting American policy toward Iraq before the war: the tilt had to be evil, not merely mistaken balance-of-power policy.

• *That said, thus far the public concerns over economics seem persistent.* The trends that began several years ago—a turning away from military and toward economic concerns—have endured. Even the euphoria over America's victory in the Persian Gulf was short-lived, as Americans turned back to economic and domestic problems. In February 1991, 58 percent of those polled felt that the country was moving in the "right direction." By April only 42 percent believed so.[25] While specific evaluations of economic prospects rise and fall with circumstances, the higher priority to economics seems likely to endure, in part because America's economic weaknesses will not soon go away and in part simply because the big security threat has evaporated.

• *Chunks of policy might simply be appropriated by groups in American domestic society that care the most.* If overarching national concern over the Soviet Union is gone, what remains might be limited domestic interests. Peter Peterson's chapter argues that domestic policy has produced less a resolution than an accumulation of competing interests, each defending its stakes. Foreign policy might come to look like that as well.

To switch the analogy, more of American foreign policy might come to look like past American policy toward second-order regions like Latin America or Africa. Since there was only intermittently an overriding security interest (virtually never in Africa's case), American policy tended to reflect the wishes of whichever groups in American society cared the most at any given time. For Latin America, in the 1950s and 1960s those were mostly U.S. based multinational corporations, in the 1970s and early 1980s human rights and church groups, and so on.[26]

• *At the same time, if national security becomes more diffuse, new groups will acquire influence.* If the process of defining policy opens, it will become so to many groups. And it is not inevitable that each will merely appropriate a chunk of policy. Single-issue groups are not necessarily pernicious. It may be, for instance, that environmental groups will succeed in doing what civil rights groups did a generation ago—put "their" issue higher on the agenda than before. If they succeed, it will be not just because the issue is "theirs"; it will be because other Americans look at the evidence and share the conviction that a change in priority is needed.

• *Americans may simply want a respite from international extension.* The cold war's over and we won it, so why not come home? So far there is not much evidence in public opinion polls of such an attitude. Yet it also seems a mistake to assume too easily, after the last forty years, that America will continue to be internationalist, but just in a new form. Since the change in the Soviet threat is real, a shift in public concern from it to drugs, terrorism, and the domestic economy is not necessarily a mistake. It would be an argument for a foreign policy of relative "disengagement," if not "coming home," then limiting our international projects lest pushing too hard increase the chances of the worst outcomes.

The danger with this mood is that it could turn not inward to serious problems but nastily outward to new enemies. For better or worse, the last forty years have conditioned Americans to define their security in terms of external threats. That search for external enemies has been evident in attitudes toward the drug issue, for instance, though time and thought have diminished it. It would be unfortunate if such attitudes persisted as the nation moved to tackle problems of trade and competitiveness. Whether or not Japan has played unfairly on the fields of international trade, *its* behavior is a small part of *our* current economic problem. It is not the enemy; rather, as Pogo would say, the enemy is us.

Is it important, then, that America find a new polestar to replace the one containment provided during most of the cold war? As military spending has risen and fallen over the past decades, it has often been led by shifts in public opinion. Congress is attentive to public concerns, and the congressional hand in national security issues has been large, certainly since the late 1960s. In the instance of the Gulf War, the question of public support for a war hung over the debate. Those in Congress who were reluctant to go to war argued that without public support a long, drawn-out war could result in the same type of "failure" that has lingered from Vietnam. It was difficult to fashion policy in the absence of public consensus concerning the nature of the problems and what to do about them.

Before institutional changes or even changes in the roles, missions, and authority of current institutions can be expected, some consensus on the definition of the problem seems purposeful, even necessary. Absent such a consensus in the near term, "new" security concerns will most likely be addressed in an ad hoc manner, using task forces and the like, much as the United States has recently approached the drug problem. American public processes tend toward muddling through—toward responding rather than getting out ahead of problems and public crises.

Yet the connection between public opinion and policy is at best a dotted line; public views are at once a cause and an effect of those held by the political leadership. Public opinion influences foreign affairs and defense policy on broad, persisting issues. Its influence is usually indirect, its views often rather ambivalent and uninformed beyond broad, long-run concerns. Presidents usually get their way in foreign policy if they are determined.

For instance, while public attitudes on defense capabilities and budgets seemed to respond to national or international events—such as budget deficits or the ending of the cold war—those attitudes were, unsurprisingly, uninformed about the specifics of the defense budget. In the mid-1980s, during the spare parts scandal, the majority of Americans estimated that 46 percent of the federal budget went to defense expenditures (about 26 percent was the actual figure in 1986). And nearly 40 percent of the public believed that the largest share of the defense budget went for nuclear weapons (the actual share was 11 percent).[27]

It is trite to say so, but if the public mood will be more volatile than in the past, the need for leadership will be all the greater lest unhappy outcomes ensue from inattention. If volatile, the public mood will also be relatively permissive. It will indicate what is on people's minds but not define policy. Over the past few years, it has seemed to some that presidential leadership might be a thing of the past—witness the budget battles of the late 1980s and Congress's increased role in influencing national security policy. In 1990 the inability of the political system to produce a viable budget agreement cast a blow to the power of the presidency. When the House of Representatives rejected the president's budget plan, Mr. Bush's popularity sank more than 20 percentage points in two months, to a low of 51 percent.[28]

The Gulf War has done much to attenuate that view; it perhaps confirms what history has shown: in foreign policy, presidents generally reign; Congress becomes critical only when presidents are badly out of step with the public mood. President Bush, along with the military leadership, led the country through the crisis. Shortly before ground forces were sent to the region, public opinion suggested only shaky support for such a move. But within a week of troop deployment, a strong majority of the public was on the president's side. Plainly, his personal leadership was decisive.

In many ways though, the Gulf looks more like a cold war security issue than security issues the United States might face in the future. The Gulf crisis had all the elements of a "military" security threat—clear aggression and a threat to U.S. interests. What about "crises" that do not involve such clear threats, or involve "new" threats to which the public is less accustomed? What happens when Americans are not supporting "the troops"—when the response is not so clearly military?

In those situations and about those issues, the role for leadership in articulating interests and specifying threats will be more essential still. And it will be more difficult. There will be less by way of a backdrop consensus like that provided by the Soviet threat. With a more diffuse threat, security debates will more resemble debates over domestic and economic policy—messier, often split down party lines, and influenced by a wider cast of characters.

It is hard to escape the conclusion that, for all the shortcomings diagnosed in this chapter, the United States has done better for the last forty years at issues of national security than those of domestic policy. The Soviet threat has at least provided some sense of *national* interest above the claims of specific groups. And while we are by now familiar with the effects of nearly permanent divided government, with Democrats controlling Congress, Republicans the presidency—almost institutionalized partisanship, along with weak incentives both for coherent opposition in Congress and for political risk taking on the president's part—those were somewhat attenuated in national security by the continuing Soviet imperative.

If national security is becoming more like the rest of American public policy, then perhaps it is time to contemplate radical changes in the way that business is conducted, changes hinted at in

Peter Peterson's chapter. He must be right that affection for a parliamentary system should be tempered by having seen the British example; yet it is intriguing that when the United States installed regimes in Japan and Germany, it put in place parliamentary, not presidential, forms, in the German case in a nation as federal in structure as the United States.

Again, purposes are paramount, not organization for its own sake, and the purpose is simple to state if implausible to achieve: to shape and give pride of place to long-term and national interests over short-run and parochial ones. It is to rectify a system that has become too Madisonian in its capture by those specific interests that yell the loudest, spend the most, or vote most often. If it is premature to make radical changes in America's national security establishment, it is surely too soon to make them in how the nation does all its public business. But it is not too soon to think about them.

Notes

[1] This section draws from Millett and Maslowski (1984), pp. 471–588, and Huntington (1988), pp. 409–432.

[2] May (1990), pp. 33–35.

[3] The best treatment of this case is Destler et al. (1976).

[4] The best brief account is a case now being completed at Harvard University's Kennedy School of Government, "The Reagan Administration and the Soviet Pipeline Embargo," available in Treverton (forthcoming).

[5] Speech to the Council on Foreign Relations, New York, January 12, 1954.

[6] For background, see Cohen (1988), p. 78ff.

[7] "The Congress, the Executive and Intermestic Affairs: Three Proposals," *Foreign Affairs,* January 1977, pp. 306–24.

[8] See Allison and Szanton (1976), p. 78ff.

[9] See Destler (1972), p. 26ff.

[10] Roper commercial survey 24; and Gallup surveys 412K, 436K, and 458, respectively, as cited in Huntington (1961), p. 236.

[11] The results in the paragraph are cited in Huntington (1961), pp. 238–39.

[12] See discussion in Schneider (1983), pp. 33–64.

[13] Discussed in Mandelbaum and Schneider (1979), pp. 40–63.

[14] Millett and Maslowski (1984), p. 579, and Schneider (1983), p. 36.

[15] Yankelovich and Doble (1984), pp. 41–42.

[16] Yankelovich and Doble (1984), pp. 38–39.

[17] Americans Talk Security (ATS), *A Series of Surveys of American Voters: Attitudes Concerning National Security Issues,* Survey No. 4, April 1988, pp. 38, 44.

[18] For a more detailed discussion see Yankelovich and Smoke (1988), pp. 1–17.

[19] Sixty-four percent felt that Soviet nuclear weapons were a very serious threat; 56 percent felt that Soviet aggression was.

[20] The results in this paragraph and in Table 2 are in Americans Talk Security, *Serial National Surveys of Americans on Public Policy Issues,* Survey No. 13, April 1990, pp. 5, 6.

[21] See, for instance, Treverton (1990).

[22] Huntington (1986).

[23] A number of studies have discussed the merits of a flexible acquisition strategy. Among them are *A New Military Strategy for the 1990s, Implications for Capabilities and Acquisition,* The Final Report of the CSIS Conventional Arms Control Project, January 1991, and Paul H. Richanbach et al., *The Future of Military R & D: Towards a Flexible Acquisition Strategy,* Institute for Defense Analyses Paper P-2444, July 1990.

[24] See, for instance, Blechman (1990).

[25] As reported in the *Washington Post,* April 12, 1991, p. A4.

[26] See, for instance, Treverton and Lowenthal (1978).

[27] *A Quest for Excellence,* Final Report to the President by the President's Blue Ribbon Commission on Defense Management, June 1986, Appendix, pp. 208–12.

[28] *Washington Post* poll, April 12, 1991.

Bibliography

Adelman, Kenneth L., and Norman R. Augustine. 1990. *The Defense Revolution: Strategy for the Brave New World*. San Francisco: ICS Press.

Adomeit, Hannes. 1982. *Soviet Risk-taking and Crisis Behavior: A Theoretical and Empirical Analysis*. London: Allen and Unwin.

Allison, Graham. 1988. "Testing Gorbachev." *Foreign Affairs*, Fall 1988.

Allison, Graham, and Peter Szanton. 1976. *Remaking Foreign Policy: The Organizational Connection*. New York: Basic Books.

Aron, Raymond. 1966. *Peace and War*. Garden City: Anchor Press/Doubleday.

Babst, D. 1972. "A Force for Peace." *Industrial Research*.

Banks, Arthur, and William Overstreet. eds. 1983. *A Political Handbook of the World*. New York: McGraw Hill.

Baritz, Loren. 1964. *City on a Hill: A History of Ideas and Myths in America*. New York: John Wiley and Sons.

Bergsten, C. Fred, et al. 1978. "The Reform of International Institutions." in *Trilateral Commission Task Force Reports: 9–14*. New York: New York University Press.

Betts, Richard K. 1987. *Nuclear Blackmail and Nuclear Balance*. Washington, D.C.: The Brookings Institution.

Blechman, Barry M. 1990. *The Politics of National Security: Congress and U.S. Defense Policy*. New York: Oxford University Press.

Borrus, Michael G. 1988. *Competing for Control: America's Stake in Microelectronics*. Cambridge: Ballinger.

———. 1990. "Chips of State." *Issues in Science and Technology*, Fall 1990.

Brierly, J.L. 1963. *The Law of Nations*. Oxford: Oxford University Press (Clarendon Press).

Bundy, McGeorge. 1988. *Danger and Survival: Choices about the Bomb in the First Fifty Years*. New York: Random House.

Caidin, Martin. 1960. *A Torch to the Enemy: The Fire Raid on Tokyo*. New York: Ballantine Books.

Claude, Inis. 1962. *Power and International Relations*. New York: Random House.

Cohen, Stephen. 1988. *The Making of United States International Economic Policy*. New York: Praeger Publishers.

Cohen, Stephen, and John Zysman. 1987. *Manufacturing Matters*. New York: Basic Books.

———. 1988a. "Manufacturing Innovation and American Industrial Competitiveness." *Science*, March 4, 1988.

———. 1988b. "Business Economics and the Oval Office: Advice to the New President and other CEOs." *Harvard Business Review*, November–December 1988.

Cohen, Stephen, David J. Teece, Laura Tyson, and John Zysman. 1984. "Global Competition: The New Reality." *Working Paper of the President's Commission on Industrial Competitiveness*, Vol. III.

Conference on Security and Cooperation in Europe. 1990. "Charter of Paris for a New Europe." Paris: CSCE. (available from the U.S. Department of State.)

Cooper, Richard N., et al. 1978. "Towards a Renovated International System." *Trilateral Commission Task Force Reports: 9–14*. New York: New York University Press.

Coriat, Benjamin. 1990. *L'Atelier et le Robot*. Paris: Christian Bourgeois.

Crowe, William J. Jr., and Alan D. Romberg. 1991. "Rethinking Security in the Pacific." *Foreign Affairs*, Spring 1991.

Cutler, Lloyd N. 1985. "The Right to Intervene." *Foreign Affairs*, Fall 1985.

David, Paul. 1989. "Computer and Dynamo: The Modern Productivity Paradox in Historical Perspective." Working Paper No. 172. Stanford: Center for Economic Policy Research.

Davis, Tami, and Sean Lynn-Jones. 1987. "City Upon a Hill." *Foreign Policy*, Spring 1987.

Dertouzous, Michael, et al. 1989. *Made in America*. Cambridge: MIT Press.

Destler, I.M. 1972. *President, Bureaucrats and Foreign Policy: The Politics of Organizational Reform*. Princeton: Princeton University Press.

Destler, I.M., et al. 1976. *Managing an Alliance: The Politics of the U.S. Japanese Relationship.* Washington, D.C.: The Brookings Institution.

Diamond, Larry. 1989. "Beyond Authoritarianism and Totalitarianism; Strategies for Democratization." *The Washington Quarterly,* Winter 1989.

Doyle, Michael. 1983a. "Kant, Liberal Legacies, and Foreign Affairs: Part I." *Philosophy and Public Affairs.*

————. 1983b. "Kant, Liberal Legacies, and Foreign Affairs: Part II." *Philosophy and Public Affairs.*

————. 1986. "Liberalism and World Politics." *American Political Science Review,* December 1986.

Drucker, Peter. 1990. "The Emerging Theory of Manufacturing." *Harvard Business Review,* May/June 1990.

The Europa Yearbook for 1985. London: Europa Publications.

Evans, Richard J. 1989. *In Hitler's Shadow: West German Historians and the Attempt to Escape from the Nazi Past.* New York: Pantheon.

Freedom House. 1991. *Freedom in the World 1989–1990.* New York: Freedom House.

Freeman, Christopher. 1987. *Technology Policy and Economic Performance: Lessons from Japan.* London: Pinter Publishers.

Gaddis, John L. 1977. "Containment: A Reassessment." *Foreign Affairs,* July 1977.

————. 1982. *Strategies of Containment.* New York: Oxford University Press.

Gastil, R. ed. 1985. "The Comparative Survey of Freedom." 82 *Freedom at Issue.*

Gellner, Ernest. 1983. *Nations and Nationalism.* Ithaca: Cornell University Press.

Gerlach, Michael. 1989. "Keiretsu Organization in the Japanese Economy: Analysis and Trade Implications." in Johnson, Tyson, and Zysman 1989.

Gilpin, Robert. 1975. *U.S. Power and the Multinational Corporation.* New York: Basic Books.

————. 1981. *War and Change in World Politics.* Cambridge: Cambridge University Press.

————. 1987. *The Political Economy of International Relations.* Princeton: Princeton University Press.

Hatsopoulos, George N., Paul R. Krugman, and Lawrence H. Summers. 1988. "U.S. Competitiveness: Beyond the Trade Deficit." *Science,* July 15, 1988.

Hayes, Robert H., Steven C. Wheelwright, and Kim B. Clark. 1988.

Dynamic Manufacturing: Creating the Learning Organization. New York: The Free Press.

Herrigel, Gary. 1989. "Industrial Order and the Politics of Industrial Change: Mechanical Engineering." in Katzenstein 1989.

Hirsch, Fred, and Michael Doyle. 1977. "Politicization in the World Economy." in Hirsch, Doyle, and Morse 1977.

Hirsch, Fred, Michael Doyle, and Edward Morse. eds. 1977. *Alternatives to Monetary Disorder.* New York: Council on Foreign Relations/ McGraw Hill.

Holmes, Stephen. 1979. "Aristippus In and Out of Athens." 73 *American Political Science Review.*

Howard, Michael. 1990. "The Remaking of Europe." *Survival,* March/ April 1990.

Huntington, Samuel P. 1961. *The Common Defense.* New York: Columbia University Press.

———. 1986. "American Military Strategy." Policy Papers in International Affairs, No. 28. Institute of International Studies, University of California, Berkeley.

———. 1988. "Defense Organization and Military Strategy." in Kozak and Keagle 1988.

Inoguchi, Takashi. 1989. "Shaping and Sharing Pacific Dynamism." *The Annals of the American Academy of Political and Social Science,* September 1989.

Ishihara, Shintaro, and Akio Morita. 1989. "The Japan that Can Say 'No.' " translation, U.S. Department of Defense.

Israel, Fred I. ed. 1966. *The State of the Union Messages of the Presidents* (3 volumes). New York: Acropolis Press.

Jaikumar, Ramchandran. 1988. "From Filing and Fitting to Flexible Manufacturing: A Study in the Evolution of Process Control." Working Paper. Cambridge: Harvard Business School.

Japan Economic Institute. 1990. "Economic Regionalism: An Emerging Challenge to the International System." *JEI Report,* No. 25A, June 29, 1990.

Johnson, Chalmers, Laura Tyson, and John Zysman. eds. 1989. *Politics and Productivity.* New York: Ballinger.

Katzenstein, Peter. ed. 1977. *Between Power and Plenty.* Madison: University of Wisconsin Press.

———. ed. 1989. *Industry and Politics in West Germany.* Ithaca: Cornell University Press.

Kaysen, Carl. 1990. "Is War Obsolete? A Review Essay." *International Security,* Spring 1990.

Kennedy, Paul. 1987. *The Rise and Fall of the Great Powers: Economic Change and Military Conflict from 1500 to 2000.* New York: Random House.

Keohane, Robert. 1984. *After Hegemony: Cooperation and Discord in World Political Economy.* Princeton: Princeton University Press.

Kershaw, Ian. 1989. *The Nazi Dictatorship: Problems and Perspectives of Interpretation,* 2nd ed. London: Arnold.

Kindleberger, Charles. 1973. *The World in Depression.* Berkeley: University of California Press.

Kozak, David C., and James M. Keagle. eds. 1988. *Bureaucratic Politics and National Security.* Colorado: Lynne Reiner Publishers.

Krasner, Stephen. 1977. "United States Commercial and Monetary Policy: Unravelling the Paradox of External Strength and Internal Weakness." in Katzenstein 1977.

Krause, Lawrence B. 1990a. "Trade Policy in the 1990s: Good-bye Bipolarity, Hello Regions." in *World Today,* Vol. 46, No. 5. Royal Institute of International Affairs, May 1990.

———. 1990b. "Pacific Economic Regionalism and the United States." Paper prepared for the Symposium on Impact of Recent Economic Development on U.S.–Korea Relations and the Pacific Basin, University of California, San Diego, November 9–10, 1990.

Kupchan, Charles, and Clifford Kupchan. 1991. "Concerts, Collective Security, and the Future of Europe." *International Security,* Summer 1991.

Langer, William L. ed. 1968. *The Encyclopedia of World History.* Boston: Houghton-Mifflin.

Lawrence, Robert. 1984. *Can America Compete?* Washington, D.C.: The Brookings Institution.

Levy, Jack S. 1983. *War in the Modern Great Power System, 1495–1975.* Lexington: University Press of Kentucky.

Lukas, Richard C. 1986. *Forgotten Holocaust: The Poles under German Occupation, 1939–1941.* Lexington: University Press of Kentucky.

Maier, Charles. 1977. "The Politics of Productivity: Foundations of American International Economic Policy after World War II." in Katzenstein 1977.

———. 1988. *The Unmasterable Past: History, Holocaust, and German National Identity.* Cambridge: Harvard University Press.

Mandelbaum, Michael, and William Schneider. 1979. "The New Internationalisms: Public Opinion and American Foreign Policy." in Oye, Lieber, and Rothchild 1979.

Maresca, John. 1985. *To Helsinki: The Conference on Security and Cooperation in Europe.* Durham, N.C.: Duke University Press.

Mason, Henry L. 1981. "Imponderables of the Holocaust." *World Politics,* October 1981.

———. 1988. "Implementing the Final Solution: The Ordinary Regulating of the Extraordinary." *World Politics,* July 1988.

Mattingly, Garrett. 1963. "No Peace beyond What Line?" *Transactions of the Royal Historical Society.*

May, Ernest R. 1990. "Cold War and Defense." in Neilson and Haycock 1990.

Mearsheimer, John J. 1983. *Conventional Deterrence.* Ithaca: Cornell University Press.

———. 1990a. "Back to the Future: Instability in Europe after the Cold War." *International Security,* Summer 1990.

———. 1990b. "Why We Will Soon Miss the Cold War." *The Atlantic,* August 1990.

Millett, Allan R., and Peter Maslowski. 1984. *For the Common Defense: A Military History of the United States of America.* New York: The Free Press.

Ministry of International Trade and Industry. 1987. *1987 White Paper on International Trade and Investment.* Tokyo: MITI.

Mischel, Lawrence. 1989. *Manufacturing Numbers.* Washington, D.C.: Economic Policy Institute.

Monden, Tasuhiro. 1983. *The Toyota Production System.* Norcross, Ga.: Industrial Engineering and Management Press, Institute of Industrial Engineers.

Moran, Theodore H. 1990. "The Globalization of America's Defense Industries: Managing the Threat of Foreign Dependence." *International Security,* Summer 1990.

Mueller, John E. 1989. *Retreat from Doomsday: The Obsolescence of Major War.* New York: Basic Books.

Nau, Henry. 1990. *The Myth of America's Decline: Leading the World Economy into the 1990's.* New York: Oxford University Press.

Neilson, Keith, and Ronald Haycock. eds. 1990. *The Cold War and Defense.* New York: Praeger Publishers.

Noonan, Peggy. 1990. *What I Saw at the Revolution: A Political Life in the Reagan Era.* New York: Random House.

Nye, Joseph S. 1990. *Bound to Lead: The Changing Nature of American Power.* New York: Basic Books.

Office of Technology Assessment, Congress of the United States. 1988. *Paying the Bill: Manufacturing and America's Trade Deficit.* Washington, D.C.: U.S. Government Printing Office.

Oye, Kenneth A., Robert J. Lieber, and Donald Rothchild. eds. 1979.

Eagle Entangled: U.S. Foreign Policy in a Complex World. New York: Longman.

———. 1983. *Eagle Defiant: U.S. Foreign Policy in the 1980's.* Boston: Little, Brown.

Perkins, Dexter. 1963. *A Histroy of the Monroe Doctrine.* Boston: Houghton-Mifflin.

Piore, Michael, and Chuck Sable. 1984. *The Second Industrial Divide.* New York: Basic Books.

Posen, Barry R. 1991. *Inadvertent Escalation: Conventional War and Nuclear Risks.* Ithaca: Cornell University Press.

Reisman, Michael. 1984. "Coercion and Self Determination: Construing Charter Article 2(4)." 78 *American Journal of International Law.*

Rosenman, Samuel I. 1972. *Working with Roosevelt.* New York: Da Capo Press.

Rummel, R. 1983. "Libertarianism and International Violence." *Journal of Conflict Resolution.*

Russett, Bruce. 1985. "The Mysterious Case of Vanishing Hegemony." *International Organization,* Spring 1985.

Safire, William. 1975. *Before the Fall: An Inside View of the Pre-Watergate White House.* Garden City: Doubleday.

Sandholtz, Wayne, and John Zysman. 1989. "1992: Recasting the European Bargain." *World Politics,* October 1989.

Schachter, Oscar. 1984. "The Legality of Prodemocratic Intervention." 78 *American Journal of International Law.*

Schneider, William. 1983. "Conservatism, Not Interventionism: Trends in Foreign Policy Opinion, 1974–1982." in Oye, Lieber, and Rothchild 1983.

Segal, Gerald. 1990. *Rethinking the Pacific.* Oxford: Clarenden Press.

Shott, Jeffrey. 1989. "Is the World Devolving into Regional Trading Blocs?" Washington, D.C.: Institute for International Economics.

Silverberg, Gerald, Giovanni Dosi, et al. 1988. *Technical Change and Economic Change.* London: Pinter Publishers.

Solow, Robert. 1957. "Technical Change and the Aggregate Production Function." *The Review of Economics and Statistics.*

Stowsky, Jay. 1986. "Beating Our Plowshares into Double-Edged Swords: The Impact of Pentagon Policies on the Commercialization of Advanced Technologies." Research Paper No. 17, Berkeley Roundtable on the International Economy. April 1986.

Streit, Clarence. 1939. *Union Now.* New York: Harper & Brothers.

Thompson, Kenneth. 1953. "Collective Security Re-examined." *American Political Science Review,* September 1953.

Treverton, Gregory F. 1990. "The Defense Debate." *Foreign Affairs.*

———. ed. forthcoming. *Making American Foreign Policy.* Englewood Cliffs: Prentice-Hall.

Treverton, Gregory F., and Abraham F. Lowenthal. 1978. "The Making of U.S. Policies toward Latin America: Some Speculative Propositions." Working Paper No. 4, Latin American Program. Washington, D.C.: The Wilson Center.

Tucker, Robert W. 1990. *Empire of Liberty: The Statecraft of Thomas Jefferson.* New York: Oxford University Press.

Tyson, Laura, and John Zysman. eds. 1983. *American Industry in International Competition.* Ithaca: Cornell University Press.

———. 1989. "Developmental Strategy and Production Innovation in Japan." in Johnson, Tyson, and Zysman 1989.

Ullman, Richard. 1975–76. "The Foreign World and Ourselves: Washington, Wilson, and the Democrat's Dilemma." *Foreign Policy,* Winter 1975–76.

———. 1991. *Securing Europe.* Princeton: Princeton University Press.

U.K. Foreign and Commonwealth Office. 1980. *A Yearbook of the Commonwealth 1980.* London: HMSO.

U.S. Department of Defense. 1990a. *A Strategic Framework for the Asian Pacific Rim: Looking Toward the 21st Century,* April 1990.

———. 1990b. Defense Science Board. *Foreign Investment and the Defense Industrial Base.* in draft April 1990.

U.S. Department of State. 1981. *Country Reports on Human Rights Practices.* Washington, D.C.: U.S. Government Printing Office.

Van Evera, Stephen. 1990. "Why Europe Matters, Why the Third World Doesn't: American Grand Strategy after the Cold War." *The Journal of Strategic Studies,* June 1990.

Vogel, Steven. 1989. "Japanese High Technology, Politics, and Power." Research Paper No. 2, Berkeley Roundtable on the International Economy, March 1989.

Walt, Stephen M. 1989. "The Case for Finite Containment: Analyzing U.S. Grand Strategy." *International Security,* Summer 1989.

Waltz, Kenneth N. 1979. *Theory of International Politics.* Reading, Mass.: Addison-Wesley.

Walzer, Michael. 1977. *Just and Unjust Wars.* New York: Basic Books.

Williams, William Appleman. 1962. *The Tragedy of American Diplomacy.* New York: W.W. Norton.

Yakushiji, Taizo. 1985. "The Dynamics of Techno-Industrial Emulation: An Essay on the Growth Patterns of Industrial Pre-eminence and U.S.–Japanese Conflicts in High Technology." Working Paper

No. 15, Berkeley Roundtable on the International Economy, Summer 1985.

Yankelovich, Daniel, and John Doble. 1984. "The Public Mood: Nuclear Weapons and the USSR." *Foreign Affairs,* Fall 1984.

Yankelovich, Daniel, and Richard Smoke. 1988. "America's 'New Thinking.' " *Foreign Affairs,* Fall 1988.

Zysman, John. 1977. *Political Strategies for Industrial Order.* Berkeley: University of California Press.

———. 1991. "Trade, Technology and National Competition." *International Journal of Technology Management,* 1991.

Final Report of
the Seventy-ninth
American Assembly

At the close of their discussions, the participants in the Seventy-ninth American Assembly, on *Rethinking America's Security*, at Arden House, Harriman, New York, May 30–June 2, 1991, reviewed as a group the following statement. This statement represents general agreement; however, no one was asked to sign it. Furthermore, it should be understood that not everyone agreed with all of it.

Rethinking America's Security

"Life, liberty, and the pursuit of happiness." In the wake of the cold war and a hot battle, America's goals in the Declaration of Independence now seem ascendant in a world of increasing interdependence. Our security, traditionally defined, has never appeared more certain. The political values of freedom and the market pursuit of prosperity inspire the globe.

And yet, in a shrinking world, security must be redefined. It acquires new external dimensions, and it begins at home. We must act to secure the "blessings of liberty . . . for our posterity" by investing in our future rather than consuming our inheritance. If we fail, we will forfeit a historic opportunity. If we succeed, we can lead the way toward a more secure, prosperous, and just community of nations.

For forty years America knew what its national security meant: protection against the overriding threat of the Soviet Union and communism, often seen as linked, was priority number one. With the end of communism and the rise of democracy, America finds itself at the moment of re-creation, to paraphrase Dean Acheson, akin to that before American leaders a half century ago. The need for American leadership on the international stage has not changed. Of that, the Gulf War was testimony; no one else could mobilize the anti-Saddam coalition.

Yet the challenges to and instruments of that leadership have changed. The challenges are now less military and more economic or political, at home as well as abroad. And the leadership must be collaborative, a genuine sharing of responsibility as well as burden. America's alliances with Europe or Japan are one form; other multilateral institutions such as the General Agreement on Tariffs and Trade (GATT) and the Organization of American States (OAS) are another; ad hoc coalitions of the willing, like that assembled during the Gulf War, are another; still another, and crucial, is the United Nations.

The most urgent challenge for America is to get its own house in order. There is no contradiction between doing so and simultaneously sustaining America's international leadership. If its domestic problems went unaddressed, its capacity to take necessary actions internationally would, over time, diminish. Americans would then turn inward or be tempted to find external scapegoats for their problems.

With threat from the Soviet Union declining, the central values for which America stands—the rule of law, democracy, and human rights—become even more central in driving and building public support for America's security policy.

Rethinking the Concept of National Security

The full implications of the dramatic reduction of the threat that was for forty years the polestar of American security policy are still being assessed. Even to talk of "threats" now smacks of the past age of the cold war. But while everything can be a challenge, not everything is a threat. It is a sense of priorities that is critical.

The underlying concept of security has not changed. But as the challenges to that security change, along with the place of the United States in the world, America cannot retreat from the world nor "go it alone"; interdependence is a fact of life.

Military Interests

- Sustaining America's sovereignty and territorial integrity, neither of which has been at risk, save for the prospect of nuclear war, for over a hundred years.
- Protecting allies and friends from armed attack.
- Forestalling regional conflicts that might threaten the interests of the United States or its allies.
- Restraining the proliferation of armaments, especially weapons of mass destruction, but also conventional weaponry.
- Multilateralizing the use of force, and its human and fiscal costs, through collective security, including UN mechanisms whenever possible.

Economic and Systemic Interests

- Sustaining an open international trading order in the interests of an expanding American prosperity as well as that of others.
- Assuring access to energy and other natural resources.
- Promoting the dynamism that new immigrants bring to American society while acting to diminish the risk of waves of migration.
- Containing the risk of harm to the global environment.
- Promoting human rights and democratic institutions.
- Diminishing the widening gap between rich and poor across the globe to stabilize the world political economy.

These interests are not so much new as newly prominent given the changes in the world. For much of the cold war, for instance, there was little inclination to question whether the United States could afford international leadership, even international beneficence; the need for both seemed self-evident.

Interests in the Domestic Base

As President Dwight D. Eisenhower pointed out more than three decades ago, to undermine from within what one is seeking to protect from without is folly. Precise prescriptions for domestic reconstruction were beyond the agenda before us. But no agenda could hope to provide a secure domestic base from which to conduct an effective international policy that did not include urgent attention to:

- The transformation—not tinkering or reform—of education at all levels to assure an adequately educated, socially secure work force.
- The significant restructuring of social programs to provide more effective, accessible services at a cost that is sustainable.
- The development of corporate cultures that significantly shorten the time required to convert technology into products of truly world-class quality.
- The social and tax incentives to convert a debt-burdened culture of public and private consumerism to a nation of savers and investors for the longer term.
- The rebuilding of existing physical infrastructure and the creation of vital telecommunications and other infrastructures critical to economic success in the twenty-first century.
- Serious, effective, and continuing attention to rebuilding a gathered political community that shares purposes rather than accentuating differences, facilitates difficult choices in the public sphere, and is less generally hostile to the very idea of leadership, even while decrying its absence.

There is also no doubt that the domestic agenda can more readily be addressed with the necessary resources and urgency because external dangers have diminished. Some of those domestic problems are already undercutting our ability to compete in the international economy or promote its values abroad; left untended, they could eventually threaten the ability to defend ourselves in traditional military terms.

In sum:

1. The Soviet Union will remain an object of concern while not a threat of the sort it presented during the cold war. Sustaining military forces as insurance is essential.

2. American security by the traditional military definition is less at risk. This circumstance inevitably brings to the surface with fresh urgency the other dimensions of security, and in particular, the need for greater attention to America's domestic agenda. Yet it is mistaken to think of a "zero-sum" trade-off between America's international and its domestic agendas. The two must be addressed together. Some of our domestic problems require international cooperation, while domestic ills, if left unaddressed, would risk turning Americans inward, against their international interests and commitments.

Rethinking the Military Dimension

The United States is now safer in military terms than at any time in the postwar era. We support the administration's determination to shrink defense forces by about a quarter over the next five years and urge deeper reductions to follow if circumstances permit. That said, the Gulf War was a sharp reminder, if any were needed, that the world remains both dangerous and uncertain.

Soviet Union and Eastern Europe

The Soviet Union, which focused America's fears, now presents both threats and opportunities. Soviet cooperation in the UN was essential during the Gulf War and had been important before it; if less cooperative, Moscow could again obstruct a range of American policies. Hopefully, the transformation of the Soviet Union over a generation or more into one or several democratic and economically reformed states would be tantamount to removing it as a military threat—a tremendous, if far from certain, undertaking.

The Soviet Union still remains a nuclear superpower and has the most powerful army on the Eurasian land mass. Yet its retreat from Eastern Europe means that for it once again to pose a cold war type threat to Western Europe would require much more than a new Stalinist regime. While such a threat cannot be ruled out, it could not arise quickly.

However, a quite different risk from the Soviet Union must now be faced. If increasing economic disruption and disintegration result in civil war, frightening questions arise whether centralized command and control of 30,000 nuclear weapons spread over a half dozen republics can be maintained. Precise contingencies cannot be forecast, but the risk of nuclear artillery shells or advanced conventional weapons finding their way into the international arms bazaar can hardly be excluded.

Plainly, the security of Eastern Europe will be affected by the course of events in the Soviet Union. Some of those countries have done what the Soviet Union so far has not—made the leap to fully democratic politics and free market economics. Their chances for a successful transition are thus all the greater, and should things go badly in the Soviet Union, it would become even more important to deepen the West's engagement with them.

This assessment indicates several lines of policy:

- *Nuclear deterrence* remains essential but can be accomplished with much smaller forces than before. Active pursuit of arms control agreements will permit even greater reduction.
- *Military insurance for Europe.* U.S. forces in Europe supplemented by forces at home serve such a function while also providing a stabilizing factor as Germany unifies and Europe seeks to rejoin its two halves. Numbers can be pared sharply from their 300,000-plus of the 1980s down to 70,000–100,000 as the North Atlantic Treaty Organization (NATO) revises its military structure; equipment for reinforcements should be left behind. At the same time, the United States should support a European defense structure as a complement to NATO, perhaps through the Western European Union (WEU), which might, in due course, become the focal point for European contributions to actions outside Europe.

  By the same token, the Conference on Security and Cooperation in Europe (CSCE) is not a competitor to NATO but a complement. It is very much in the American interest to see it develop as a forum for building military transparency, for moni-

toring human rights, and for helping to resolve or to mediate the conflicts that surely lie ahead in Eastern Europe.
* *Broadened engagement with Eastern Europe and the Soviet Union.* "Broadened engagement" is the watchword for American policy toward both Eastern Europe and the Soviet Union, though the policy has different implications for the two.

Specifically, we recommend with regard to Eastern Europe:

* Expanded programs, in cooperation with America's partners in Europe and Japan, to provide support and technical assistance to democratic politics as well as economic reform.
* Freer access to Western markets, especially that of the European Community, as well as new forms of political relationships between Europe's eastern and western halves—including an intensification of parliamentary contracts.
* Arrangements to help reduce the region's energy dependence on Soviet supplies.
* Closer contacts between these countries and the North Atlantic Treaty Organization. The issue is sensitive; explicit security guarantees to Eastern Europe would risk feeding Soviet paranoia. But closer connections—the new liaison relationships, for instance, or sending soldiers to NATO training facilities—build deterrence against any Soviet adventure by identifying Eastern Europe as part of the democratic family of nations. Over the long term, this is an additional argument for creating a "European" security arrangement.

With respect to the Soviet Union, participants debated the idea of a "Grand Bargain." If the Soviet leadership—union and republic—was prepared to make a decisive political commitment to democracy and market economy, should the West engage in this process, including through financial assistance on the scale of the Marshall Plan? Some thought so, while others doubted that any Soviet government could now credibly give such commitments or adopt a coherent economic program for such a transition. Still others worried about the U.S. willingness to pay its share of the cost.

There was strong support for an ongoing bargaining process,

one designed to strengthen the hand of the Soviet reformers. Working with other nations and through international agencies, the United States should stand ready to help the Soviet Union qualify as soon as possible for membership in all the UN international economic agencies, including the GATT, the International Monetary Fund (IMF), and the World Bank. The United States should also consider proposals to assist the Soviet government to move rapidly to a free market and open policy. A joint program might provide significant financial assistance but on a strictly conditional and step-by-step basis. The conditions might include not only specific steps to a market economy but also progress on security issues.

Proliferation

This is now a major threat. While the threat of nuclear attack on the American homeland from, say, a Third World nuclear force remains remote—and does not alone justify the Strategic Defense Initiative (SDI)—American forces abroad, as well as the interests of U.S. allies, are increasingly at risk. The Soviet nuclear problem is best considered in this broader context of proliferation, for it seems far-fetched to imagine Soviet nuclear weapons being used in a civil war. More likely, as discipline broke down and personal risk increased, desperate people might be willing to sell nuclear materials for private gain.

The spread of technology continues, and now includes ballistic and long-range missiles. Thus, distance has been reduced while regional antagonisms in the Third World persist, thus increasing the urgency of the proliferation problem.

- In the Soviet case, proliferation is both an additional argument for broadened engagement and a strong one for negotiations to sharply reduce numbers of weapons (to zero in the case of short-range nuclear missiles and artillery).
- Arms control in the Middle East is an imperative, one that bears on America's own arms sales policies. Reducing and ultimately eliminating chemical weapons are a priority, and the current negotiations for a treaty to eliminate all chemical weapons

should be accelerated. In the nuclear area, a simple freeze on nuclear weapons runs the risk of seeming to freeze an Israeli advantage; the right long-term objective is a nuclear-free zone. That is only plausible if strict restraints on conventional weapons are also imposed.

- More generally, there is the need to strengthen the range of antiproliferation efforts—for example, the nuclear suppliers group and the missile transfer control regime, both of which need to include China as well as the Soviet Union; and the Non-Proliferation Treaty (NPT). To retain the support of the 140 parties to the Non-Proliferation Treaty, the nuclear weapons states need to respond to the demand for further restraints on nuclear weapons tests, including at least a tight annual quota and a reduction in the yield of such tests. A UN agreement to label any new possessor of nuclear, biological, or chemical weapons a "threat to peace and security" would be a step in the right direction. So is the draft treaty on chemical weapons now under consideration, especially since it contains far-reaching and intrusive verification provisions.

  These efforts do little more than buy time in the hopes that particular conflicts will be resolved—as has that between Brazil and Argentina—and so nations will see it in their interest not to acquire weapons of mass destruction. But at least they do buy time.

- SDI as currently conceived does little to help defend against proliferated nuclear threats. If military responses are considered, the right ones are antitactical missiles designed to defend American forces or other specific targets overseas.

- Weapons of mass destruction get most of our attention, but existing "conventional" weapons are also appallingly destructive. Thus there is a need for new ideas and possible new institutions to staunch the international trade in arms. Thought should be given to ways of compensating, for example, the Eastern Europeans for reducing or eliminating production. The United States, as well as other aid donors, should consider following the Japanese suggestion of linking economic assistance to a reduction of defense spending by recipient countries.

- The spread of weapons should also be dealt with at its causes, by attempting to defuse the regional antagonisms that impel those who acquire them, not just by dealing with its symptom, the weapons themselves. In the Middle East, for example, the Gulf War has again highlighted the need for a breakthrough to durable peace. Contingency arrangements by U.S. military operations to bolster stability in the region are prudent, but the fundamental challenge is to expedite a political settlement. American diplomacy should continually press Arab states to deal directly with Israel and Israel to remove the obstacles it raises to negotiation. Under no circumstances should the United States support an Israeli policy of "settlements instead of a settlement."

Insurance in Asia

The U.S.–Japan security relationship and the broader American presence in Asia will remain important to the stability of the region. While the declining Soviet threat makes possible commensurate reductions in it presence, the United States, by history and geography, is the only global power not seen as a threat by nations of the region, with the single exception of North Korea. Precipitous withdrawals would be destabilizing. They would also run the risk of making Japan feel pressure to fill the vacuum—something in the interest of neither Asian stability nor the United States.

Terrorism

This issue ranks high on the list of public concerns. However, thanks in no small measure to quiet international cooperation, the task is to make sure it remains under control.

America's Forward Presence

American forces and bases abroad will shrink, and we regard that as appropriate. Much of that presence was driven by the Soviet threat, and so the waning of the threat also reduces the need for our presence. Moreover, many of the countries that played host to American forces are less willing to do so now. The United States will need to shift from fixed bases to access for air and naval forces of the sort it had during the Gulf War. In the Middle East and Gulf, there surely is a case for sustaining a naval presence, an intelligence capacity, and some infrastructure of bases in reserve. But even there, a higher profile seems to us to run political risks that probably are not worth the military gain.

In this context, the need for an effective, generously supported diplomacy and intelligence community can only increase in a multipolar world in which opportunities, challenges, and threats will likely be more frequent than in the past generation. American diplomacy, in particular, has been starved of vital resources in recent years.

Rethinking the Broader Dimensions of Security

Since the collapse of the Berlin Wall, it has become apparent that the Soviet threat served as a glue holding the industrialized democracies together. As that unifying threat disappears, the danger now grows of economic frictions dividing the United States, Europe, and Japan. Relations between the United States and Japan have sunk to an uncomfortably low ebb. According to a number of public opinion polls, many Americans view Japan's economic power as a greater threat to U.S. security than Soviet military power. Europe and Japan are also increasingly at odds on trade. Bonds between the United States and Europe remain strong, but there is significant risk that the GATT talks will fail, and Americans will blame Europe.

America must act now to ensure that economic competition with Japan, Europe, and other nations does not lead to a deterioration in relations with nations friendly to us:

- Bring the final round of GATT talks to the highest level of concern with other key governments in order to produce a successful outcome—a reflection of America's stakes in preserving and expanding an open world trading order.
- While moving toward a free trade zone with Mexico, Canada, and perhaps other nations of the hemisphere, work to prevent a division of the world into two or three major trading blocs.

- Intensify its efforts to engage the Japanese in a wide range of economic measures designed to redress the chronic trade imbalance with Japan. The United States should also seek more active Japanese participation in international scientific and technological cooperation to the benefit of the peoples of many nations.

Perspective is critical. Despite incremental reforms, Japan's markets do remain relatively closed, and some Japanese business practices hurt particular economic interests of the United States—fostering a public perception of foul play. However, America's problems of competitiveness are rooted at home, not overseas. To label Japan the "enemy" is only to see the world through the prism of the cold war.

The United States today is saving too little, consuming too much, and continuing to create a mountain of public debt. We have been a major debtor nation before, but today's indebtedness is of a different character because too much of our borrowing is directed toward consumption, not investment in the future. Our lifestyle has become dependent on foreign creditors as well as oil producers. Political leadership in the United States has not yet made the case with the majority of American voters that additional revenues are necessary to deal with burgeoning domestic problems.

It is also essential that America move decisively to reduce energy dependence. Our imports of foreign oil are growing ominously—more than half of our oil now comes from overseas. If current trends continue, payments for oil could reverse the current downward trend in our trade deficit. The Organization of Petroleum Exporting Countries (OPEC) will also grow in power. To address its energy needs, the United States should:

- Enact a gasoline tax of $1 a gallon, phased in over three to five years. Each penny of tax is estimated to produce $1 billion in revenue, so the annual gain would ultimately amount to $100 billion.
- Assist the development and modernization of safe, clean, comfortable, and reliable systems of public transport.
- Pursue a far more rigorous program of energy conservation and

develop sources of energy other than oil, including nuclear power.

- Assist the modernization and development of oil resources in the Soviet Union and other nations outside the Middle East.

America's capacity to rapidly produce quality goods and services based on emerging high technologies essential to our industrial and military strength is more and more in question. The nation must rethink the appropriate roles of government and the private sector in ensuring that America does not lose its technological superiority in key fields. This is not only a matter of military security, for the Pentagon now lags behind civil industry in many sectors of high tech. The failure of the United States to maintain its lead in electronics, for example, is being replicated in other fields, such as parallel processing. America's universities must be recognized as a vital resource, essential to new scientific and technological developments. Our leadership is eroding in fields where we now excel, such as biotechnology, where advances would create jobs, save lives, and enhance the image of America as the leader of scientific achievement. Only a more coherent federal effort to support progress in education in science and technology can remedy such losses.

Other so-called transnational challenges now demand greater attention. We may debate the extent to which they pose a "national security threat" to the United States, but there is no gainsaying their importance. To postpone vigorous moves to address global warming and ozone depletion would be to create irreversible damage for coming generations.

Addressing the challenges posed by the large-scale movement of people across borders, and the social catastrophe that they may reflect and entail, requires collaborative leadership. The United States has a particular interest in ensuring an orderly transition to democratic freedom and economic prosperity in Mexico. The United States should also be at the forefront in helping to address the problems of 18 million refugees in the world and in preventing new waves of migration arising from ethnic and nationalistic conflicts, as well as poverty.

Much of the world is deeply concerned about a population explosion, even if the United States is not, for very special political reasons of its own. America was once a pioneer in population programs, and should resume that role.

As a nation comprising 5 percent of the world's population but consuming half of its cocaine, the United States has a direct and immediate interest in curbing the flow of international drugs. However, here as with competitiveness, the enemy is us, as Pogo might have put it; dealing with the problem begins at home.

America's Role in the New International Order

National security is not simply a matter of identifying threats and defending them, especially not in the world aborning. Security is international, and it is not a zero-sum game. States depend on each other, and the security of all can be enhanced if they agree on the rules of their system. When Moscow realized, perhaps too late, that command economics would not produce and Communist politics could not last, it let loose the spectacular changes of the last two years. Those in turn have opened up the possibility of a better organized, more consensual international system—what President Bush has called "a new world order."

Visions of this new order are the backdrop for thinking about the future of America's security. One vision is "unipolar." The effective withdrawal of the Soviet Union from the global contest has left the United States the only and unchallenged superpower. The American people should not underestimate the opportunities, nor the responsibilities, that this unique position brings with it. The opportunity is not a license for unilateralism. The Gulf War, for example, was a success achieved by leadership exerted in concert with, and largely financed by, allies, and through multilateral institutions, notably the UN. Without such allied support and international authority, America's action would have been difficult to finance and would have lacked legitimacy in the eyes of the world.

A view of the future as one of great power cooperation within a multipolar world may thus be realistic. The end of the cold war with its bipolar balance of terror has returned us to the uncertainties familiar to our ancestors, particularly in Europe, but with the added danger of nuclear weapons. This view was, in fact, assumed by the founders of the United Nations Organization in 1945, who supposed that international order could only be maintained by the five great powers of that time acting in concert—hence the permanent membership of the Security Council.

Yet the world also can be seen as one of equal sovereign states, all enjoying equal rights under the same international law. If the vision of great power cooperation reflects some of the reality of the 1990s, it still smacks too much of realpolitik, of a world where the strong dominate the weak. The concept of sovereign states also inspired the authors of the UN Charter. Under it, the duty of the strong is to uphold the law, by force if necessary, in order to protect the weak. The action to liberate Kuwait is a textbook example, suggesting that this model may now at last be applicable, thanks to entente among the great powers, in a way that their mutual antipathy and mistrust previously made impossible.

A community of liberal democracies, though, better reflects American ideals. This vision rejects the idea that all states are equal no matter how they treat their citizens or how much say those citizens have in choosing their government. History holds few, if any, examples of wars pitting liberal democracies against each other. Even overwhelming military power, such as America has wielded since 1945, does not inspire fear in other liberal democracies. Thus, the spread of democracy in Latin America, Eastern Europe, and parts of East Asia, and its acceptance as an aspiration in most of Africa, is the most encouraging long-term development of recent years.

Plainly, these are visions, not blueprints for the future. The first—the unipolar moment—is at best a partial description of the present unique historical period. The last—a community of peaceable democracies—reflects an aspiration and an ideal. America must promote the adoption of liberal democratic values.

However, the second and third models—a concert of powers working together, and a world of independent nations equal before the law—between them provide the most fruitful guide to American policy. The United States will need to act in concert with other major powers in order to sustain a stable balance, indeed its citizens will demand that it do so; but it will also need to work through the UN and other intergovernmental organizations, showing respect for other sovereign states and their legal rights. Only in extreme cases of emergency or humanitarian need will it be right to set aside the sovereignty of other states.

We recommend:

- Recognizing the responsibility that comes with economic weight. In particular, Japan and Germany should have a greater role and be encouraged to contribute to multilateral security operations. For now, the most that can be envisaged and should be attempted is the removal of the "enemy" clause from the UN Charter. Possible ways of enabling Germany and Japan, as well as major states of the developing world, to be involved in consultation with permanent members of the Security Council should be put in place as soon as possible.

  As politics permit, the UN Security Council should be restructured, bringing in Japan and Germany as permanent members. Alternatively, Germany might be represented by Britain and France ceding their places to a single delegate of the European Union.

- Creating a command and control mechanism for a UN Rapid Deployment Force and earmark units—including, but not limited to, those from the present members—which could be used for timely intervention in international crises.

- Mounting a major multilateral effort to prevent the further spread of technologies and weapons of mass destruction. This involves setting up an international regime to control the transfer of technology and materials capable of use in the construction of such weapons, backed by intrusive verification procedures. Existing bodies entrusted with such inspections, for instance, the International Atomic Energy Agency, are not up to the task and should be strengthened. The Security Council should adopt a resolution declaring possession of nuclear, biological, and chemical weapons in violation of existing agreements a threat to peace and security, thereby opening the way to mandatory sanctions against states found to possess them.

- Developing far more stringent monitoring and control of conventional arms transfers. Drawing on the experience of CoCom in limiting West-East transfers of sensitive technology during the cold war, the monitoring should cover high-technology weapons, equipment, delivery systems, and electronic components, as well as lower-technology weapons of more conventional type. America should seek support from the relatively small number of principal arms producers for the establishment of an international control agency, to be entrusted with the task of monitoring, controlling, and when necessary limiting the sale of such weaponry by its member states.

- Fostering voluntary restraints by private industry to control improper weapons exports that might slip through official controls.
- Devising more imaginative financing for core UN operations, so that the UN could maintain a permanent capacity for reacting to humanitarian crises. (The regular UN budget is roughly equivalent to that of the New York City Fire Department; the peacekeeping budget only double that.)
- Giving the UN a permanent capability to put police, as opposed to troops, into countries where it is asked to help end a civil conflict; and a staff of people qualified to supervise elections.
- Encouraging regional bodies to strengthen their peacekeeping and dispute-settling machinery, so that the UN is not the only resort in all conflicts. These bodies should also develop mechanisms for protecting human rights in member countries, following the example of the Council of Europe.
- Building on the embryonic CSCE machinery for helping political development and defusing ethnic conflicts in Europe. It could be replicated at a world level, or by other regions.

The fundamental implication of our Assembly is this: the United States is required to think again, at a depth not required in two generations. What we lack is less the material resources than the resources of spirit—new concepts for a world beyond the cold war and the sense of national purpose to make choices, not evade them. Some dangers loom but more opportunities beckon, if we stretch our minds, then our politics, then our policies, to embrace them. The re-creation is up to us.

Participants

+ DAVID L. AARON
Senior Fellow
Twentieth-Century Fund
New York, New York

CHARLES F. ADAMS
Chairman
Finance Committee
Raytheon Company
Lexington, Massachusetts

+ GRAHAM ALLISON
Douglas Dillon Professor of
Government
John F. Kennedy School of
Government
Harvard University
Cambridge, Massachusetts

J. BRIAN ATWOOD
President
National Democratic Institute
for International Affairs
Washington, DC

DOUGLAS BALL
Princeton, New Jersey

BARBARA A. BICKSLER
Institute for Defense Analyses
Alexandria, Virginia

+ ROBERT D. BLACKWILL
Lecturer in Public Policy
John F. Kennedy School of
Government
Harvard University
Cambridge, Massachusetts

PHILIP BOFFEY
Deputy Editorial Page Editor
The New York Times
New York, New York

ROBERT R. BOWIE
Dillon Professor of
International Affairs,
Emeritus
Harvard University
Washington, DC

CHARLES W. BRAY III
President
The Johnson Foundation, Inc.
Racine, Wisconsin

L. PAUL BREMER III
Managing Director
Kissinger Associates
New York, New York

BARRY E. CARTER
Professor of Law
Georgetown University Law
Center
Washington, DC

RICHARD F. CELESTE
Celeste & Sabety Ltd.
Columbus, Ohio

ANTONIA H. CHAYES
ENDISPUTE, Inc.
Cambridge, Massachusetts

LESTER M. CRYSTAL
Executive Producer
MacNeil/Lehrer News Hour
New York, New York

+ JOHN DESPRES
Select Committee on
Intelligence
United States Senate
Washington, DC

MICHAEL DOYLE
Professor of Politics &
International Affairs
Princeton University
Princeton, New Jersey

GLORIA DUFFY
President
Global Outlook
Palo Alto, California

JAN ELIASSON
Permanent Representative of
Sweden to the United
Nations
New York, New York

+ AHMED FAKHR
The National Center for
Middle East Studies—Cairo
Cairo, Egypt

STEPHEN FLANAGAN
Policy Planning Staff
United States Department of
State
Washington, DC

THOMAS M. FRANCK
Murry & Ida Becker Professor
of Law
Director
Center for International
Studies
New York University School of
Law
New York, New York

ALTON FRYE
Vice President & Washington
Director
Council on Foreign Relations
Washington, DC

RICHARD N. GARDNER
Henry L. Moses Professor of
Law
& International
Organization
Columbia University Law
School
New York, New York

**DAVID R. GERGEN
Editor-at-Large
U.S. News & World Report
Washington, DC

GEORGIE ANNE GEYER
Universal Press Syndicate
Washington, DC

*STEPHEN R. GRAUBARD
Editor
Daedalus
Cambridge, Massachusetts

EDWARD K. HAMILTON
President
Hamilton, Rabinovitz &
Alschuler, Inc.
Los Angeles, California

DAVID C. HENDRICKSON
Department of Political
Science
The Colorado College
Colorado Springs, Colorado

NORMAN M. HINERFELD
Chairman & Chief Executive
Officer
Tica Industries, Inc.
New York, New York

JOHN HUDSON
Vice President
Amalgamated Clothing &
Textile Workers Union
New York, New York

SAMUEL P. HUNTINGTON
Director
John M. Olin Institute for
    Strategic Studies
Harvard University
Cambridge, Massachusetts

+ J.C. HUREWITZ
Professor Emeritus
Columbia University
New York, New York

+ B.R. INMAN
Chairman of the Executive
    Committee
Science Applications
    International Corporation
Austin, Texas

*KARL KAISER
Director
Research Institute of the
    German Society of Foreign
    Affairs
Professor of Political Science,
    Cologne
Bonn, Germany

+ KOJI KAKIZAWA
Director
National Defense Division
Liberal Democratic Party
Member of The House of
    Representatives
Tokyo, Japan

ZALMAY KHALILZAD
Assistant Deputy
    Undersecretary of
    Defense for Policy Planning
Department of Defense
Washington, DC

CHARLES A. KUPCHAN
Department of Politics
Princeton University
Princeton, New Jersey

BETTY GOETZ LALL
Co-Director, National Security
    Studies
Council on Economic
    Priorities
New York, New York

THOMAS W. LANGFITT
President
The Pew Charitable Trusts
Philadelphia, Pennsylvania

RICHARD LATTER
Associate Director
Wilton Park Conference
    Center
West Sussex, United Kingdom

+ ROBERT LEGVOLD
Director
The W. Averell Harriman
    Institute for Advanced Study
    of the Soviet Union
Columbia University
New York, New York

**WINSTON LORD
New York, New York

DONALD F. McHENRY
University Research Professor
    of
    Diplomacy & International
    Affairs
Georgetown University
Washington, DC

EDWARD C. MEYER
Managing Partner
Cilluffo Associates
Arlington, Virginia

*EDWARD MORTIMER
Foreign Affairs Columnist
Financial Times
London, United Kingdom

+ RICHARD N. MURPHY
Senior Fellow for the Middle
East
Council on Foreign Relations
New York, New York

JOSEPH S. NYE, JR.
Director
Center for International Affairs
Harvard University
Cambridge, Massachusetts

**MICHAEL PALLISER
Chairman
Samuel Montagu & Co.
London, United Kingdom

ELIZABETH R.
RINDSKOPF
General Counsel
Central Intelligence Agency
Washington, DC

ENID C.B. SCHOETTLE
International Affairs Program
The Ford Foundation
New York, New York

DANIEL L. SCHORR
Senior News Analyst
National Public Radio
Washington, DC

ELIZABETH D.
SHERWOOD
Associate Director
Strengthening Democratic
Institutions Project
John F. Kennedy School of
Government
Harvard University
Cambridge, Massachusetts

+ PETER TARNOFF
President
Council on Foreign Relations
New York, New York

GREGORY F.
TREVERTON
Senior Fellow
Council on Foreign Relations
New York, New York

CARLO TREZZA
First Counsellor
Embassy of Italy
Washington, DC

RICHARD H. ULLMAN
David K.E. Bruce Professor of
International Affairs
Woodrow Wilson School of
Public and International
Affairs
Princeton University
Princeton, New Jersey

ITARU UMEZU
Acting Director
The Japan Institute of
International Affairs
Tokyo, Japan

STEPHEN VAN EVERA
Department of Political
   Science
Massachusetts Institute of
   Technology
Cambridge, Massachusetts

PAUL R. VIOTTI
Professor and Department
   Head
Department of Political
   Science
United States Air Force
   Academy
Colorado Springs, Colorado

PAUL A. VOLCKER
Chairman
James D. Wolfensohn, Inc.
New York, New York

WALLACE EARL WALKER
Professor of Public Policy
Department of Social Science
United States Military
   Academy
West Point, New York

THOMAS G. WESTON
Deputy U.S. Representative to
   the European Communities
U.S. Mission to the European
   Communities
Brussels, Belgium

MALCOLM WIENER
Chairman of the Board
The Millburn Corporation
New York, New York

EDWIN D. WILLIAMSON
Legal Adviser
United States Department of
   State
Washington, DC

+ AHARON YARIV
   Head of The Jaffee Center for
      Strategic Studies
   Tel Aviv University
   Tel Aviv, Israel

+ GRIGORY A. YAVLINSKY
   Former First Deputy, Prime
      Minister of the Russian
      Federation
   Moscow, USSR

 *Rapporteur
**Discussion Leader
+ Panelist

STEERING COMMITTEE AND ADVISERS

for International Series of American Assemblies

About the Council
on Foreign Relations

Founded in 1921, the Council on Foreign Relations is an educational membership institution and a forum bringing together leaders from the academic, public, and private worlds. The Council is nonpartisan and takes no institutional positions. It conducts meetings that give its members an opportunity to talk with invited guests from the United States and abroad who have special experience and expertise in international affairs. Its studies program explores foreign policy questions through research by the Council's professional staff, visiting fellows and others, and through study groups and symposia. The Council also publishes the journal *Foreign Affairs*, in addition to monographs.

About The American Assembly

The American Assembly was established by Dwight D. Eisenhower at Columbia University in 1950. It holds nonpartisan meetings and publishes authoritative books to illuminate issues of United States policy.

An affiliate of Columbia, the Assembly seeks to provide information, stimulate discussion, and evoke independent conclusions on matters of vital public interest.

American Assembly Sessions

At least two national programs are initiated each year. Authorities are retained to write background papers presenting essential data and defining the main issues of each subject.

A group of men and women representing a broad range of experience, competence, and American leadership meet for several days to discuss the Assembly topic and consider alternatives for national policy.

All Assemblies follow the same procedure. The background papers are sent to participants in advance of the Assembly. The Assembly meets in small groups for four or five lengthy periods. All groups use the same agenda. At the close of these informal sessions participants adopt in plenary session a final report of findings and recommendations.

THE AMERICAN ASSEMBLY

Columbia University

Index

Acheson, Dean, 16, 446
Adams, John Quincy, 107
Afghanistan, 224, 260, 368, 417
Agriculture Department, U.S., 30, 50, 51, 425
Aid Consortia, 64
Aid to Families with Dependent Children (AFDC), 82
Air Force, U.S., 26, 173*n*, 192–93, 409
    force reductions of, 191
    force structure of, 342–43, 344
Albania, 256, 284–85
Alexander VI, Pope, 106
Algiers Accords (1981), 293
Allison, Graham T., 15–31, 35–56, 375–85, 415
American Arbitration Association (AAA), 286
American Association of Retired Persons (AARP), 81–82
American Civil Liberties Union (ACLU), 91
American Israel Public Affairs Committee (AIPAC), 356–57
American Red Cross, 40, 43
Americans Talk Security (ATS), 419
"American system," 106, 107
Angola, 260, 272
Anti-Ballistic Missile (ABM) Treaty (1972), 340–41
Aquino, Corazon, 62, 320
Arab-Israeli conflict, 233, 244, 349–61
    arms control and, 360–61
    Bush and, 354
    European Community and, 355
    Middle East arms race and, 355–58
    occupied territories and, 349–52
    Palestinian issue and, 359–61
    Resolution 242 and, 350–51, 353–55, 359–60
    Resolution 338 and, 354
    Soviet Jews' immigration and, 352
    UN and, 350–51, 353–54, 359–60
    U.S. as peacemaker in, 353–55
    see also Middle East
Argentina, 277, 303, 320, 453
arms control, 46, 291, 450, 452–54
    Arab-Israeli conflict and, 360–61
    collective security and, 258

Arms Control Advisory Board, 60
Army, U.S., 409
    force reductions of, 191
    force structure of, 342, 343–46
Asia, 21, 22, 28, 137, 146, 150, 164, 173*n*–74*n*, 224, 248, 343, 404, 459
    as economic region, 159–61
    electronics industry and, 153
    GDP of, 158–59
    growth rate of, 169*n*
    Japanese vs. U.S. influence in, 138
    new international system and, 227–28
    nuclear proliferation and, 231, 232
    ongoing changes in, 363–65
    U.S. alliances in, 365–66
    U.S. defense strategy and, 187–88
    U.S. foreign policy and, 190
    U.S. markets and, 160–61
Aspen Institute, 176
Aspin, Les, 36
Assad, Hafez, 240, 406*n*
Australia, 46, 174*n*, 374*n*
    U.S. defense strategy and, 188
Australia-New Zealand-U.S. (ANZUS) Alliance, 186, 188, 309, 320, 374*n*
Austria, 113, 225, 254, 309

Bailey, Thomas A., 107
Baker, James, 55, 353, 355, 383
balance of power, 238–39, 312
    19th-century Great Britain and, 301–2
    Persian Gulf and, 242–45
    Soviet Union and, 245–48
Ball, George, 27, 29, 349–61
Baltic States, 27, 182, 247, 252, 377
Bandung conference (1955), 196
Barton, John H., 25, 279–94
Bay of Pigs, 101
Bemis, Samuel Flagg, 107
Bennett, William, 425
Benvenisti, Meron, 351
Berlin Wall, 30, 203, 419, 455

Bicksler, Barbara A., 29, 407–32
bipolarity, 225–27, 254
Blackwill, Robert, 26–27, 375–85
Blix, Hans, 276–77
Blue Ribbon Commission on Defense Management,
     411
Borrus, Michael, 20, 21–22, 28, 136–75
Brandt, Willy, 82–83
Brandt Commission, 82
Brazil, 210, 277, 453
Bretton Woods agreements, 88
British Guiana, 97
British Loan, 327
Burke, Edmund, 387
Burton, Daniel F., Jr., 20, 21, 117–35
Bush, George, 24, 31, 55, 94, 113, 114, 183, 186, 195,
     271, 308, 347, 352, 361, 386, 400, 405, 425, 458
  Arab-Israeli conflict and, 354
  Aspen Institute address of, 176
  Gulf War leadership of, 240, 241, 244, 396, 399,
     427–28, 431
  Israeli loan guarantees denied by, 353
  Kurdish rebels and, 305
  "new world order" concept of, 112, 238, 272
  Reagan Doctrine endorsed by, 307
  rejected budget plan of, 430
  UN addressed by, 272

Cambodia, 101, 178, 272, 364, 368
Camp David Accord (1978), 58, 355
Canada, 43, 95, 158, 242, 256, 287, 312, 331n, 455
Canada–U.S. Free Trade Agreement, 287, 292, 293
Caradon, Lord, 350
Carter, Barry E., 25, 279–94
Carter, Jimmy, 55, 103, 301, 339, 394, 411
Center for Conflict Prevention, 271
Central Intelligence Agency (CIA), 29–30, 50, 408
Chad, 271
Chalwood, Robert Cecil, Viscount, 359
Chamarro, Violeta Barrios de, 294n
Chancellor, John, 68–69
Cheney, Dick, 36, 182, 185, 190, 193, 194, 276, 302
Chernobyl disaster, 205
China, People's Republic of, 60, 100, 103, 210, 227,
     248, 277, 298, 304, 306, 319, 322, 357, 364,
     365–66, 368, 369, 398, 403, 453
  nuclear weapons and, 228
  population growth in, 201
  U.S. and, 239
  Vietnam's border conflict with, 234
"choiceless society," 19, 29, 59, 77–89
  federal deficit and, 71–74
  oil dependency and, 70–73
Churchill, Winston, 242
Civil War, U.S., 97, 151, 378, 388
Claude, Inis, 253
Clay, Henry, 106, 107
Cleveland, Grover, 97, 107
cold war, 23, 30, 112, 178, 197, 198, 213, 214, 221–30,
     240, 295, 297, 316
  bipolarity and, 225–27
  East-West balance and, 226
  end of, 395–96, 421, 458–59
  European peace and, 224
  national security establishment and, 408
  nuclear proliferation after, 225, 228–30
  political cooperation and, 216–17
  public perception of, 100–101
  Third World and, 224, 232–34, 337–38
  Vietnam War and, 393

collective security, 249–66, 271
  arms control and, 258
  concert based system and, 253–55
  conditions for, 251–52
  criteria for, 255–56
  foreign policy and, 263–65
  France and, 250, 254, 257, 260, 263
  Germany and, 250, 251, 257, 260, 263
  goals of, 250
  Great Britain and, 250, 254, 257, 260, 263
  nationalism and, 261–63
  national security and, 263–65
  NATO and, 257–58, 264–65
  nuclear proliferation and, 258–59
  peacekeeping and, 259
  regional conflicts and, 259–60
  security group for, 257
  Soviet Union and, 250, 257, 259–60, 263, 265
  U.S. policy and, 263–65
College of Europe, 263
Commerce Department, U.S., 30, 50, 87, 126, 130, 425
Commission on Democracy (COD), 262, 263
Commission on Political Development (CPD), 262
Committee on Economic Development (CED), 86–87,
     89
Compromise of 1850, 97
Computer Systems Policy Project, 169n
Concert of Europe, 24, 249, 254
Conference on Security and Cooperation in Europe
     (CSCE), 24, 38, 46, 187, 250, 256–57, 260, 261,
     262, 264–65, 269, 271, 381, 450–51, 461
Conflict Prevention Center (CPC), 260, 261
Congress, U.S., 62, 93n, 95, 97–98, 114, 275, 294n, 342,
     343, 353, 368, 371, 408, 412, 417, 422, 429, 430–31
  annexation of Mexico rejected by, 106
  armed forces reductions and, 366–67
  defense issues and, 410–11
  defense reform and, 425–26
  executive and, 44
  federal deficit and, 35
  Gulf War and, 399
  Israel and, 27, 354
  national security and, 425–26
  science budget of, 130
  special interests and, 82
  U.S.–Japanese relations and, 28
Congress of Vienna (1815), 254
Constitution, U.S., 92n, 95, 288, 293
containment policy, 30, 53, 102, 185, 263, 317, 393,
     407–8, 421
  national security and, 407–8, 415–20
  nuclear proliferation and, 452–53
  Vietnam War and, 417
conventional forces in Europe (CFE) agreement, 54,
     184, 194, 258, 376, 379
Convention on the Law of the Sea (1982), 288
Coolidge, Calvin, 111, 391
Coordinating Committee on Export Controls
     (COCOM), 303, 461
Council of Europe, 271, 288, 461
Council on Competitiveness, 126, 127
Council on Foreign Economic Policy (CFEP), 413
Cuba, 106, 189, 403
Cuban Missile Crisis, 101, 102, 415
Cyprus, 272
Czechoslovakia, 177, 247, 288, 326–27

Defense Advanced Research Projects Agency
     (DARPA), 130, 132
Defense Authorization Act (1990), 374n

Defense Department, U.S., 29, 36, 38, 41, 44, 50, 157,
        176–77, 368, 374n, 408, 410, 411, 412, 417, 425, 457
    budget and, 192, 420, 422
    defense strategy and, 178–80, 185, 191–92, 194–95
    force reconstruction and, 193
    force reductions in Asia by, 366
    Soviet turmoil and, 182
    technology and, 21, 52–53, 122–26, 131, 132, 133,
        422–23
defense spending, 35–44
    Korean War and, 416–17
    since Pearl Harbor, 299
    public support for, 416–18, 430
    Vietnam War and, 417
deficit, *see* federal deficit
de Gaulle, Charles, 65
Democratic party, U.S., 307, 310, 393, 431
Deng Xiaoping, 298
Denmark, 171n
Dionne, E. J., Jr., 91
Doyle, Michael W., 25, 307–33
Dukakis, Michael, 307
Dulles, John Foster, 47–48, 413

Economic Commission for Europe, 271
economic liberalism, 221–23
economic security council, 424
Edison, Thomas A., 118
education, 74, 75, 181–82, 299, 448
    national security and, 67
    technology and, 131, 134
Egypt, 47, 61, 189, 197, 218, 233, 240, 276, 398
Eisenhower, Dwight D., 16, 19, 47, 58–59, 61, 68, 100,
        101–2, 104–5, 108, 409, 413, 448
El Salvador, 272, 300
Energy Department, U.S., 130
entitlement(s), 74, 299
    deficit and, 74–77
    in Japan, 76–77
    nonpoor and, 90
    revolution in, 81
    tax rate and, 299
environment, 204–6, 291
Ethiopia, 260
Europe:
    cold war stability in, 224
    as economic region, 161–64
    imperialism in, 107
    military insurance for, 450
    military potential of, 164–67
    Monroe Doctrine and, 96–97, 107
    NATO and future of, 186–87
    new international system and, 227–28
    nuclear energy and, 205
    nuclear-free zone in, 229
    population migration to, 203
    Soviet gas pipeline case and, 413
    unification of, 197
    U.S. and economic position of, 161–62
    U.S. defense strategy and, 186–87
    U.S. foreign policy and, 190
    see also collective security
Europe, Eastern, 31, 46, 49, 75, 92, 135, 162, 166, 168,
        183, 185, 194, 197, 207, 209, 246, 251, 252, 270,
        320, 333n, 362, 365, 370, 377, 395, 449–52, 459
    "broadened engagement" in, 451
    cold war and, 224
    European Community and, 247–48, 451
    future conflicts in, 227
    NATO and, 184, 451

nuclear weapons and, 229, 231, 453
    state system of, 215, 216
    transformation of, 177–78
    U.S. aid to, 38, 62
    U.S. global strategy and, 177–78
Europe, Western, 38, 47, 108, 137, 198, 209, 224, 247,
        404, 412, 449–50
    economic integration of, 215–16
    environmental movement in, 205
    political cooperation in, 216–17
    population migration to, 202–3
    state system of, 215–16
    U.S. leadership and, 199
European Atomic Energy Community (Euratom),
        294n
European Bank for Reconstruction and Development,
        269
European Central Bank, 159
European Coal and Steel Community (ECSC), 294n
European Commission on Human Rights, 283
European Community (EC), 126, 159, 214, 217, 241,
        260, 264, 270, 280, 282, 288, 297
    Arab-Israeli conflict and, 355
    Court of Justice of, 287
    Eastern Europe and, 247–48, 451
    unification and, 199
European Convention for the Protection of Human
        Rights and Fundamental Freedoms, 288
European Court of Human Rights, 282–83, 287–88
European Economic Community (EEC), 162, 174n,
        358
European Free Trade Association (EFTA), 162–63
European Union, 460
"executive committee of the cabinet" (ExCab), 415
Export-Import Bank, 357

Falklands War, 273
federal deficit, 61, 63–64, 110, 430
    balance of trade and, 142–43
    "choiceless society" and, 71–74
    consumption tax and, 72–73, 92n
    electronics industry and, 119
    entitlements and, 74–77
    industry and, 138, 141
    investments and, 74–75
    Japan and, 64–65
    oil dependency and, 70–72
    U.S.–Japanese trade imbalance and, 369
five-year defense plan (FYDP), 410
Ford, Gerald R., 46, 108, 414
Foreign Affairs, 360
foreign policy:
    allied burden sharing and, 63
    Asia and, 190
    collective security and, 263–65
    defense strategy and, 190–91
    depleted resources and, 137
    of "disengagement," 429
    domestic concerns and, 85–86
    economy and, 167, 300
    end of cold war and, 395–96
    free trade and, 241–42
    Gulf War and, 396–97
    "new world order" and, 239–40
    population growth, 202–3
    of post-Communist Soviet Union, 251–52, 268, 395
    post–World War II alliances and, 392
    trade policies and, 413
    Vietnam War and, 393–94
    World War I and, 390–91

Forrestal, James, 409
Fourth Geneva Convention, 351
France, 24, 27, 105, 217, 219, 227, 229, 230, 270, 296,
    305, 311, 314, 316, 327, 357, 359, 389, 391, 423
    collective security and, 250, 254, 257, 260, 263
    European bill of rights adopted by, 288
    European unification and, 216
    GNP of, 171*n*
    Great Britain's relationship with, 309
    Gulf War and, 398
    Mexico and, 97
    nuclear energy used by, 71
    nuclear weapons and, 228
    Suez crisis and, 64, 138
    UN restructuring and, 460
Friedman, Thomas L., 355

Gaddis, John, 332*n*
Galbraith, John, 80
Gardner, Richard N., 24, 267–78
General Agreement on Tariffs and Trade (GATT), 44,
    51, 63, 251, 269, 280, 291, 292, 327, 446, 452, 455
General Services Administration, U.S., 147
Georgia (Soviet republic), 384
Germany, Democratic Republic of (East): NATO and,
    297
Germany, Federal Republic of (West), 19, 21, 47, 56,
    90, 108, 113, 217, 221, 222, 234, 323, 327, 432
    GDP of, 137
    investment in production by, 143–44
    special interests in, 82–83
    World War II aftermath in, 79
Germany, Imperial, 109, 246, 309, 313–14, 327, 390
Germany, Nazi, 282, 303, 304, 318, 326–27, 354, 392,
    393, 401
Germany, unified, 24, 73, 75, 162, 163, 171*n*, 177, 270,
    274, 286, 295, 296, 304, 321, 346, 450, 460
    collective security and, 250, 251, 257, 260, 263
    Gulf War and, 55, 398
    nationalism and, 216
    new international system and, 227–29, 231
    U.S. fiscal policy and, 138
Germany, Weimar, 109
Gettysburg Address, 110
Ghent, Treaty of (1814–15), 105
global strategy, U.S., 176–95
    allied participation in, 180, 185–89
    deterrence and, 194–95
    East Europe's transformation and, 177–78
    force structure and, 191–94
    forward presence and, 190–91
    regional contingencies and, 178–80
    Soviet Union and, 182–84
global warming, 205
Goldwater-Nichols Defense Reorganization Act
    (1986), 411, 421
Gomery, Ralph, 156
Gorbachev, Mikhail, 182, 247, 251, 255, 297, 318, 364,
    367, 377, 378, 380, 384, 396, 418
Gramm-Rudman Act (1985), 76
Grand Coalition, 396
Great Britain, 19, 24, 47, 93*n*, 95–96, 113, 217, 227, 229,
    283, 296, 300, 305, 311, 314, 316, 327, 333*n*, 357,
    359, 389, 391, 432
    Albania and, 284–85
    collective security and, 250, 254, 257, 260, 263
    European Court of Human Rights and, 288
    foreign debt of, 64–65
    France's relationship with, 309
    Gulf War and, 398

international stability and, 301–2
    key interests of, 108–9
    Latin America involvement of, 97
    nuclear weapons and, 228
    Suez crisis and, 64, 138
    UN restructuring and, 460
    U.S. relationship with, 308–9
    U.S. security and, 108–9
    War of 1812 and, 96
Great Depression, 88, 100, 317
Greek-Turkish aid program, 109
Grenada, 44, 324, 326
Gross Domestic Product (GDP), 169*n*–70*n*
    of Asia, 158–59
    global, 158–59
    of Japan, 137
    of U.S., 137, 142
    of West Germany, 137
Gross National Product (GNP), 207–8
    of France, 171*n*
    rankings of nations and, 111
    of U.S., 23, 37, 48, 68, 72, 74, 75, 76, 77, 137, 142,
        171*n*, 192, 197–98, 210, 299, 411
    of world, 240, 299–300
Group of Seven, 138
Guatemala, 100
Gulf Cooperation Council, 189
Gulf War, *see* Persian Gulf War

Hadashot, 353
Haiti, 326
"Hama rules," 399, 406*n*
Hamilton, Alexander, 95
Harding, Warren G., 98, 99, 111, 112
Havel, Vaclav, 182
Headstart program, 87
Heisbourg, Francois, 165
Helsinki Final Act (1975), 46
Hendrickson, David C., 28–29, 30, 386–406
Hersh, Seymour, 311
Hitler, Adolf, 83, 181, 219, 246, 311
Hong Kong, 113, 203
Horton, Willie, 91
House, Edward Mandell, 391
House of Lords, British, 354
House of Representatives, U.S., 301, 430
    Armed Services Committee of, 36, 426
Housing Ministry, Israeli, 353
Howard, Michael, 259
human rights, 282–83, 322–23, 325, 333*n*
    domestic courts and, 290
    UN and, 324
Hungary, 20, 62, 113, 177, 247, 288
Huntington, Samuel, 323, 421
Hussein, Saddam, 16, 18, 22, 25, 36, 60, 183, 240, 244,
    297, 299, 301, 303, 305, 342, 396, 398, 399, 400

imperialism, 107, 221, 234, 308, 317, 332*n*
income redistribution, 207–10
India, 64, 109, 197, 198, 210, 227, 271, 276, 326, 333*n*,
    398
India-Pakistan conflict, 233
Indonesia, 64, 271
Inman, B. R., 20, 21, 117–35
Inter-American Treaty of Reciprocal Assistance (1947),
    186
Intermediate Nuclear Forces (INF) Treaty (1987), 54,
    277–78, 364
International Atomic Energy Agency (IAEA), 188, 269,
    276–77, 373*n*–74*n*, 460

International Centre for the Settlement of Investment Disputes (ICSID), 286
International Chamber of Commerce (ICC), 286
International Court of Justice (ICJ), 25, 281, 283–85, 288–89, 292
international law, 279–94, 392
  arbitration and, 285, 291–93
  changes in, 280–81
  domestic courts and, 289–92
  enforcement of, 283–85
  Gulf War and, 397
  legal network and, 290–94
  New York Convention and, 285–87, 289
  reciprocity and, 281
  specialized courts and, 287–89
  UN and, 283–84
International Monetary Fund (IMF), 51, 197, 208, 251, 269, 327, 382, 452
International Postal Union, 208
International Tribunal for the Law of the Sea, 288
interservice rivalry, 409
Intifada, 351, 358
investment, 456
  deficit and, 74–75
  in production, 143–44
  resources and, 76
  savings and, 74–75
  in technology, 132–33
Iran, 55, 100, 181, 240, 242–43, 248, 276, 284, 293, 303, 398, 417
Iraq, 29, 52, 53, 60, 61, 63, 76, 176, 186, 189, 197, 231, 238, 242–43, 248, 251, 268, 271, 273, 276, 291, 298, 301, 303, 305, 339, 341–42, 354, 356
  see also Persian Gulf War
Iraq-Iran conflict, 233, 242, 369
Ireland, 359
isolationism, 25, 267, 311, 321, 339, 396, 403–4
  costliness of, 317–18
  resurgence of, 296, 300–302
  after World War I, 391
Israel, 47, 61, 178, 179, 189, 231, 276, 321, 398, 453, 454
  Intifada and, 351, 358
  Johnson's guarantee to, 356
  nuclear weapons and, 218, 228, 234
  occupied territories and, 349–51
  peace process and, 244, 245, 354–55
  Resolution 242 and, 350–51
  Suez crisis and, 64, 138
  U.S. Congress and, 27, 354
  U.S. loan guarantees to, 352–53
  U.S. policy and, 27, 186
  wars of, 218
Italy, 171n–72n, 227, 286, 288, 309, 357
Izvestiya, 183

Jackson, Henry, 415
Japan, 17, 19, 21, 26, 46, 53, 57, 63, 79, 83, 90, 108, 109, 113, 142, 148, 162, 167n, 180, 209, 217, 221, 231, 234, 239, 241, 248, 271, 274, 295, 296, 306, 318, 319, 320, 321, 323, 327, 354, 364, 365, 366, 382, 392, 394, 401, 432, 456, 460
  domestic economy of, 144
  domestic investment by, 161
  electronics industry and, 121, 153–56
  energy program of, 71–72
  entitlement policy in, 76–77
  export dependency of, 173n
  GDP of, 137
  Gulf War and, 27, 369, 398
  intra-Asian trade and, 158–61

  military potential of, 164–67, 175n
  new international system and, 227, 229–30
  nuclear energy in, 205
  production investment by, 143–44
  Soviet relationship with, 368, 370–71, 377
  trade structure of, 174n
  UN and, 373
  U.S. defense strategy and, 187
  U.S. deficit and, 64–65
  U.S. economy vs. economy of, 74–75, 171n
  U.S. fiscal policy and, 138
  U.S. GNP and, 372
  U.S. relationship with, 27, 55–56, 362–63, 367–69, 371–74, 423, 454, 455
  U.S. security treaty with, 186
  U.S. technology contrasted with, 150
  in World War II, 218, 219, 222
Jay Treaty (1794), 316
Jefferson, Thomas, 96, 106, 388
Johnson, Andrew, 97
Johnson, Lyndon B., 100, 101, 102, 356, 414, 424
Joint Chiefs of Staff, 36, 60, 185, 408–9, 410, 411–12, 420
Jordan, 189, 358

KAL 007 disaster, 311
Kansas-Nebraska Act (1854), 97
Kant, Immanuel, 25, 312–13, 331n, 332n, 333n
Kennan, George F., 316–17, 332n–33n
Kennedy, John F., 100, 101, 272, 278, 299, 307, 410, 413–14, 415, 424
Key West agreement, 409
Kim Il-Sung, 188
Kissinger, Henry A., 24, 58, 238–48
Kohl-Gorbachev summit, 297
Korea, People's Republic of (North), 55, 60, 187, 276, 298, 303, 366, 454
  nuclear program of, 188, 373–74
  South Korea contrasted with, 365
  Soviet Union and, 364–65
  UN and, 365
Korea, Republic of (South), 63, 173n–74n, 180, 234, 304, 333n, 343, 344, 346, 371, 374n
  North Korea contrasted with, 365
  Soviet relations resumed by, 188, 364–65
  U.S. defense strategy and, 186–87
Korean Airlines (KAL) 007 disaster, 311
Korean War, 92, 99, 102, 108, 181, 218, 224, 272, 298–99, 365, 416–17
Krauthammer, Charles, 25, 295–306, 402
Kupchan, Charles A., 24, 25, 249–66
Kupchan, Clifford A., 24, 25, 249–66
Kuwait, 70, 112, 176, 181, 189, 240, 244, 251, 268, 271, 273, 282, 291, 296, 298, 301, 305, 339, 341–42, 343, 347, 354, 357, 396, 397, 399, 404, 459

Laos, 100, 101
Latin America, 19, 46, 47, 62, 97, 178, 317, 428, 459
  U.S. defense policy and, 189–90
  U.S. intervention in, 234
League of Nations, 254, 284, 298, 317, 391
Lebanon, 100, 243, 245, 272
Levy, Frank, 68
liberal community, 329–31
Liberia, 180
Libya, 271, 276, 285–86, 303, 340
  U.S. bombing of, 268
Lincoln, Abraham, 97, 110–11
Lloyd George, David, 354, 359

Lodge, Henry Cabot, 390
"long telegram," 102
Louis XIV, King of France, 311
Luxembourg, 205

McCarran Act (1950), 203
McGroddy, James, 172n
McKinley, William, 317
McNamara, Robert, 410, 411
Malcolm Baldrige Quality Award, 133
Manifest Destiny, 316
Manning, Bayless, 414–15
Marine Corps, U.S., 26, 343, 345
Marshall, George C., 385
Marshall Plan, 23, 27, 40, 88, 92, 109, 138, 197–98,
    208, 210, 327, 380, 381, 385, 412–13, 451
mass production, 143, 145 46, 155, 171n
Mattingly, Garret, 107
May, Ernest R., 19, 20, 28, 94–114, 425
Mearsheimer, John J., 24, 213–37
Merger Treaty (1967), 294n
Mexican War, 311, 316, 389
Mexico, 43, 62, 96, 97, 106, 242, 293, 320, 455, 457
Mexico–U.S. free trade agreement, 292
Michel, Richard, 68
Middle East, 17, 24, 26, 27, 50, 55, 56, 75, 246, 270,
    299, 343, 349, 362
    arms race in, 355–58
    nuclear proliferation in, 276–77
    Soviet Union and, 239
    U.S. defense strategy and, 189
    U.S. foreign policy and, 190
    see also Arab-Israeli conflict
migration, 200, 202–4
Military Staff Committee, 274, 275
Mill, J. S., 326, 333n
Millikan, Max, 208
Ministry of Defense, Soviet, 373n
Ministry of International Trade and Industry (MITI),
    Japanese, 126, 160, 174n
missile transfer control regime, 453
Missouri Compromise, 97
MIT Commission on Industrial Productivity, 171n
Mitterrand, François, 423
Mohammed Reza Shah Pahlevi, 55
Moiseyev, Mikhail, 183
Mongolian People's Republic (MPR), 363
Monroe, James, 96, 97, 99, 105, 390
Monroe Doctrine, 19, 96–98, 103, 105, 107, 316
    security of foreign states and, 389–90
Montreal Protocol, 209
Moynihan, Daniel Patrick, 68
Mutually Assured Destruction (MAD), 66

Namibia, 272
Napoleon I, Emperor of France, 246, 311, 390
Nasser, Gamal Abdel, 64
National Aeronautics and Space Administration
    (NASA), 130
National Commission on Excellence in Education, 67
National Guard, U.S., 26, 191, 344–45, 347
National Institute for Standards and Technology
    (NIST), 130, 132, 133
National Institutes of Health, 130
nationalism, 216, 304
    collective security and, 261–63
National Science Foundation, 130, 132
national security:
    alliances and, 45–46, 53–54, 320, 392, 404
    conventional forces and, 51–52

definitions of, 57–58, 63–64, 94, 200
diplomacy and, 45, 54–56
domestic aspects of, 47–48, 66–69, 99–101, 448–49
economic aspects of, 101–3, 222–23, 241, 412–15,
    422, 447
"empire for liberty" concept and, 106–9, 112–13
end of cold war and, 395–96
energy and, 54, 204–5
evolution of, 95–103
expenditures for, 39, 40, 41–42
external vs. domestic policy and, 18–19, 58, 85–86,
    104
foreign policy debates and, 316
free world and, 99–101
global dimension of, 23
hemispheric independence and, 97–99
intelligence and, 54
international order and, 24–25
legal network and, 290–94
military dimension of, 22, 408–12, 423–25, 447,
    449–52
national purpose and, 388–90, 403–5
new era in, 167–69
"new world order" and, 458–61
non-American nations and, 107–9
nuclear forces and, 51
overseas bases and, 53
perception of U.S. influence and, 66
political goodwill and, 47
presidential leadership and, 422, 427–30
prevention of war and, 236, 237
regional economic structure and, 157–58
safe borders and, 95–97
single-issue groups and, 428–29
Third World intervention and, 236–37
threats to, 60–61, 420
U.S. economy and, 49–50, 61
National Security Act (1947), 408–10, 412
National Security Council (NSC), 30, 57, 87, 102, 133,
    408–9, 410, 412, 414, 415, 416, 422, 424
Navy, U.S., 26, 36, 185, 192–93, 409
    force reductions and, 191–92
    force structure of, 341–42, 343
Nepal, 271
Netherlands, 327
New Deal, 100
new trade theory, 166–67
"new world order," 112, 238–40, 248, 305,
    386–406
    foreign policy and, 239–40
    U.S. role in, 458–61
New York Convention on the Recognition and
    Enforcement of Foreign Arbitral Awards (1958),
    285–87, 289, 292
New York Times, 355
New Zealand, 186, 188, 374n
Nicaragua, 260, 284, 285, 294n, 324
NICS, 158, 159–60, 173n–74n
Nigeria, 201, 202, 203
"nine-plus-one" agreement, 182–83, 384
Nitze, Paul, 420
Nixon, Richard M., 102, 103, 414
Nixon doctrine, 101
Noriega, Manuel, 55, 112, 283, 308
North Atlantic Treaty Organization (NATO), 24, 31,
    38, 45, 46, 57, 88, 109, 163, 208, 217, 247, 252,
    260, 270, 309, 320, 327, 344, 345, 346, 355, 392,
    404, 417, 450
    collective security and, 257–58, 264–65
    concert of nations and, 257–58

Eastern Europe and, 184, 451
East Germany and, 297
Europe's future and, 186–87
Havel's address to, 182
Soviet threat to, 177–78
Northwest Ordinance (1787), 106
Nuclear Non-Proliferation Treaty (1968), 232, 453
nuclear proliferation, 225, 228–32, 302–3, 377
  Asia and, 231, 232
  collective security and, 258–59
  containment and, 452–53
  deterrence of, 450
  in Middle East, 276–77
  national security and, 402–3, 452–54
  superpowers and, 234–35
  technology and, 304, 452
  in Third World, 234–35, 419, 452
  UN and, 276–77, 453
nuclear weapons, 46, 54, 60, 254, 321
  China and, 228
  developing nations and, 179
  in Eastern Europe, 229, 231, 453
  France and, 228
  in future war, 338
  Great Britain and, 228
  Iraq's quest for, 400
  Israel and, 218, 228, 234
  in Japan, 368
  likelihood of war and, 219–20, 226–27
  in new international system, 228–29
  Soviet, 27, 54, 240–41

occupied territories, 349–51
October War, 178, 233
Odom, William E., 26, 29, 337–48
Office of Free Elections (OFE), 262–63
Office of Management and Budget (OMB), 87
Office of Science and Technology Policy, 132
oil, 92n
  "choiceless society" and, 70–73
  deficit and, 70–72
  Soviet exports of, 71
  Third World conflicts and, 234
  U.S. dependence on, 54, 70–73, 243, 456–57
Organization for Economic Cooperation and
  Development (OECD), 270–71
Organization of American States (OAS), 446
Organization of Petroleum Exporting Countries
  (OPEC), 70–71, 73, 456

Packard, David, 411
Packard, Vance, 80
Packard Commission, 411
Paine, Thomas, 316
Pakistan, 197, 227, 228, 243, 276, 303, 326
Palestine Liberation Organization (PLO), 244–45
Panama, 44, 55, 112, 322, 324, 326, 346
  U.S. invasion of, 283, 308
Pax Americana, 304–5, 339, 359
Permanent Court of International Justice, 281
Perpetual Peace (Kant), 312
Persian Gulf War, 16, 47, 56, 66, 73, 110, 111–12, 117,
  122, 168, 179, 191, 195, 218, 219, 234, 272, 274,
  298–99, 304, 340, 345, 347, 349, 353, 357, 359,
  387, 417, 420, 429, 446, 454, 458
  Air Force capability and, 342
  Bush's leadership in, 240, 241, 244, 396, 399,
    427–28, 431
  Congress and, 399
  diplomacy and, 54–55

future capacities and, 137
France and, 398
Germany and, 55, 398
Great Britain and, 398
international coalition and, 180, 186, 398–99,
  427–28
international law and, 397
lessons of, 401–3
outcome of, 399–401
Soviet Union and, 183, 297, 398
technology and, 181, 184, 193
UN and, 282, 397, 398, 449
U.S. defense spending and, 36, 180
U.S. foreign policy and, 396–97
"Vietnam syndrome" and, 396
Peter I (the Great), Emperor of Russia, 246
Peterson, Peter G., 18–20, 22, 29, 30, 57–93, 428, 432
Philippines, 46, 53, 61–62, 106, 188, 300, 320, 326, 366,
  371
Pirate, The (Scott), 107
planning, programming, and budget system (PPBS),
  410
Poland, 177, 219, 221, 234, 247
political action committees (PACs), 84, 86
Polk, James K., 106
population growth, 200–202, 457–58
Powell, Colin, 36, 185
practical internationalism, 267–78
  armed force and, 270–75
  international organizations and, 268–69
  UN and, 272–75
  weapons of mass destruction and, 276–78
Prodi, Romano, 172n
production, 143–46
  flexibility and, 144–46, 171n
  mass, 143, 145, 145–46, 155, 171n
  revolution in, 143–45
protectionism, 317, 321
Public Papers, 114n

Qadhafi, Mu'ammar al-, 285–86

Raspberry, William, 83
Reagan, Ronald, 103–4, 307, 310, 328, 351–52, 394,
  402, 411, 414, 417, 418
"Reagan Doctrine," 307
Reagan Revolution, 77
Reform Bill (1832), 308
Regional Development Banks, 269
Republican party, U.S., 307, 393, 431
Rio Treaty (1947), 186
Rockefeller, Nelson, 415
Romberg, Alan D., 28, 362–74
Roosevelt, Franklin D., 98, 99, 102, 108
  Four Freedoms speech of, 271–72
Roosevelt, Theodore, 95, 97–98, 110
Rostow, Walt, 208
Russia, 18, 254, 378, 384

Saudi Arabia, 47, 53, 70, 111, 179, 186, 189, 240, 276,
  341–42, 346, 357, 397, 398, 399–400
savings, 80, 299, 456
  investment and, 74–75
Schelling, Thomas C., 23–24, 196–210
Schiff, Ze'ev, 360
Schlesinger, Arthur, Jr., 83, 114n
Schmidt, Helmut, 83
Schwarzkopf, Norman, 350, 420
Scott, Walter, 107
Sebenius, James K., 18–20, 22, 29, 30, 57–93

Senate, U.S., 86, 275, 317, 426
  Armed Services Committee of, 35–36, 185, 193, 426
  Foreign Relations Committee of, 332*n*–33*n*, 426
Serbia, 378
Shamir, Yitzhak, 353, 354, 358
Sharon, Ariel, 353, 358
Shevardnadze, Eduard, 182
Singapore, 90, 188–89, 333*n*
Single European Act, 294*n*
Sino-Soviet Treaty of Friendship, Alliance, and
  Mutual Security (1950), 363
Solow, Robert, 135*n*
South Africa, 23, 113, 200, 228, 245, 276, 303, 333*n*
Southeast Asia Collective Defense Treaty, 186
South Sea Bubble, 66
"sovereignty-at-bay" thesis, 216–17
Soviet Union, 16, 17–18, 22, 24, 35, 36, 37, 38, 40, 46,
  49–50, 53, 60, 90, 100, 101, 102, 103, 111, 135, 137,
  162, 163, 209, 217, 232, 304, 316–17, 322, 357, 392,
  393, 403, 416, 417, 427, 428, 446, 449–53
  German invasion of, 219
  Jewish emigration from, 203
  October War and, 233
  public perception of, 418–19
Soviet Union, post-Communist, 18, 28, 66, 75, 164,
  180, 185, 189, 193, 270, 277, 295, 296, 297, 338–39,
  341, 362
  Asia allies of, 363–64
  August coup in, 27
  balance of power and, 245–48
  collective security and, 250, 257, 259–60, 263,
  265
  CSCE and, 256, 381
  domestic struggle of, 375–79
  external aid to, 382–83
  foreign policy of, 251–52, 268, 395
  future of, 26–27
  Gulf War and, 183, 398
  Japan's relationship with, 368, 370–71, 377
  Jewish emigration from, 352
  Middle East and, 239
  military modernization and, 184
  Muslim republics of, 243
  new international system and, 227–30
  new Union Treaty proposed for, 183, 380–81
  "nine-plus-one" agreement of, 182–83, 384
  North Korea and, 364–65
  nuclear weapons and, 27, 54, 240–41
  oil exports of, 71
  Persian Gulf aims of, 243
  regional conflicts and, 178
  South Korea relations resumed by, 188,
  364–65
  Soyuz movement in, 384
  strategic deterrence and, 194–95
  Third World and, 251
  transformation of, 177–78
  turmoil within, 182–83
  U.S. arms control agreement with, 291
  U.S. global strategy and, 182–84
  U.S. loans to, 252
  U.S. military and, 51–52
  U.S. relations and, 183
  Vietnam's relationship with, 363–64
  see also specific republics
Soyuz movement, 384
Spain, 96, 326, 327, 389
special interests, 80–83, 88
State Department, U.S., 30, 41, 50, 61, 410
"Statement of the Ten," 380–81

state system, 213–17, 221–23, 235
  future of, 214–16
  nationalism and, 216
Stein, Herb, 91
Stewart, Michael, 64
Strange, Susan, 64–65
Strategic Arms Reduction Treaty (START), 379
Strategic Defense Initiative (SDI), 195, 340, 452, 453
Suez crisis (1956), 19, 64, 65, 138
supply:
  technology and, 148–51
  U.S. economy and, 146–51
Supreme Court, U.S., 286, 287
Switzerland, 112, 286
Syria, 218, 234, 240, 248, 276, 360, 398, 427
Szanton, Peter, 415

Taiwan, 90, 100, 173*n*–74*n*, 234, 333*n*
Tanzania, 271, 326
Taylor, Zachary, 97
technology, 117–35
  consumer electronics industry and, 118–19, 140–41
  Defense Department and, 21, 52–53, 122–26, 131,
  132, 133, 422–23
  economics of, 119–22
  education and, 131, 134
  export controls and, 122–23
  Gulf War and, 181, 184, 193
  interdependence and, 119–22
  investment in, 132–33
  military vs. commercial, 21, 118, 123–26, 129, 131,
  141, 151–57, 173*n*, 422–23, 457
  national economy and, 52–53, 119–22
  national security and, 20–21, 52–53, 122–23, 135
  proliferation and, 304, 452
  research and development and, 130–32
  supply base of, 146–51
  trade patterns and, 170*n*–71*n*
  U.S. decline in, 21, 118, 123, 126–29
  U.S. influence and, 138–39
Thailand, 100, 186, 188
Thatcher, Margaret, 163, 216
Third World, 196–97, 225, 318, 323–24, 333*n*, 394
  cold war and, 224, 232–34, 337–38
  conflicts in, 224, 232–34, 259, 271
  nuclear proliferation and, 234–35, 419, 452
  Soviet Union and, 251
  state system and, 215, 216
  superpower involvement in, 233–34
Thomas Aquinas, Saint, 399
Tiananmen Square, 239, 298
Time, 271
Treasury Department, U.S., 43, 50, 414
Treaty of Mutual Cooperation and Security, 186
Treverton, Gregory F., 15–31, 35–56, 407–32
Triple Alliance, 309
Truman, Harry S., 88, 99–100, 102–3, 104, 108, 109,
  316, 416
Turkey, 64, 113, 243, 305, 357

Uganda, 271, 326
Ukraine, 20, 113, 378, 384
United Arab Emirates, 357
United Nations, 25, 27, 88, 112, 114, 208, 238, 242, 245,
  251, 253, 271, 280, 446, 452, 458–59
  Arab-Israeli conflict and, 350–51, 353–54, 359–60
  Bush's address to, 272
  effectiveness of, 268–69, 272
  "enemy" clause in Charter of, 460
  Gulf War and, 282, 397, 398, 449

human rights and, 324
international law and, 283–84
Japan and, 373
new international order and, 297–98
North Korea and, 365
nuclear proliferation and, 276–77, 453
practical internationalism and, 272–75
Resolution 242 of, 350–51, 353–54, 355, 359
Resolution 338 of, 353–54
restructuring of, 460–61
Uniting for Peace Resolution of, 275
weapons of mass destruction and, 276–78
United Nations Environmental Program (UNEP), 269, 291
United Nations Reconstruction and Rehabilitation Administration (UNRRA), 208
UN Participation Act, 274–75
United States:
covert action by, 100
as debtor nation, 456
defense industry of, 124
demand-side economy of, 79–80
diplomatic establishment of, 45
economic decline of, 139–43
global intervention and, 240
immigration policy of, 202, 203–4
international legal system and, 292–94
leadership of, 198, 240
military forces of, 45
national purpose of, 388–90
political system in, 86
preeminence of, 297, 299
as service economy, 142
withdrawal from public life in, 83–85
United States–Iran Claims Tribunal, 25, 286–87, 292
United States–Japan Mutual Cooperation and Security Treaty (1960), 57, 367–69
United States–Philippines Mutual Defense Treaty (1951), 186, 374n
United States–Republic of Korea Mutual Defense Treaty, 186

Vandenberg, Arthur, 268
Vatican, 112, 283
Venezuela, 97
Vienna, Treaty of (1814–15), 105

Vienna Convention on Diplomatic Relations (1961), 283
Viereck, Peter, 74
Vietnam, 234, 366, 368, 393
Soviet relationship with, 363–64
Vietnam, Republic of (South Vietnam), 393
"Vietnam syndrome," 394, 396
Vietnam War, 28, 60, 65, 80, 84, 100, 101, 102, 218, 224, 344, 368, 393–94, 410–11, 417, 418

War of 1812, 96, 105
Warsaw Pact, 60, 177, 195, 257, 270
Washington, George, 19, 94, 95, 96, 97, 316, 388, 404
Watergate affair, 84
weapons of mass destruction, 179, 301, 453–54
practical internationalism and, 276–78
proliferation of, 302–3, 377, 402
UN and, 276–78
Webster, Daniel, 389
Webster, William, 35–36
Weinberger, Caspar, 411
Western Alliance, 241
Western European Union (WEU), 187, 264, 270, 450
Western Hemisphere Free Trade Area, 242
White House Office of Science and Technology Policy, 126
William II, Emperor of Germany, 109, 313
Wilson, Woodrow, 98, 99, 107–8, 310, 390
Wolfowitz, Paul D., 22, 24, 26, 36, 176–95
World Bank, 51, 197, 208, 251, 269, 286, 382, 452
World Health Organization, 269
World War I, 99, 106, 113, 241, 297, 311, 327, 332n
prelude to, 309
U.S. foreign policy and, 390–91
World War II, 19, 29, 47, 51, 68, 80, 95, 99, 104, 106, 108, 111, 112, 122, 143, 151, 208, 214, 219, 279, 290, 297, 300, 304, 311, 323, 354, 385, 392, 396, 401, 404, 407, 412, 418
aftermath, 79
Eastern Front in, 218, 220–21

Yankelovich, Daniel, 69
Yeltsin, Boris, 182, 333n
Young, John A., 67
Yugoslavia, 259

Zysman, John, 20, 21–22, 28, 136–75